READING ASIA

Curzon-IIAS Asian Studies Series

Series Co-ordinator: Dick van der Meij
Institute Director: Wim A.L. Stokhof

The International Institute for Asian Studies (IIAS) is a postdoctoral research centre based in Leiden and Amsterdam, The Netherlands. Its main objective is to encourage Asian Studies in the Humanities and the Social Sciences and to promote national and international co-operation in these fields. The Institute was established in 1993 on the initiative of the Royal Netherlands Academy of Arts and Sciences, Leiden University, Universiteit van Amsterdam and Vrije Universiteit Amsterdam. It is mainly financed by The Netherlands Ministry of Education, Culture, and Sciences. IIAS has played an active role in co-ordinating and disseminating information on Asian Studies throughout the world. The Institute acts as an international mediator, bringing together various entities for the enhancement of Asian Studies both within and outside the Netherlands. The Curzon-IIAS Asian Studies series reflects the scope of the Institute. The Editorial Board consists of Erik Zürcher, Wang Gungwu, Om Prakash, Dru Gladney, Amiya K. Bagchi, James C. Scott, Jean-Luc Domenach and Frits Staal.

Images of the 'Modern Woman' in Asia
Edited by Shoma Munshi

Nomads in the Sedentary World
Edited by Anatoly M. Khazanov & André Wink

Reading Asia
Edited by Frans Hüsken & Dick van der Meij

Tourism, Heritage and National Culture in Java
Heidi Dahles

Asian-European Perspectives
Edited by Wim Stokhof & Paul van der Velde

Law and Development in East and Southeast Asia
Edited by Christoph Antons

The Indian Ocean Rim
Edited by Gwyn Campbell

Rethinking Chinese Transnational Enterprises
Edited by Leo Douw, Cen Huang & David Ip

'Hinduism' in Modern Indonesia
Edited by Martin Ramstedt

The History of Tibet
Edited by Alex McKay, 3 vols.

Diasporas and Interculturalism in Asian Performing Arts
Edited by Hae-Kyung Um

READING ASIA

New Research in Asian Studies

EDITED BY

Frans Hüsken
and
Dick van der Meij

LONDON AND NEW YORK

First published in 2001
by Curzon Press

Published 2004 by Routledge
2 Park Square, Milton Park, Abingdon, Oxfordshire OX14 4RN
711 Third Avenue, New York, NY 10017

First issued in paperback 2015

Routledge is an imprint of the Taylor and Francis Group, an informa business

Editorial Matter © 2001 Frans Hüsken and Dick van der Meij

All rights reserved. No part of this book may be reprinted or reproduced or utilised in any form or by any electronic, mechanical, or other means, now known or hereafter invented, including photocopying and recording, or in any information storage or retrieval system, without permission in writing from the publishers.

British Library Cataloguing in Publication Data
A catalogue record of this book is available from the British Library

ISBN 13: 978-1-138-86329-3 (pbk)
ISBN 13: 978-0-7007-1371-4 (hbk)

TABLE OF CONTENTS

Contributors   vii

Introduction:
God's Mountain: An Asian Anthology
Frans Hüsken and *Dick van der Meij*   ix

PART ONE: COPING WITH THE PRESENT

1   Ethnicity, Law and Development in Southeast Asia
    Christoph Antons   3

2   Development, Media and Youth Issues in Malaysia
    Samsudin A. Rahim   29

3   Kreteks Crackle in Children's Hands: The Impact of
    Advertisements and Peers on Smoking Behaviour
    of Adolescents in Bandung, Indonesia
    Freek, Hans and Max Colombijn   49

4   China in Reform: Structural Problems in the
    Economy and Society of Contemporary Zhejiang Province
    Keith Forster   64

PART TWO: HISTORICAL LEGACIES

5   The Seventeenth-Century Acehnese Model of Malay Society
    Leonard Y. Andaya   83

6   Accumulation of Knowledge: Piligrimage as Leitmotif
    in the Indian Ocean in the Ancient Period
    Himashu Prabha Ray   110

7   Scientific Forestry: History, Boundary Making,
    and Power in Malaysia
    Fadzilah Majid Cooke   128

8 Providence and Power: Korean Protestant Responses
   to Japanese Imperialism
   Kenneth M. Wells — 154

9 The Central-European Jewish Community in Shanghai, 1937-45
   Pan Guang — 173

PART THREE: PERFORMANCE AND PRESENTATION

10 Reading for Performance:
   A Cirebonese Romance as a Narrative Model for Wayang
   Matthew Isaac Cohen — 197

11 Modelling and Measuring the Parametres of Performance
   Hae-Kyung Um — 219

12 The Maithili Language
   Yogendra P. Yadava — 240

13 A New Approach to an Old Problem:
   On Chinese Discourse *LE*
   Guo Wu — 261

14 A Comparative Study of the Instruments of the Sarangi Family
   from an Ethnographic Perspective
   Suvarnalata Rao — 279

15 Karma Gling Pa: Treasure Finder or Creative Editor?
   Henk Blezer — 292

Contributors

LEONARD Y. ANDAYA is Professor of History at the University of Hawaii at Manoa in Honolulu.

CHRISTOPH ANTONS is a senior lecturer in the School of Law and director of the Centre for Southeast Asian Law at Northern Territory University in Darwin, Australia

HENK BLEZER is an affiliated fellow at the International Institute for Asian Studies, Leiden, the Netherlands.

MATHEW I. COHEN is a lecturer in Theatre Studies at the University of Glasgow.

FREEK COLOMBIJN is an anthropologist at IIAS, Leiden, and a lecturer in the Department of the Languages and Cultures of South-East Asia and Oceania at Leiden University

HANS COLOMBIJN is a psychologist at the Regional Mental Health Institute (RIAGG) Parnassia, The Hague, the Netherlands.

MAX COLOMBIJN is a paediatrician at the Beatrix Hospital, Gorinchem, The Netherlands.

FADZILAH MAJID COOKE is a research fellow in the Resource Management in Asia Pacific Project, Department of Human Geography, Research School of Pacific and Asian Studies, Australian National University, Canberra, Australia.

KEITH FORSTER teaches at Southern Cross University in Australia

PAN GUANG is Dean of Jewish Studies Shanghai, Director of the Institute of European and Asian Studies, Shanghai Academy of Social Sciences and Director of the Centre for International Studies, Shanghai Municipality.

FRANS HÜSKEN is Professor of Anthropology at the Catholic University of Nijmegen, the Netherlands.

CONTRIBUTORS

DICK VAN DER MEIJ is acting head of the Projects Divion, Department of Languages and Cultures of Southeast Asia and Oceania, Leiden University, Leiden, the Netherlands.

SAMSUDIN A. RAHIM is Professor of Communication and Dean of the Faculty of Social Sciences, Universiti Kebangsaan Malaysia.

SUVARNALATA RAO is a research scientist and co-ordinator for music programmes at The National Centre for the Performing Arts Nariman Point, Mumbai, India.

HIMANSHU PRABHA RAY is an associate professor at the Centre for Historical Studies, Jawaharlal Nehru University, New Delhi, India.

HAE-KYUNG UM is an affiliated fellow at the International Insitutute for Asian Studies, Leiden, the Netherlands.

KENNETH WELLS is a fellow in the Research School of Pacific and Asian Studies, The Australian National University, Canberra, Australia.

GUO WU is a senior lecturer in Chinese at the School of Language and Linguistics, University of Western Sydney, Australia.

YOGENDRA P YADAVA is Professor of Linguistics at the Central Department of Linguistics at Tribhuvan University, Kirtipur, Kathmandu, Nepal.

Introduction:

God's Mountain: An Asian Anthology

Frans Hüsken and Dick van der Meij

Bu Lu and Bu Kyaw, two twelve-year old twin brothers from the Ka Mar Pa Law village in the Karen hill region, made a stunning impression on the world at the beginning of the twenty-first century. Overnight, they became known under their Christian names as Luther and Johnny Htoo, supreme commanders and revered leaders of God's Army – a force of a few hundred Karen hill tribesmen in the mountainous region of Burma, close to the Thai border.

What brought these youngsters into the limelight of world-wide news coverage, was when on the 24th of January, 2000, ten fighters from Luther's and Johnny's Army left their base on Kersay Doh (God's Mountain) on the Burmese side of the border, and started a raid on the hospital of the Thai town of Ratchaburi. For more than a day, they held some 500 patients and staff hostage. However, none of these fighters survived when a day later, Thai commandos stormed the building and freed the hostages.

International news agencies reporting on the affair, stressed the spectacular part of it: "jungle fighters commanded by illiterate messianic twins forcing their way into a modern medical facility" (Time 7 February 2000). A camera crew of Associated Press in December 1999 shot images of the teenage soldiers playing with their guns as if they were toys. The news item conveyed an image of a people living at subsistence level, in a village that recalls the "primitive settlement presided over by Marlon Brando in *Apocalypse Now*". Living in a faraway hide-out, infested with endemic cerebral malaria, the fighters of God's Army had rallied behind the twin brothers who are shorter than the M-16 rifles some of their followers carry. Johnny and Luther having a black tongue, which in the Karen tradition is taken to be a sign of divinity, are believed to offer divine protection.

It is easy to see why the raid by God's Army provided the international press with a perfect news item as it combined exotic stereotypes of mountain Asia with the thrill of Crocodile Dundee bravado. There is, of course much more to their performance than just the bizarre and romanticised image of primitive rebels fighting for a good cause who had entered the international political highway by accident to be overrun by the first lorry that happened to pass.

The other side of the Karen coin was covered by several news agencies which went beyond the quixotic and delved a bit deeper into the historical and political backgrounds of God's Army's, a guerrilla group that in 1997 had split from the mainstream Karen National Union. They related the story of the Karen, who for half a century had been bravely clashing with the Burmese army and fighting for their independence as a non-Burman, non-Buddhist minority group. Their zeal in resisting Burmese domination was articulated by ethnic and religious differences. They particularly stressed their distinct religious position as a group where from the 1820s onwards, US Baptist missionaries had found a fertile ground for their biblical message as the Karen accepted it readily, merging it with native beliefs and practices and a strong reliance upon ancestral spirits.

For many years, the Karen had been relatively successful in securing their terrain and in keeping the Burmese army at bay. In 1997, however, Burmese troops had launched a massive attack in which many Karen died and tens of thousands were displaced. While the army of the Karen National Union proved to be no match for the Burmese and fled in disarray, a small group of fighters held out, reportedly inspired by the Htoo brothers who told them that an army of spirits would come to help them. Subsequent successes of this small band of guerrilla fighters attracted others who the formed God's Army, led by Johnny and Luther who took up rank as colonels. They also used the special powers attributed to them to establish a fundamentalist brand of Christianity with strong messianic overtones insisting upon rigorous observance of the strict rules the twins have introduced.

After their defeat at the Thai hospital which so dramatically ended with the death of all ten hijackers, little has been heard on the fate of God's Army. However, the two days at Ratchaburi are one out of many examples of how present-day events in Asia can puzzle an international audience as well as many Asians themselves. From the turbulent twentieth century, in which most Asian countries fought for independence from colonial domination to embark on a voyage to 'modernity' and 'progress', Asia has carried a range of tension areas into the new millennium. Old problems like the tension between a central, or even centralist, state and centrifugal tendencies in the regions have again become acute with the rise of separatist movements in the 1980s and 1990s, contesting the ideals of national unity. At the same time, like elsewhere in the world, stressing ethnic differences has become part of present-day Asian political vernacular, more often than not in combination with emphasising religious as well as cultural distinctions. Tensions like these ones have been exacerbated by growing socio-economic inequalities as whatever kind of 'development' has been going on in the individual countries during the past decades, it has generally been the national centres that could reap the major benefits of it while

Introduction: God's Mountain: An Asian Anthology

peripheral regions were left behind. Asian states, half a century after national independence during which they tried to get rid of colonial legacies, are still looking for a suitable political as well as cultural format. And while the erstwhile nationalists may have felt very strongly about the ideals of modernity, the formation of a rationalised nation-state and the creation of a homogeneous national identity, late twentieth-century processes of globalisation have generated or strengthened cultural, religious and linguistic identification. At the micro-level of the Karen raid on the Ratchaburi hospital, several of these macro-political tensions of modern Asian states seem to have converged.

The essays collected in this volume, written by scholars while they worked as research fellows at the International Institute for Asian Studies at Leiden, can be read in a similar way as miniatures of general Asian themes. They address from a variety of angles and case-studies (i) contemporary political and social problems and the ways Asian states are coping with them; (ii) the pre-colonial and colonial legacies that have shaped present Asian states and political discourse in general; and (iii) the cultural traditions which not only have survived centuries of profound changes but which also are being revived and reconstructed.

The contributions to the first part of this volume concern present-day Asia and the ways in which states are engaged in a process of shaping the modalities of everyday life of their citizens and the ways in which these citizens respond to such policies. *Christoph Antons* discusses the ethnic diversity of Southeast Asia and the ways in which former colonial masters through legislation have modelled present interethnic relations. He focuses upon the trading minorities (in particular, the Chinese) that can be found in all Southeast Asian countries, and shows that current legal policies towards them has not changed sharply since independence. It seems that initially the colonial powers used prevailing trading customs and that favouritism towards trading minorities were a prerequisite for the coloniser to survive. Later this attitude was more deliberately used as a way to develop the colonies. Having been close to colonial masters, the minorities found themselves often in a difficult position vis-à-vis the post-colonial governments in Southeast Asia, and have become the objects of negative of positive discrimination policies. These policies have caused considerable economic set-backs and the author therefore concludes that as long as ethnicity remains an issue in legislation, long-term economic development in Southeast Asia, relying upon export-oriented growth, will be at risk.

Nevertheless, during the 1980s and 1990s, up to the crisis of 1997, many Southeast Asian economies have boomed which in general has diminished poverty, but which also has brought new problems. Rapid economic development and the changing landscape of the media industry in Malaysia have contributed to what government spokesmen have described as 'unhealthy life styles' and 'moral decadence', especially among the urban youth. *Samsudin Rahim*'s contribution to this volume discusses these social problems. One the one hand, young people are seen by the Malaysian government as a national asset and of pivotal importance for the future of the nation. However, a rapidly expanding media industry has brought an upsurge of entertainment magazines and so-called 'low-quality programmes' which promote a lifestyle that is contrary to the one promoted by the government which stresses thriftiness and dedication. Samsudin Rahim accepts the view that 'Malaysia would like to preserve its values and traditions as its cultural identity' and that therefore the media need to be urged to act as socialising agencies supporting a more responsible lifestyle. Whether such a role can be fulfilled in an era in which young people have easy access to global media and in which they are not confined to national media, is questionable, but the discussion in itself refers to the much-debated issue of 'Asian values' that need to be protected against 'Western contamination'.

One of the nowadays fashionable fights against 'social evils' which threaten the health of people in general, but youth in particular, concerns smoking behaviour. Indonesia is one of few countries in the world where the smoke of cigarettes, especially in the national dress of clove cigarettes (*kretek*), is everywhere. *Freek, Hans and Max Colombijn* address the question why young people start smoking. In a 1988-study among school children, no significant effect was measured of peers on the smoking behaviour of adolescents. A follow-up study in 1995, using a different research strategy, revealed that there was an important impact of peers. Another determinant of smoking behaviour is the omnipresent advertising of the Indonesian cigarette industry which transmits the prestigious image of modernity.

The fourth essay in this section analyses economic growth in the Chinese province of Zhejiang. During twenty years of the post-Mao reform period, this coastal province experienced rapid economic growth. The factors which *Keith Forster* holds responsible for that astonishing growth are to be found in extensive small-scale rural industrialisation which was largely initiated by local peasants-cum-entrepreneurs. Such a strategy has been highly successful, but as Forster concludes, the social and economic structures of Zhejiang's industry which in the past decades have brought growth, now stand in the way of its transformation into a more modern, efficient and outward-oriented socio-economic organisation. The province has made considerable progress in the transition from a planned economy to a market system, but needs considerable guidance from the provincial government to make it into the twenty-first century.

Introduction: God's Mountain: An Asian Anthology

While the essays in the first section concentrate upon the economic and socio-political dynamics of contemporary Asia, the second section is historical in orientation. The contributions to this section present both indigenous and colonial models of society and of individual life. *Leonard Andaya* discusses the role of the North Sumatran sultanate in the history of the Malay. Due to historical circumstances, the Malay world has not only been divided geographically but also intellectually. The territory on the east coast of Sumatra which has been regarded as the historical mainland became marginalised in the course of history, while the kingdoms of the Malay peninsula aimed at becoming the new centre. These efforts later on were supported by the British colonial regime eager to avoid confrontation with the Dutch across the Straits of Malacca. This historical background is needed to assess the role of Aceh in Malay history. Many of its achievements in the sixteenth and seventeenth centuries have been appreciated not as part of the evolution of the Malay world but of a uniquely Acehnese contribution. Andaya argues that the sultanate at that time occupied a central position in the Malay world and that Aceh should be regarded as a major player in the Malay tradition. Only in the nineteenth century as a result of colonial efforts was Aceh relegated to a regional identity which became increasingly distinct from that of the Malay.

Like the Malay tradition and Islam have been shared by communities scattered over Southeast Asia, at a much earlier stage Buddhism, *Himashu Prabha Ray* contends, has created a cultural bond between different parts of Asia. Ray discusses the significance of the story of Sudhana prominently sculpted on the classic Buddhist monument of the Borobudur (Central Java), in the context of the cultural realm extending across the Bay of Bengal in the ancient period. The Buddhist Order provided a potent bond between the communities of South and Southeast Asia, leading to travel across the Indian Ocean both for pilgrimage and for the accumulation of knowledge. This quest, in Ray's view, is represented in stone at the Borobudur, as well as vividly portrayed by Sudhana's visits to various centres in India to learn from a broad range of teachers.

Colonial expansion and control brought often completely different models for society. The essay by *Fadzilah Majid Cooke* examines the institutionalisation of 'scientific forestry' in colonial Malaya and Sarawak. At present, scientific forestry is being criticised for its narrowness of focus. In Malaysia, the debates have centred on sustained-yield management practices: criticism is raised against the way in which this type of forestry privileges industrial production over subsistence and local use; the manner in which the well-being of forests is treated as separate of that of the people living in the forests; and finally against the premise that complex ecosystems like tropical forests can be regarded as sufficiently resilient in the long run so that logging can proceed if only the appropriate technology is applied. What is often overlooked in these criticisms is that most of the problems faced by contemporary forestry are a legacy of processes which have been set in motion by colonial forestry and appropriated after independence for purposes of national development. Cooke concentrates on colonial Malaya and examines the first forty years of the Forest department since its formation in 1901. In Sarawak, a similar department was only founded by the Brooke administration in 1919. A survey if the history of both departments sheds light on the way forest reserves have been established, often against the wishes of regional colonial administrators and contested by native people. The colonial discourse of needs for timber (of the population versus those of industrial forestry) feeds into practices that relegate as unimportant other needs (of native peoples for subsistence) and practices (like trade in non-timber forest products). It turns out that in this field, administrative and ideological continuity between colonial and post-colonial policies is high.

The next two contributions concern specifically the fate of some Western or Westernised communities in colonial Asia. A remarkable group of foreigners settling in China has been the Jewish community of Shanghai. Between 1937 and 1945, more than 25,000 Jewish refugees from Central Europe escaped to Shanghai. *Pan Guang* in his article depicts the reasons why Shanghai became such a haven, and how the Jewish community fared during the Second World War. Even at some stage, the Japanese occupation forces, under the pressure from Nazi-Germany, considered setting up concentration camps for the Jews, this so-called 'Meisinger Plan' was never implemented. The Jewish community depended heavily for their survival on their Chinese neighbours and ties have remained cordial after the end of the war when the Jews left Shanghai again.

Kenneth Wells' essay on Protestantism in Korea during the Japanese occupation focuses upon the activities and the writings of two Korean Christian leaders, Yun Ch'iho and Kim Kyoshin. In Korean historiography, the two are invariably contrasted as Yun is considered to have been a collaborator while Kim is seen as the good nationalist and patriot. Wells aims at an alternative interpretation of Yun's and Kim's responses to Japanese colonial domination. In his view, their positions have been first of all understood in relation to the secular categories of imperialism and nationalism, and not in terms of their religious beliefs; as a result, they have been measured against criteria they did not for the most part subscribe to. If, however, their own professed starting point (divine providence and the will of God in history) are taken seriously, Wells argues, we find that the motives that have been commonly attributed to the two men's actions are often directly contradicted by their own statements. He concludes that once their writings and lives are examined in relation to their own principles, Tun's and Kim's positions on imperialism appear remarkably similar; the divergence in their activities reflects different positions with regard to the place of politics in Christian life, rather than political collaboration or resistance.

With the final section of this volume we enter the domain of Asian arts in a broad sense. It covers contributions on theatrical traditions as well as on philological and linguistic topics. Together these contributions present texts, perceptions and performances and the ways in which they have been preserved and shaped as cultural legacies.

While some essays point to the dimensions of 'high culture' by concentrating upon texts, others have directed their attention towards the role of these traditions in the here and now. In that latter vein, *Matthew Cohen* takes us to the fascinating world of Javanese shadowplay (*wayang*) as it is being performed in the Cirebon area, along the north coast of West Java. The often-studied *wayang* is presented here from a new angle: the interplay of performer, text and audience. As Peter Burke observed, we tend to see folk performances through the texts that have survived and which are brought to us by literate outsiders while we want to see the performances through the eyes of (usually peasant) audience. Cohen aims at such a presentation, using the theory of narrative performance, and applying it to the story of Jaka Menyawak ('The Lizard Boy'). That brings him to the conclusion that stories are appropriated by the audience and that '*wayang* drama does not transport spectators into a sublime alternate dimension, rather it intensifies worldly conflicts'.

The contribution of *Hae-Kyung Um* illustrates the practice of performance through an analysis of the traditional Korean musical *p'ansori* drama. The original performers were itinerant entertainers working on markets alongside acrobats, clowns and tight-rope-walkers, but *p'ansori* has been 'upgraded' to the status of a drama being performed on stage, and regularly 'exported' as a representation of Korean cultural traditions. Um analyses one *p'ansori* performance staged in Los Angeles and New York, and shows how a performance is built upon multiple layers of practice with varying aims and purposes and that their interactions produce different meanings, values and identities, rather than standard interpretations. Systems of patronage, *inter alia*, have influenced or shaped *p'ansori*, and present-day state patronage is closely related to the efforts of the Korean government to construct a modern national identity.

The subsequent essays address linguistic and ethnomusicological topics. *Yogendra Yadava* discusses the Maithili language, spoken in Bihar (India) and the adjoining Terai region in Nepal. He focuses on major grammatical characteristics of the language and shows how there converge with or diverge from genetically and regionally related languages. He finally analyses efforts aimed at promoting the use of Maithili in education and administration next to Hindi and Nepali. A more analytic approach to language use is taken by *Guo Wu* who examines the use of the particle *le* in Mandarin Chinese. He does so from a discursive point of view: discourse is social interaction and language serves as underspecified, but contextually efficient 'clues and cues' to prompt the cognitive constructions for the understanding of discourse. From an ethnographic perspective, *Suvarnalata Rao* investigates musical instruments from the *sarangi* family (bowed cordophones) in the north-western Indian state of Rajasthan which is well known for its rich musical heritage. His analysis of the cordophones aims at providing insight into the socio-cultural significance of the traditions associated with these instruments. The final contribution to this section and to the volume is by *Henk Blezer* who starts with the discovery of an anonymous and not yet dated Tibetan Buddhist text *Man ngag snying gi dgongs pa rgyal ba'i bka'zhes bya ba'i rgyud*. It turned out that half of the text is almost completely identical to two better-known texts. The author attempts to make a preliminary comparison of the three texts involved and concludes that they are based upon an earlier source which can even partially be reconstructed.

The panoramic view of Asia as seen through the lenses of historians, anthropologists, sociologists, linguists, political scientists and philologists who contribute to this volume, is kaleidoscopic. Each of them is a miniature text in itself, but together they provide often fascinating insights into the socio-cultural dynamics of Asia, just as the local raid of God's Army on a Thai hospital sheds light on issues which are shared by most Asian countries.

PART ONE

COPING WITH THE PRESENT

CHAPTER 1

ETHNICITY, LAW AND DEVELOPMENT IN SOUTHEAST ASIA*

CHRISTOPH ANTONS

Over the past decade, the political leadership of ASEAN countries has at times shown considerable interest in Japanese and East Asian approaches to economic development. Malaysia even propagated a 'look East' policy in contrast to the former reliance on Western development models.[1] With the Japanese economy in its heaviest recession since World War II, such recommendations are now becoming rarer. However, before the onset of the Asian crisis many commentators warned already that Japanese and East Asian experiences would be difficult to repeat in the countries of Southeast Asia.[2] Some observers noted that those Asia-Pacific countries with the most impressive growth rates shared a common cultural basis in Confucianism, which is largely absent in Southeast Asia,[3] although observations like this often seemed to overlook the marked differences between Japanese and Chinese Confucianism.[4] This idea of a common cultural basis should not be discarded out of hand as it contains a further thought which is less often directly expressed: the political and economic power structure of these Northeast Asian countries is not as pluralist as it is in Southeast Asia.[5]

The result of this pluralist power structure in Southeast Asia is a division between political and economic power along ethnic lines. In other words: political power is exercised by indigenous power holders, while a large part of the economic power is concentrated in the hands of ethnic minorities which have migrated to Southeast Asia over the last few centuries. 'Ethnicity' in this contribution, therefore, refers to these 'trading minorities' as the Dutch sociologist Wertheim has called them.[6] Most notable among these trading minorities are the Chinese, who play an important role in the economic life of all Southeast Asian countries, but there are also significant communities of Indians and Arabs, in particular in Indonesia, Malaysia, and Singapore. There are of course many more ethnic minorities in ASEAN countries, such as the hill tribes of North-Western Thailand, the Dayaks of Borneo, and the Papuas of Irian Jaya. While research into the fate of these minorities is certainly very important, they are largely marginalized and have little impact on the development of the national economies surveyed. They will, therefore, be ignored for the quite limited purpose of this contribution which is concerned with minorities which have played a major role in the economic development process of Southeast Asian countries.

Prior to the arrival of the Europeans in Southeast Asia, foreign traders from different parts of Asia had been prominent there since many centuries. Besides the different Chinese, Indian, and Arab communities, there were many other Asian traders such as Japanese, Armenians, Turks, and Persians. In the lively trading ports of Southeast Asia, they met Southeast Asian traders, traders from the East Coast of Africa and an increasing number of Europeans.[7] However, after the Portuguese capture of Malacca in 1511, the size and significance of trading communities from South and West Asia declined. The necessity to buy naval passes from the Portuguese to gain the guarantee of free passage was presumably eating a large hole into their profits.[8] As from then on European ships carried an increasing amount of the goods in the Eastern part of the Indian Ocean, West and South Asian merchants began to concentrate their activities on trading in the Near and Middle East.[9] Although they had bowed out, the Europeans failed to achieve the same dominance in the long-distance trade with East Asia, which remained largely in Chinese hands.[10] This increased the visibility of the Chinese as the most important Asian trading community in Southeast Asia during the colonial period.

As a consequence of these developments, the position of the Chinese in Southeast Asia is much better documented and has been researched much more intensively than the circumstances of other trading minorities.[11] In comparison with the Chinese, the relationship of the indigenous population with Arabs and Indians as the most important other 'trading minorities' in Southeast Asia has been less problematic and it is perhaps for this reason that it has attracted relatively little attention. Arab immigration, numerically also far less significant than that of the Chinese, followed the spread of Islam to the Malay-speaking countries of Southeast Asia.[12] When indigenous traders began to organize themselves at the beginning of the twentieth century to face Chinese competition, they did this in religiously inspired organizations such as the *Sarekat Dagang Islam* in the Netherlands East Indies and Arab merchants played a prominent role in these organizations.[13] In spite of their foreign origins, the Arabs were, therefore, welcomed as allies in the struggle against the Chinese, an approach that was also aided by the growth of Pan-Islam.[14] In Indonesia today Arabs are largely assimilated and Indonesians of Arab descent have become prominent ministers in the Suharto and Habibie governments, for example the long serving foreign minister, Ali Alatas.[15]

The situation of the Southeast Asian Indian communities is less problematic than that of the Chinese but more problematic than that of the Arabs. In comparison with the Chinese, the number of Indians in Southeast Asia is fairly insignificant. During a conference at the India International Centre in 1980 their numbers were estimated at about 200 in Vietnam, 4000 in the Philippines,

30,000 in Thailand, 40,000 in Indonesia, 170,000 in Singapore and 1,400,000 in Malaysia.[16] In contrast to the Arabs, racial problems have been reported from Malaysia, which has a comparatively large Indian population and from Indonesia where the conflict between India and Pakistan led to widespread rioting against Indians and the destruction of Indian property towards the end of the Soekarno era in 1965.[17] A further reason for the relatively limited attention paid to the Indian minority in Southeast Asia is the fact that many of them came under the indenture system to work as labourers on plantations in Malaysia and Sumatra.[18] Uneducated, from poor backgrounds, and contractually bound for years to repay their passage from India and without a network comparable to that of the Chinese, these people were hardly perceived to be a threat by the upcoming class of indigenous traders.

This contribution will attempt to outline how the colonial powers used legal instruments to shape the economic roles of different minorities in accordance with the overarching colonial strategy of 'divide and rule.' The contribution will then proceed to show the problems that the system posed to the newly independent states of Southeast Asia and their different reactions which ranged from upholding relevant colonial legislation, the abolition of such legislation, to the enactment of new discriminative laws to achieve a reversal of the colonial power structure. At the end of the contribution, an attempt will be made to assess the economic impact of these legal policies on the economic development process of the countries concerned.

In view of the large number of countries surveyed, this contribution can provide only a brief survey of the issues. The essay is based on the assumption that an analysis of the legal framework of racial distinctions might give an additional explanation for ethnic tensions that is at least as important as cultural preferences or political alliances.

THE COLONIAL ROOTS OF THE POSITION OF DIFFERENT TRADING MINORITIES

As outlined above, different trading communities of Chinese, Arabs, and Indians had been influential in Southeast Asian countries long before the arrival of the European powers. The Indian influence especially goes back to the proto-historic period. This is not the place to repeat the discussion among historians whether this influence was the consequence of large-scale immigration from India or whether the propagation of Indian culture was mainly the work of traders and religious teachers.[19] What cannot be disputed is the presence of Indians in Southeast Asia since the early days of Southeast Asian history. The Chinese appeared in the area they called Nanyang in significant numbers only much later. They had entered and finally conquered most of present-day Vietnam during the last three centuries BC, but significant trade with the remaining parts of Southeast Asia began only towards the end of the Sung dynasty and again particularly after the Mongol conquest of China when the Nanyang trade was strongly encouraged.[20] However, this policy was once again reversed by the Ming dynasty after the end of the Mongolian rule. Those Chinese who refused to return home after this reversal and decided to settle in Southeast Asia were henceforth regarded as outlaws and they would have been severely punished had they returned to China.[21] This policy was continued by the Ch'ing dynasty, partly because the Overseas Chinese were regarded as supporters of the former government and consequently Overseas Chinese settlements were considered as potential breeding grounds for rebel movements. Even after the ban on overseas trade was lifted, an imperial decree of 1712 stipulated that 'those who stayed overseas permanently are liable to capital punishment, and will be extradited from foreign countries by the provincial governors for immediate beheading.'[22] Therefore, when the Chinese community of Batavia was massacred in 1740, the Emperor Ch'ien-lung merely remarked that .'...these people are deserters of the Celestial Empire, they deserted their ancestral tombs and sought benefits overseas, and the court is not interested in them.'[23]

The relationship between these early settlers and the local population seems to have been relatively unproblematic, although contemporary reports about occasional racial tensions suggest that this was probably more true for the upper than for the lower strata of society.[24] Initially, the foreign merchants lived in the multi-ethnic trading ports of Southeast Asia in their own quarters, where they were allowed to choose their own head administrator (*shahbandar*). While they were supposed to settle their internal conflicts peacefully within their respective communities, universally valid commercial laws and customs helped to prevent legal disputes between members of different communities.[25] If they decided that their stay would be of a more permanent nature, intermarriages with locals were frequent. As far as the Chinese were concerned, intermarriages might have also been facilitated by the fact that in the fourteenth century many of them were already Muslim, because during the period their faith was on the rise in China, the Mongols preferred to grant trade privileges to Muslim Chinese.[26]

The relatively tolerant attitude of Southeast Asians during this period has been attributed to the different nature of Asian trade at that time and the relative lack of competition in a pre-capitalist society.[27] Occasionally, Southeast Asian feudal rulers would grant preferential treatment in the form of tax exemptions and the like to Chinese traders, as reported for instance for Thailand in the seventeenth century[28] and for Vietnam at the beginning of the nineteenth century.[29] Although Tran Khanh reports restrictions concerning the movement of Chinese in Vietnam and requests that they settle within separate quarters and assimilate to Vietnamese customs.[30] He explains these restrictions in the light of hostilities between the Ming government and the Vietnamese government at the time.[31] With the arrival of the colonial powers, the differentiation between ethnic groups gradually became more accentuated. Distrustful of the local population and by implementation of the strategy of 'divide and rule,' the colonial powers soon encouraged the immigration of foreign minorities to their trading ports. The Portuguese, as the first colonial power in the area, did little to develop a specific administrative or legal structure. They confined themselves to separate quarters within their strongholds and kept the Malay administration more or less intact. The *shahbandar* system was continued and all non-Portuguese traders remained subjected to their own tribunals.[32] In their commercial activities besides their reliance on the Chinese the Portuguese also leaned heavily on non-Muslim Indian traders. Because of this collaboration with the Portuguese, the Indians lost their influential position in Melaka to the Chinese after the city was taken over by the Dutch.[33]

Like the Portuguese in Melaka, the Spaniards in the Philippines preferred to seek the security of Manila's inner city (*intramuros*), from which the local population and other Asian traders were excluded.[34] The commercial attractiveness of the Philippines depended on the galleon trade with Mexico. In Manila, Chinese goods were purchased with Mexican silver and loaded on ships bound for Acapulco. Many of the Chinese traders who brought these goods from the Chinese mainland decided to stay and the Chinese population of the Philippines grew rapidly.[35] The Spaniards began to rely on the different skills the Chinese brought with them, in spite of a certain mutual dislike and distrust that lasted throughout the entire Spanish colonial period and resulted in frequent Chinese revolts and anti-Chinese riots and massacres.[36] However, because of their indispensable role in the colony, the Chinese were also legally protected by the Spaniards and the *parian*, a separate area consisting of shops and apartments, was constructed for them outside of the inner city in 1581. Contemporary commentators remarked at the turn of the sixteenth and seventeenth centuries: 'It is true the town cannot exist without the Chinese as they are workers in all trades and business, and very industrious and work for small wages' and 'without the trade and commerce of the Chinese these dominions could not have subsisted.'[37]

Intermarriages between the Chinese traders and local women soon became frequent, resulting in a growing Mestizo population. As a consequence, the Spaniards began to distinguish legally between China-born Chinese (*Chinos* or *Sangleys*), Chinese Mestizos, and the *Indios*, as they called the indigenous population.[38] Apart from differences in taxation, the Chinese were restricted to the *Parian* and needed permission to travel or to trade in the interior. It seems, however, that at least initially the distinction was largely based on religion as

Chinese who converted to Roman Catholicism were allowed to settle in the provinces.[39]

Swayed by religious fervour and racial prejudices, the legal policies of the Spaniards constantly shifted between a certain degree of protection and encouragement and grave forms of legal discrimination and expulsion orders which, when the crunch came, were not strictly enforced in the interest of the economy.[40] The parallel with the legal policies of some Southeast Asian countries over the last few decades is striking. An edict of 1755, for instance, provided for the expulsion of all non-Christian Chinese but a large number of Chinese evaded the edict by the simple expedient of converting to Christianity. An earlier expulsion order issued by the Indian Council in Madrid had been ignored by the governor who judged it to militate against public interests. The expulsion orders and the subsequent conversion of many Chinese to Roman Catholicism had a further important effect on the economic position of those Chinese in that it gave them access to credit and land via the Roman Catholic religious orders. They were able to work on *encomiendas* which were administered by Catholic orders.[41] Mestizo Chinese were even able to acquire land mortgaged to them by *Indios* who were then unable to repay their debts.[42] In this way, the Mestizo Chinese became gradually distinguishable from the *Sangleys* as landholders in the provinces. Their original position in the retail trade in the provinces was later filled by newly arrived Chinese immigrants.[43]

As in the Philippines, after the foundation of Batavia in 1619 contemporary Dutch commentators praised the local Chinese for their skills. The Chinese were described as 'an industrious people...on whom the well-being of Batavia completely depends, because without them no markets would be held, neither houses nor defence works would be made' and other sources stated that 'the Chinese form the foundation of this colony' and 'the Chinese have the greatest trade here, they form most of the excise and customs.'[44] In the first century of VOC rule, the Chinese were also still important in farming and market-gardening in the environs of Batavia.[45] In fact, Jan Pieterszoon Coen, the founder of Batavia, was so impressed by the Chinese that in 1622 ships were sent to China to kidnap Chinese and to bring them to Batavia.[46] Coen envisaged a separate trading quarter like the one that the Spaniards had opened in Manila and as the Spaniards and Portuguese before them, the Dutch left the administration of Chinese affairs in the hands of Chinese captains who were responsible for their communities.[47] Nevertheless, some provisions in the first piece of VOC legislation, the so-called '*Indische plakaten*,' already began to make distinctions between the European, the Chinese, and the indigenous population.[48] The Chinese were the only population group which had to pay a poll tax, accounting for a large part of Batavia's income,[49] and it was decreed that Chinese could be sold as slaves by their creditors should they not be able to pay back their debts.[50] Chinese who settled outside the immediate surroundings of Batavia (the so-called *Bataviase Ommelanden*) remained subject to their own customary law. A collection of Chinese customary laws was published in 1761 and named after its editor *Compendium Haksteen*.[51]

The original enthusiasm for the Chinese traders lessened after they became successful competitors of the Dutch in the sugar industry. With the end of the boom in sugar, a large number of Chinese lost their work and when the Dutch authorities started to round them up and news spread of a decision to deport them to Ceylon accompanied by rumours that they would be thrown overboard during the voyage, the Chinese revolted in 1740 and were killed in a massacre that claimed about 10,000 lives.[52] Immediately after the massacre the '*wijkstelsel*' was introduced which, like the *Parian* in Manila,[53] confined the Chinese to a particular quarter of a city, 'within range of the city's guns' as Lynn Pan remarks.[54] Moving around from then on was only possible after obtaining '*permissiebriefjes*,' official permits to travel. Go Gien Tjwan[55] claims that this and other measures finally succeeded in driving the Chinese out of their original position as primary traders and importers and exporters into a role as intermediate retail traders in the interior, whereas the VOC monopolized the international trade.

While the Dutch encouraged, but also strongly controlled the Chinese trade, they crushed the indigenous economy. A new chapter in colonial history was begun in 1800 when the Dutch state was forced to take over the administration of the colony from the bankrupt VOC. Military force was repeatedly used, especially against enterprising states in the Eastern archipelago and these states were finally subdued only early this century.[56] On the main island of Java, the Java War, which ended in 1830, broke the economic power of the aristocracy and turned the Javanese aristocrats into powerless instruments of the Dutch administration.[57]

Towards the middle of the nineteenth century, the colonial economies underwent a profound change.[58] Britain considerably expanded its interests in the area and with France and later the United States new colonial powers appeared on the scene. These changes brought capitalist concepts of production with them. The first steps towards industrialization were taken and in the field of agriculture, large-scale production on plantations began to replace the former method of forced cultivation by small-holders.[59] The increasing need for labourers was once again met by importing foreign minorities. Initially many Chinese and later an increasing number of Indian labourers were brought to the Straits Settlements.[60] At the time, the Straits Settlements were still under the administration of British India and no immigration law restricted the flow of Indians to Southeast Asia. Most of them received advances which were deducted from their wages under the indenture system. This was regulated at first by the British Indian government and later on by the Indian Immigrants Protection Ordinance of the Straits Settlements. Most of these regulations granted the Indian labourer a basic protection against grossly inhumane practices, but also contained harsh penalties for 'absence from work' or 'disobedience of orders.'[61] In the early days of the Straits Settlements it was also common to use convict labourers from India.[62] The flow of Chinese labourers to Southeast Asia increased greatly after the conclusion of the Treaty of Nanking between China and Britain in 1842 and subsequent treaties between China and other Western powers.[63] As a result of these treaties it was no longer possible for the Manchu dynasty to enforce their restrictions on the travel and settlement of Chinese subjects abroad.[64] Lynn Pan has pointed out that the coolie immigration system was a replacement for the African slave trade, since slavery had been abolished in the British colonial possessions two years before the outbreak of the Opium War.[65] With a rising demand for labour on the plantations of Sumatra, Chinese plantation workers were often transferred from the Straits Settlements to the Netherlands East Indies.[66]

The Spaniards, in spite of their ambivalent feelings about Chinese commercial activities in the Philippines, nevertheless towards the middle of the nineteenth century began to use Chinese labour to achieve a modernization of the agricultural sector. In 1839 travel permits similar to those in the Netherlands East Indies were introduced. Initially they were valid for three months outside of Metropolitan Manila. In 1850, taxes to be paid by Chinese agricultural labourers were reduced and in 1863 restrictions on occupations for foreigners were lifted.[67] As a result, recently immigrated Chinese began to fill the position in retail trade in the provinces, which had earlier been vacated by the new landholding Chinese Mestizo elite.[68] In the Netherlands East Indies, coolie labour from China and India was used mainly on the plantations in Sumatra. In Java, where indigenous labour was abundant, the foreign minorities continued in their role as intermediate traders into which they had been pushed during the previous century.[69]

An Agrarian Law of 1870 attempted a liberalization of land ownership, but its effects on the Chinese who had acquired rights to land earlier in the century were not always clear. The *'Reglement omtrent de particuliere landerijen ten Westen der Rivier Tjimanoek'* (Ordinance over the private landholdings West of the Cimanuk River) led to a discussion between lawyers which lasted for almost a century about whether the term 'occupants' (*opgezetenen*) of the land, who were able to acquire long term leases (*erfpachten*), would include the Chinese. As a result of contradicting court decisions and in spite of a final decision in favour of the Chinese, many Chinese farmers were driven from their land.[70] The situation was finally clarified in a decree of 1912[71] which recognized Chinese farmers as 'occupants' but contained also a prohibition forbidding 'natives' (*inlanders*) to transfer their rights to Chinese or Europeans. In 1913, a separate long-term lease for Chinese which later became known as '*landerijenbezitsrecht*' was introduced.[72] Consequently in his '*Hukum*

Antargolongan' Professor Sudargo Gautama differentiates between three different land rights, namely those of Europeans, those of native Indonesians, and those of Chinese.[73] General prohibitions forbidding indigenous Indonesians to transfer land to non-indigenous people (*vervreemdingsverbod*) has been introduced via several decrees since 1972.[74]

By the mid-nineteenth century the differences in the legal and economic position between indigenous Indonesians and foreign minorities had become so numerous that the foreign minorities were classified as a legal group on their own. The first constitution of the Netherlands East Indies of 1855, the so-called '*Regerings-Reglement*,' still classified Indians, Arabs, and Chinese as 'natives' for legal purposes and subjected them to their own customary laws.[75] However, the Governor-General was authorized to make exceptions to this rule. Such an exception was promptly made by a decree in 1855 which created a new group, the so-called 'foreign Orientals' (*vreemde oosterlingen*). These 'foreign Orientals' were from now on subject to the European civil and commercial codes except for their family and inheritance matters in which customary laws still applied.[76] In 1919, a decree of 1917 came into force which subjected the Chinese, with some minor exceptions, to the entire European civil law so that henceforth in fact a legal distinction was made between four different groups: the Europeans, the Chinese, the 'foreign Orientals' other than Chinese, and the native Indonesians.[77] The economic motives behind the system can be seen from the fact that the Japanese and later the Thai were classified as 'Europeans' after 'modernizing' their legal system,[78] whereas the Chinese in spite of such a 'modernization' in China nevertheless remained categorized as 'foreign Orientals.' The system was reconfirmed Arts. 131 and 163 of the *Indische Staatsregeling* of 1925.[79]

Since the different population groups did not confine themselves to dealings within their own communities, it was necessary to regulate which law applied to contracts, to marriages and a host of other agreements concluded between members of different groups. This produced a complicated mixture of statutes, decrees, case law, and customs which the Dutch called *intergentiel recht* (inter-communal law).[80] This body of law also contained regulations for a complete transfer from one population group to the other in the form of a so-called 'equalization' (*gelijkstelling*) with Europeans or 'assimilation' with indigenous Indonesians (*vermenging met de autochtone bevolking*). The main criteria for such a transfer were name, religion, and way of life. Inter-ethnic marriages often led to a presumption of a change of lifestyle. Interestingly, the lifestyle of the husband's community seemed to be decisive here for marriages between non-Europeans, whereas a marriage with a European woman would lead to an 'equalization' of the non-European husband.[81] The importance attached to Islam in this classification resulted in the assimilation of a large number of Arabs and Muslim Indians.[82] However, with the rise of Pan-Islam,

Arabs were increasingly seen as a political threat. Immigration of Arabs was made more difficult and the segregation of Arabs through the *wijkstelsel* and the travel permits (*passenstelsel*) was strictly enforced, before it was finally abolished early in this century.[83]

On establishing themselves in Vietnam the French were eager to participate in the China trade. They had apparently learned from other colonial powers and allowed the Chinese a generous amount of freedom under their own organizations and headmen, provided that they paid their poll taxes.[84] Vietnamese legislation early in the nineteenth century had established a distinction between recent migrants (*Thanh*) and mixed Sino-Vietnamese (*Minh Huong*). The latter were finally granted political rights in 1829, but they were also prohibited from travelling to China.[85] This policy was initially continued by the French. Later, however, they created a new category of French Asian citizens.[86] French civil and commercial law applied to such 'Assimilated Asians' (*Asiatiques assimilés*) and they were legally distinguished from the indigenous population.[87]

The British colonial possessions in Malaya and Borneo were gradually subjected to the statutory introduction of English law between 1807 and 1951.[88] As the British applied English law only if 'suitable to local conditions,' the customary laws of the various communities were recognized as 'personal laws' for such fields as family law and land law.[89] In British Malaya, a land reservation policy blocking Malay land sales to non-Malays was introduced in 1913, a policy that drove land values down and reduced the creditworthiness of the Malays.[90] This in turn required that a definition of who was 'Malay' be made. The definition adopted regarded as Malay someone 'who habitually speaks the Malay language or any Malayan language and professes the Muslim religion.'[91] This definition facilitated the assimilation of many immigrants from the different islands of the Indonesian archipelago, but it excluded the Chinese and those Indians who were not Muslims. The Chinese were denied the right to enter Malaya's civil service and a three-to-one quota in favour of Malays was established at the University of Malaya.[92]

ETHNIC TENSIONS, LAW AND DEVELOPMENT IN THE ASEAN COUNTRIES

After independence, the new leadership of the ASEAN countries had to face the legacy of the 'divide and rule policy' of their colonial predecessors. While indigenous Indonesians, Filipinos, and Malays were largely in charge of politics, administration, military and police, large parts of the economy were controlled by the Chinese. As many of the countries chose to keep the colonial order at least partially intact for the time being, among the many legal problems arising were unclear citizen status and confusion as to what law was applicable to what had originally been foreign trading minorities. Apart from Singapore, which is officially propagating a policy of multiracialism, all of the countries surveyed in this contribution have at some stage enacted laws or issued decrees which were targeted either directly at the Chinese community or that targeted activities in which the Chinese were predominantly involved. While these measures were often meant to increase the popularity of a particular government with the indigenous population, such governments soon had to face the same dilemma as the colonial administrations which preceded them, namely that to get rid of the Chinese would severely damage the economy. As in colonial times, such discriminating legislation was, therefore, often only half-heartedly enforced.

Many problems resulted from complicated citizenship statutes that often dated back to the colonial period. The American administration which followed the Spaniards in the Philippines applied the Chinese Exclusion Act, a piece of legislation which was originally conceived to stop Chinese immigration to the United States.[93] As a consequence, the *ius soli* principle applied to determine citizenship during that period did not apply to Chinese.[94] The Commonwealth Constitution of 1935 replaced the *ius soli* principle with the *ius sanguinis* principle which was, however, interpreted in such a way that only children of Filipino fathers could acquire the Filipino citizenship.[95] Because of this it remained difficult for Chinese to acquire citizenship even after the exclusion of Asians was removed from the Philippine Naturalization Law in 1939.[96] These difficulties came to a head in 1954, when the Philippines enacted the Retail Trade Nationalization Law in 1954. The Retail Trade Nationalization Law restricted retail trade to companies that were 100 per cent Filipino-owned. There was a ten-year transition period for foreign companies and traders who were active in retail trading before 1954. The latter were allowed to continue their trade until their death or retirement. After this, however, their companies ceased to exist.[97]

The Retail Trade Nationalization Law was one of the strictest pieces of legislation engendered by economic nationalism in Southeast Asia and went considerably further than earlier legislation which provided for the nationalization of public utilities, banks, shipping, civil aviation, and mining and usually required an indigenous ownership of sixty per cent.[98] Since 1936, agricultural land had been reserved for Filipino nationals and since 1949 the government of the Philippines reserved an ever-growing percentage of import quotas for new Filipino importers.[99] It was, however, the Retail Trade Nationalization Law which hit the Chinese hardest, since retail trade was their classical domain in Southeast Asia. While some family companies managed to survive by having some of their members naturalized and by transferring shares from the remaining members to the naturalized members, many companies had no option but to dissolve in 1964. The situation eased somewhat after the adoption of the Constitution of 1973 which granted equal status to male and female Filipino nationals.[100] In addition, following Presidential Instructions from Marcos the conditions for naturalization were relaxed and many Chinese were able to acquire Filipino citizenship on the basis of these instructions.[101]

In comparison to the situation in the Philippines, it was relatively easy for 'foreign Orientals' to acquire Indonesian citizenship.[102] However, Art 26 of the Indonesian Constitution of 1945 and Art 1 of the Nationality Act of 1946 nevertheless distinguished between indigenous Indonesians (*orang Indonesia asli*) and persons of other ethnic origin (*bangsa lain*).[103] From this developed the widespread distinction between the indigenous '*pribumi*' (sons of the soil) and the '*non-pribumi*,' persons of foreign descent. Indonesians of foreign descent are also commonly distinguished from indigenous Indonesians by simply referring to them as 'WNI' for '*warga negara Indonesia*' (Indonesian citizen) in contrast to themselves who are 'WNA' (*warga negara asli*) or native citizens. A common and less discriminating term in Indonesia is also '*orang keturunan*' (a person of descent). In spite of the fact that the terms mentioned could in fact be used for all the different groups of 'foreign Orientals' of the colonial period, the use of the term in Indonesian publications shows that it is predominantly meant for the Chinese.[104] There is little official clarification given to explain why Indians and Arabs are no longer mentioned in this context. One clue is the fact that the first vice-president of Indonesia, Mohammad Hatta, wrote in a letter in 1975 that the Arabs had shown loyalty to Indonesia and should no longer be regarded as '*non-pribumi*.'[105] A little later, in an official instruction to the Governor of Central Java the then Minister for State Apparatus Reform, Sumarlin, wrote, how the term '*non-pribumi*' had to be interpreted: '..for the group of non-indigenous people who has already been assimilated and integrated themselves and considered by the local community to be indigenous people, such as those of Arab descent who have achieved complete integration with the local Indonesians, they have to be treated as '*pribumi*' (indigenous) group...'[106] Presumably the same would apply to Indian adherents of the Islamic faith.

Siddique and Suryadinata,[107] however, quote a 'secret circular' issued by the Bank Indonesia containing a 'practical guide to the definition of *pribumi*' which was published in the daily newspaper *Kompas* of 24 March 1976. According to this definition, *pribumi* are people who are not foreign citizens, do not belong to the legal categories of 'Europeans' or 'foreign Orientals,' and are not Indonesians of Chinese descent. If one follows this definition, then it seems that the acceptance of Arabs and Indian Muslims as *pribumi* is based on the concept of assimilation of the *intergentiel recht*. The *intergentiel recht* and the classification of the population into different ethnic groups based on Art

163 *Indische Staatsregeling* survived independence on the basis of a transitional article in the 1945 Constitution, which kept all former regulations of the Netherlands East Indies in force, unless and until they would be replaced by new regulations of the Republic of Indonesia.[108] The field is known in Indonesia as '*hukum antargolongan*' ('intergroup law'). An instruction of the Cabinet of the Indonesian Government of 1966 directed the Civil Registry (*Kantor Catatan Sipil*) no longer to make a distinction between different population groups and in future to distinguish only between Indonesian citizens and foreigners. However, as Gautama correctly points out, the instruction does not invalidate the distinction itself and consequently, different regulations for different groups continue to be applied.[109]

The distinction between '*pri*' and '*non-pri*' has become important to many business sectors which have been reserved for '*pribumi*.' In this context, '*pribumi*' have also been often referred to as 'the economically weak group' (*golongan ekonomi lemah*). For example, Presidential Decree No. 14 A of 1980 reserved all government contracts in the construction industry under a certain value for the 'economically weak group.'[110] Similarly, the investment priority scales issued by the Capital Investment Co-ordinating Board (*BKPM - Badan Koordinasi Penanaman Modal*) have been used to preserve certain sectors for the *pribumi* and small-scale capital investors or to prescribe some form of participation for these local businesses.[111] For a company to be recognized as a 'national company' it is necessary that at least 50 per cent of the shares are owned by indigenous Indonesians. The Indonesian National Banks have also given priority to *pribumi* in granting low-interest credits.[112] As early as the early 1950s when the citizen status of many Chinese was still unclear, the Indonesian government had initiated the so-called Benteng programme which reserved certain categories of goods for indigenous importers and provided credit for these importers through the Indonesian National Bank (BNI). This led to abuses as many of the indigenous licence-holders did not work the licences themselves but sold them to Chinese. The result was a growth of so-called 'Ali-Baba firms' where Ali, referring to the indigenous Indonesian, would hold the licence and the Baba, a Chinese term referring to a Southeast Asian born Chinese, would run the business.[113] The programme was finally abrogated in 1957.[114]

Another blow against Chinese business interests during the Soekarno period occurred in 1959 when the Minister for Trade issued Government Regulation No. 10, known in Indonesia as 'PP10' (Peraturan Pemerintah No.10, 1959) revoking licences for alien Chinese to participate in the retail trade at village level. The regulation led to an exodus of about 120,000 Chinese from Indonesia. Others moved to the cities or established 'Ali-Baba firms.' When indigenous traders failed to fill the gap, PP10 was no longer so rigorously enforced. After a while, the retail trade in rural areas was again dominated by the Chinese.[115]

Even in Thailand, which was never colonized, a series of measures to nationalize the economy and to diminish the Chinese share in it was introduced after the nationalist revolution in 1932. By 1942, twenty-seven trades and professions were reserved for Thais[116] and in 1952, the annual residence tax for aliens was raised considerably. However, most of these measures were reversed during the 1950s. In 1972, the so-called Alien Business Law reserved retail trade for Thais and Thai companies, but unlike the situation in the Philippines, Thai companies were defined as those in which Thais owned more than 50 per cent of the capital.[117] In Vietnam, immediately after the departure of the French, the South Vietnamese government enacted decrees which closed certain key sectors of the economy in which the Chinese were active to foreigners and thereby forced the Chinese to take Vietnamese citizenship.[118] After the socialist government came to power, the government crackdown on capitalists affected a large number of Chinese and many decided subsequently to leave the country.[119]

The most far-reaching redistribution of shares in the economy along ethnic lines was undertaken by Malaysia which introduced the 'New Economic Policy' (NEP) in 1971, following the ethnic turmoil and widespread rioting that occurred in 1969. The goals of the NEP were: (1) to eliminate absolute poverty, especially among the Malay peasantry; (2) to abolish the correlation between occupation and ethnicity through an 'affirmative action' programme requiring quotas for Malays in education, employment, and government contracts; and (3) to restructure the ownership of corporate equity holdings through state funding of *Bumiputera* (i.e. Malay and other indigenous peoples) 'trust agencies' that purchase and hold equities for the *Bumiputera* community. The aim was to raise *Bumiputera* ownership in the economy from 1.9 per cent to 30 per cent, that of other Malaysians from 23.5 per cent to 40 per cent and to reduce the share of foreigners from 60.7 per cent to 30 per cent.[120] The 'New Economic Policy' has renewed a debate about the legal definition of the term '*bumiputera*.' This debate became particularly relevant after Singapore, Sabah, and Sarawak joined the Federation of Malaysia in 1963. Suddenly the Malay majority of Peninsular Malaysia was joined not only by non-Malay Singaporeans but also by the non-Malay indigenous population of Sabah and Sarawak. After this, it became difficult to uphold the original identification of '*bumiputera*' with Malays. For a while, the term 'Malays and other indigenous people' became common and apparently a distinction was being made between indigenous majorities in Peninsular Malaysia on the one hand and those in Sabah and Sarawak on the other hand.[121] As far as Peninsular Malaysia is concerned, the debate with reference to the definition of 'Malay' in the Constitution continues. According to this definition, a 'Malay' is someone who habitually speaks the Malay language, practises Malay customs, and is a Muslim.[122] Given the considerable economic incentives provided by the Government for Malays under the 'New Economic Policy,' the question arises whether Indian and Chinese Muslims, Pakistanis and Arabs qualify for these benefits. In a parliamentary debate of 1978, Malaysia's then Prime Minister, Datuk Hussein Onn, remarked on this issue that a non-Malay Muslim would not be included under the constitutional definition.[123]

CONCLUSION:
THE IMPACT OF RACIALLY DISCRIMINATIVE LEGISLATION ON ECONOMIC DEVELOPMENT

In studying the different legal policies towards Southeast Asian trading minorities over a longer period of time, it becomes clear that it would be wrong to see the pre-colonial, colonial, and post-colonial periods as sharply divided. In fact, some of the feudal rulers of pre-colonial Southeast Asia applied similar discriminative measures as those usually attributed to colonialism. It seems that in the initial phases of the European expansion to the region, the favouritism shown to trading minorities was simply a necessity for survival. The Portuguese attempted to continue the trading emporia tradition of Melaka and, since they were distrustful of Muslims, they began to rely heavily on Hindus from the southern parts of India. In fact, it seems to have been the original *shahbandar* system that inspired the Europeans to keep the different trading minorities separate and governed by their own rules. The VOC and the British East India Company were giant enterprises aiming to derive profits from the region and they were little concerned with the administration of justice. It tended to be rather towards the later period of the colonial rule that policies were no longer *ad hoc* but deliberately designed to use different trading minorities as instruments to develop the colonies and to avoid a concentration of power in the hands of the indigenous elite. During this process the Chinese, who became the main target of this policy, were distinguished more sharply from the Indians, who were less important in trade, and from the Arabs, who managed to become part of the growing movement of nationalist indigenous traders which had its roots in Pan-Islam.

Looking at the difficulties that this colonial legacy poses for the independent ASEAN countries today, it is interesting to note that the only ASEAN country that has so far been able to join the ranks of the 'Newly Industrializing Countries' (NICs) is Singapore, a country where political and economic power is not defined in ethnic terms. In those countries where the political and economic power is divided along ethnic lines, some of the discriminating colonial legislation has been retained. The picture is made more complicated because governments have attempted to reduce the dominant position of the Chinese in the economy through 'affirmative action' legislation. This 'affirmative action' legislation has been repeatedly criticized for putting enormous costs on the economy[124] and for creating a 'rentier entrepreneurial class.'[125] Yoshihara Kunio has identified the relative lack of discriminating legislation in Thailand, as compared to the Philippines, as one of the reasons responsible for the economic rise of Thailand and the relative decline of the Philippines over the last few decades.[126] Commenting on Malaysia, Paul M. Lubeck has pointed out that changes in foreign investment patterns created a situation in which much of the new investment in Malaysia arrived from the NICs, Taiwan, Singapore, and Hong Kong, and as a consequence the foreign Chinese presence in Malaysia was increasing. Discriminating legislation under the 'New Economic Policy' then actually resulted in a denationalization of industries, because Malaysian Chinese were discouraged from developing supplier firms, while foreign Chinese firms were encouraged to bring their own suppliers.[127] Given the current structure of the Southeast Asian economies and their reliance on export-oriented growth models, ASEAN governments would, therefore, be well advised to abolish discriminating legislation targeted at citizens of ASEAN countries of foreign descent and to secure their position. Following the recent economic turmoil and the anti-Chinese riots in Indonesia, both the Malaysian and Indonesian governments have taken first steps to achieve this aim. In September 1998, Indonesia's President Habibie issued a Presidential Decree that abolished the distinction between *'pribumi'* and *'non-pribumi.'*[128]

NOTES

* This is an amended version of a paper originally submitted at the 1995 Annual Meeting, Research Committee on Sociology of Law, International Sociological Association at the University of Tokyo on 2 August 1995. A draft of the paper was subsequently published in the conference proceedings. I would like to thank Alice Erh-Soon Tay and Rosy Antons-Sutanto for helpful comments on this earlier draft.

1 See P.M. Lubeck, 1992, p. 177. Cf. also Lim Chong-Yah, 1990, pp. 38-56; Lee Poh Ping, 1991, pp. 23-9; Lim Chong Yah, 1991, pp. 137-67.

2 See for example Yoshihara Kunio who in 1988 used the term 'ersatz capitalism' for Southeast Asian economic development, see Yoshihara K., 1988, pp. 130-1. Cf. also P.M. Lubeck, 1992, pp. 176-98.

3 See the discussion in J. Henderson and R.P. Appelbaum, 1992, pp. 15-17.

4 Lim Chong-Yah, 1991, pp. 163-4. M. Morishima, 1982, pp. 11-28. See

generally on this discussion The Institute of East Asian Philosophies, *A Forum on 'The Role of Culture in Industrial Asia - The Relationship between Confucian Ethics and Modernisation,'* Singapore: Institute of East Asian Philosophies, 1988.
5   See P.M. Lubeck, 1992, p. 177.
6   W.F. Wertheim, 1980, pp. 104-20. More recently and not confined to Southeast Asia, Christine Dobbin has used the term 'Asian entrepreneurial minorities,' see C. Dobbin, 1996.
7   See K.N. Chaudhuri, 1985, chapter 5, pp. 98-118.
8   K.N. Chaudhuri, 1985, p. 69.
9   Ibid., pp. 100-1.
10 A. Reid, 1992, pp. 494-5.
11 See for example C. Coppel; Wang Gungwu, 1991; Yen Ching-hwang, 1995; L. Suryadinata, 1992. See also the various contributions in J.A.C. Mackie, 1976.
12 H.J. Benda, 1958, pp. 1-2.
13 H. Algadri, 1994; B. Dahm, 1971, pp. 38-9.
14 For Pan-Islam in Southeast Asia, see P. Kratoska and B. Batson, 1992, Volume Two, p. 310.
15 H. Algadri, op. cit., p. 161.
16 S.R. Sudhamani, 1982, p. 9.
17 B.D. Arora, 1982, pp. 123-4.
18 See the extract from R.N. Jackson, 1979, pp. 257-66.
19 See D.G.E. Hall, 1981, pp. 12-24; J.G. De Casparis and I.W. Mabbett, 1992, Volume One, pp. 286-8.
20 Wang Gungwu, 1992, pp. 11-13.
21 Wang Gungwu, op. cit., p. 14; A. Reid, 'Flows and Seepages in the Long-term Chinese Interaction with Southeast Asia,' in: A. Reid (ed.), 1996, p. 26.
22 See Yen Ching-Hwang, op. cit., pp. 3-4.
23 Ibid., p. 5.
24 Go Gien Tjwan, 1972, pp. 8-9; Go Gien Tjwan, 1971, p. 567.
25 K.N. Chaudhuri, op. cit., pp. 112-13; A. Reid, op. cit., pp. 483-8; C.M. Turnbull, 1980, pp. 31-2.
26 Wang Gungwu, op. cit., p. 16; C.M. Turnbull, 1980, p. 21.
27 Go Gien Tjwan, 1971, pp. 567-9.
28 G.W. Skinner, 1957, pp. 7-8.
29 Tran Khanh, 1993, pp. 19-20.
30 Tran Khanh, 1997, p. 271.
31 Tran Khanh, 1993, p. 17.
32 M.B. Hooker, 1988, pp. 4-6; C.M. Turnbull, op. cit., p. 39.

33 L.Y. Andaya, 1992, Vol. 1, p. 368.
34 L.Y. Andaya, op. cit., p. 366.
35 See C. Dobbin, op. cit., pp. 21-2.
36 Major riots and massacres are reported for 1603, 1639, 1662 and 1686 and again in 1762, see Teresita Ang See, 1996, pp. 3-7; C. Dobbin, op. cit., p. 24.
37 Quotations from the works of Antonio Morga and Juan de la Concepcion in J. Foreman, 1899, pp. 117-18. See also H.C. Stuntz, 1904, pp. 265-6; R. Oades, 1974, pp. 191-2.
38 G.W. Skinner, 1996, p. 67.
39 See Andaya, 1992, pp. 368-9 and Dobbin, op. cit., p. 23.
40 A. Reid, 1996, p. 46. Cf. also R. Oades, op. cit., pp. 192-3.
41 As to the encomienda system see Andaya, 1992, p. 366.
42 Dobbin, op. cit., pp. 32-8.
43 See N.G. Owen, 1984, pp. 68-71.
44 L. Blussé, 1988, pp. 74-5.
45 Go Gien Tjwan, 1966, 68; Andaya, 1992, p. 367.
46 Go Gien Tjwan, 1966, p. 50; L. Pan, 1991, pp. 34-5.
47 L. Blussé, 1989, pp. 114-15.
48 Go Gien Tjwan, 1966, p. 74.
49 L. Blussé, 1988, pp. 80-3.
50 Go Gien Tjwan, 1966, p. 66.
51 E. Utrecht and M. Saleh Djindang, *Pengantar dalam Hukum Indonesia*, 11th ed., Jakarta: Sinar Harapan, 1983, p. 176.
52 L. Pan, op. cit., 35-7; L. Blussé, 1988, pp. 94-5.
53 See J. Foreman, op. cit., 117-18.
54 L. Pan, op. cit., 37.
55 Go Gien Tjwan, 1966, pp. 67-8; Go Gien Tjwan, 1971, pp. 564-75.
56 M.C. Ricklefs, 1981, pp. 60-1 and 129.
57 M.C. Ricklefs, op. cit., p. 113.
58 See R.E. Elson, 1992, pp. 131-95.
59 R. Robison, 1986, pp. 6-7 has described these changes for the Netherlands East Indies. See also M.C. Ricklefs, op. cit., pp. 143-7.
60 R.E. Elson, op. cit., p. 163; C.M. Turnbull, op. cit., p. 104; Fukuda Shozo, 1995, pp. 55-60. The word 'coolie' is originally derived from the name of an aboriginal Gujarat tribe of India, see L. Pan, op. cit., p. 45.
61 R.N. Jackson, 1979, pp. 257-61.
62 T.H. Silcock and Ungku Abdul Aziz, 1979, p. 273.
63 As to these treaties see J.D. Spence, 1990, pp. 158-64.
64 Tran Khanh, 1993, p. 21.
65 L. Pan, op. cit., pp. 45-6.

66 Fukuda Shozo, op. cit., p. 57.
67 R. Oades, op. cit., pp. 196-8.
68 C. Dobbin, op. cit., pp. 164-71; N.G. Owen, op. cit., pp. 68-71.
69 Cf. C.P. FitzGerald, 1972, p. 177.
70 Go Gien Tjwan, 1966, above note 26, pp. 74-93.
71 Stbl 1912 No 442, see Gautama, *Hukum Antargolongan*. p. 90.
72 Stbl. 1913 No 702 cited in Gautama, *Hukum Antargolongan*, pp. 91-2; See also Go Gien Tjwan, 1966, op. cit., pp. 92-6.
73 S. Gautama, *Hukum Antargolongan*, p. 88. See also S. Gautama, 1995, pp. 119-32.
74 *Staatsblad van Nederlandsch-Indië* 1875 No. 179. See also Stbl. 1872 No 117, art 19, Stbl. 1906 No 431, art 2, Stbl. 1915 No 98, arts 17-18 and Stbl. 1923 No 475, art 2, cited in: S. Gautama (Gouw Giok Siong), op. cit., pp. 89-90; see also S. Wignjosoebroto, 1994, pp. 91-4.
75 Stbl. 1855 No 2. This confirmed an earlier classification in the *Algemeene Bepalingen van Wetgeving voor Nederlandsch-Indië*, Stbl. 1847 No 23.
76 See Stbl. 1855 No 79. See also C. Fasseur, p. 37; Yoe-Sioe Liem, 1986, p. 404.
77 S. Gautama and R.N. Hornick, 1983, pp. 13-14; C. Fasseur, op. cit., p. 43.
78 S. Gautama and R.N. Hornick, op. cit., p. 3.
79 Stbl. 1925 No 415, see Gautama, 1995, p. 5.
80 The term was derived from the Latin '*ius intergentes.*' As to different translations of the term into English see S. Gautama, *Hukum Antargolongan*, op. cit., p. 19-20.
81 Gautama, *Hukum Antargolongan*, pp. 105-7. The 'equalization' of the Non-European husband was even legally prescribed after 1848, see Gautama, p. 129.
82 Gautama, *Hukum Antargolongan*, pp. 107-9.
83 See Algadri, op. cit., pp. 57-8, 74-81, 91-100.
84 Tran Khanh, 1993, p. 22; V. Thompson, 1968, pp. 167 and 170.
85 Tran Khanh, 1997, op. cit., p. 272.
86 Ibid.
87 M.B. Hooker, pp. 240-1; V. Thompson, op. cit., p. 167.
88 Wu Min Aun, 1982, pp. 1-21.
89 Wu Min Aun, op. cit., p. 47; M.B. Hooker, 1978, pp. 129-43.
90 P.M. Lubeck, op. cit., 187.
91 S. Siddique and L. Suryadinata, 1997.
92 Li Dun Jen, 1982, pp. 170-1.
93 See the critical remarks as to this policy by H.C. Stuntz, above note 37, p. 280. See also I.R. Cortes and R.P.M. Lotilla, 1990, p. 345.
94 Yoshihara Kunio, 1994, p. 30.

95 Yoshihara, K., op. cit., p. 30. The *ius soli* principle continued to be applied, however, to a small group of people born in the Philippines of foreign parents, who, before the adoption of the Constitution, had been elected to public office in the Philippines, see Cortes and Lotilla, op. cit., p. 346.
96 Cortes and Lotilla, op. cit., p. 346.
97 Yoshihara K., op. cit., pp. 28-30; A. Doronila, 1992, pp. 71-2.
98 Yoshihara K., op. cit., p. 28.
99 Yoshihara K., op. cit., pp. 28-9; Doronila, op. cit., p. 71.
100 Cortes and Lotilla, op. cit., p. 347.
101 Yoshihara K., op. cit., 31.
102 For details see Ko Swan Sik and T.M. Rhadie, 'Nationality and International Law in Indonesian Perspective,' in: Ko Swan Sik (ed.) 1990 pp. 125-76; C.A. Coppel, H. Mabbett and Ping-ching Mabbett, 1982, pp. 4-5; H. Thoolen (ed.), 1987, pp. 151-2.
103 Ko Swan Sik and T.M. Radhie, pp. 130, 139-40.
104 H. Junus Jahja (ed.), 1991.
105 Algadri, op. cit., Appendix 2, pp. 169-70.
106 Cited after the translation by Algadri, op. cit., Appendix 5, p. 176.
107 Op. cit., 85.
108 S. Gautama, 1993, p. 13; See also S. Pompe and C. de Waaij-Vosters, 1989, pp. 365-9.
109 Gautama, 'An Overview of the Indonesian Legal System,' op. cit., p. 14; Gautama, 1995, op. cit., p. 8.
110 R. Robison, op. cit., p. 185; L. Suryadinata, 1997, p. 62.
111 R. Robison, op. cit., p. 184.
112 H. Thoolen, op. cit., p. 153; Siddique and Suryadinata, op. cit., p. 85. As to the economic effects of these policies see A.J. MacIntyre, 1993, pp. 123-64.
113 Siddique and Suryadinata, op. cit., p. 86.
114 R. Robison, op. cit., pp. 44-6.
115 R. Robison, op. cit., pp. 86-7.
116 As to this period see Supang Chantavanich, 1997, pp. 240-1. Cf. also Fukuda Shozo, op. cit., pp. 168-70.
117 Yoshihara K., op. cit., pp. 32-6.
118 Tran Khanh, 1993, pp. 28-9; Tran Kanh, 1997, p. 274.
119 Tran Kanh, The Ethnic Chinese, pp. 81-7; Tran Khanh, 1997, pp. 276-7.
120 P.M. Lubeck, op. cit., 180. See also Siddique and Suryadinata, op. cit., pp. 84-5 and D. Brown, 1994, pp. 243-57.
121 Siddique and Suryadinata, op. cit., pp. 79-83.
122 Ibid., p. 79.

123 Ibid., pp. 87-9.
124 Yoshihara K., 1988, pp. 130-1.
125 P.M. Lubeck, op. cit., pp. 194-5.
126 Yoshihara K, 1994, pp. 28-40.
127 P.M. Lubeck, op. cit., pp. 195-6.
128 Inpres No. 26/1998 of 16 September 1998, quoted in H. Junus Jahja, 1999, p. 1.

REFERENCES

Algadri, H. (1994) *Dutch Policy Against Islam and Indonesians of Arab Descent in Indonesia*. Jakarta: LP3ES.

Andaya, L.Y. (1992) 'Interactions with the Outside World and Adaptation in Southeast Asian Society, 1500-1800,' in: N. Tarling (ed.) *The Cambridge History of Southeast Asia, Volume One: From Early Times to c. 1800*. Cambridge: Cambridge University Press.

Ang See, Teresita (1996) *The Ethnic Chinese in the Philippine Revolution*. Manilla: Kaisa Para Sa Kaunlaran.

Appelbaum, R.P. and J. Henderson (eds) (1992) *States and Development in the Asian Pacific Rim*. Newbury Park-London-New Delhi: Sage Publications.

Arora, B.D. (1982) 'Indians in Indonesia,' in: I.J. Bahadur Singh (ed.) *Indians in Southeast Asia*. New Delhi: Sterling Publishers.

Benda, H.J. (1958) *The Crescent and the Rising Sun: Indonesian Islam Under the Japanese Occupation 1942-1945*. The Hague-Bandung: W. van Hoeve.

Blussé, L. (1988) *Strange company: Chinese settlers, mestizo women and the Dutch in VOC Batavia*. Dordrecht: Foris Publications.

--(1989) *Tribuut aan China: Vier eeuwen Nederlands-Chinese betrekkingen*. Amsterdam: Otto Cramwinckel Uitgever

Brown, D. (1994) *The State and Ethnic Policies in Southeast Asia*. London-New York: Routledge.

Casparis, J.G. De and I.W. Mabbett (1992) 'Religions and Popular Beliefs of Southeast Asia before c.1500,' in: N. Tarling (ed.) *The Cambridge History of Southeast Asia, Volume One: From Early Times to c. 1800*. Cambridge: Cambridge University Press.

Chantavanich, Supang (1997) 'From Siamese-Chinese to Chinese-Thai: Political Conditions and Identity Shifts among the Chinese in Thailand,' in: L. Suryadinata (ed.) *Ethnic Chinese as Southeast Asians*. Singapore: Institute of Southeast Asian Studies.

Chaudhuri, K.N. (1985) *Trade and Civilisation in the Indian Ocean: An Economic History from the Rise of Islam to 1750*. Cambridge: Cambridge University Press.

Coppel, C.A. (1983) *Indonesian Chinese in Crisis*. Kuala Lumpur: Oxford University Press.

Coppel, C.A., H. Mabbett and Ping-ching Mabbett (1982) *The Chinese in Indonesia, the Philippines and Malaysia*. Minority Rights Group, Report No.10, Revised edition.

Cortes, I.R. and R.P.M. Lotilla (1990) 'Nationality and International Law from the Philippine Perspective,' in: Ko Swan Sik (ed.) *Nationality and International Law in Asian Perspective*. Dordrecht-Boston-London: Martinus Nijhoff Publishers.

Dahm, B. (1971) *History of Indonesia in the Twentieth Century*. London-New York-Washington: Praeger Publishers.

Dobbin, C. (1996) *Asian Entrepreneurial Minorities: Conjoint Communities in the Making of the World-Economy, 1570-1940*. Richmond: Curzon Press.

Doronila, A. (1992) *The State, Economic Transformation and Political Change in the Philippines, 1946-1972*. Singapore-Oxford-New York: Oxford University Press.

Elson, R.E. (1992) 'International Commerce, the State and Society: Economic and Social Change,' in: N. Tarling (ed.) *The Cambridge History of Southeast Asia, Volume One: From Early Times to c. 1800*. Cambridge: Cambridge University Press.

Fasseur, C. (1994) 'Cornerstone and stumbling block: Racial Classification and the late colonial state in Indonesia,' in: R. Cribb (ed.) *The Late Colonial State in Indonesia: Political and economic foundations of the Netherlands Indies 1880-1942*. Leiden: KITLV Press.

FitzGerald, C.P. (1972) *The Southern Expansion of the Chinese People: 'Southern Fields and Southern Ocean.'* Canberra: Australian National University Press.

Foreman, J. (1899) *The Philippine Islands: A Political, Geographical, Ethnographical, Social and Commercial History of the Philippine Archipelago and its Political Dependencies Embracing the whole Period of Spanish Rule*. 2nd ed., New York: Charles Scribner's Sons.

Gautama, S. (1993) *Hukum Antargolongan*, 11th ed., Jakarta: PT. Ichtiar Baru Van Hoeve.

--(1993) 'An Overview of the Indonesian Legal System (With Special Reference to Foreign Investments),' in: The Ministry of Law/The Singapore Academy of Law/Faculty of Law, National University of Singapore, *Business and Investment Laws in Indonesia*. Proceedings of the First Indonesia-Singapore Law Seminar, 26-27 February 1993.

--(1995) *Indonesian Business Law*. Bandung: PT. Citra Aditya Bakti.

Gautama, S. and R.N. Hornick (1983) *An Introduction to Indonesian Law: Unity in Diversity*. Bandung.

Go Gien Tjwan (1966) *Eenheid in verscheidenheid in een Indonesisch dorp*. Sociologisch-Historisch Seminarium voor Zuidoost Azië - Universiteit van Amsterdam, Amsterdam.

--(1971) 'The changing trade position of the Chinese in South-East Asia,' *International Social Science Journal* XXIII(4).

--(1972) 'Chinezen in Indonesië: Schets van een gediscrimineerde minoriteit,' *Intermediair*, vol 8 no 36, pp. 7-9, 15.

Hall, D.G.E. (1981) *A History of South-East Asia*. 4th ed., Houndmills-London: Macmillan.

Henderson, J. and R.P. Appelbaum (1992) 'Situating the State in the East Asian Developmental Process,' in: R.P. Appelbaum and J. Henderson (eds) *States and Development in the Asian Pacific Rim*. Newbury Park-London-New Delhi: Sage Publications.

Hooker, M.B. (1975) *Legal Pluralism: An Introduction to Colonial and Neo-Colonial Laws*. Oxford: Clarendon Press.

--(1978) *A Concise Legal History of South-East Asia*. Oxford: Clarendon Press

--(1988) 'Introduction: European Laws in South-East Asia,' in: M.B. Hooker (ed.) *Laws of South-East Asia, Volume II: European Laws in South-East Asia: Essays on Portuguese and Spanish Laws, the Netherlands East Indies, English Law, American Law in the Philippines and the 'Europeanization' of Siam's Law*. Singapore: Butterworths.

Institute of East Asian Philosophies (1988) *A Forum on 'The Role of Culture in Industrial Asia – The Relationship between Confucian Ethics and Modernisation,'* Singapore: Institute of East Asian Philosophies.

Jackson, R.N. (1979) 'Immigrant Labour and the Development of Malaya 1786-1920,' Kuala Lumpur 1961, reprinted in: J. Bastin and R.W. Winks (eds) *Malaysia: Selected Historical Readings*. Nendeln: KTO Press.

Jahja, H. Junus (ed.) (1991) *Nonpri di mata pribumi*. Jakarta: Yayasan Tunas Bangsa.

--(1999) *Acong Kemana...?* Jakarta: Lembaga Pengkajian Masalah Pembauran.

Ko Swan Sik and T.M. Rhadie (1990) 'Nationality and International Law in Indonesian Perspective,' in: Ko Swan Sik (ed.) *Nationality and International Law in Asian Perspective.* Dordrecht-Boston-London: Martinus Nijhoff Publishers.

Kratoska, P. and B. Batson (1992) 'Nationalism and Modernist Reform,' in: N. Tarling (ed.) *The Cambridge History of Southeast Asia, Volume One: From Early Times to c. 1800.* Cambridge: Cambridge University Press.

Lubeck, P.M. (1992) 'Malaysian Industrialization, Ethnic Divisions and NIC Model: The Limits to Replication,' in: R.P. Appelbaum and J. Henderson (eds) *States and Development in the Asian Pacific Rim.* Newbury Park-London-New Delhi: Sage Publications.

Lee Poh Ping (1991) 'A political framework for an economically resilient Southeast Asia and Japan's role,' in: Institute of Strategic and International Studies (ISIS) Malaysia/The Sasakawa Peace Foundation (SPF), *Towards an Economically Resilient Southeast Asia: Proceedings of the Second Japan-Southeast Asia Conference.* Kuala Lumpur, January 14-16, 1991, Kuala Lumpur-Tokyo: Institute of Strategic and International Studies (ISIS) Malaysia/The Sasakawa Peace Foundation (SPF).

Li Dun Jen (1982) *British Malaya: An economic analysis.* 2nd ed., Kuala Lumpur: Institut Analisa Sosial.

Liem, Yoe-Sioe (1986) *Überseechinesen - eine Minderheit: Zur Erforschung interethnischer Vorurteile in Indonesien.* Aachen: Edition Herodot/Rader Verlag.

Lim Chong-Yah (1990) 'Taiwan's Economic Miracle: A Singaporean Perspective,' in: S. Naya and A. Takayama (eds) *Economic Development in East and Southeast Asia: Essays in Honour of Professor Shinichi Ichimura.* Singapore-Honolulu: Institute of Southeast Asian Studies-East West Centre.

--(1990) *Development and Underdevelopment.* Singapore: Longman

MacIntyre, A.J. (1993) 'The Politics of Finance in Indonesia: Command, Confusion and Competition,' in: S. Haggard, Chung H. Lee and S. Maxfield (eds) *The Politics of Finance in Developing Countries.* Ithaca and London: Cornell University Press.

Mackie, J.A.C. (1976) *The Chinese in Indonesia.* Honolulu: The University Press of Hawai'i.

Morishima, M. (1982) *Warum Japan so erfolgreich ist.* München: C.H. Beck.

Oades, R. (1974) *The Social and Economic Background of Philippine Nationalism, 1830-1892.* Ph.D. thesis, Ann Arbor.

Owen, N.G. (1984) *Prosperity without Progress: Manila Hemp and Material Life in the Colonial Philippines.* Berkeley-Los Angeles-London: University of California Press.

Pan, L. (1991) *Sons of the Yellow Emperor: The Story of the Overseas Chinese.* London: Mandarin.
S. Pompe and C. de Waaij-Vosters (1988) 'The End of Hukum Antargolongan?,' in: *Bijdragen tot de Taal-, Land- en Volkenkunde* 145.
Reid, A. (1992) 'Economic and Social Change, c. 1400-1800,' in: N. Tarling (ed.) *The Cambridge History of Southeast Asia, Volume One: From Early Times to c. 1800.* Cambridge: Cambridge University Press.
--(1996) 'Flows and Seepages in the Long-term Chinese Interaction with Southeast Asia,' in: A. Reid (ed.) *Sojourners and Settlers - Histories of Southeast Asia and the Chinese in Honour of Jennifer Cushman.* St. Leonards NSW: Allen & Unwin.
Ricklefs, M.C. (1981) A History of Modern Indonesia – c.1300 to the present, London-Basingstoke: Macmillan.
Robison, R. (1986) *The Rise of Capital.* Sydney-Wellington-London: Allen & Unwin.
Shozo, Fukuda (1995) *With Sweat and Abacus: Economic Roles of Southeast Asian Chinese on the Eve of World War II.* Singapore: Select Books.
Siddique, S. and L. Suryadinata (1997) 'Bumiputera and Pribumi: Economic Nationalism (Indigenism) in Malaysia and Indonesia,' in: L. Suryadinata (ed.) *Chinese and nation-Building in Southeast Asia.* Singapore: Singapore Society of Asian Studies.
Silcock, T.H. and Ungku Abdul Aziz (1979) 'Nationalism in Malaya,' in: J. Bastin and R.W. Winks (eds) *Malaysia: Selected Historical Readings.* Nendeln: KTO Press.
Skinner, G.W. (1957) *Chinese Society in Thailand: An Analytical History.* Ithaca/New York: Cornell University Press.
--(1996)'Creolized Chinese Societies in Southeast Asia,' in: A. Reid (ed.) *Sojourners and Settlers – Histories of Southeast Asia and the Chinese in Honour of Jennifer Cushman.* St. Leonards, NSW: Allen & Unwin.
Spence, J.D. (1990) *The Search for Modern China.* New York-London: W.W. Norton & Company.
Stuntz, H.C. (1904) *The Philippines and the Far East.* Cincinnati-New York: Jennings and Pye/Eaton and Mains.
Sudhamani, S.R. (1982) 'Indians in Southeast Asia: An Approach Paper,' in: I.J. Bahadur Singh (ed.) *Indians in Southeast Asia.* New Delhi: Sterling Publishers.
Suryadinata, L. (1992) *Pribumi Indonesians, the Chinese Minority and China.* 3rd ed., Singapore: Heinemann Asia.

--(1997) 'Government Policies towards the Ethnic Chinese: A Comparison between Indonesia and Malaysia,' in: L. Suryadinata (ed.) *Chinese and Nation-Building in Southeast Asia*. Singapore: Singapore Society of Asian Studies.

H. Thoolen (ed.) (1987) *Indonesia and the Rule of Law: Twenty Years of 'New Order' Government*. London: Frances Pinter (Publishers).

Thompson, V. (1968) *French Indo-China*. New York: Octagon Books.

Tran Khanh (1993) *The Ethnic Chinese and Economic Development in Vietnam*. Singapore: Institute of Southeast Asian Studies.

--(1997) 'Ethnic Chinese in Vietnam and Their Identity,' in: L. Suryadinata (ed.) *Ethnic Chinese as Southeast Asians*. Singapore: Institute of Southeast Asian Studies.

Turnbull, C.M. (1980) *A Short History of Malaysia, Singapore and Brunei*. Stanmore-North Melbourne: Cassell Australia.

Utrecht, E. and M. Saleh Djindang (1983) *Pengantar dalam Hukum Indonesia*, 11th ed., Jakarta: Sinar Harapan.

Wang Gungwu (1991) *China and the Chinese Overseas*. Singapore: Times Academic Press.

--(1992) *Community and Nation: China, Southeast Asia and Australia*. St. Leonards NSW: Allen & Unwin.

Wertheim, W.F. (1980) 'The Trading Minorities in South-East Asia,' in: H.D. Evers (ed.) *Sociology of South-East Asia: Readings on Social Change and Development*. Kuala Lumpur: Oxford University Press.

Wignjosoebroto, S. (1994) *Dari Hukum Kolonial ke Hukum Nasional: Dinamika Sosial-Politik dalam Perkembangan Hukum di Indonesia*. Jakarta: Raja Grafindo Persada.

Wu Min Aun (1982) *An Introduction to the Malaysian Legal System*. 3rd ed., Petaling Jaya: Longman.

Yen Ching-hwang (1995) *Studies in Modern Overseas Chinese History*. Singapore: Times Academic Press.

Yoshihara, Kunio (1988) *The Rise of Ersatz Capitalism in South-East Asia*. Singapore: Oxford University Press.

--(1994) *The Nation and Economic Growth: The Philippines and Thailand*. Kuala Lumpur: Oxford University Press.

Chapter 2

Development, Media and Youth Issues in Malaysia

Samsudin A. Rahim

Prior to the spread of the ripples of the financial and economic crisis in to Asia in the middle of 1997, the Malaysian economy was brimming with confidence, indicated by an economic growth rate of 8.9 per cent annually since 1988, and an unemployment rate of only 2.8 per cent. The per capita income showed an improvement of RM 1,106 in 1970 to RM 9,786 in 1995, which is equivalent of a rise from US$ 978 to US$ 9,470 respectively in terms of purchasing power parity (PPP). This gave the government the confidence, that given such economic growth rate, Malaysia could embark on a more accelerated growth spurt and hence be transformed from its present NIC status to a developed nation. Hence, in a 1991 speech 'The Way Forward' the prime minister, Dr Mahathir Mohammed, set the Malaysian national objective of becoming a fully industrialized country by the year 2020.

Since independence in 1957, Malaysia has experimented with several social engineering processes in its development plan. From 1960-70, the emphasis was on uniting a nation of multi-ethnic (indigenous groups 59 per cent, Chinese 32 per cent, and Indians 9 per cent) and multi-religious (Islamic, Buddhist, Hindu, and Christian) entities into a more cohesive unit as a nation. Then, from 1970-90 the development strategy shifted to the distribution of wealth among the multi-ethnic population to overcome disparities between ethnic groups, regions, and occupational opportunities through offering increased opportunities for participation in the expanding commercial and industrial sector to economically backward regions. Finally, since 1991 the country has begun to lay the foundation for becoming a developed nation by mobilizing the population towards the future and gearing it towards using science and information technology, forging the basis for it to remain competitive.

In his 1995 New Year speech, Prime Minister Mahathir made a remark indicating that he thought that Malaysia's development progress was being tainted by what he termed moral decadence and an unhealthy lifestyle among its young people. He reminded Malaysians of the importance of curbing social ills such as loafing and indolence, *bohsia* (teenage girls involving themselves in free sex) and drug abuse especially among the young. These 'social maladies' identified among young people, if left unchecked could set the country's development goals back. The remark was made in reference to a cabinet paper prepared by the Ministry of Youth and Sports in 1994 highlighting unhealthy lifestyles among young people which included issues of loafing, drug abuse, juvenile delinquency, pre-marital sex, HIV cases, deviant religious teachings, and disturbing symptoms of social malaise.

The young population is important to a country's development. Griffin (1995) suggested that 'youth should be treated as key indicator of the state of a nation, it is expected to reflect the cycle of booms and troughs in the economy, shifts in cultural values over sexuality, morality, and family life, concepts of nationhood, and occupational structures.' It is expected that in the year 2020, 41 per cent of the Malaysian population will constitute what is presently categorized as a young population. The young population between the age of 15-39 years constituted 34 percent of the 1980s population of eighteen million. In 1990 it increased to 42 per cent of the population of nineteen million.

There is a significant increase in young people migrating from the rural to urban areas. In 1995, the number of young people working in urban areas increased to 56.5 per cent compared to 33.6 per cent in 1990. Youth participation in the declining agricultural sector dropped from 19.3 per cent in 1990 to 13.1 per cent in 1995. In the manufacturing sector, youth participation increased from 32.8 per cent in 1990 to 37.9 per cent in 1995. The government is also depending on the young people as a repository of human resources required in the information technology sector. It is predicted that there will soon be a demand for a 27,174 work force in this area (Malaysia 1996).

In the Seventh Malaysia Plan (1996-2000), the government commitment towards youth development was enhanced by an allocation of RM 2.7 billion. Out of which, RM 900 million has been allocated to programmes to increase the capacity of young people to meet the demands of the employment market. Another RM 160 million is to promote the *Rakan Muda* (Friends of the Youth) healthy lifestyle programmes for youth. The *Rakan Muda* programmes started off with a media blitz in the form of thirty-second commercial spots. The publicity generated by the media drawing attention to social maladies among the young and the media blitz of the *Rakan Muda* healthy lifestyle programmes successfully grasped the imagination of the population and drew its attention to the social issues at hand. Its slogan *Yakin Boleh* (Yes We Can) has become a morale booster not only among the younger group, but to the entire nation. It has somewhat lifted the self-esteem of the population, leading it to believe that if we set our goal right, we as a nation can be successful in our endeavour.

The debate on 'social maladies' among young people is still going on. Is it an exaggeration, making a mountain out of a molehill? Or, is such a phenomenon a normal developmental process of being young? Furthermore, is the phenomenon a direct result of incompetent social planning on the part of the government? Or, is it an outcome of the new society created by present and past development policies? It is not possible to come up with a single answer to address the issues. The Ministry of Youth and Sports cited several factors that have influenced the value system and lifestyle of young Malaysian people. Among them are the peer group, the family, educational institutions, religious teaching, youth organizations, and, last but not least, the mass media.

In the 1960s, UNESCO encouraged developing countries to invest in communications infrastructures, which were considered to be 'tools' for development. The infrastructure facilitates diffusion of information, which is a catalyst for economic and social development. However, the 1980s, with the emergence of global communication and new communications technologies, brought a new approach known as 'media imperialism' which views the media, situated in a transnational context, as obstacles to meaningful and well-balanced socio-economic progress.

Malaysia is one of those developing countries that has invested in communications technologies and the expansion of the mass media in order to facilitate its development, hoping eventually to 'catch up' with the advanced industrialized countries. It has been suggested that there is a correlation between increment in GNP and investment in telecommunications and communications infrastructures. Rahim (1987) found such a correlation does exist in ASEAN countries. With per capita income improving from RM 1,106 in 1970 to RM 9,786 in 1995, it was expected that the Malaysian media landscape would change and subsequently media penetration among its population would increase.

The communication medium is fast emerging as an important agent of socialization among youth, especially in this era of globalization in which the world is described as a 'global village' and information is at our fingertips. Critics see the easy access to foreign programmes as encouraging higher exposure to 'undesirable alien values and permissiveness.' Bank and Collins (quoted in Morley and Robins, 1995:44) argue that 'the integrity and continued existence of communities and their political institutions depends crucially on their communication sovereignty, and that if a community consumes too much unspecified exogenous information the legitimacy of the native political institutions will come under threat and the community will untimely cease to exist.'

Studies have shown that, in their development, young people tend to spend less time with their family and spend more time with the media. It is getting difficult to define young people in terms of their age and developmental stage. This has become more so since the young are now being easily identified by their lifestyle. Youth lifestyle has been developing in the United States where the emphasis is on entertainment like music, dance, and fashion, since the 1960s. According to Fornas and Bolin (1995), 'interest in pleasure is stronger for the majority of young people than interest in more serious activities, and pleasure is more important for youths than it is for adults. This orientation unites youth: it exists almost independent of socio-economic background.'

This paper will discuss the development of the communications industry and hence the new media environment among Malaysian youth. It will argue that if communications are going to be an important socializing agent among young people, expansion of the media environment should be regulated through a comprehensive communications policy so as to contribute to the development of young people as an asset to the country. Bowes (1984) pointed out that government planners should be cautious regarding a laissez-faire policy on communications development because 'information pollution will spread just like industrial pollution,' if planning is not oriented to social planning and human development.

Development and Social Issues among Young People

The development of a country has always been measured by its economic performance in such terms as growth rate and per capita income. To encompass the non-economic aspect of development, indicators of the physical quality of life index (PQLI) were also used. The PQLI indicates, among other things, mortality rate, life expectancy, and doctor per 1,000 population and so on. While these indicators cover the economic and non-economic well being of a country, they fall short of determining the real quality of life of the population.

What is missing in many development indicators are the intangible human aspects such as changes in values, morality, family life, stress, and self-esteem to name but a few. In many societies, while development and modernization are welcome, there is a sort of bond which allows them to retain their identity, which is characterized by their values, families, morality, and other matters. Needless to say, all these intangible aspects of life are very much affected by the changes in the economic indicators.

In its process of development Malaysia turns to the West for guidance in terms of its industrialization and technological know-how, but Malaysia also turns to the East, as in its Look East Policy for a work ethic and management style. In its way of life, Malaysia tries to uphold and maintain Asian values which include professing Islamic doctrine. As development progresses, the well being of the people improves and their lifestyle changes and so do their values and perceptions of things around them. This is exactly what is happening to the present-day Malaysian society, succumbing to the process of development and youths are the product of the present new environment.

As in many East Asian societies, economic growth has led to the emergence of a middle-class society. In Malaysia, the middle class was about 24 per cent in 1980 and 37.2 in 1986 (Khan, 1995). According to Rahman (1997), middle-class Malaysians have experienced cultural differentiation through the acquisition of status symbols which are considered to be symbols of modernity and of having 'arrived,' such as home-ownership, membership of a country club, having credit cards, personal computers, dining at hotels, patronizing coffee-houses and karaoke centres, owning cellular telephones, and driving luxury cars.

The process of development and change has been stressful on families and their children. Many families now have both parents working, both out of choice and out of necessity. Women's entry into the work force had increased to 47 percent (2.9 million) in 1995. In land settlement schemes, such as Felda schemes, housewives are being recruited to work in electronic factories where there is an acute shortage of workers. While both parents are out working, children are left unattended after they come home from school. The fortunate ones will have domestic helpers to keep an eye on them. In many urban centres, school children are seen roaming in shopping complexes and eateries after school hours.

There are fairly common instances of many working parents being involved in part-time jobs such as becoming dealers for direct selling companies and becoming petty traders in the local government-sponsored *pasar malam* (night market). Those doing part-time jobs are not necessarily poor in absolute terms. They need the extra income to acquire the material things necessary to achieving social status such as home and car ownership.

A family's status is also enhanced by their children's academic performance. Parents expect their children to score maximum As in public examinations. Good academic performances guarantee these children a place in boarding schools (several categories and status) and also the possibility of studying overseas. In many instances such opportunities are fully financed by the government, semi-government, or private agencies

Those who are not fortunate enough to continue their tertiary education will enter the work force. The private sector, especially the industrial sector, has been the major employer of the new school-leavers. Blue-collar jobs in the industrial and manufacturing sectors offer better remunerations (salary, overtime, and bonuses) than do traditional white-collar jobs such as administrative and teaching occupations in the public sector. Youth participation as a work force in the manufacturing sector has increased from 32.8 per cent in 1990 to 37.9 per cent in 1995 (Malaysia, 1996).

Young people in urban areas usually find accommodation in *rumah bujang* (bachelor houses), where a group of them rents a house or apartment and shares the costs. Major companies are providing free accommodation to their young employees on the same basis as *rumah bujang*, but the companies take care of the rent. Depending on the ability to pay the rent and the comfort they wish to have, in many instances *rumah bujang* are crowded and their occupants do not have the privacy to do their own thing. Many spend their free time outside the house, and only return to sleep. Shopping complexes become places for 'retreat' because they provide a more conducive, cool, air-conditioned environment to the otherwise humid and crowded home environment.

There is another category of young people who commute to work daily in urban areas from their suburb and rural homes. They live with their parents and commute either on buses provided by their employers or using their own transport. They may have the comfort of their own home, and mothers' cooking, but find life at home unexciting. They have a sea of free time outside their working hours. Many will spend this free time with friends either at nearby stalls, at public places in the vicinity of their houses, or in nearby towns.

Lepak or hanging out without much purpose is a label that has been ascribed to Malaysian youth. At weekends and on public holidays, young people congregate to *lepak* in many public places such as shopping malls, the five-foot pavements in front of shop houses, cinemas, junctions in a village and other like places. In the federal capital of Kuala Lumpur, the young congregate at places such as Dataran Merdeka, Central Market, various shopping malls such as Bukit Bintang Plaza, Lot 10, Pertama Kompleks, and Sogo. In smaller towns they gather together in pedestrian malls or along river or sea fronts. In the rural land settlement schemes, areas near foodstalls at the entrance to the land scheme are favourite meeting places. Notable among them are Malay youths with a fine range of hairstyles from a short haircut to those sporting long hair emulating rock singers.

The Ministry of Youth and Sports commissioned a study to determine the profile of these young people - who they are, what activities they get up to while *lepak*, and what attracts them to those public places. A sample of 6,110 young people interviewed revealed that they spend an average of 16.3 hours per week idling in public places (Samsudin et al., 1994). Initially it was assumed that this is an urban phenomenon, but data shows that young people in rural areas loaf around much longer hours (24 hours in a week) than their counterparts in urban areas (15.6 hours). Asked why they congregate in public places, the most common answers given are a way to relax, meeting friends in a conducive environment, or something similar. What are the activities they engage in while with friends? Among other things the young people admit that they are involved in drug-taking (14 per cent), cigarette smoking (70 per cent), reading and viewing pornographic materials (40 per cent), drinking alcohol (25 per cent), and gambling (28 per cent).

Who are these youths who frequent and loaf in public places? The study shows that majority of these youths come from families with an average income of RM 700 a month, an income considered insufficient to meet the ever-rising cost of living. Their parents have had primary or lower secondary school education only. These youths are not task-oriented, meaning that they were not keen to improve their performance in carrying out their work. They are more interaction-oriented, meaning that they would prefer spending more time with peer groups. Young people who spend more time loafing tend to be those who have lower self-esteem, spending more time on entertainment programmes offered by the media. They generally suffer from a lack of role models with which they can identify.

The result of the study found mixed reactions. What is wrong with young people spending free time in the malls? Adults seem to get away with it when they hangout at country or golf clubs. Nevertheless, the government has heeded the warning that the present development policies are having undesirable social implications. Social development is not keeping pace with economic development. The government's concern is that the findings, especially activities that young people get involved with in their so-called free time, correlate with a spate of social issues that the government finds alarming.

The Task Force on Drugs at the Ministry of Home Affairs reported that there are 200,000 reported drug addicts. If for the estimate of every drug addict reported, there is another who goes unreported, the actual number could easily soon reach half a million. Related to illegal drug use is the number of HIV/AIDS cases. The Ministry of Health reported that there were 12,000 HIV cases in 1995. The first HIV case was reported in 1987. The pattern of transmission in Malaysia is different from other countries like Thailand, Vietnam, and Western countries. In Malaysia, 76 per cent of HIV transmission is through intravenous needles. The World Health Organization (1997) estimated HIV cases in Malaysia to be around 21,863.

HIV cases and illegal drug use should be tackled holistically since they are related. A study by the Ministry of Health on 'AIDS and Youth' (Samsudin and Iran, 1976), indicates that the major reasons young people resorted to taking drugs are the stress of life, experimentation, and peer influence. The study shows that drug users who were interviewed in a rehabilitation centre, admitted to being heavy smokers compared to those not taking drugs. Thus we have an intertwining relations between cigarette smoking, drug taking, and HIV. Unfortunately, officials are not too keen on looking at data and listening to expert opinions. Problems, they are convinced, are not to be solved holistically, but at the sectarian level, piecemeal by bits and pieces.

About 70 per cent of young people admitted that they smoke cigarette (Samsudin et al., 1994). The high percentage of smoking is still prevalent in spite of various measures taken by the government. The Ministry of Health passed a law prohibiting smoking in public places and punishing adults who ask minors to buy cigarettes for them. The Ministry of Information has legislated so that direct cigarette advertising is banned. Despite all these efforts, the cigarette companies still have a field day in terms of their promotion - indirect promotion of their brand name.

Dunhill, a major cigarette trademark has opted to promote its brand name indirectly through men's wear and accessories. *Dunhill* is the major sponsor of sporting events, including the Malaysian football premier league. *Dunhill* is also the major sponsor of television programmes dubbed the Dunhill Double on TV3 and Movie Magic on TV2. *Salem*, another cigarette brand name, is now synonymous with the music industry. *Salem* established *Salem Powerhouse* a chain of shops that sells CDs and cassettes. *Salem* is also behind *Salem Concert*, organizer of concerts by popular local and foreign recording artists. In 1995 the Ministry of Youth and Sports cancelled its concert because it was alleged that free cigarettes were to be distributed to the audience, the majority of whom were young people. Another cigarette brand name, *Peter Stuyvesant*, was not given licence by the local authorities to stage *KRU Megamania*, a concert involving a well-known local rap group. It was alleged that the concert would have a bad influence on the younger population. *Benson and Hedges* promotes its brand name through a popular television series *Benson and Hedges Golden Dreams*.

In its effort to disassociate cigarette companies from sporting events, the Ministry of Youth and Sports has come up with the idea of *Rakan Sukan* (Friends of Sports). The programme encourages big corporations to adopt certain sports associations by giving them annual grants. Since sports have always been associated with the younger population, the campaign has managed to dislodge several big cigarette companies as major sponsors of sporting events. Under the *Rakan Sukan* programme, companies associated with the national car project, Proton and EON have sponsored badminton; Petronas, the national oil company, has sponsored netball; Time

Engineering, a telecommunications company sponsors cycling; one of the leading banks, Maybank, has chosen to give its support to aquatic events.

Another major concern about young people is their sexual values. In a conservative society such as Malaysia, premarital sex is strictly not permitted, especially among Muslims. Social mixing with the opposite sex is not encouraged. The scene has changed with development. It is not so much that the overall societal values have changed, but with development and urbanization, more nightspots have sprung up. Nightclubs, discos, karaoke lounges, and *dangdut* lounges have become prominent landmarks in the lives of young people, especially in big cities. Close proximity between the sexes in leisure and entertainment centres has become commonplace in their lifestyle.

Sexual values are inextricably linked to this lifestyle. There is evidence that there has also been a rise in sexual promiscuity among young people. More young people nowadays admit that they have had sexual relations with their partners before marriage. Two studies (Samsudin et al., 1994; and Samsudin and Iran, 1996) found that 17 to 25 per cent of the respondents admitted having premarital sex. In the capital city of Kuala Lumpur it is common knowledge that a group of young girls are happy to exchange sexual favours in return for a good time in pubs or motorcycle rides. These girls have been labelled *bohsia* (sex-for-pleasure-girl). Corresponding to these changing sexual values, there has been an increasing number of reported cases of babies having been abandoned in public lavatories, rivers, bushes, bus shelters, and even in front of prayer houses. In 1988 there were only eighteen, but in 1993 has increased to fifty-six.

DEVELOPMENT OF THE COMMUNICATIONS INDUSTRY

The development of the communications industry in Malaysia is closely related to the development objectives and the social transformation of Malaysian society in general. In addition, it is impossible to discount the effect of trends in the world communications industry. Malaysia's vision of becoming an industrialized country with active participation in international forums has had an undisputed influence on the development of the communications industry especially those related to broadcasting and information technology. To be effective in putting across Malaysia's position on international issues, it needs adequate communication channels. In retrospect, to be a global player in either the economic or political sphere, Malaysia cannot afford to isolate itself from the rest of the world. In other words, Malaysia must be competitive. Hence, the inception of the Multimedia Super Corridor and the launching of Malaysia's own satellite have been part of the overall effort to prepare Malaysia to be an active player in the global arena.

Malaysia launched its East Asia Satellite (MEASAT 1) on January 13, 1996. Subsequently the first satellite television was commissioned in October 1996. The direct-to-user (DtU) broadcasting service with twenty-two television channels and eight radio channels marked a major shift in communications policy in Malaysia. Prior to this date, broadcasting services were confined to terrestrial broadcasts and satellite dishes were strictly prohibited. With the launching of MEASAT2 in October 1996, the MEASAT system has a footprint covering Southeast Asia, India, Vietnam, Taiwan, and Eastern Australia. .

The All Asia Radio and Television Company (ASTRO), the operator of the DtU satellite broadcasting, broadens the choices of television and radio preferences. ASTRO radio channels are broadcast in English. Responding a shift in programming policy, ASTRO was reported to have closed down its news and current affairs division thus depriving its Malay channel *Astro Ria*, of the opportunity to air two current affairs programme in the national language. Commenting on this, critics have been sceptical of how ASTRO would fit in with the overall national aspiration to build up a united nation. Even more they have doubted its commitment to achieve a civil society through building a knowledgeable society. The prime minister was stated to have said that a 'knowledgeable society must also become a civil society. The transition from merely accessing information to infusing knowledge and becoming a civil society is subtle but critical' (*New Straits Times*, Dec. 20, 1996).

It is important to acknowledge at this point that in the past broadcasting services has been a catalyst to national development. Broadcasting services have been in the forefront of the social engineering process especially in the promotion of the national language, the fostering of unity, encouraging and changing people's attitude towards development, inculcating a savings ethic among the indigenous people through government trust funds to name but a few instances. Television and Radio Malaysia (RTM) were entrusted with carrying out these responsibilities. RTM, which was the pioneer of broadcasting services, operates two television stations TV1 and TV2, and eighteen radio stations (five national and thirteen regional stations). Until recently it enjoyed the monopoly of broadcasting services and true, to its status as a public broadcasting station, was able to promote 'public interest' through programmes that inform, educate, and entertain its audience.

The RTM reliance on predominantly local Malay programmes and imported English programmes has not been able to attract audiences who are not proficient in Malay or English. Yeo et al. (1993) found that Chinese who were not proficient in Malay or English were not watching programmes on Television Malaysia, and this has somewhat affected the government's strategy to reach the masses with its development and national unity messages. Linguistically isolated, this segment of the population turned instead to their video cassette player to view videos from Hong Kong and Taiwan as their form of entertainment. Many of the videos were released simultaneously in Malaysia and in Hong Kong television broadcasts. *Media Guide* (1997) estimated at its height about seven million videos were rented out each month.

Basically for strategic and tactical purposes, the government gave permission for the commissioning of a private television station to provide alternative programming in order to win back that segment of the population. TV3, as the new private station is popularly known, made its debut in June 1984 and created specific time belt for Chinese serials in the evening and late at night. The Chinese belt programmes, slowly but surely, have won back the Chinese audience and in the process the programmes have become a hit among the non-Chinese audience too. By 1988, there was a decline in video viewing.

It could be argued that although TV3 was set up as a commercial station, it was nevertheless guided by the notion that public broadcasting is there to serve the 'public interest.' TV3 has brought an important segment of the population back within 'government reach.' Having achieved its 'public interest' objectives, it is no coincidence that the operator of TV3 found the commercial value of the station. There was a substantial advertising market still untapped. RTM had not seriously tapped the advertising market since it was not a commercial station and most of its operating costs were borne by the treasury from general taxation revenue and radio and television licences. TV3 driven by its market instinct created niche programming and in its few years of operation has managed to enjoy the lead in advertising revenue outstrippiing the RTM channels, TV1 and TV2.

While toying with the idea of corporatization, RTM has privatized the selling of airtime on TV1 to GT Consultants and on TV2 to Commark. By privatizing its airtime, RTM is squaring up to claim its fair share of the advertising market. So the war breaks out and commercialism creeps in the television industry. In 1996, from a total of RM 7,72 million advertising spending on television, TV3 commanded a 44 per cent share. TV2 share had 31 per cent and TV1 16 per cent (*Media Guide*, 1997). In the process, RTM had adjusted its programming from the traditional unity, development, and education, to that suitable to a more commercial outlook.

The rapid development in the broadcasting industry which began in 1995 has caused confusion about where broadcast services are heading. The Minister of Information announced in 1994 (*New Straits Times*, March 2, 1994) that the government would carefully consider proposals for new television stations because the government does not want Malaysians to be too preoccupied with watching television. Nonetheless, two other stations, Metro Vision and Mega TV (cable television offering five channels), were given licences to operate television services in July and November 1995 respectively.

Compared to television, radio services have been commercialized at a later date. Besides the nineteen national and regional public radio services operated by Radio Malaysia, there are five other commercial radios: the Time Highway Radio, Suara Johor-Best 104, Radio Rediffusion, and Radio Kenyalang.

Associated with the broadcasting services, especially radio, is the music industry. It was suggested that local music changed from the traditional style to popular music in the 1960s. It was suggested that the local music industry flourished at a rapid pace stimulated by the socio-economic change in the Malaysian society.

The popularity of Western heavy metal, rock, and rap groups encourages the formation of their 'local counterparts.' Local groups such as Gersang, Headwind, Search, Wings, Ella and the Boys were in the forefront in the mid-1980s. In the early 1990s, groups such as 4U2C and KRU were popularizing local version of rap music. Lent (1995) points out that, 'the heavy metal music appealed chiefly to frustrated urban blue collars workers and unemployed youth, among them the alienated Malay youngsters known locally and figuratively as *kutu* (head lice), who congregate around shopping malls and adopt a punk lifestyle.'

The popularity of such genres on the music scene at times occasions criticism as it encourages the growth of a subculture that challenges the dominant culture and the socio-economic norms of the Malaysian society. The principle followers of the local music scene are Malay youngsters. In 1987, the WEA successfully promoted a new genre on the local music scene with an introduction of *dakwah* songs (songs with an Islamic religious message) by a group known as Raihan. The first album reached a record sale of 600,000, a rare achievement for any locally produced and what more a religious album. Raihan's success proved a bandwagon for other *dakwah* groups who have also met with considerable success.

Compared to the development in the broadcasting services, the growth of print media has been almost imperceptible. The liberalization policy towards the print media in the early 1980s has not changed much in the major national newspaper landscape. What has actually emerged from such a liberalization has been the emergence of tabloid newspapers with political undertones. These tabloids, such as *Watan* and *Mingguan Perdana* do not command large markets and many of them wrapped up after some years.

The most noticeable development in the print media has been the emergence of entertainment magazines and humorous comics. These publications have been targeted mainly towards the younger population. One of the early entertainment magazines, URTV, published fortnightly has a circulation of 120,000. By Malaysian standards, this circulation figure is substantial and commercially viable. This magazine mainly publishes news and information about the personalities of those involved in the radio, television, film, and music industries. Encouraged by the success formula of URTV, several other entertainment magazines, notable among them is *Mangga* a weekly publication with a circulation of 205,000. *Mangga* has been described as a magazine that has stretched the limits of decency, because most of its articles focus on gossip and sexy pictures of entertainment personalities. Other entertainment magazines such as *Bacaria*, *Media Hiburan*, and *Remaja* have a circulation of 58,000, 83,000, and 60,000 respectively. Most of the readers are those between 17-25.

Another significant development in the print media has been the influx of humour magazines. *Gila-Gila*, an imitation of the American humour magazine MAD, has a circulation of 120,000 fortnightly. Following the success of *Gila-Gila*, more humorous magazines have flooded the market. Notable among them are *Ujang*, *Geli Hati*, *Gado-Gado*, and *Humor* with a circulation of 156,000, 45,000, 50,000, and 15,000 respectively.

Another phenomenon in the print media is the influx of magazines portraying popular animated characters on television. These magazines are translated into the national language from their original Japanese and printed locally. At first glance there seems to be no significant educational element in the magazine, yet titles such as *Doremon* and *Sailormoon* are popular, especially among the lower age group in the teens

Malaysians read an average of 1.5 pages of book a day. Therefore, the present trend towards reading light entertainment magazines is not likely to augur well for the future intellectual development of the younger population. In addition, the younger population who have had the opportunity to have a better education should more inclined to reading better quality reading materials. Entertainment magazines seem to have more fervent devotees than educational magazines. Except for *Dewan Pelajar* and *Dewan Siswa*, which are targeted towards school children, other educational magazines have a relatively small circulation. In a study on young people Samsudin et al. (1994) highlighted that they spent more time reading entertainment magazines than educational ones.

Ownership of personal computers (PCs) and access to the Internet is another development. Although in many developed countries such as in the United States where the sales of personal computers have surpassed those of television sets, efforts are being made in Malaysia to encouraged ownership and accessibility. This is in line with the government's information technology policy and other efforts such as the Multimedia Super Corridor and the paperless administration in the new federal capital. Computer loans were made available to government staff and rebates for purchasing computers were instituted in the 1996 budget. Access to Internet has been rising significantly. *Media Guide* (1997) reported that there are 250,000 Internet subscribers. This figure is relatively high compared to subscribers in other ASEAN countries such as Thailand (120,000), the Philippines (20,000), Indonesia (100,000) and Singapore (195,000). It is estimated that 90 per cent of Internet users are under thirty-nine years of age (*The Star*, Sept. 1996).

MEDIA PENETRATION AMONG YOUTH

The communications revolution has made media hardware cheaper and easily accessible. Cogently, the communications revolution has also made possible the free flow of information across national boundaries through the direct broadcasting satellite (DBS) and the Internet. If accessibility to media facilities to facilitate development in developing and underdeveloped countries was the major concern of UNESCO in the 1960s and 1970s, this is no longer the case. It has been replaced by a concern about the flow of information and its effect on the recipient countries. The McBride Report (1983) addresses the effect of imbalances in information flow between developed and developing countries.

The issue is now becoming more acute. With globalization and further advances in communications technology, it is becoming difficult to restrict access to information. Much of the information, including pornographic material, is now in public domain and easily accessible to many through the Internet. DBS has made censorship of broadcast materials irrelevant. The physical movement of media software is becoming more efficient and it is distributed almost simultaneously all over the world. The mode of communication is secondary to the software or contents which finally reach the audience. According to Taylor (1997), modern communication is indeed about technology, but it is also about creativity, because when something is communicated to someone, an impact or influence is likely to be the result, with the provision it often depends on how creatively the contents of the communication are deployed.

In Malaysia, young people now have better access to media facilities. This could translate into better access and exposure to transnational information. Accessibility can be direct, through DBS and the Internet, and indirect through local media which becomes the conveyer of foreign information and programmes.

A study of 850 youths in Klang Valley, an area around the vicinity of Kuala Lumpur (Samsudin, 1998), indicates that more than 90 per cent have access to the three main media of mass media, that is television, radio, and newspapers. Access to satellite and cable television is still marginal at 11 per cent. There is a growing number of young people who have access to computers, an average of 36 per cent. About 37 per cent have access to computer-based video game facilities. With regard to access to personal media, 67 per cent of the young people studied has access to a video recorder and 80 per cent has access to cassette players.

Although young people have a high rate of access to television, radio, and newspapers, there is a big difference in their use of the medium. While young people spend 14.6 hours and 16.3 hours per week respectively watching television and listening to the radio, their use of newspapers is very much lower, namely around 7.1 hours a week. Although access to computers is still low, young people spend about 6.2 hours per week using them, almost catching up with the time spent reading the newspaper. They also spend time listening to their cassette players and watching videos up to a total of eight hours a week. Overall, it can be safely said that media penetration among young people is relatively high at around 58.2 hours a week, which works out at 8.3 hours per day.

The relatively high penetration of the media among young people in terms of time spent using the various media is not surprising. It is to be expected that in their developmental stage they will tend to shift their attention from family to media. As they grow a little older, young people will spend more time with the media than with their families. This shows that the media constitute a major element in youth socialization, alongside other agents such as family, peer groups, and educational and religious institutions.

How do media organizations position themselves as socializing agents for young people? In an era of commercial media, market forces will determine media agenda for young people. But again, who determines the agenda for the media? Media content in many instances reflects demand from the market place, cultivating and perpetuating the interest of young people in entertainment. A study on the portrayal of young people in the print media (Samsudin and MusCharil, 1995) suggests that 54 per cent of news about young people was dominated by personalities from the entertainment industry. Another study on young people who like to loof around (Samsudin et al., 1994) showed that they prefer an entertainment-oriented content when they watch television (55 per cent), listen to radio (70 per cent), read newspaper (57 per cent) or read magazines (56 per cent). The same trend can be traced in the smaller and personal media. Young people show considerable interest in puzzle games, virtual sports such as NBA, basketball, soccer, and ice hockey, and flight simulators such as US Navy Fighter, Flight Sim 5, and War Craft 2 (Samsudin, 1997).

A Need for a Communications Policy

At the present moment there is no communications policy in Malaysia. There was an effort to formulate a policy during a symposium held in 1983, but the idea was later abandoned and only emerged again in 1992 when a panel was formed to formulate a national information policy. The panel has submitted a draft to the Minister of Information, but so far there has been no official announcement of any policy. With the rapid development in the communications industry and the social issues related to young people which have arisen in its train, it is necessary to have a policy to address such developments.

It is rather convenient to blame the media industry for the social problems related to young people. While it is not easy to contemplate a simple notion of the direct effect of media on youth, nonetheless we could not prove that it does not have some effect on the values and behaviour of young people. The fact that even the neo-liberals want the government to regulate the media shows that the media is a useful tool by which young people can interpret their realities. If this be so, regulating the media is necessary to serve national priorities.

The regulating bodies which oversee the communications industry are the Ministry of Home Affairs and the Ministry of Information. The Ministry of Home Affairs has jurisdiction over issues pertaining to print media while the Ministry of Information takes charge of the broadcasting services and the film industry. Local councils under the Ministry of Housing and Local Government approve licences for videotape rentals and video and computer games outlets. There is a possibility that a new ministry, a Multi-media Ministry, will be set up before the end of 1998. This move is considered appropriate because there is a considerable convergence of functions and media in the communications field as a result of developments in communications and telecommunications technologies. A single regulatory agency would be able to co-ordinate efforts to address social issues pertaining to youth most effectively.

Globalization has affected Malaysia in a number of ways. One of the concerns arising from globalization is the unrestricted flow of information across national boundaries. Many national governments are concerned about having less control over incoming information and the effect of this flood of information on their national identities. The European Union in its Green Paper has recommended steps to protect children and young people from against programmes and news items that could be harmful to them.

Malaysia has not made any explicit effort to regulate media agencies forcing them to adhere to any standards with regard to its younger population. In the broadcasting services, the most noticeable ruling has effected the use of the national language. Television stations are required to have 80 per cent local programmes in the national language by the year 2000. Lately, the Minister of Information has warned television stations that they must broadcast only locally-produced programmes in the national language during prime time between 8.30 to 10.00 PM (*New Straits Times*, July 10, 1998). The same minister has warned radio stations of the excessive use of English above the national language in their announcements.

The emphasis on the use of the national language is certainly welcome because it has to do with the national identity. But, what is missing is the same emphasis on good programmes, either imported or local, which could help young people through the portrayal of good role models. In the past, the ministry has issued a policy to restrict violence, horror, sex and counter-culture (VHSC), prohibiting programmes which include portrayals of lifestyles which are considered to be 'morally wrong.' As a follow-up there is a classifications system (U, 18SG, 18SX etc.) to regulate the VHSC guidelines.

This move is more reactive than proactive in attempting to cultivate the values and aptitudes of the young population. Programmes should build up their stories around the kind of young people the nation should have in the future. A consultative meeting between youth associations and government agencies to come up with guidelines on a youth behavioural index study suggested several characteristics with which young people should be imbued, including having good family values, patriotism, confidence in their future, high self-esteem, and good parents-children relations (Samsudin, Rokiah and Muhammad, 1997). Not denying the young population the entertainment they yearn for, efforts should be made to integrate good educational and entertainment elements into the so-called edutainment genre for television programmes. Production houses should also take into consideration incorporating storylines which help to build up positive self-esteem among youth. Media content should also ensure that young people are portrayed positively. It is up to the media to highlight role models for young people.

Regulating the media is not a popular move. But to emulate commercialization in the media where market forces determine the content is not popular either. Somehow, a middle-of-the-road approach is necessary in order to achieve Malaysia's aspiration of achieving an informed and knowledgeable society. To this effect, there is an imbalance of entertainment and serious publications. For the young population, there is an imbalance in the number of serious publications to stimulate their minds. The regulatory agencies should ensure a fairer share of distribution of different types of magazines for the younger population.

In this era of globalization, while we cannot do much to stop the information flow, the least we could do is to help build in greater resilience among our young population to ensure the maintenance of the cultural identity. The purpose of encouraging the development of media industry has been achieved to a certain extent and Malaysians are now exposed to diverse information. Somehow, policy planners have overlooked the younger population, but advertisers have certainly not done so. Advertisers have targeted the younger population by sponsoring popular programmes, which are usually popular, but not necessarily, educational or informative.

A policy to accommodate the role of media in inculcating a healthy lifestyle among young people is urgently required. Although the social issues, which are rearing their heads among young people, are considered alarming, they could be addressed adequately with the help of a comprehensive communications policy. The policy should address the role of the media and their responsibility towards bringing about a positive media environment encouraging young people to reflect on the realities around them.

As mentioned in the introduction, UNESCO encouraged the development of communications facilities in developing countries in the hope these would accelerate the development process. Disseminating messages could be accomplished in many different ways. In the final analysis, the media create awareness, build aspirations, and bring about positive changes in the population. Let us remain true to such noble ideas. Commercialization might be the most efficient vehicle to operate media organizations in the present era of competition and globalization, but, let us not be swallowed up by commercialization and lose sight of the real purpose of the role of communications organizations in developing countries.

Conclusion

Social issues effecting younger people in Malaysia should be understood from a Malaysian perspective. In some societies, the so-called issues related to younger people are no issues at all. Malaysia would like to preserve its values and traditions as its cultural identity in its acceleration towards becoming an industrialized nation.

Young people are regarded as a national asset in Malaysia. Investing in them either through education, vocational training, or the inculcation of social values is important because it will ensure future human resources for the country. The media being the prime socializing agent among young people, should play its role in moulding them as future human resources. With the rapid development in the communications industry, a policy to address the positive as well as negative impact of the media on young people should properly be addressed.

REFERENCES

Abdul Rahman Embo (1997) 'Cultural transformation of the Malay middle class in Malaysia,' Paper presented at the *International workshop on the South East Asia Middle Classes in comparative perspective*. Taipei, Taiwan, June 1997.

Fornas, J and G. Bolin, G. (1995) *Youth culture in late modernity*. London: Sage Publications.

Griffin, C. (1995) *Representations of youth: The study of youth and adolescents in Britain and America*. Cambridge: Polity Press.

Khan, J. (1996) 'Growth, economic transformation, culture and the middle class in Malaysia,' in: R. Robinson and D. Goodman (eds) *The new rich in Asia: mobile phone, McDonalds and middle-class revolution*. London: Routledge.

Lent. J. (1995) *Asian popular culture*. Boulder: Westview Press.

Malaysia (1996) *The seventh Malaysia plan*. Kuala Lumpur: Percetakan Nasional Bhd.

Mc Bridge, S. (1993) *Many Vioces, One World*. Paris: UNESCO.

Media Guide (1997) *Kuala Lumpur*. White Knight Communications.

Morley, D. and K. Robins (1995) *Spaces of identity, global media, electronic landscape and cultural boundaries*. London: Routledge.

New Straits Times. Dec 20, 1996; Dec 27, 1989; July 10, 1998.

Rahim, S. (1987) *Computerization and development in Southeast Asia*. Singapore: AMIC.

Said, E.
--(1981) *Covering Islam*. New York: Random House.

Samsudin A. Rahim (1994) *Youth and social issues*. Kuala Lumpur: Ministry of Youth and Sports.

--(1997) *Media penetration among youth*. Preliminary findings to International Centre for Media Studies. Kuala Lumpur, Malaysia.

Samsudin A. Rahim and S. MusCharil (1995) *Portrayal of Youth in Print Media*. Report submitted to the Ministry of Youth and Sports. Kuala Lumpur, Malaysia.

Samsudin, A. Rahim and H. Iran (1996) *Youth and AIDS*. Report to the Ministry of Health, Kuala Lumpur, Malaysia.

Samsudin A. Rahim, Rokiah Ismail and Mohammed Awang (1997) Youth Lifestyle andf Behavioural Index. Research report to the committee on the Intensification of Research in Priority Areas (IRPA), Ministry of Science and Environment.

Taylor, P. (1997) *Global communication, international affairs and the media*. London: Routledge.

WHO (1997) STD, HIV and AIDS Surveillance Report. Issue 10, Oct. 1997.

Yeo, Y.K. (1983) *Exposure to development messages on Malaysian television*. Report submitted to the Dept. of National Unity. Kuala Lumpur, Malaysia.

CHAPTER 3

KRETEKS CRACKLE IN CHILDREN'S HANDS: THE IMPACT OF ADVERTISEMENTS AND PEERS ON SMOKING BEHAVIOUR OF ADOLESCENTS IN BANDUNG, INDONESIA

FREEK, HANS AND MAX COLOMBIJN

The relationship between smoking tobacco and death rates has been known since the publication of a seminal article by Hammond and Horn (1958). Undeniably, smoking tobacco also has several positive effects: it oils social contacts, it can ease the nerves, and heighten concentration (Knol, 1993). The normative proposition taken here is that there are alternatives by which to obtain these positive effects, but no remedy for death, and that early death is unwanted. Therefore, smoking is considered undesirable behaviour that, on balance, damages human welfare and must be reduced. Tobacco smoking is addictive. Ensuring that more people do not start to smoke is a faster track to the reduction of the number of global smokers than making more people abandon the habit. And since most starting smokers are adolescents and not adults, an anti-smoking campaign should best be directed towards the prevention of smoking among adolescents (Knol, 1993:24, 27).[1] Research into why children start to smoke can provide the scientific background for such campaigns.

Smoking cigarettes is a global phenomenon and some brands are known all over the world, but the local significance of smoking and the social context varies from place to place. Indonesia not only has its own smoking culture (or cultures), but also an idiosyncratic product: the clove cigarette or *kretek*. Researchers have begun to map the incidence of the smoking of conventional cigarettes and *kretek*s by Indonesian adolescents. In 1988, an important survey was conducted at three senior secondary schools (SMA, Sekolah Menengah Atas), three junior secondary schools (SMP, Sekolah Menengah Pertama), and one technical school (STM, Sekolah Teknik Menengah) in Bandung (West Java), using a questionnaire that had previously been successfully presented to schoolchildren in Groningen, the Netherlands. It found that 39.8 per cent of the 804 boys (aged from twelve to eighteen) and 2.9 per cent of the 566 girls were smokers; the percentage of male smokers increased from 0 per cent among the twelve-year olds to 55 per cent among the eighteen-year old.[2] About six out of seven boys and one out of seven girls had smoked a cigarette at least once. A 1986 survey among 1547 SMA pupils (age fourteen to twenty) in Semarang, Surabaya, and Kudus reported that 22.5 per cent of the boys was a smoker and 1.3 per cent of the girls.[3] A survey in Jakarta, specifying neither the number of respondents nor the criterion for 'smoker,' reported the following incidence of smokers: 52 per cent of SMA pupils, male and female, 50 per cent of SMP boys, 9 per cent of SMP girls, 41 per cent of primary school boys and 10 per cent of primary school girls. An often-quoted piece of research estimated that 51 per cent of schoolchildren in Jakarta began smoking between the ages of twelve and sixteen. Today (1998) the Indonesian Health Department estimates that between 22 and 25 per cent of ten-year-old boys smoke (Colombijn et al., 1993; Kartasasmita et al., 1990; Lapau et al., 1991:38, 46; Reynolds, 1998; Saptari, 1996:177; Schwarz, 1990:33). The inconsistent outcome may be largely explained by a varying definition of 'smoker' and a different sample population.

Research about the question of why Indonesian children start to smoke is still in its infancy. It has run aground either because of vagueness (Lapau et al., 1991:48, 65; Nawawi et al., 1996:94-103) or inconclusive results (Colombijn et al., 1993). The Bandung survey mentioned above found no correlation between smoking behaviour of children on the one hand, and types of school or smoking behaviour of parents on the other. In marked contrast to the results in Groningen, where five times more children smoked when they had smoking friends, no effect from peers could be proven in Bandung. It was impossible to attest the peer effect in Bandung, because 95 per cent of all Indonesian children reported having smokers among their friends (Colombijn et al., 1993). The failure to attest the impact of peers in Bandung was due to a classical methodological problem: the translation of a questionnaire from one to another language without sufficient attention being paid to cultural differences. In Indonesia the concept of friend (*teman*) is used liberally and also extends to acquaintances, whereas in the Netherlands friend (*vriend*) is virtually synonymous with close friend. Indonesian adolescents will therefore have a much bigger network of friends than young Dutch people and almost everybody will have some 'friend' who smokes. The question about smoking friends was therefore irrelevant in Bandung (Colombijn et al., 1996). However, fieldwork experience in a small Javanese village, an intermediate Sumatran town, and the capital city, Jakarta, by one of us made us suspect that the impact of peers must be very important. This is, in fact, even indicated by the survey in Bandung, since 64 per cent of the respondents said he, or she, had obtained the first cigarette from a friend (Colombijn et al., 1993:233).

We therefore decided to concentrate a follow-up study in Bandung on the role of peers through participant observation, a method that places the researcher in the habitual environment of the researched, disturbs the daily social processes as little as possible, and by and large circumvents the pitfall of intercultural surveys. Immediate feedback between interviewer and interviewee reduces the risk of misunderstanding terms like 'friend.' (Becker and Geer, 1969; Johnson, 1975; Spradley, 1980). The research was carried out during one week in 1995. In our analysis we combined the fieldwork data with a learning theory of the psychologist Bandura (1969), in order to point out the direction towards a prevention policy. We discarded individual-psychological and genetic factors that may influence smoking behaviour, because the latter factors are less susceptible to 'social engineering' than social factors. Since advertising campaigns appeared to be relevant, we include a section about the cigarette industry in Indonesia.

THE HEALTH EFFECTS OF SMOKING *KRETEKS*

Tobacco fumes consist of gases and solid particles, 'tar'; among the gases are carbon monoxide, ammonia, hydrocyanic acid, and phenol, and in the list of solid matters are nicotine, benzene, cadmium, and nickel. Many of these matters are irritating, promoting inflammations, and are carcinogenic or toxic in another way. In countries where smoking is a common habit, the World Health Organization has estimated that it causes 90 per cent of lung cancer deaths, 75 per cent of bronchitis deaths, and 25 per cent of heart disease deaths in men under sixty-five years of age. The WHO has also estimated that 57,000 Indonesians die each year as a result of tobacco use. Moreover, at an older age the lung capacity declines faster than among non-smokers (Hammond and Horn, 1958; Knol, 1993:14-16; Reynolds, 1998; Saptari, 1996:171).

The specific health risks of *kreteks* are not known precisely. Compared with conventional cigarettes, 20-40 per cent of the tobacco is replaced by clove, which may be less unhealthy. The cloves, however, probably contribute more to total particulate matter and carbon monoxide to the smoke, and also contain a potential carcinogen, eugenol. Experiments with rats and hamsters were contradictory; sometimes *kreteks* caused less negative effects in the rodents and sometimes more. Regardless of the inconsistent outcome, the value of these experiments is limited anyway, because statistical power was weak (one brand of *kretek* compared with one American cigarette and only five to ten test animals in each group) and the exposure of the animals was not identical to the deep inhaling by humans (Clark, 1990; Guidotti, 1989). The risk of *kreteks* does not lie predominantly in the composition of the clove, but in its tobacco: the average *kretek* has 56.0 mg tar and 2.8 mg nicotine per cigarette (Schwarz, 1990:32, see further Table 1).

Table 1. Smoke analysis of *kretek*s and conventional cigarettes

Brand	Carbon monoxide	Tar	Nicotine
Gudang Garam (*kretek*)	14.9-18.2 mg	44.5-49.7 mg	5.3-5.4 mg
Djarum (*kretek*)	18.9-19.5	51.3-51.6	5.0
Bentoel (*kretek*)	n.a.	45.0	2.2
Dji Sam Soe (*kretek*)	n.a.	38.6	5.3
Marlboro (conventional)	n.a.	12.0	0.9
Marlboro Light (conventional)	n.a.	8.0	0.6
Dunhill (conventional)	16.4	12.0	0.9

Source: Gudang Garam, Djarum, and Dji Sam Soe: Reid, 1985:541; Bentoel and the carbon monoxide content in Dunhill: Saptari, 1996:175; Marlboro, Marlboro Light and Dunhill: the legally obligatory information on packets sold in the Netherlands. The figures are a rough indication and vary with other types of the same trademark; *kretek*s sold in the West have considerably lower tar and nicotine contents than those mentioned in this table.

Smoking has special effects on children: it reduces the normal growth of lung capacity, both measured in VC (vital capacity: the total volume of air breathed out after fully breathing in) and FEV1 (forced expiratory volume, breathed out in one second). The average difference of FEV1 between smokers and non-smokers at the age of twenty years is 400 ml. The maximum level of VC and FEV1, usually maintained from the twenty-fifth to the thirty-fifth year by non-smokers, is either shorter or absent. Autopsy of young smoking adults who died suddenly revealed inflammations of the bronchial tubes (Knol, 1993:20; Knol and Colombijn, 1988).

Smoking is, of course, especially dangerous because it is addictive, the nicotine in particular. Neurological research has shown that negative effects of nicotine, such as nausea, rapidly disappear (so-called down-regulation), whereas some positive effects, such as relaxation, are self-enforcing (up-regulation). Up- and down-regulation operate so quickly that children can become addicted after four or five cigarettes (Knol, 1993:9-12). We guess that *kretek*s are addictive even faster, because the sweetness helps to overcome the antipathetic taste that every experimenting smoker must experience with his or her first cigarette: the punishment for lighting the first cigarette is less than is the case with a conventional cigarette. Moreover, as one study found, eugenol numbs the lungs, reducing the 'noxious effects of smoking and inhaling. [This enables] the youthful user to learn more easily how to inhale deeply without experiencing ... coughing or throat irritation' (Schwarz, 1990:33). The tobacco industry exploits the addictive nature of its product. People who succumb to the temptation once may be trapped for good. Advertisements lure people into experimenting, and once these people have tried a few cigarettes, they may become life-long customers (Knol, 1993:26-7).

IT PAYS TO ADVERTISE:
THE *KRETEK* INDUSTRY IN INDONESIA

The year of the introduction of tobacco in Asia is known precisely: 1575, when the Spanish brought it to the Philippines from Mexico. In 1601 it was introduced to Java, where it was being cultivated a few decades later. In the mid-seventeenth century tobacco was used in Java in pipes and in indigenous cigarettes, and it became popular among women and men throughout the Archipelago as an additive to the betel quid.[4] The indigenous cigarettes, later known as *kelobot* (in Javanese) or *strootje* (in Dutch), were made of shredded tobacco wrapped up in dried maize, banana, or palm leaves (Boomgaard, 1997:421; Mangoenkoesoemo, 1929:7; Reid, 1985:535-6).[5]

The first Western cigarette, wrapped in paper, was imported into Batavia in 1845. European men, who considered betel chewing and spitting the excess saliva on the ground indicative of the low status of the indigenous people, abandoned betel chewing and began to consume tobacco in the form of cigars and cigarettes. In a process of modernization, the cigarette spread to groups with lower social status. The fashion that descended from the Dutch was exclusively a male image of cigarette smoking. Prestige was derived only from smoking the conventional, Western, paper-wrapped cigarettes; the *strootjes* were considered almost as backward as a betel quid. The first factory for the local manufacture of conventional cigarettes was opened by the British American Tobacco (BAT) Company in Cirebon in 1924, and the second, also by BAT, in Surabaya in 1928 (Budiman and Onghokham, 1987:173; Reid, 1985:538-9).

The *strootjes* made a comeback by mixing tobacco with clove buds and a little flavour (*saus*). The result was the *kretek*; the name is onomatopoeic of the crackling sound of burning cloves. The first *kretek* is attributed to Haji Jamahri of Kudus (Central Java), who invented it as a medicine. The manufacture of *kretek*s began in the 1870s and gradually the new product became popular outside Kudus. It was mainly a home industry using hand-operated rollers; the conical shape of the *kretek* and the use of irregular dried maize leaves prohibited mechanization. The factories were places for the collection, quality control, packaging, and distribution. At first, the industry was in Javanese hands, but its success attracted Chinese entrepreneurs too and mounting competition led to an outbreak of violence on 31 October 1918: factories and houses were burnt down and some people were even killed. After the indigenous culprits had been sent to jail, the Chinese manufacturers could consolidate and strengthen their position. (Budiman and Onghokham, 1987:105-8; Mangoenkoesoemo, 1929:5-9, 43, 58-9; Tarmidi, 1996:86).

An important weapon in the stiff competition, 175 factories in Kudus in 1933 (Budiman and Onghokham, 1987:124) were advertising. The *kreteks* were put in packets of ten, twenty-five, or fifty pieces, and a number of packets were then combined in packages. It was these packages, and not the packets, that were done up in attractively printed paper. Most paper was printed in Kudus, but some was imported from Malang or even as far away as Japan. Another way to advertise, that is obvious today but new at the time, was to cover vans with billboards. The very idea of advertising and its forms were copied from Western cigarette companies (Mangoenkoesoemo, 1929:50-1, 59). The copying of Western promotion techniques was more than the adoption of an innovation: by itself it gave *kreteks* a Western (thus high) status.

In 1921 a *kongsi* (partnership of Chinese entrepreneurs) built the first factory for *kreteks* using paper wrappers. It was a major breakthrough, for the use of paper instead of maize allowed the mechanized production of *kreteks* that from then on necessarily acquired a cylindrical form. The stepped-up speed of production compensated for the more expensive wrapper. In the 1920s production expanded rapidly. The investment in mass-production technology was only economical if it coincided with mass-consumption. But the market of Kudus and environs was saturated, and moreover, the local people preferred the old conical *kretek* with maize wrapper, so that the Chinese entrepreneurs had to find a new market for the paper *kretek* outside Kudus (Budiman and Onghokham, 1987:115-17; Mangoenkoesoemo, 1929:11, 43).

The markets of East Java and the rest of Central Java were conquered by using full-scale promotion campaigns. A pioneer in this field was Mas Nitisemito, born in Kudus in 1863. In a period when many people were illiterate, he had a powerful trademark: Bal Tiga ('Three Balls'). For promotion he dispensed glasses, plates, cups, watches, bicycles, clocks and other items with the characteristic three green balls. He often organized a stand during night fairs (*pasar malam*). At the turn of the century he was also the first to cover his cars with posters. He once even rented a plane to drop pamphlets. The West Java market remained averse to the new product, however, and there he, and other producers, used so-called *stambul* groups. These popular theatre troupes wandered through the countryside and whenever they performed painted the stage in the colours of the trademark (Budiman and Onghokham, 1987:128-9; Mangoenkoesoemo, 1929:12-14, 59; Saptari, 1996:182).

According to Saptari (1996:173), after Independence, many people were smoking cheap brands of locally made, conventional cigarettes. We can only guess the reason why, apparently, *kretek*s had lost terrain again: higher prices, lower status? After the establishment of the New Order regime, in 1965, when the standard of living began to rise, the pattern of smoking began to change once again. The emerging middle class turned to expensive foreign brands, but also reverted to *kretek*s. The *kretek* companies made a comeback with a much glossier appearance and expensive packaging, mimicking Western trademarks. Also the adoption of filters was probably more to give *kretek*s a modern image than a health measure. Currently *kretek*s have almost pushed the foreign brands out of the market. In 1971, 18 billion conventional cigarettes and 20 billion *kretek*s were produced in Indonesia; in 1991 these figures were respectively 19 and 130 billion (Saptari, 1996:174; Tarmidi, 1996:86-91).[6] The rapid increase was made possible by the adoption of mechanized production by the big companies: Bentoel (in 1968), Djarum (1976), Gudang Garam (1978) and Sampoerna that also holds Dji Sam Soe (1983) (Tarmidi, 1996:90). The mechanization has led to a shakeout of firms and the concentration of market shares in a few hands: Gudang Garam and Djarum each holding 31 per cent (in 1989), Bentoel 12 per cent, and Sampoerna 5.5 per cent (Tarmidi, 1996:97).

The heavy investments were only viable if they expanded their market share, or increased total consumption. The way to do this was advertising. Djarum, for instance, experimented with sponsoring sporting matches and cultural events and providing free cigarettes on domestic flights.[7] As in the 1920s, a number of packets could be exchanged for glasses, and this was such a success that in the late 1970s the glass factories in Jakarta and Surabaya were no longer able to meet other orders. The first massive co-ordinated campaign was the launching of a new product Bentoel Biru International ('Blue International Bentoel') in 1976 (Saptari, 1996:182-3). The most important images used in the *kretek* advertisement are: modernity, Western pictures (Marlboro country, statue of liberty, skyscrapers), hard work or leisure, and respect for Indonesia (the Borobudur and the colours of the national flag in the background) (Saptari, 1996:182-5). Some adverts are only understandable in a Western context. For instance, in the eyes of urban Indonesians the jungle is a backwater, a place to avoid; the Djarum image of a man and woman driving a jeep through the jungle only makes sense in Indonesia if one knows that Western brands such as Camel use the same icon.

The industry maintains that promotion is meant to make users switch from one brand to another. Opponents of the industry, pointing out the minor shifts in market shares, consider this argument unconvincing. This objection against the industry's argument is not fully convincing either, because it is very possible that trademarks only maintain their market share because they uphold it with their adverts. It is even possible that smokers switch constantly from one brand to the other, but that the net effect is zero. Whatever the truth of the market share, promotion must at least also be seen as a joint effort by trademarks to lure new people into addiction, and therefore the adverts are meant for potential smokers. Since few adults start smoking, the advertisements are directed towards the adolescents (Knol, 1993:26-8; Saptari, 1996:186-7).

Smoking celebrates modernity and masculinity.[8] Smoking has an increasing role in the status system based on wealth. The great variation in price range of cigarettes, from the cheapest home made *strootje* to the most expensive *kretek*, serves as a precise marker of the achieved status of the man who offers cigarettes to his companions (Reid, 1985:542). In the 1980s one could still observe scavengers collecting butts from the street in baskets to recycle them; the cigarettes produced from these butts were very cheap, but also extremely unhealthy because of the increased concentration of nicotine. Parvenus put cheap cigarettes in the packages of expensive brands, but often betray themselves by the little singe marks on their clothes, because the cheap brands use coarser pieces of cloves that fall out of the cigarettes as glowing embers.

The Indonesian government faces the dilemma of having to choose between the tax revenues, employment (of tobacco cultivators, factory labourers, suppliers, distributors, and street hawkers), and sponsor money[9] from the *kretek* industry and public health. Its priority lies clearly with the economic gains,[10] and for instance, in 1990, the Youth and Sports Minister of all people, lobbied hard to ensure that no government policy would crimp sponsorship money from cigarette companies to youth groups. According to Catherine Reynolds the government received US$ 1.3 billion in taxes in 1997 and 4.3 million people were directly or indirectly involved in producing cigarettes. However, some sections in the government, notably the Department of Health, backed by the Indonesian Heart Foundation, the Association Against Cancer and a non-governmental consumers' association, form an anti-smoking lobby. As early as 1978 smoking was prohibited in public transport in Jakarta, but this has not been enforced. In 1990 cigarette commercials were banned from television (but short takes for the cinema are still very common) and more recently health warnings were stamped on the packets (Reynolds, 1998; Saptari, 1996:172, 176-7; Schwarz, 1990:33).

FIELDWORK RESULTS: THE IMPACT OF PEERS

During one week in 1995, one researcher made observations on the premises and in the vicinity of the seven schools of the 1988 Bandung survey and in popular streets. He also interviewed twenty-five schoolboys and eleven schoolgirls, often in small groups, where he met them on location, with the help of a short standard list of items. These thirty-six interlocutors were selected by theoretical sampling (Glaser and Strauss, 1967), purposefully searching for variation in type of school (discernible from the school uniform), gender, group size, and apparent status as smoker or non-smoker. The informal setting gave the advantage that the schoolchildren interviewed felt at ease, but the disadvantage that less articulate children agreed with the opinion of a group's spokesperson, rather than giving their own view. The researcher was clear about his intentions; he did not smoke himself. Additional information was obtained in formal interviews with three headmasters.

About half of the boys interviewed and none of the girls smoked. Almost all smokers had had his first cigarette from a friend. Most adolescents were met on the street, in-groups of two to four peers. Members of these groups displayed physical contact: girls walked hand in hand, boys flung their arms around each other's shoulders. All interviewed and observed groups consisted completely of either smokers or non-smokers; no mixed groups of smokers and non-smokers were found. As far as we observed, smokers never lit a cigarette when they walked alone.

All interviewees knew the detrimental effects of smoking. A strong norm about sharing cigarettes prevailed among smokers: one was expected to buy a packet for the whole group in turns, and one took a cigarette from somebody else's packet without asking for it.

The most popular cigarettes were Marlboro (the 'cowboy,' as somebody said), Gudang Garam, and Sampoerna. They belong to the more expensive brands, costing respectively 1,450, 800, and 900 *rupiah* per packet at that time. The cheaper brands were about 500 *rupiah*. Cigarettes were most often bought with pocket money from parents and one headmaster therefore concluded that only the children of better-off parents could afford cigarettes. One smoker envied non-smokers since the latter had more money to spend on other things.

One unanimously held the opinion that smoking was unseemly for girls and women, but not inappropriate for elder boys (of about SMA age and older); therefore smoking was associated with adulthood. Some children associated smoking girls with *kupu-kupu malam*, 'night-butterflies.'[11] Smoking boys and some girls deemed smokers more *jantan*, virile. Some girls, in part the same ones who considered smokers virile and non-smoking boys believed smokers to be rowdy and cocky. One person said that there is a stench from the mouth of smokers. Some smokers regarded non-smoking boys as unsociable and effeminate. There were no nicknames for either smokers or non-smokers.

Smoking was prohibited in schools. When smoking on the school premises was discovered, the cigarettes were confiscated. Now and then anti-smoking posters were hung in the schools.

DISCUSSION OF FIELDWORK FINDINGS

Smokers did not light a cigarette when they were alone, and apparently smoking is a social act (and not, or not only, for personal indulgence; see also Reid, 1985:540). The trip from home to school and back is a moment when the adolescents are free from control by parents and teachers. The groups that are formed on these trips show a strong solidarity, expressed, for instance, by bodily contact. These groups either smoke in their entirety or do not smoke. Contrary to the Bandung survey, the impact of peers appears to be very important now.

The norm of sharing a packet of cigarettes strengthens group cohesion and, moreover, is practical. Schoolteachers confiscate cigarettes, and cigarettes are also better kept hidden from parental eyes. A packet when bought must be emptied quickly, which can only be done by sharing the contents. Not smoking within smokers' groups is therefore asocial behaviour, punished by social pressure (Soekanto, 1993:19). Smoking, on the other hand, is rewarded; it gives prestige through the association with the qualities displayed by *kretek* adverts (virility, modernity et cetera). Joining the smokers also increases social cohesion, because, we believe, it reduces the guilt felt by other smokers (who all know about the bad health effects and are aware of the prohibition by teachers and many parents).

The adolescents prefer the expensive brands of *kretek*, or the even more costly Marlboro. Precisely these brands dominate advertising with references to youth, wealth, success, and America (see also Danusantoso, 1991:17-18). They are most prestigious. The girls gain prestige by conforming to the norm of not smoking.

In order to propose a strategy to reduce the incidence of smoking, we connect our fieldwork results with a theoretical model derived from A. Bandura (1969). Bandura's social learning theory describes how the example of others may be followed. If an example of one certain type of behaviour looks attractive, it may be tried out; and when the test is appreciated, the new pattern of behaviour will become enduring. Bandura predicts two ways by which the adoption of the example, in our case smoking, can be prevented: either the example is removed or the example is robbed of its attractiveness. When cigarette adverts are banned and smoking in school is prohibited, the example is removed. But what is prohibited is often especially attractive and after school-hours boys will continue to stimulate each other to smoke.[12] Therefore, a solution must be sought in a change of the meaning of the example (Korrelboom and Kernkamp, 1993).

At present, the anti-smoking campaigns try to give smoking a new meaning, by pointing out the risk of premature death. We believe that this campaign is ineffective for two reasons. First, in the perception of adolescents death is far away. Social ostracism is a much more acute danger than death. Second, adolescents can underscore their own vitality by reckless behaviour: in a psychological sense, smoking is an exorcism of Death, a challenge to mortality (Yalom, 1980). Well-intended slogans like 'smoking is a deadly sin' (launched in the Netherlands in 1995 and again in 1999) appeal to an aspect not so relevant or not so relevant yet, to the life of youths. Anti-smoking campaigns will be more effective when they associate smoking with lack of will or a non-sexy stench from the mouth.

CONCLUSION

Contrary to the inconclusive results of the 1988 survey in Bandung, participant observation among schoolchildren showed that peers are very important in the decision of Indonesian adolescents to smoke. Smoking is social behaviour and groups of friends either smoke completely or not at all. The meaning of this social behaviour is derived from the image conveyed by commercial advertisements.

The *kretek* industry obeys the logic of capitalism and creates its own demand. History repeats itself in this respect, for both in the 1920s and the period from about 1970 until recently, periods of prosperity in Indonesia, the industry mechanized the production process and subsequently had to find a new outlet for the increased output that must make good the capital investment. The means for finding new markets has been by launching promotion campaigns, especially directed at the most promising potential customers: adolescent boys. Even the contents of the adverts in the 1920s and today were similar: the message transmitted is that smoking is modern, virile, Western, in short: prestigious.

An anti-smoking campaign will be most effective when it attempts to give smoking a new meaning: it should be associated with lack of will and unattractive stench.

NOTES

1. A survey conducted in Jakarta under the auspices of the World Health Organization supports this general statement. Of 986 men between twenty-five and sixty-four years, 59.9 per cent was a smoker, 22.6 per cent an ex-smoker, and 17.4 per cent a non-smoker (of 1085 women these percentages were respectively 5.9, 4.7, and 89.4). 63.3 per cent of the smoking men had started between the ages of ten and twenty, and 3.6 per cent had started before the age of ten (Boedhi-Darmojo, 1993:120).
2. A smoker was somebody who had smoked at least one cigarette in the two weeks preceding the survey.
3. The definition of smoker was much stricter than in Bandung: somebody who had smoked at least one cigarette every day in the year preceding the survey.
4. Tobacco also spread to other Indonesian islands. In Borneo, the Dutch exploited the tobacco addiction of Dayak and Banjarese to defeat them in the Banjarmasin War (1859-63); strict regulation on the salt and tobacco imports helped to subdue the indigenous peoples (Han Knapen, personal communication, cf. Arsip Nasional Republik Indonesia, Jakarta, Zuid-Oost Borneo 7-10, Algemeen verslag 1860, f. 4v).
5. The cigarette was also introduced in Indonesia from Mexico. The cigarette is an invention derived from poor Spanish people, who rolled cigar butts into paper.
6. A similar process has happened with soft drinks, where a bottled lemon tea, Teh Botol, has conquered a considerable market share on Coca-Cola and Sprite.
7. In Padang (West Sumatra) one of us observed that cigarettes were handed out during a rock concert; the music was so loud that the visitors used the cigarette filters as earplugs.
8. A curious consequence of the male association is that in some shops placing a blue packet of Bentoel Biru on the counter signifies that one wishes to rent a blue movie.

9   Cigarette companies sponsor sports events and musical happenings, but in places like Kudus also pay for public facilities, road construction, mosques, and scholarships.
10 A typically Indonesian financial interest is the Badan Pembelian dan Penyangga Cengkeh (BPPC, 'Clove Trade Agency') headed by the former president's son, Hutomo Mandala Putra Suharto ('Tommy'). It was instituted to guarantee a minimum price for the peasants growing cloves, but effectively gained a monopoly over the clove trade (Tarmidi, 1996:106). The monopoly was among the first to be dismantled by the IMF when Indonesia was plunged into a financial crisis at the end of 1997.
11 Night-butterfly is the literal translation of *kupu-kupu malam;* the word is used for streetwalkers and girls in bars who provide company, but not necessarily sex, against payment. Smoking a cigarette on the pavement is a discreet way for a woman to make known that she is a streetwalker.
12 In our view, Danusantoso (1991:27) is right when he states that smoking should be bereft of its glamorous meaning, but wrong when he believes that a prohibition by teachers and parents can achieve this change of meaning.

REFERENCES

Bandura, A. (1969) *Principles of behavior modification.* New York: Holt, Rinehart and Winston.

Becker, H.S. and B. Geer (1969) 'Participant observation and interviewing: a comparison,' in: G.J. McCall and J.L. Simmons (eds) *Issues in participant observation.* Massachusetts: Addison-Wesley, pp. 322-31.

Boedhi-Darmojo, R. (1993) 'The pattern of cardiovascular disease in Indonesia,' *World Health Statistics Quarterly* 46, pp. 119-24.

Boomgaard, Peter (1997) 'Gevolgen van de introductie van nieuwe landbouwgewassen (1600-1900),' *Spiegel historiael* 32, pp 418-23.

Budiman, Amen and Onghokham (1987) *Rokok kretek; lintasan sejarah dan artinya bagi pembangunan bangsa dan negara.* Kudus: PT Djarum.

Clark, Gerald C. (1990) 'Comparison of the inhalation toxicity of *kretek* (clove cigarette) smoke with that of American cigarette smoke. II. Fourteen days exposure,' *Archives of toxicology* 64, pp. 515-21.

Colombijn, R.M., H.J.Th. Colombijn and F. Colombijn (1996) 'Intercultureel onderzoek naar de invloed van (anti-) rookreclame op scholieren,' *Tijdschrift voor sociale gezondheidszorg, gezondheid en samenleving* 7, pp. 362-3.

Colombijn, R.M., et al. (1993) 'Roken door kinderen: Groningen versus Bandung, Indonesia,' *Tijdschrift Kindergeneeskunde* 61, pp. 232-4.

Danusantoso, Halim (1990) *Rokok dan perokok*. Jakarta: Arcan.

Glaser, Barney G. and Anselm L. Strauss (1967) *The discovery of grounded theory; strategies for qualitative research*. Chicago: Aldine Publishers.

Guidotti, Tee L. (1989) 'Critique of available studies on the toxicology of *kretek* smoke and its constituents by routes of entry involving the respiratory tract,' *Archives of toxicology* 63, pp. 7-12.

Hammond, E.C. and D. Horn (1958) 'Smoking and death rates,' *Journal of the American Medical Associaton* 166, pp. 1294-308.

Johnson, John M. (1975) *Doing fieldwork*. New York: The Free Press.

Kartasasmita, Cissy B., et al. (1990) 'Faktor risiko pada kebiasaan merokok pada siswa Sekolah Lanjutan Atas,' *Pediatrica Indonesiana* 30, pp. 31-41.

Knol, K. (1993) *Kinderen en tabak; afscheidscollege uitgesproken op 26 oktober 1993*. Groningen: Regenboog.

Knol, K. and R.M. Colombijn (1988) 'Daarom moeten kinderen niet roken,' *Nederlands Tijdschrift voor Geneeskunde* 132, pp. 2047-8.

Korrelboom, C.W. and J.H.B. Kernkamp (1993) *Gedragstherapie*. Muiderberg: Coutinho.

Lapau, Buchari, Mon Dastri, Korib Sudaryo and Aulia Sani (1991) *Study kepustakaan tentang merokok dan kesehatan*. Jakarta: Yayasan Jantung Indonesia dan Perhimpunan Ahli Epidemologi Indonesia.

Mangoenkoesoemo, Darmawan (1929) *Bijdrage tot de kennis van de kretekstrootjes-industrie in het regentschap Koedoes*. Weltevreden: Landsdrukkerij [Mededeelingen van de afdeeling nijverheid 6].

Nawawi, Abdullah, J. Marsaman, Marulah Pribadi, et al. (1996) *Selamatkan generasi muda bangsa dari bahaya penyalahgunaan narkotika; dilengkapi analisa tentang kriminalitas remaja dan pemuda*. Jakarta: Badan Kerjasama Pembinaan Warga Tama, YPLNP and Yayasan Titian Bhakti Jenderal Oerip Soemohardjo.

Reid, Anthony (1985) 'From betel-chewing to tobacco-smoking in Indonesia,' *Journal of Asian studies* 44, pp. 529-47.

Reynolds, Catherine (1998) 'Worshipping cancer sticks,' *Inside Indonesia*, October-December 1998, pp. 28-9.

Saptari, Ratna (1996) 'The political economy of smoking; the case of the *kretek* cigarette industry in Indonesia,' in: P. Boomgaard, R. Sciortino and I. Smyth (eds) *Health care in Java; past and present*, pp. 171-89.

Schwarz, Adam (1990) 'Battle of the brands,' *Far Eastern Economic Review* 19 April 1990, pp. 32-3.

Soekanto, Soerjono (1993) *Remaja dan masalah-masalahnya*. Yogyakarta: Kanisius and Jakarta: Gunung Mulia.

Spradley, J.P. (1980) *Participant observation*. New York: Holt, Rinehart and Winston.

Tarmidi, Lepi T. (1996) 'Changing structure and competition in the *kretek* cigarette industry,' *Bulletin of Indonesian Economic Studies* 32-3, pp. 85-107.

Yalom, I.D. (1980) *Existential psychotherapy*. New York: Basic Books.

CHAPTER 4

CHINA IN REFORM: STRUCTURAL PROBLEMS IN THE ECONOMY AND SOCIETY OF CONTEMPORARY ZHEJIANG PROVINCE

KEITH FORSTER

China is currently in the twentieth year of its ambitious programme of reform and opening to the outside world. The past two decades have witnessed a shift of major proportions in the social and economic contours of the country, which has far-reaching importance for the Asian region and the world as a whole. The economic and social structures which are in the process of formation in the transition from a command to market economy, and from a closed to more open and accessible society, clearly bear the legacy of the previous Maoist years as well as exhibiting patterns of behaviour which have occurred in other countries of the region during their period of economic take-off. This essay briefly examines the economic and social structure of one of the most economically successful provinces, Zhejiang, and explains the paradoxical nature of the structures which have emerged and the problems these pose for its continued economic development and social cohesion.

Since 1978 Zhejiang has experienced rapid and sustained economic growth. The average annual growth rate in its GDP has been second only to Guangdong province, while in per capita GDP growth rate it has ranked first in China (because it has done better in controlling population growth than Guangdong). From being a middle-ranked province in 1978 Zhejiang's economy now ranks fifth in the country, while the gross value of its industrial output (GVIO) ranks fourth.[1] For a province with only about 3.5 per cent of the country's population it is possible to agree with the characterization of this achievement by local commentators as a 'miracle,' while keeping in mind another, sharper assessment which sums up these decades as having 'obvious achievements, outstanding problems.'[2]

It is claimed, with some justification, that Zhejiang has passed through the initial stage of the industrialization process and has entered a new, higher phase of economic development. While the province has changed from an agricultural to an industrial, and from a small to a large economy, for various reasons, which will be outlined below, it cannot be considered to possess a balanced or a strong economy.

What could be called the Zhejiang pattern of development (and this is not to say that such a pattern has not been followed or has not manifest itself in other provinces but the pattern does seem somewhat paradoxical for an economically advanced province such as Zhejiang, as measured by its location and per capita GDP) has relied on crude, extensive, small-scale, rural-based, domestically-financed industrialization involving the processing of cheap and low-grade consumer goods for the Chinese market. The degree of development of Zhejiang's regional economy is linked closely with this pattern, that is the closer a locality's economy has simulated these conditions the faster it has grown during the reform period. The pattern also illustrates the role of peasants and entrepreneurs in the economic development of Zhejiang, which in many respects signifies a return to influence in new guises and new forms of traditional and historically-important commercial and business patterns stifled but not extinguished during thirty years of Maoism.

Partly as a result of this style of economic development, social development in the province has lagged behind in terms of many national indicators, particularly in the fields of education, and science and technology. The incongruities inherent in this lag reveal the peculiarities and weaknesses of Zhejiang's economic development which until recently have been obscured by phenomenal rates of economic growth.

This essay will outline the features and deficiencies of the socio-economic structure of the province and the reasons behind the emergence of these structures. It will conclude with speculations concerning the future direction of and challenges confronting Zhejiang as it heads into the next century.[3]

POPULATION[4]

Between 1949 and 1995 Zhejiang's population increased by an annual average rate of 1.62 per cent, doubling the total population from nearly 21 million to over 43 million. Between 1979 and 1995 the average annual rate of population increase dropped to only 0.9 per cent. In 1996, the rate of the natural increase in population over 1995 was only 0.55 per cent, just over half the national rate of increase for the same year.[5] Zhejiang has now shifted from a pattern of population trends exemplified until the mid 1960s by a high birth rate, relatively high death rate, and high rate of natural population increase, to a modern structure with a low birth rate, low death rate and low rate of natural increase. It is important to emphasize that this transformation occurred in the early 1970s, that is during the latter stages of the Cultural Revolution, when China introduced birth control measures to limit the birth rate as well as disseminating medical facilities and personnel into rural areas which helped lower the death rate. In Zhejiang, the death rate in 1996 was in fact slightly higher than that in 1967, and the province's lowest death rate since 1949 was recorded in 1969.[6]

It appears that when a systematic birth control programme was introduced in the early 1970s the authorities in Zhejiang implemented it more successfully than their counterparts in other localities. After seventeen successive years when the birth rate exceeded 3 per cent, commencing in 1967 it began to fall. At the national level, during the 1970s the birth rate fell 0.37 per cent compared to the 1960s while in Zhejiang the fall was over twice this magnitude at 0.83 per cent. The dramatic slowdown in the rate of population increase in Zhejiang achieved during the final years of the Maoist period and continued into the present, has played a major part in the dramatic increase in per capita economic indices during the reform period. In 1996 the rate of natural increase in the population in Zhejiang over 1995 was just over one-half of the national average. With the death rate in Zhejiang a fraction higher than the national average, the reason for Zhejiang's rate of population increase being only half that of the national average was that its birth rate at 1.21 per cent was only 70 per cent that of the national average of 1.7 per cent. The rate of natural increase in the population in Zhejiang is about the same as that of its northern neighbour Jiangsu, and considerably lower than that in Guangdong, where the birth rate and rate of natural increase are above the national average.[7]

Looking at the quality of Zhejiang's population from the perspectives of education (the crude illiteracy rate and average length of education) and health (the infant death rate and average life expectancy), we find a picture of contrasts. The 1 per cent sample population survey carried out in 1995 found that the proportion of the provincial population aged over 15 who are illiterate or semi-illiterate came to 13.3 per cent. This was a fall on the three previous censuses of 1964, 1982, and 1990. The average length of education had risen from 5.6 years in 1990 to 6.3 years in 1995, that is the first year of junior secondary school. Both the infant death rate and average life expectancy approached levels found in developed countries.

Zhejiang's population structure (both its natural structure and socio-economic structure) also show contrasting trends. In particular, Zhejiang's population has prematurely, for an economy which has only recently entered the phase of economic take-off, and because of the great success of the population control policy pursued for over twenty years, become an ageing population. The population aged over sixty-five years now exceeds the 7 per cent proportion considered by international demographers as an indication of an aged population, and has reached 8.7 per cent. The repercussions of this skewed age structure for the immediate future, in terms of social welfare and employment, are significant.

Looking at the socio-economic structure of the provincial population (in terms of its urban/rural and industrial structures), we find that in 1995 the urban population comprised 30 per cent of the total population, compared to 12 per cent in 1949 and to 15 per cent in 1980. However, the agricultural population (as against the non-agricultural population, which was formerly so defined because under the planned economy it was issued grain coupons) has only fallen marginally from 85 per cent of the total population in 1949 to 82 per cent in 1995. Zhejiang remains overwhelmingly a province of peasants and rural communities living in villages and towns. The great majority of cities are classified as small (having a population between 50,000 and 200,000), and even in the province's third largest city, Wenzhou, the non-agricultural population is outnumbered by the agricultural population.

Thus, Zhejiang's population structure reveals contrasting features. Some population indices are modernizing while others are in the process of approaching this stage. The patterns of reproduction and birth have achieved modernization, the health index is approaching the levels of developed countries, while education levels are far below. The age structure has surpassed the stage of economic development, while the urban/rural and industrial structures are lagging well behind economic development, which acts as a major constraint on the transfer of the surplus rural labour force.

While Zhejiang's birth rate has slowed to beneath replacement levels, the absolute increase in numbers has become a constraining factor on sustained economic growth, in terms of pressure on limited and non-renewable resources and employment. In 1995 the work force in Zhejiang comprised 74 per cent of the population. The newly-employed urban population increased at an annual average of 6 per cent between 1985 and 1995, and in addition, two million rural labourers entered cities looking for work each year. The lag in raising population quality also constrains sustained economic development by preventing the province's industrial structure from being upgraded because of the lack of skilled technical and managerial personnel. In the 20s and 30s of the next century the natural structure of Zhejiang's population will constrain economic development in that the ageing population will impose a heavy burden on the working population, a burden beyond the capacity of the economy to bear. The lag in the transformation of the socio-economic structure of the population seriously affects the shift of excess rural labour and in turn the adjustment of industrial structure. The speed of the shift to a more urbanized population should be compatible with economic development, but to date it has lagged behind.

KEITH FORSTER

ECONOMIC STRUCTURE[8]

Zhejiang's population structure is both partly the cause of, and in turn also the consequence of, its economic structure. While the province has now entered the middle stage of industrialization, by international criteria the structure of its GDP is unbalanced, in that the proportion of secondary industry is too high and that of tertiary industry too low (it is, in fact, paradoxically for one of the most developed provinces in the country, below the national average) given the level of per capita GDP attained.

Looking at the structural composition of Zhejiang's GDP we discover that it possesses a weak agricultural base, with little per capita cultivated land (one-half the national average and below the danger line as defined by the United Nations' Food and Agricultural Organization), and an unfavourable topography comprised of seven parts mountains, one part water and two parts arable land. Because of the concentration of investment in secondary industry there is a critical lack of investment in agriculture, and land holdings are small, dispersed, and uneconomic in scale. Zhejiang's agricultural sector has been boxed in by the national policy of self-sufficiency in grain production, when it would be more rational and economic to import grain from other provinces or overseas, and to devote grain fields to cash crops or to other economic endeavours.

The industrial structure of Zhejiang is renowned as being low-grade, small-scale, dispersed, and crude, and heavily biased toward light industry and the processing of consumer goods principally for the domestic market. In many respects the fundamentals of the industrial structure have changed little since 1978, except from the ownership perspective where a major shift from the public to the non-public sectors has taken place. For example, between 1985 and 1995 the proportion of industrial output coming from the state sector fell from 37 per cent to 17 per cent.[9] The state sector continues to play an important role in basic industries, energy, raw materials, and high-tech industries, mainly, one suspects, because the non-public sector is forbidden from investing or running enterprises in these sectors.

Although government and commentators have called for a basic change to this industrial structure, as a result of an unbalanced pattern of investment whereby funds flow into those areas of the economy which provide large and rapid returns, there is little, although some, signs of such a transformation taking place.[10] Ironically, given the so-called business acumen of the people of the province and the importance of markets to its economic success, Zhejiang's industry now finds that it cannot respond rapidly enough to changes in consumer demand, particularly from the newly-emerging bourgeoisie who demand more sophisticated and higher grade consumer goods which it is often beyond the capacity of Zhejiang's industry to supply. In a country known for its cheap and shoddy consumer goods, *Zhe huo* (Zhejiang goods) are found at the bottom end of this scale.

This industrial structure is replicated in cities and towns across the province, resulting in the duplication of production, the high demand for supplies of raw materials (supplied principally by the agricultural sector) and subsequent waste of resources. Basic materials and energy industries play a disproportionately small role in the provincial economy, and the recent upsurge in investment in social infrastructure facilities such as power, transport, and water- conservancy has been unable to compensate for previous years of neglect. The failure to maintain coastal and river embankments adequately has caused enormous economic losses to the province in recent years. For example, in 1994 a typhoon caused damage that amounted to one-tenth of the GDP.[11]

Township and village enterprises contribute over one-third of GVIO, and have led to a remarkable industrialization of the countryside of Zhejiang.[12] However, the great majority of these enterprises is small-scale, and employs even fewer trained and educated personnel and technical staff than larger scale and state-owned enterprises. While rural industrialization has soaked up many unemployed or under-employed labourers from the agricultural sector, it has held back the growth of cities and tertiary industry, which in turn has fed back into an inability to create jobs for larger numbers of the potential work-force, created horrendous pollution to the environment, particularly in such industries as cement-making, tanning, and dyeing, and reinforced feudal, old-fashioned, and outdated views about population and education which have in turn slowed the transition to more contemporary attitudes found in urban, modern societies.

Although the province has on the whole met the standards of a wide range of criteria proving that it has entered the stage of *xiaokang* (initial prosperity), the regional structure of Zhejiang's economy reveals a substantial gap between advanced and backward sub-regions, cities, and counties, with the gap tending to widen in the 1990s.[13] The six district-level cities of the Jiangnan plains of the northeast share approximately 50 per cent of the land area and population of the province with the mountainous and coastal region encompassing the four cities and one district of the southwest. However, economic resources and wealth are highly unbalanced in favour of the north-east, although the gap between the two in terms of their share of industrial output has narrowed somewhat in the mid 1990s. Still effected by the unbalanced pattern of state investment during the Maoist years the state sector of the industrial economy is much more influential in the northeast, as is the foreign-invested sector, profiting from advantages in location and infrastructure. Conversely, the non-public sectors are stronger in the south-west of the province. Zhejiang is a province where the proportion of budgetary revenue relative to provincial GDP is very low, which means that the government lacks the ability to extract and redistribute financial resources to reduce regional economic disparities.

There is very little difference in the kinds of industries pre-eminent in the two regions. One peculiar feature of Zhejiang's regional development is that with the exception of the port-city of Ningbo, where a major upgrading of port facilities has occurred boosted by the bestowal of a series of state preferential policies, the coast, islands, and ports of the province have suffered years of neglect.

The structure of enterprises in Zhejiang is, as has been suggested above, characterized by smallness of scale, backwardness in use of technology, and deficient in the proportion of skilled and educated technical staff and management employed, particularly in rural industry. Plant and equipment is often outdated or not operating at efficient levels because of to the lack of skilled personnel. The smallness of scale is particularly evident in the heavy industrial sector, such as the chemical fibres industry, where efficiencies of scale are critical.

Products produced by Zhejiang industry are sold principally on the domestic market. About 45 per cent is sold to the 'three norths' (north, northwest, and northeast China), 30 per cent is sold within the province, and the remaining 25 per cent exported. In their own market, Zhejiang goods are under threat from better quality goods both from overseas and from other provinces, while in the 'three norths' cheaper goods produced with lower-cost labour in interior provinces threaten to displace products from Zhejiang. Because of their poor quality, Zhejiang goods find it difficult to make inroads into the more sophisticated and demanding markets of large cities.

The nature of its products and the location of its markets mean that Zhejiang's economy is highly sensitive to fluctuations in domestic social demand. When growth in the national economy slows, as it has done in 1982, 1989, and 1997 this is reflected immediately and strongly in Zhejiang, where falls in growth rate tend to exceed national averages (just as increases do). Zhejiang's industry is in an unenviable transition from low cost inputs and low quality outputs to high cost inputs and low quality outputs, and there is a structural surplus in output because of the duplication of plant and products across the province. It lacks key, core enterprises to pull its economy along.

The overseas component of Zhejiang's economy also shows some interesting anomalies. Both foreign trade and investment as a proportion of GDP and total investment in fixed assets respectively demonstrate a below average and lagging performance. Exports by town and village enterprises as a proportion of their total output are below that of neighbouring coastal provinces, while exports from foreign-invested enterprises as a proportion of total provincial exports are well below the national average.

In terms of foreign investment Zhejiang was late out of the blocks, and the gap which opened up with other coastal provinces is widening. This is the principal reason for the trends referred to in the previous paragraph. Rather than viewing foreign investment, particularly direct foreign investment, as a means of upgrading and restructuring industry by introducing advanced technology, management experience and new industries, it has mainly been looked at from the perspective of providing jobs and making up deficiencies in construction funds. One reason for the relatively low levels of foreign investment in Zhejiang is the alleged adequate supply of domestic funds, which deters enterprises and departments from putting in the effort required to negotiate deals with foreign businesses.

The provincial government has not provided policy incentives to attract foreign investment, and there are no clear goals (for example, there is no focus on a region from which to attract foreign investment). As a result, foreign investment, principally from Hong Kong, has been directed into increasing the over-supply of light, small-scale processing enterprises concentrated in the wealthier cities of the north-east of the province and the two most advanced cities in the south-west. In the tertiary sector foreign investment has gravitated towards real estate and hotel construction. In the foreign funds which have come into the province, there has been a high proportion of short-term borrowing from foreign financial institutions.[14]

Zhejiang is known for the size and number of its markets, which are mainly commodity exchange markets for wholesale consumer goods (both industrial and agricultural).[15] There are few factor markets for labour, finance, real estate, and technology, however. Most of the markets are located in towns and small cities. The market in Yiwu city (county-level) in central Zhejiang has the highest turnover of any commodity market in the country.

In examining the urban-rural structure of the province,[16] we find, first of all, that there has been a major problem regarding the definition of the term 'city' during the reform period. Cities as places have now, with the administrative reform whereby cities rule their surrounding counties, become conflated and confused with the old term 'district,' which indicated an area. Hangzhou city proper, which has six city districts and a population of less than two million, as Hangzhou City, rules seven surrounding counties (county-level cities), with a total population of over six million.

Zhejiang is a province of small cities and towns scattered around the countryside. Urbanization lags well behind industrialization and economic growth, resulting in or exacerbating the dispersal of inputs, the small scale of industry and its lack of specialization. The cities of the province tend to have poor infrastructure because of the lack of investment (although this trend may be changing) and the under-development of service industries is noticeable. The low level of urbanization is largely responsible for the lag in tertiary industries, and the accompanying relatively weak growth of core cities and their subsequent radiating influence on surrounding rural areas. In a total population of nearly 44 million there are only six cities in the province with populations in excess of 200,000.

A comparison of urban development in Guangdong is instructive.[17] Both provinces posses a similar topography and resource base, but Guangdong's location is more favourable than Zhejiang's and it has received more preferential policies from the state and at an earlier time. In 1990 the total non-agricultural population in Zhejiang was 16.4 per cent compared to 23.1 per cent in Guangdong. In 1995 gap had widened, with Zhejiang's non-agricultural population having grown to 18.1 per cent while Guangdong's had reached 34.9 per cent. The bulk of Guangdong's cities are medium-sized (200,000 to 500,000) while in Zhejiang the majority is small. This means that investment in fixed assets and its scale and distribution in Guangdong tends towards large and medium cities, while in Zhejiang it is toward small cities. The spatial distribution of cities in both provinces is similar, and most cities are found on plains, and near the coast and highways and railway lines. While there are no great individual characteristics or clear division of labour between the cities of both provinces those in Guangdong have a superior infrastructure and better quality transport links. Consequently, the proportion of provincial GDP provided by the cities of Guangdong is higher than in Zhejiang and is beneficial to the adjustment of its industrial structure.

SOCIAL STRUCTURE[18]

Based on ten comprehensive indicators drawn up by the state bureau of statistics Zhejiang's social development ranked around ninth in the mid-1990s, an indication that the quality of life in Zhejiang is above the national average. However, Zhejiang ranked only thirteenth in 1990 in terms of social structure, and in 1995 its indices were below the national average. In key indicators of social structure Zhejiang has both strengths and weaknesses. While those indices reflecting economic development and standard of living - such as per capita GDP, labour productivity, urban and rural income, and the ratio of television sets and telephones to population - ranked high, those in the spheres of education, science and technology, and general cultural facilities performed badly.

For example, the amount of provincial investment in education in 1996 as a proportion of GDP was lower than that in Japan thirty years earlier, when it had a substantially lower per capita GDP than contemporary Zhejiang. In 1970 South Korea invested a greater proportion of its GDP in Research and Development than Zhejiang in 1994, and between 1955 and 1976 the contribution of technology to economic development in South Korea was substantially higher than that in Zhejiang in 1996. In 1995 Zhejiang lagged behind national levels in terms of the ratio of tertiary and senior secondary students to population, funds for scientific and technological activities as a proportion of GDP, the number of personnel engaged in science and technology, the proportion of tertiary industry to GDP and the proportion of the population enjoying social security. The proportion of mental workers in the work force actually fell between 1990 and 1995.

In terms of cultural facilities such as theatres and cinemas, health resources (the ratio of doctors and hospital beds to population), the number of schools and sports ovals, and the per capita area of open public space in cities,[19] Zhejiang performs badly. The backwardness of social development is a constraining factor on economic development, particularly in the areas of personnel, land, and resources. Zhejiang's per capita water resources, which are unevenly distributed, are only one-third of the world average, and are affected by serious pollution. Urban pollution has spread to rural areas and inland pollution is spreading to the sea. Its environment has been battered by air pollution (widespread acid rain, dust from construction sites and exhaust fumes from cars), solid waste pollution of frightening proportions, noise pollution in cities, and soil erosion in the wake of the indiscriminate felling of trees on slopes.

There is unevenness in the internal composition of the province's social structure as well as in the regional development of social institutions. This means that there is a disproportionate development between public-use and commercial social institutions. There are plenty of restaurants, discotheques, and karaoke clubs in Zhejiang, but few public libraries, museums or sports ovals and stadiums. This imbalance is directly related to the quality of the population (in terms of its low educational standards) and the trend whereby market forces rather than government intervention and guidance play the major role in determining cultural activities. There is also a strikingly disproportionate regional distribution of social facilities between urban and rural areas, and developed and undeveloped localities.

Zhejiang has set itself the goal of attaining initial modernization by the year 2010. Just how difficult that task will be can be seen from comparing the present state of three key indicators with their ambitious targets. The ratio of population with higher education is now 1.5 per cent (goal 15 per cent), the ratio of doctors per 10,000 people is now 15.3 (goal eighty), and the ratio of the non-agricultural population to the total population is now 18.3 per cent (goal over 50 per cent). And recent performance has not been encouraging. In 1992 the provincial authorities decided that by the end of 1995 outlays on science and technology would come to 2.9 per cent of fiscal expenditures, but the outcome fell well short of the target.

FUTURE CHALLENGES

The substantial but distorted transformation of Zhejiang's economic system has been a process instigated from the bottom, not imposed from the top, and was forced on rural organizations and individuals by the failure of old planned economy to distribute needed goods in the absence of markets.[20] The depth and speed of this transformation has been related to locational factors, natural endowments (particularly per capita cultivated land area) incentives, anticipated benefits, the strength and influence of the structures of the former command economy, the effectiveness and durability of collective economic and administrative systems, the distance from the political centre (Hangzhou), and historically-formed social customs, values and outlook. However, this process of transformation eventually reaches a stage where government intervention is required (see the change in the pattern of government behaviour in Wenzhou)[21] to direct this spontaneous, erratic and distorted pattern of development.

During the reform period government in Zhejiang has, for various reasons, been largely unable (strapped by its lack of budgetary revenue) or unwilling to play an active role in the process of economic development by focusing on issues which are relevant to local circumstances rather than to those which the centre considers important (for example the role of state industry and grain production). Zhejiang's party-government state has, for the most part, been conservative, reactive, and compliant in its behaviour.[22]

Stern tests lie ahead for Zhejiang's economy. Additional to the structural problems and imbalances pointed out in this essay are question of what role Zhejiang will play in the regional economy of East China centred on Shanghai as the heart of the Yangtze River Delta. To date, Zhejiang appears to have been hesitant in taking the initiative to establish closer economic links with the great metropolis for fear of playing a supporting role (what other role can it play?), stemming from parochial pride, and afraid of being outsmarted by the worldly and capable Shanghainese.[23] The development of Zhejiang's coastal and maritime resources are beyond the capacity of the province alone, and require regional and national support.

The challenge for the province is how to change its industrial structure, which has to date provided Zhejiang with a prolonged period of rapid economic growth, without threatening the basis on which this economic growth has been built, with the consequent threat to social stability. Not to act indicates procrastination and lack of purpose, but to do so could be fatal. China has moved into a situation where a perennial seller's market has now turned into a buyer's market, placing new and onerous demands on industrial and commercial enterprises.

In early 1998 there were startling images on the provincial television of workers and officials wielding sledge-hammers to smash old and out-dated looms in textile mills, while their erstwhile operatives looked on with a mixture of stupefaction and regret. The textile industry, the backbone of the traditional industries which have powered economic growth in Zhejiang, is in crisis, and new industries have not yet been established to take its place. The continual widening of income gaps (between urban and rural areas, different localities, industries, and rich and poor) will certainly lead to discontent and social instability, given their low degree of social acceptability. In 1998 the socio-economic issue of greatest concern in China has been employment, and the lack of an adequate social welfare net for those stood down or thrown out of work. This issue has the potential to pose the greatest test yet to the authorities in Zhejiang.

China's economy is still in transition from a planned to a market system. While this fundamental transformation has proceeded further in Zhejiang than in many other provinces, it has been an unbalanced and distorted process with somewhat paradoxical outcomes for the province's economic structure. The population and social structures have impeded, and have themselves been influenced by, this economic structure where the urban has played a secondary role to the rural, the foreign to the domestic, the large to the small, and the traditional to the modern. The problems these structures are creating for continued economic growth have been apparent for several years. Whether the provincial authorities have the will or the ability to intervene to correct and readjust Zhejiang's socio-economic structures is yet to be shown.

NOTES

1   For a description and analysis of Zhejiang's economic progress during the reform period, see Keith Forster, *Zhejiang Province in Reform*, 1998.
2   See Guo Zhanheng, 1996, pp. 34-44. I am preparing to edit an issue of *Chinese Economic Studies* in which this article, together with other recent commentaries and analyses concerning the economic and social situation in Zhejiang referred to in this essay, will appear.

3   This paper stems from a three-year research project, funded by the Australian Research Council, which will culminate in a monograph regarding the political economy of Zhejiang under reform.
4   This section of the paper draws extensively on Ye Juying, 1998.
5   See *Zhongguo renkou tongji nianjian* (China's population statistics yearbook), 1997, p. 3.
6   See *Zhejiang tongji nianjian* (Zhejiang statistical yearbook), 1994, p. 32. Of course, the average age of the population in 1996 was higher than in the 1960s.
7   *Zhongguo renkou tongji nianjian*, 1997, p. 3.
8   This section has drawn extensively on Zhang Renshou. 1998; the forum in *Zhejiang jingji*, No. 7, 1997, pp. 4-7 entitled '*Zhejiang jingji bianlengde yuanyin fenxi*' (Analysis of the reasons behind the cooling in Zhejiang's economy); and Zhou Bijian, 1997, pp. 10-11.
9   Third industry survey leading small group of the Zhejiang provincial people's government and the provincial bureau of statistics, 'Zhejiangsheng disanci gongye pucha gongbao' (Bulletin of the third industrial survey of Zhejiang province), December, 1996, in *Zhejiang zhengbao* (Zhejiang government gazette), No. 8, 1997, pp. 27-31.
10 See Zhuo Yongliang, 1997.
11 Guo Zhanheng, 'Problems and trouble-spots in the economic development of Zhejiang province under reform.'
12 See Zhao Yannian et al., 1997, pp. 36-8.
13 See Huang Yong (ed.), 1997); Chen Zifang et al., 1998, pp. 65-70; and Wang Jie, 1998.
14 See Shen Guangming, 1997, pp. 51-3; Xie Xiaobo, 1998, pp. 28-32; Shen Guangming, 'Yanhai shengshi jingji fazhan zhong waizi zuoyongde bijiao', pp. 12-20; and Jiang Wenjie, 1997, pp. 52-4.
15 Zhu Aiwen, 1997, pp. 10-14; Leng Xiao, 1997, pp. 33-7; Lin Jin and Zhu Guofan, 1997, pp. 36-7.
16 'Zhejiang sheng zhongxin chengshi fazhan guihua yanjiu' ketizu, 'Jingji zengzhang fangshi zhuanbian yu qianghua zhongxin chengshi gongneng' (The shift in the style of economic growth and strengthening the function of core cities), *Zhejiang jingji*, No. 3, 1997, pp. 42-4.
17 See Li Wangming et al., 1997, pp. 58-60.
18 This section has drawn extensively on Gu Yinchun and Yang Jianhua, 1997, pp. 12-21 and 'Zhejiang shehui fazhan xianzhuang yu duice' yanjiu ketizu, 1992-1996 Zhejiang shehui fazhan zhuangkuang (The state of Zhejiang's social development from 1992 to 1996), (Hangzhou: Zhejiang renmin chubanshe, 1997).
19 For information concerning Hangzhou, the capital city of Zhejiang, see Jin Yuanhuan and Wang Jianyu, 1997.

20 Zhuo Yongliang, 'Touzhixing zhidu bianqian yu Zhejiang jingji tizhi zhuanhuan' (Induced system transformation and the shift in Zhejiang's economic system), *Zhejiang jingji*, No. 8, 1997, pp. 54-56.
21 See Keith Forster and Yao Xianguo, 1999.
22 I have elaborated this argument in my 'Reform in Zhejiang' and in 'The Political Economy of post-Mao Zhejiang'.
23 Zhejiang shengwei zhengyanshi, Zhejiang sheng jiwei 'Zhe-Lu jingji hezuo yanjiu' ketizu, 'Tuijin Zhejiang yu Shanghai jingji hezuo xiang jinmixing fazhan' (Push forward economic cooperation between Zhejiang and Shanghai into an inseparable-type development), *Zhejiang jingji*, No. 1, 1997, pp. 46-50.

REFERENCES

Chen Zifang et al. (1998) 'Zhejiang quyu jingjide bu pingheng fazhan ji qi chajude shoulianxing' (Zhejiang's uneven regional development and its ability to narrow the gap), *Zhejiang shehui kexue* (Zhejiang social sciences), no. 1.

Forster, Keith (1997) 'Reform in Zhejiang: The Paradoxes behind Restoration, Reinvigoration and Renewal,' in: David S.G. Goodman (ed.) *China's Provinces in Reform: Change, Community and Political Culture*. London: Routledge, pp. 233-71.

--(1998) *Zhejiang Province in Reform*. Sydney and Honolulu: Wild Peony Press and University of Hawaii Press. (Published under the auspices of the Centre for Research on Provincial China, Sydney)

--(1998) 'The Political Economy of post-Mao Zhejiang: Rapid Growth and Hesitant Reform,' in: Peter Cheung, Jae Ho Chung, and Lin Zhimin (eds) *Provincial Strategies of Economic Reform in Post-Mao China: Leadership, Politics, and Implementation*. New York: M.E. Sharpe, pp. 145-211.

Forster, Keith and Yao Xianguo (1999) 'A Comparative Analysis of Economic Reform and Development in Hangzhou and Wenzhou Cities,' in Jae Ho Chung (ed.) *Cities in Post-Mao China: Recipes of Economic Development in the Reform Era*. London: Routledge.

Gu Yinchun and Yang Jianhua (1997) 'Zhejiang shehui fazhan xianzhuang yu sikao' (The present state of Zhejiang's social development and reflections thereon), *Dangdai xueshu xinxi* (Contemporary academic information), nos. 5-6.

Guo Zhanheng (1996) 'Gaige yilai Zhejiang sheng jingji fazhande wenti yu nandian' (Problems and trouble-spots in the economic development of Zhejiang province under reform), *Jingji yanjiu cankao* (Economic research papers), no. 892, June 14, pp. 34-44.

Huang Yong (ed.) (1997) *Zhe dongbei gaizao lun* (On the transformation of north-east Zhejiang). Hangzhou: Zhejiang renmin chubanshe.

Jiang Wenjie (1997) 'Dangqian Zhejiang liyong waizi xianzhuang ji duice fenxi' (The present situation regarding Zhejiang's use of foreign investment and thoughts on counter-measures), *Zhejiang jingji*, no. 5.

Jin Yuanhuan and Wang Jianyu, 'Zhejiang liangge zhongxin lun' (On Zhejiang's two centres), *Zhejiang shehui kexue* (Zhejiang social sciences), No. 2, 1997, pp. 30-3.

Leng Xiao (1997) 'Lun Zhejiang sheng shichang jianshe ji jinhou zou xiangde duice' (On the construction of Zhejiang's markets and counter-measures for their future direction), *Shangye jingji yu guanli* (Commercial economics and management), no. 1.

Li Wangming et al. (1997) 'Zhe-E chengzhen fazhan duibi jiqi qishi' (An illuminating comparison of urban development in Zhejiang and Guangdong), *Zhejiang jingji*, no. 7.

Lin Jin and Zhu Guofan (1997) 'Zhejiang zhuanye shichang fazhan xianzhuang ji qi mianlinde tiaozhan' (The present state of the development of Zhejiang's markets and the challenges ahead), *Gaige yu shichang* (Reform and markets), no. 2.

Shen Guangming (1997) 'Zhejiang waishang zhijie touzide xianzhuang ji zhengce jianyi' (The present state of direct foreign investment in Zhejiang and policy suggestions), *Zhejiang jingji* (Zhejiang's economy), no. 10.

--(1997) 'Yanhai shengshi jingji fazhan zhong waizi zuoyongde bijiao' (A comparison of the utilisation of foreign investment in the economic development of coastal provinces and cities), *Diaocha yu sikao* (Investigation and reflections), no. 50.

Wang Jie (1998) 'Zhejiang jumin shouru chaju kuodade qushi ji qi fenxi' (Trends in and analysis of widening income gaps in Zhejiang), *Gaige yu fazhan yanjiu* (Studies in reform and development), No. 42, February 5.

Xie Xiaobo (1998) 'Zhejiang liyong waizi fangshi xianzhuang ji duice jianyi' (Zhejiang's mode of use of foreign investment and suggestions for counter-measures), *Zhejiang shehui kexue*, no. 1.

Ye Juying (1998) 'Zhejiang renkou yu ke chixu fazhan' (Zhejiang's population and its sustainable development), *Zhejiang xuekan* (Zhejiang studies), no. 1, pp. 55-9.

Zhang Renshou (1998) 'Jiegou tiaozheng: Zhejiang jingji kua shiji fazhande zhuti' (Structural adjustments: key issues concerning the development of Zhejiang's economy into the next century), *Zhejiang Ribao*, March 9.

Zhao Yannian et al. (1997) 'Zhejiang xiangzhen gongye zengshu huiluo yuanyin poxi' (An analysis of the slowdown in the growth rate of Zhejiang's township and village industry), *Zhejiang jingji*, no. 9,

Zhejiang tongji nianjian (Zhejiang statistical yearbook) (1994).

Zhongguo renkou tongji nianjian (China's population statistics yearbook), 1997. Beijing: Zhongguo tongji chubanshe.

Zhou Bijian (1997) 'Dangqian Zhejiang gongye fazhan zhongde sanda jiegouxing maodun' (Three major structural contradictions in Zhejiang's current industrial development), *Zhejiang jingji*, no. 10, pp. 10-11.

Zhuo Yongliang (1997) 'Touzi xuqiu zengzhangde xin qushi' (New trends in the growth in investment demand), *Gaige yu fazhan yanjiu* (Studies in reform and development), no. 34, August 20.

Zhu Aiwen (1997) 'Zhejiang de zhuanye shichang ji sikao' (Reflections on Zhejiang's specialised markets), *Zhejiang shehui kexue*, no. 1.

Part Two

Historical Legacies

CHAPTER 5

THE SEVENTEENTH-CENTURY
ACEHNESE MODEL OF MALAY SOCIETY

LEONARD Y. ANDAYA

When the Dutch and the English signed an international agreement in 1824 drawing the boundaries between their respective spheres of influence in the Indo-Malaysian archipelago, the repercussions extended beyond the political and economic arenas. Political borders came to delimit the extent of historical investigations, resulting in artificial divisions of subjects. For many Malaysians the story of the Malays begins with Melaka at the beginning of the fifteenth century, ignoring the ancient and glorious heritage of Srivijaya in southeast Sumatra between the seventh and the eleventh centuries. Srivijaya is located in present-day Indonesia and is therefore regarded as belonging properly to the sphere of 'Indonesian' history. Indonesians themselves view Srivijaya as part of an older Sumatran-Java rivalry with barely a mention of its links to the Malay Peninsula.

This intellectual and academic divide has unfortunately influenced our understanding of the *Melayu* or Malay past. European scholar-officials in British Malaya, particularly O.W. Winstedt and R.J. Wilkinson, were influential not only in their own scholarly productions, but also in collecting and copying a large number of Malay documents in a variety of Malay genres. Their activities did more than simply structure what was known about the Malays; they created the whole 'Malayistics' enterprise by setting the boundaries of Malayness.[1] By focusing their investigations on the 'natives' of the Peninsula, they were able to reinforce the British justification that their colonial rule was a partnership between themselves and the Malay rulers.[2] This, then, was the beginning of the notion of Malay culture and history beginning with the kingdom of Melaka in the fifteenth century.

Only by disregarding this entire colonial premise underlying Malay history can one come closer to an understanding of the development of the Malay heritage. It was not an uncontested heritage, and for more than a century after the fall of Malay Melaka to the Portuguese in 1511, Aceh could legitimately claim to be Melaka's heir. Aceh's example, like that of Melaka before it, became a model of proper Malay behaviour and institutions which were already being emulated on the west coast and the northern half of east-coast Sumatra, as well as in Perak and Kedah on the Peninsula. Had Aceh maintained its dominance over Johor, it would have offered the Malay world a different model from that which we now identify as being 'authentically Malay.'

THE MALAY HERITAGE

By ignoring nineteenth-century classifications, it is possible to see continuity in the history of the Melayu people on both sides of the Straits of Melaka.[3] It begins, if archaeologists and comparative linguists are correct, with the 'homeland' of the Malayic-speaking peoples in western Borneo. Sometime around 100 BCE some of the group left Borneo via the Tambelan and Riau islands and then moved in two different directions. Some went to south-east Sumatra, where they used the Musi and the Batang Hari rivers to penetrate far into the interior; others followed the coasts up the Malay Peninsula, then further northwards and westwards, perhaps as far as central Vietnam. While the former met little resistance in their progress, the latter group could not dislodge the well-established agricultural Austro-Asiatic speakers on the mainland. It was therefore in southeast Sumatra that Malayic-speakers became established and developed a distinctive 'Malay' culture.

The story of the Malays in Sumatra is well documented, with the name 'Melayu' first appearing in a mission to China in 644. Seventh-century inscriptions written in Old Malay found near present-day Palembang refer to a powerful and prosperous trading entrepôt and kingdom known as Srivijaya. Although both Palembang and Jambi were associated with this kingdom, Jambi came to be known as 'Melayu.' Srivijaya's commercial success aroused the envy of the Cholas of India, who launched a successful invasion of Srivijaya's lands in 1024-5. Though the memory of Srivijaya/ Melayu's greatness was preserved, international trade in the western part of the archipelago became dominated by the Javanese. The name Melayu then came to refer to the interior areas of Palembang and Jambi, where some of the Srivijayan subjects had retreated to safety. This is confirmed in a 1286 inscription left by the conquering Javanese in the upper reaches of the Batang Hari River, which refers to the people as inhabitants of Melayu.

The name Melayu appears to have persisted into the fourteenth century in interior Jambi, where a 1347 inscription attributed to Adityavarman mentions Melayupura (City of Melayu). But reference to Melayu was not limited to the old centre of Malayic-speakers in southeast Sumatra. When the Majapahit court poet Mpu Prapanca wrote his *Desawarnana* in 1365, he listed the 'Melayu lands' as comprising among others Lampung, Jambi,

Palembang, Minangkabau, Siak, Rokan, Kampar, Pane, Kampe, Aru, Mandailing, Tumiang, Perlak, Barat, Lwas, Samudra, Lamuri, and Barus. They are place-names located along the entire East Coast of Sumatra and around to the West Coast to Barus, plus the interior areas of Minangkabau. Names on the Malay Peninsula, on the other hand, are referred to as being the territory of 'Pahang.'[4] The association of the name Melayu with the Peninsula appears to have been a later development which came with the founding of Melaka at the turn of the fifteenth century.

In a tradition from Melaka known as the *Sejarah Melayu* (Story of Melayu), the origins of the rulers and the people of Melaka are traced to a Palembang prince and his followers who leave their country and move to Bintang, Singapore, Muar, Bertam, and eventually to Melaka. In Melaka the exiled court and followers 're-establish' Srivijaya, and the kingdom quickly regains the prestige, wealth, and power of its illustrious predecessor. The rapidity with which Melaka gained dominance in international trade demonstrates experience, skills, and connections which seem to support *Sejarah Melayu*'s origin stories.[5] Even the sagacity of its founder in winning the favour of the Chinese over its main rival, Ayudhya, to become the leading commercial entrepôt in the region appears to reflect an understanding of China's crucial role in Srivijaya's success.[6]

With increasing prosperity came prestige. Melaka's government, customary practices (*adat*), style of dress, version of the Malay language, and newly-adopted religion of Islam became the standard for many archipelagic societies seeking to emulate or at least bask in Melaka's success. So dominant was the image of Melaka that the name Melayu and all things Malay came to be equated with Melaka. What was Melakan was Malay, what was truly Malay was Melakan. Hence in one episode in Malay folklore which came to be written down and known as the *Hikayat Hang Tuah* (The Romance of Hang Tuah), the people of Indrapura in Siak in east-coast Sumatra are reluctant to entertain their Melakan guest, Hang Tuah, with their songs. They explain, 'we speak a bastard form of the language and not the pure Malay of Melaka.' To put them at their ease Hang Tuah suggests that the people of Melaka may in fact be speaking a bastard form of Malay themselves because of their mixing with Majapahit Javanese.[7] Hang Tuah's words acknowledge the long intermingling of the fortunes of the Malays of south-east Sumatra and the Javanese, a relationship which dates at least from the seventh century.[8]

Melayu areas on Sumatra were now forced either to conform to these Melakan prescriptions of being Malay, or search for another meaningful identity. Paradoxically, as the determinants of Malayness came to be defined by and restricted to Melaka's example, they opened the door to 'new Malays' by offering a precise recipe for Malay identity. It was now possible for groups throughout the archipelago, but particularly the former Melayu areas on Sumatra, to assume Malay identity in a maritime international atmosphere of trade and diplomacy, and another identity for the interactions of ethnies in a more localized area.

The Portuguese conquest of Melaka in 1511 shattered the prestige of the kingdom and loosened its dominance as the model of Malayness. After the ignominious flight of the ruler and his court, and their peripatetic existence for a number of years to escape the relentless Portuguese, the reconstituted kingdom on Johor no longer was the unchallenged leader of things Malay. Melaka's splendour and vibrant court and cultural life could not be sustained in Johor, and the rise of Aceh in the latter half of the sixteenth century came to challenge Johor's position as the standard-bearer of Malay culture and identity. For much of the sixteenth and seventeenth centuries, Aceh became a serious contender for leadership in the Malay world by setting new standards for Malayness in the court, the economy, and in Islam. Many of these standards drew upon both Melaka's experience as well as the models provided by the illustrious Muslim empires of the sixteenth and seventeenth centuries in India and the Middle East.

ACEH'S LINKS TO INDIA AND THE MIDDLE EAST

Because of Aceh's location at the northern tip of Sumatra, it was the logical first port of call for traders coming from the west. Aceh's reputation as an Islamic kingdom, and its ability to provide desired local commodities and the facilities to promote effective and profitable exchange, quickly made it a favoured entrepôt with Muslim traders. Since the fall of Malay Melaka to the Portuguese, Asian shipping had avoided that city and streamed to Aceh and Banten on the Sunda Straits. Powerful Acehnese rulers such as Sultan Alauddin Riayat Syah al-Mukamil (1589-1604) and Sultan Iskandar Muda (1607-36) wisely instituted a reorganization of the kingdom and an expansionist policy in order to assure control and delivery of pepper, tin, and elephants which were in major demand by foreign merchants. Under these two rulers, Aceh conquered pepper-producing areas on both the east and west coasts of Sumatra, as well as the tin-rich mines on Perak and Kedah on the Peninsula. Other tin areas on the west coast of the Peninsula came under its control when Iskandar Muda extended his conquests to Johor and Pahang, and to their vassal areas on both sides of the Peninsula.[9]

Among the most prominent of the Indian traders were the Muslim Gujaratis from northwest India. After 1511 they transferred their trade to Aceh, which was able to provide pepper, nutmeg, cloves, mace, tin, gold, ivory, and elephants, all of which fetched considerable profit both in India and the Middle East. Other Muslim communities, including the Malabari Mapillah and merchants representing the powerful Mughal Timurid[10] dynasty, also patronized Aceh. The Mughal Timuri princes Aurangzeb and Dara Shukoh participated in Aceh's trade, and Aurangzeb even exchanged presents with Aceh's sultan in 1641. When the Dutch conquered Portuguese Melaka in 1641, for the next two decades they attempted to restrict Muslim trade to Aceh in order to attract trade to Melaka. This angered the Mughal Timuris who then threatened retaliation in Gujarat for any losses due to Dutch intervention. A *farman*, or royal decree, was issued by the emperor 'instructing the Dutch to issue passes to any Indian ship wanting to sail to Aceh.' By the 1660s the VOC backed down and allowed Indian traders to sail to Aceh, Perak, and Kedah without restriction.[11]

Another important trading community in Aceh consisted of Indians from the Coromandel Coast who had been prominent in Malay Melaka. Golconda's ruler, nobles, and officials began investing in international shipping and trade in the last decades of the sixteenth century. In the seventeenth century they were joined by Persian merchants from the Safavid empire who were encouraged by Golconda's Sultan Muhammad Qutb Shah's (1612-24) close ties with the Safavid empire. Under Ibrahim Qutb Shah (1550-80) Golconda encouraged the immigration of Persians, especially those of Sayyid clans residing in the vicinity of Isfahan. These Persians, who arrived in substantial numbers in the late sixteenth and early seventeenth centuries, settled in both Bijapur and Golconda. The courts and administration of both kingdoms became dominated by three major Muslim factions: the Persians, the Dakhnis (local converts), and the Habshis (Abyssinian Muslims).[12] Together the Persian and Golconda Muslim communities provided the resources which fuelled this strong Muslim trade from northern Coromandel centred on the port of Masulipatnam. In southern Coromandel it was the Chulia Muslims who helped establish trade networks throughout the Straits region and beyond.[13]

In the sixteenth and seventeenth centuries the Coromandel merchants used Aceh as their primary centre for their trading activities in the region. Their textiles were especially admired, and the Coromandel factories created special designs and colours with specific names associated with the markets for which they were destined. The Coromandel traders, both Muslim and Hindu, also exported rice, iron, steel, indigo, and some slaves, and in return took pepper, tin, ivory, elephants, cloves, nutmeg, and mace. Among their many types of expertise was the proper care of elephants on their long voyage from Southeast Asia to India. The elephant trade proved to be an especially lucrative enterprise since there was a strong market in Bengal and among the Muslim kingdoms of Golconda, Bijapur, and Tanjore. Bengal merchants favoured Aceh because it could supply the burgeoning demand for elephants by the Mughal Timuri army in the seventeenth century.[14]

Aceh so valued this trade that it retained a permanent agent in Masulipatnam. It was just one of a number of Southeast Asian kingdoms, including Arakan, Pegu, Ayudhya, Kedah, Makassar, and Banten, which had agents who maintained residences and oversaw the trade of their countrymen as consular agents in that city. Golconda reciprocated and had their agents throughout Southeast Asia, and most particularly in Aceh since it was the major terminal in the Coromandel trade. Commercial ties were strongly reinforced by the personal links between the rulers. Sultan Iskandar Muda of Aceh preferred to establish state-to-state trade based on agreements between rulers, rather than merchants.[15] The Coromandel merchants continued to favour Aceh for the rest of the century, even during the reigns of its queens.[16]

The profitable trade with the Indian Muslim kingdoms brought many prominent Indian officials to Aceh. A Bengal prince in the mid-seventeenth century arrived in Aceh to present the entire cargo of his ship to the queen in return for elephants.[17] Sprinkled throughout the VOC sources are references to the presence in Aceh of important Muslim dignitaries or their representatives. A certain Nakhoda Mir Syah Mahmud came in 1642 and traded on behalf of his master, the Mughal Timuri prince, Aurangzeb,[18] and the *syahbandar* of Surat conducted his trade through his son who maintained a permanent residence in Aceh.[19] To express her delight at the ongoing profitable trade with Bengal, the queen of Aceh presented the Bengal ambassador with an enormous elephant as a gift for his lord.[20] Another ambassador from the court of Aurangzeb arrived in Aceh from Surat in 1657.[21] The exchange of envoys at the highest levels between Aceh and the Indian Muslim courts was evidence of the great importance attached to their mutually beneficial trade arrangements. Such favour showered on the Aceh court by these prestigious and powerful Indian Muslim kingdoms would not have gone unnoticed in the archipelago.

It is important to note that, though Aceh's strongest links to the Islamic world were through the Indian Muslim kingdoms, particularly the Mughal Timurid dynasty, it was also exposed to developments in the other two major Islamic empires of the Ottomans and the Safavis. In the sixteenth century the Ottomans under Sultan Suleyman (1520-66) dispatched a contingent of artillerymen to accompany some large Turkish cannon to Aceh.[22] Muslim traders and teachers from 'Rum,' the Malay designation for the fabled land of the Caliph of Turkey, were found throughout the archipelago and as far as the Spice Islands in Eastern Indonesia.[23] With the Ottomans in control of the Islamic cities of Mecca and Medina, there was a flow of ideas between the Ottoman empire and Aceh, the Southeast Asian gateway for the Muslim pilgrimage to the Holy Land. This influence is readily discernible in certain names and practices adopted by the Aceh kingdom which are traceable to the Ottoman empire.

The Safavi empire with its core in the Persian heartland had an equally important influence on Aceh, but much of it came indirectly through their subjects serving in such distant lands as Golconda and the Mughal Timurid empire. Most of the significant cultural figures in Akbar's (1556-1605) court were from abroad, particularly from the Safavi empire.[24] In the sixteenth and seventeenth centuries 'Persian' merchants living in the fringe areas of the Safavi empire, but principally in India, were influential in the affairs of Southeast Asian kingdoms, particularly Ayudhya and Aceh.[25] The Persian connection may have been at work during the annual exchange of envoys between Aceh and Ayudhya.[26] Ample evidence exists to show that Southeast Asian rulers, including those of Aceh, were eager to hear about the fabled Muslim courts of the Ottomans, the Safavis, and the Mughal Timuris from Muslim traders, envoys, and religious teachers. Islamic and secular literature written in Persian, the literary language of the Islamic court, were eagerly translated by the Muslim kingdoms of Southeast Asia into Malay, the literary language of the Muslim courts in the archipelago. Perso-Arabic-Turkic and Islamic themes and ideas were therefore transmitted to Southeast Asia, along with a large number of Perso-Arabic words and the script.[27] Persian was also the international language of diplomacy which would have contributed to its appeal to Muslim courts such as Aceh's.[28]

Although there were three distinct and powerful Muslim empires in the world in the sixteenth and seventeenth centuries, there was a remarkable intermingling of their subjects and ideas. A noted historian has indeed argued against equating 'Persia' with the Safavi empire and 'Turkey' with the Ottoman empire because both empires included Persians, Turks, and Arabs equally. Even language use was not confined within political borders. Sultan Ismail of the Safavis wrote verse in the popular tongue, Turkic, while his counterpart Sultan Selim of the Ottomans composed in Persian.[29] The sixteenth century and much of the seventeenth witnessed a period of Islamic expansion in all fields led by the brilliance of the Safavi, Ottoman, and the Mughal Timuri courts. The three major Islamic empires provided models of behaviour and statecraft, the occasional armed expedition, religious scholars, administrators, and traders to the other Islamic lands. Islamic powers thus became dominant in the Mediterranean, the Black Sea, the Red Sea, the Persian Gulf, the Indian Ocean, the various seas in the Malaysian-Indonesian archipelago, and parts of the South China Sea. Extensive seaborne trading networks of Muslim merchants were created, ensuring a steady flow of secular and spiritual goods and people along these routes. In Southeast Asia there was a noticeable increase in Muslim traders, especially

Indian Muslims and Persians. As bearers of much desired goods from the west, and as representatives of prestigious Islamic centres, these traders were welcomed by rulers in Southeast Asia.[30] The presence of foreign Muslim communities in the port cities became commonplace, and it was not unusual to find Muslim officials occupying influential positions in the courts.

Features of these three mighty Muslim empires, which shared many ideas in common, were conveyed to the Islamic periphery directly or through intermediary Muslim kingdoms. Aceh's ongoing commercial, diplomatic, and religious links with such kingdoms in India, particularly with Golconda, enabled it to seek to emulate the prestigious Islamic empires of the Ottomans, Safavis, and the Mughal Timuris. In keeping with an age-old Southeast Asian tradition, Aceh's leaders cautiously borrowed only those elements which suited their needs. It is these elements borrowed from the greater Islamic world which made Aceh unique among Malay courts and offered a model of Malayness which was distinct from that of Melaka or Johor.

THE ACEHNESE MODEL OF MALAY SOCIETY

THE COURT AND ADMINISTRATION

Melaka created the conditions for a dynamic Malay identity by focusing not on territorial or descent principles as determining factors, but on standards of language, literature, behaviour, laws, and Islam. These standards were established by a living, vibrant society, and not by any sacred command or ancestral prescription. If any primordial sentiments were evident in Malay identity, they resided in the origin story linking the Malays to both sides of the Straits of Melaka. Malayness, therefore, would forever be subject to debate and choice with the supremacy of a kingdom or society at a particular period in history being honoured by emulation by others.

With Melaka's demise in 1511 the door was open for another kingdom to assume Melaka's mantle as the most prestigious Malay centre and hence trendsetter for things Malay. Although Johor was the site chosen by the refugee rulers from Melaka, for much of the sixteenth and the first half of the seventeenth centuries, Johor was on the defensive against invasions from both the Portuguese and the Acehnese. Aceh, on the other hand, was a newly-established kingdom located at the northern tip of Sumatra and, more than any other in the Straits does, resembled Melaka in its dominance of international trade. As on the Peninsula, Sumatra, and elsewhere in maritime Southeast Asia, the Aceh court proudly proclaimed its awareness of current fashion by maintaining Melaka/Malay standards.[31] It had a thriving written literary court culture in Malay, and an equally vital oral (and later written) non-court tradition in Acehnese.

It was commonplace for Muslim courts in the archipelago to possess literary works in Malay written in *jawi*, or Perso-Arabic script, and to speak the Melakan form of Malay among themselves. Malay court culture was defined by Melaka's, and focused on ideals which were often irrelevant to the lives of the ordinary people. Beyond the courts, traditions were transmitted orally in either a localized Malay language or another entirely different local language, such as Acehnese. People spoke the local language, and they had a code of conduct expressed in that language which was more in keeping with their particular concerns. Although there was a cross-fertilization of ideas and themes between court and countryside, the former was more international in orientation and inspiration, and the latter more grounded in local concerns and traditions. The Dutch were well aware of the bilingual and dual levels of society. In 1644 a Dutch envoy in Aceh apologized to his hosts because, though he could speak Malay, he was not conversant in the Acehnese language and customs.[32] As a Malay court Aceh shared many features with Melaka of the fifteenth century. It differed fundamentally from Melaka, however, in its active pursuit of ideas and models from the mighty Islamic civilizations of the Ottoman, Safavi, and Mughal Timurid empires of the sixteenth and seventeenth centuries. The image of Malay culture as represented by Melaka and later Johor was that of an amalgam of indigenous, Hindu-Buddhist, and Islamic ideas.[33] Aceh, on the other hand, came to emphasize the Islamic underpinnings of its society. This was particularly evident in court culture.

The extensive reach of Malay court culture in the region facilitated movements of court personnel, such as the numerous peninsular Malays who came to serve Aceh's rulers.[34] The evolution of Aceh's court revealed certain institutional borrowings from Melaka, but with a uniquely Aceh flavour. As in other Malay courts, Aceh maintained the practice of dispensing titles to favoured foreigners oftentimes in exchange for specific services. One of the most profitable of offices was that of *saudagar raja*, or 'king's merchant,' who was often an Indian merchant in charge of trading on behalf of the ruler.[35] European merchants were given such descriptive titles as *raja putih*, the 'white king,' or the more Acehnese title *ulèëbalang raja*, the 'warrior king,' and were expected to offer their highly respected military skills and armaments to the ruler.[36]

As in Melaka there were four principal ministers in Aceh, but they differed in titles and functions. The first in rank and the first minister of state (*rijksraad*) in Aceh was the *Leubè Kita Kali*, who was said to be the principal judge of religious and secular law. The second minister was the *Orang Kaya Maharaja Sri Maharaja*, chief minister of state affairs, and the third was the *Orang Kaya Lakasamana Perdana Menteri*, who was also the *Panglima Dalam*. It appears that it was the *Penghulu Dalam*'s position as minister for court affairs which was of importance in the council. The fourth in rank was the *Panglima Bandara*, whose task was the regulation of international trade in Aceh's principal port and supervision of the lucrative tin and pepper trade of Aceh's territories in Perak and west-coast Sumatra.[37]

The differences between principal ministers of Aceh and Melaka are instructive. Aceh's stronger Islamic orientation is evident in the listing of the *Kali* as the *first* minister of state, who had precedence over all secular officials. Though there was also the position of *Kali* in Melaka and Johor, he was never regarded as one of the four major officials in the kingdom. The functions assigned to Aceh's *Orang Kaya Maharaja Sri Maharaja* were performed by the *Bendahara Sri Maharaja* in Melaka and Johor by the principal minister of the land. Aceh, like Melaka and Johor, had a position of *Laksamana* as commander of the ruler's fleet, but this was a function which was only activated in times of war. The greater importance of the *Lakasamana* in Melaka and Johor underlines the crucial role played by the fleets in the creation and maintenance of these kingdoms as international trading entrepôts. In Aceh, by contrast, it was the third minister of state's role as *Panglima Dalam*, not as *Laksamana*, which was emphasized. There was no equivalent of Aceh's *Panglima Dalam* as an important court official in Melaka or Johor. The fact that this office in Aceh was regarded as important enough to be included as one of the four chief ministers is an interesting comment on the organization of the state. It appears that the domains of the ruler and the state were regarded as one, a situation which may have reflected the situation under such powerful kings as Sultan Alauddin Riayat Syah al-Mukamil and Sultan Iskandar Syah. In Melaka and Johor the *Temenggung* was the third most important official in the kingdom. In Aceh that position was held by the *Penghulu Kawal*, but he was not counted among the four main ministers of state. Finally, the fourth minister of state in Aceh was the *Penghulu Bandara*, the equivalent of a 'super *syahbandar*,' in charge of international trade and revenue. In Melaka and Johor, the *Penghulu Bendahari* was also the fourth important official in the kingdom whose responsibility was the treasury.

Aceh's model for the four ministers of state owed less to Melaka than to the Mughal Timurid dynasty in India. Under Akbar (1556-1605) four ministers of equal power were appointed and met occasionally as an advisory body to the ruler. Each was independent of each other and had his own sphere of influence. One was in charge of finance and revenue; another of the army and intelligence; a third of the judiciary and religious patronage; and the fourth of the royal household, which included the maintenance of royal roads, buildings, and canals throughout the empire.[38]

Aceh introduced other innovative measures in state administration. Officials were assigned military titles, with local lords referred to as *ulèëbalang* (Mal. *hulubalang*), and governors assigned to vassal areas and certain court officials as *panglima*. Although these lords and officials were supposed to assemble and lead their forces in times of war, their primary function was non-military. The *ulèëbalang* were leaders of villages or larger units in the countryside, while the *panglima* were appointed by the court to the major fiefs in the kingdom. There were *panglima* of the major parts of the kingdom such as Pedir, Pasai, Daya, and Deli; as well as *panglima* for the pepper-producing west coast Sumatra Minangkabau settlements of Barus, Pasaman, Tiku, Pariaman, Padang, Silida, and Indrapura. Panglima titles were also assigned officials in the court itself, such as the *Panglima Bandara* in charge of international trade.

Although *hulubalang* and *panglima* are Malay terms, the use of military titles for civil functions was not a Melaka borrowing. Instead, this practice again may have come from the great contemporary Muslim empires in Asia. Both the Ottoman and the Mughal Timurid empires regarded central power with its administrative branches as one great army. This viewpoint arose from the warrior traditions which were responsible for the creation of the powerful Muslim empires. At the beginning of the sixteenth century, the Ottoman Sultan Selim I (1512-20) expanded his empire with the central administration organized as an army. Administrators held military rank and were compensated with land grants or placed on the military payroll, thus creating powerful landed military families.[39] With Aceh's continuing economic and diplomatic ties to the wider Islamic world, it would have been aware of some of these developments and may have borrowed this model in the allocating of military titles such as *panglima* and *ulèëbalang* to administrators and territorial chiefs in the kingdom.

A Malay court practice which was far more developed in Aceh than in Melaka was the use of the royal seal (Mal. *cap*). The widespread and varied uses of the royal seal in Aceh seem to be a practice borrowed from the Islamic empires' institution of the *farman*. According to a seventeenth-century Dutch source, the Acehnese made a distinction in royal seals between the *sarakata* or *tarakata* and the *éseuteumi* or *seuteumi*. In seventeenth-century usage the former was an edict sent by the ruler without the royal seal and had to be observed until it was formally retracted. The latter was the more important document, which carried the royal seal and was intended to be a permanent royal command.[40] These seals were conveyed by the ruler's officials throughout the kingdom and the vassal areas and demanded immediate obedience.[41] The young men of the court (*bujang*) were often sent to various areas carrying the ruler's *éseuteumi*.[42] When a foreign vessel arrived in Aceh's roadstead, it was not allowed to land men or goods until a *keris* bearing the royal seal on the bottom of the hilt was sent by the court. On one occasion in the early seventeenth century, a VOC merchant went ashore before being presented with a royal seal. For his effrontery he was thrown before an elephant and had his legs broken.[43]

Another Acehnese court practice which derived from the great Muslim empires was the role played by the women of the harem and the '*capados*' (Port. 'castrated,' usually translated by European commentators as 'eunuchs'). Thomas Bowrey visited Aceh in the mid 1680s and reported that the attendants to the queen 'are Said to be 100 eunuchs and 1000 of the comliest women the Countrey or Citty affordeth.'[44] Even if the numbers of women in the harem were inflated, they were indeed a formidable presence in court. As in other Muslim courts in this period, most did not actually provide sexual services to the ruler. Many were personal retainers for the ruler's mother, his consorts, and his children, with the largest number being house-servants.[45] In Aceh women for the harem came from chiefly *ulèëbalang* and noble *panglima* families, as well as from the royal households of other kingdoms. Their presence was a visible sign of the mutual trust and alliance established between the ruler and his lords, and between Aceh and other royal families. The fact that the numbers of women in the harem remained high despite the reign of queens reinforces the view that the primary importance of their presence in the court was for purposes of alliance rather than sex.

Capados or 'eunuchs' may not have been unique in the Malay world, but the nature of the *capados* and their extensive functions in the Aceh court were indeed unusual. In Classical Malay literature there is a term *sida-sida* which has been translated as 'eunuchs.'[46] A reference in the *Sejarah Melayu* to a certain court official Tun Indera Segara, who is said to be a descendant of a *sida-sida* ('Adapun akan Tun Indera Segara itulah asal sida-sida...'), raises a question whether the *sida-sida* were actual eunuchs.[47] The first definition given by Teuku Iskandar for *sida-sida* is 'a court official (perhaps a type of priest [*pendeta*]),' and the second 'a castrated [*dikasi (dikembiri)*] court official.'[48] Iskandar's first entry may have been influenced by his knowledge of the use of the term in Acehnese. According to Djajadiningrat, the word *sida* is derived from the Sanskrit *siddha*, meaning 'the learned one' or 'scholar,' hence defined in Acehnese as 'an initiate, aide to a religious teacher.' But when the word is reduplicated, *sida-sida*, it assumes the meaning of 'a court official' and 'eunuch.'[49]

Most of the references to *sida-sida* in Classical Malay literature simply list them alongside a number of other court officials who supervise ceremonies or attend court to present their obeisance to the ruler. The repetitive nature of the catalogue of officials, with *sida-sida* usually appearing before, and occasionally after, the *bentara*, suggests that the recitation of these officials may have derived from an oral tradition. One of the references in the *Sejarah Melayu* offers a further clue to the function of the *sida-sida*. In describing a ceremony at court, the *sida-sida* are said to have emerged from 'within' (*dari dalam*), which could have only meant the inner chambers of the court, or where the women of the court are housed.[50] The link between the *sida-sida* and the court women is also implied in the eighteenth-century *Misa Melayu* from Perak, which groups the *sida-sida*, the *bentara*, and the *dayang-dayang* ('court maidens') together.[51] Except for the mention of *sida-sida* in a type of formulaic recitation along with other court officials, the only clear reference to a specific duty for them is found in the *Sejarah Melayu* where the *sida-sida* are described as bearing letters (Samad Ahmad 1979:71). By contrast, in Aceh there is substantial evidence of the prominent role played by the *sida-sida*, whom the Portuguese and the Dutch referred to as '*capados*.'

Their primary function was to serve the court and the rulers, and they had free access to the innermost chambers of the court, including the harem. They served the guests at court and were the primary bearers of messages from the throne. Whenever there was a royal procession, they marched as a group and were easily recognized by their weapons. An Englishman in Aceh in 1637 witnessed a procession where the *capados* rode horses without saddles and bore on their shoulders long swords in gilt or gold scabbards. At another procession in 1642, the Dutch described some 150 *capados* carrying halberds and royal gold ornaments.[52]

One of the functions the *capados* performed at court during the reigns of Aceh's queens in the seventeenth century was as intermediaries between the throne and the guests and officials at court. Muslim propriety demanded that the queen as a woman be sequestered. She therefore conducted affairs of state somewhere behind the throne out of view of the audience, and communicated through her *capados*.[53] Because of their trusted positions in court, some of the *capados* were able to occupy positions of great importance in the kingdom. In the mid-seventeenth century the *capado* Raja Adona Lela was considered to be the equal of the four ministers of state, while the commander of all the *capados* was given the title of Maharaja Setia. Another *capado* was the bookkeeper to the Queen. These *capado* heads became close advisors to the ruler and exercised considerable power in the kingdom because of their role in determining who could gain access to the throne.[54]

The inspiration for the use of *capados* in Aceh came once again not from Melaka but from the fabled Muslim empires. In the Mughal Timurid dynasty in India castrated young boys were purchased from the slave markets of Bengal to become slave-eunuchs. They became trusted confidants and advisors to their high-born masters and mistresses, and came to fill a variety of functions. Some were servants and guards, while the most capable were entrusted with the business dealings of noble women in the harem.[55] But it was in the Ottoman empire that the institution of the eunuch was most elaborated. In the imperial household there was even a distinction between 'black' (African) eunuchs' and 'white eunuchs.' Until the end of the sixteenth century, the latter dominated the Inside Service, or the inner chambers, of the court. Most were involved in court duties and as guards of the harem, though a few reached high military or administrative positions or became scribes.[56] Not only would the Acehnese have heard of the eunuchs in the Muslim lands, but many would have dealt with eunuchs arriving on Muslim ships to trade on behalf of their masters. In 1658, for example, a *capado* called Haji Mahmet brought twenty-four packs of various cloths and some iron and steel to sell for his master, the Paleacatte Governor Mir Shah Deli.[57]

The description of certain Acehnese ceremonies in the seventeenth-century document, the *Adat Aceh*, leaves no doubt of the source of their inspiration. As Sultan Iskandar Muda reposes under his royal umbrellas and banners, he is likened to Sultan Sulayman of the Ottoman empire. Some of the Acehnese soldiers in procession bear swords, spears and muskets and are dressed in the style of the Ottoman warriors. Others carry shields which are said to have been made from iron brought from Khurasan. In describing Iskandar Muda at prayer, the *Adat Aceh* comments that his piety is known even to the Caliph in Istanbul. The grand procession from the palace to the mosque led by Iskandar Muda is said to resemble the setting out to war of the great legendary Muslim ruler, Iskandar of the Two Horns (Alexander the Great).[58]

The use of '*kerkun*' for scribe was a borrowing from the Persian, and the Chief Scribe was given a combined Malay-Persian title of '*Penghulu Kerkun.*' According to the *Adat Aceh*, the Penghulu Kerkun in the mid-seventeenth century is called Raja Setia Muda. A Dutch contemporary document around that period lists a capado as being the *Raja Setia Muda*. What these sources suggest is that the position of scribes and the Chief Scribe in Aceh, at least in the seventeenth century, was held by trusted *capado*s of the court, a practice which was also found in the Ottoman court as mentioned above. These scribes were responsible for recording goods and gifts being brought into the port by foreign merchants.[59]

In trade Aceh used the Persian term '*syahbandar*,' or harbour master, as did Melaka and Johor. But only in Aceh were the *syahbandar*s assisted by a *nazir* (Inspector of Trade) and a *dalal* (middleman), which were also Persian titles. According to the *Adat Aceh*, the *nazir* inspected all trading activity in the port, including the dispatch of the *keris* with the royal seal to each incoming vessel. He also provided valuation of gifts to the ruler, royal trade debts, and imported merchandise by the royal household. The various *dalal* operated in the customs house, where they bought and sold goods from foreign merchants on behalf of their Aceh lords.[60]

In ceremonies Aceh resembled Melaka but there was a real distinction in style and content. To entertain envoys and special visitors there were musicians, dancers, and other performers from Java, Ayudhya, India, and elsewhere. A particular sign of pleasure was an invitation to relax and be feasted at the special fishing reservoirs with their pavilions prepared for guests.[61] In the Aceh court as well as in the homes of the major officials, it was customary for foreign visitors to don 'Acehnese' clothing, i.e. Muslim dress, presented by their hosts before any business could be conducted.[62] Greater attention was paid to proper Muslim behaviour in the court of Aceh than in either Melaka or Johor.

The Islamic emphasis in Aceh did not discourage dancing and singing, which were favourite forms of entertainment. On one occasion the Dutch were summoned by the queen of Aceh and witnessed dancing between the noblemen and women of the court.[63] One of the four chief ministers of state once entertained the Dutch envoys at his home, where dances accompanied by music instruments and singing were performed. Among the expense items accounted for by the Dutch envoys were gifts for the 'instrumentalists and the male and female dancers who perform at the dinners held by the ministers of state for the benefit of the Dutch and their company.'[64]

Aceh's rulers, particularly Queen Safiyyat al-Din (1641-75), held regular Saturday audiences which were attended by the four ministers of state, the *panglima*, the *ulèëbalang*, and distinguished visitors. Their requests or complaints were heard and judgements made on criminal and civil cases. It was in these audiences that envoys, including those of the European trading companies, would submit their requests for special trading privileges or compensation for losses. At one audience a murderer tightly bound was condemned to death but had his sentence commuted by the queen.[65] There were two *balai* or meeting chambers. There was a large balai reserved for royal audiences attended by the important *ulèëbalang*, the four ministers of state and other influential officials, *capado*s, and foreign envoys; and a smaller *balai* or inner court for more intimate audiences.[66] This division into outer/public and inner/private courts resembled Akbar's General Audience Hall (*Diwan-i 'Am*) and Private Audience Hall (*Diwan-i Khas*) in the Mughal Timurid empire.[67]

In Aceh, more so than in any other court in the Indo-Malaysian archipelago, elephants and horses were an indispensable part of the royal presence. When one of the leaders of the *capado*s returned from a three-week hunt to present his eleven elephants to the queen, the animals were conducted to court with the greatest ceremony. One especially large beast was honoured by the queen by being accompanied by twelve royal umbrellas. When the queen asked the principal Muslim official, the *kali*, what he thought about the fact that such a beautiful beast had been captured in such an unlikely place, the latter replied that 'it was the work of God to have brought such a thing to past for Her Majesty.' After the queen admired the elephants, she then bestowed an especially great honour upon certain prominent officials by allowing them to feed the animals.[68]

All those who sought favour at court participated in the elephant hunt, and even Queen Safiyyat al-Din engaged in this activity.[69] So enamoured was she of her elephants that in a letter to the sultan of Perak she styled herself 'the lord of all manner of elephants, among which was one with white eyes as clear as the morning star.' She was equally proud of her collection of horses, and she boasted to the Perak ruler that she was also 'through God's Grace lord over all manner of horses from Arabia, Turkey, Rum, Tartary, Cathay, Lahore and Tanging.'[70] A common form of entertainment at court was elephant fights, though there were also contests between water buffaloes, bulls, goats, rams, and the occasional tiger vs elephant.[71]

Court protocol was adhered to rigidly. Elephants were sent by the ruler to fetch envoys to court, and it was regarded a grave affront to refuse the honour. Visiting merchants disembarking before receiving formal permission through the delivery of the royal seal by a *capado* could face punishment. The severity of Aceh's laws, which appears to have peaked during the reign of Sultan Iskandar Muda, appears unique in the Malay world. This may again be an example which was borrowed from the prestigious Islamic courts abroad.

The Economy

The economic model offered by Aceh had some similarities to that of Melaka, but with some significant differences. Indians continued to play the dominant role as in the time of Melaka, with Indian textiles maintaining their central function as the essential item of exchange. Aceh exercised the same privilege as Melaka in restricting foreign trade to the main port, and in creating institutions to facilitate trade. Both kingdoms had four *syahbandars*, though in Aceh it appears that it was the *panglima bandara* who exercised the function performed by the *syahbandars* in Melaka. To maintain law and order in the port, Aceh had a *penghulu kawal* and a *tandil kawal*, and Melaka a *temenggung*. The *Adat Aceh*, which was written sometime in the 1640s, describes a highly organized officialdom to facilitate trade in Aceh's port.[72] It was a similar attention to the needs of traders which had made Melaka the pre-eminent port in the Straits in the fifteenth and early sixteenth centuries.

The major economic difference between Aceh and Melaka was in the role of local products in international trade. Melaka had relied on the trinity of spices - cloves, nutmeg, and mace - from Eastern Indonesia, as well as on forest and sea products from the Straits of Melaka and the South China Sea. Aceh continued to attract spices from Eastern Indonesia through the Makassar traders, as well as sea and forest products brought mainly from Johor, but it was a new trinity which assured its success with international traders: pepper, tin, and elephants. It competed with Johor for the control of tin on the Peninsula by conquering Perak and Kedah in 1620 and assuring supplies from Ujung Salang, Banggarai, and Tenasserim. To gain a monopoly over the pepper trade, Sultan Iskandar Muda extended Aceh's control over the pepper-producing Minangkabau lands on the west coast of Sumatra. This policy was maintained by his successors until these Minangkabau settlements succeeded in rejecting Aceh's control with the help of the VOC.[73] In addition there was gold from the Minangkabau interior which found its way to Aceh via Bengkalis and Indragiri; rice and consumables from Javanese traders; and the highly valued cloves, nutmeg, and mace from Eastern Indonesia brought by Makassar traders. Elephants were still in plentiful supply in both Sumatra and the Peninsula, and there were always sufficient numbers to satisfy the demand from Indian courts.[74]

The key to Aceh's success as an entrepôt was its continuing ability to supply the region with a rich variety of Indian textiles brought by Muslim and Hindu traders from India. So highly desired was Indian cloth that many groups, including the interior Sumatrans who were the major suppliers of pepper and gold, refused to accept anything else in exchange. Even after the Dutch seized Melaka from the Portuguese in 1641 and brought their formidable technological and capital resources to bear on Aceh, they were unable to stem the flow of Indian ships to Aceh's roadstead. In one typical year Aceh received six Muslim ships from Bengal, another six from Gujarat, one from Pegu, five Hindu-owned ships from South India, plus numerous smaller boats manned by Malays, Javanese, Chinese, and others. The Indian traders brought so much cloth to Aceh that the whole region became saturated, much to the joy of the local populations and the dismay of the monopoly-minded Dutch.[75] Initially, the VOC employed a naval blockade and other restrictive measures to discourage Indian traders from going to Aceh. When this policy failed because of Mughal Timuri threats of retaliation, the Dutch sought to deprive the Indian traders of tin and pepper by cutting off Aceh's access to these products. These measures were more effective, though Indian ships continued to visit Aceh. The final demise of Aceh's lucrative Indian textile trade and hence its role as a leading Malay entrepôt was not due to any Dutch measures but to domestic politics in the last quarter of the seventeenth century.

ISLAM

The role of Islam in the formation of Aceh as a cultural, economic, and religious standard of Malayness was a natural consequence of the times. The sixteenth and seventeenth centuries marked the highpoint of the Islamic empires in the world. As one scholar noted, the true international language of diplomacy was Persian, the language of literature and culture in the Islamic courts. The Muslim empires of the Ottomans, the Safavis, the Ozbegs, and the Mughal Timuris controlled the greater part of the known world, with only Ming China their equal in power and prestige.[76] The splendour, the wealth, and the learning of such courts, and the incomparable strength of their armies were legend. Many lesser kingdoms around the world, most particularly Muslim ones, would have sought to model themselves after such greatness. Aceh was one such kingdom in the periphery of the Muslim world, and its ideal location between the Islamic heartland and the Indo-Malaysian archipelago enabled it to be more successful than many in this endeavour. Aceh was the first in the archipelago to be introduced to trends in religious and secular fashion from the Islamic empires. Islamic scholars, Muslim traders, and foreign envoys from Muslim lands brought their tracts, wares, and ideas to Aceh, and tempted the ruler and the people to institute changes which would update their society in the image of their illustrious co-religionists in the Ottoman, Safavi, and Mughal Timurid empires. As had always been the practice in Southeast Asia, the Acehnese only selected those aspects which they considered to be compatible with their society.[77]

The fundamental difference between Melaka and Aceh was in the emphasis given to Islam in the state, as is evident in the listing of the principal officials in the land. In Melaka none of the four was a Muslim official. There was a Kali who was chief Muslim official in the kingdom, but not regarded as one of the ministers. Aceh, on the other hand, describes the Kali as the First Minister of State (*eerste rijksraad*), and at court the Kali and the Muslim teachers (*ulama*) were allocated a separate and special section to themselves.[78] Islam's prominence in Aceh was widely acknowledged, and Islamic scholars from the heartland of Islam arrived to help make Aceh the primary centre of Islamic learning in the Indo-Malaysian archipelago.[79]

One of the practices borrowed from the illustrious Muslim empires was the appointment of a personal Islamic advisor to the ruler. In the Ottoman empire he was called the Syaikh al-Islam, a title which was used by the *Mufti* or chief jurist during the reign of Sultan Sulayman (1520-66). He was head of the *ulama*, and his *fatwa* or legal rulings were followed throughout the land. In his position as advisor to the Sultan he was able to exercise considerable political power, including the right to authorize the deposing of the ruler as unfit. In the Mughal Timurid empire, there was a tradition of dynastic intervention in religious affairs through the *sadr*, who was the scholar appointed by the ruler to take charge of land grants and income to ulama and Sufi masters (*pir*). The sadr increasingly assumed authority over all other religious personnel in the empire.[80]

In the *Hikayat Aceh*, which was written during the time of Sultan Iskandar Muda, the title 'shaikh al-Islam' is used to refer to the ruler's principal religious advisor. This would have been the well-known Sufi mystic, Syams al-Din, who may have held this position since the time of Sultan Alauddin Riayat Syah al-Mukamil (1589-1604). Nur al-Din al-Raniri served in that capacity under Iskandar Thani (1636-41), and Saif al-Rijal and Abd al-Rauf under Queen Safiyyat al-Din (1641-75). According to the *Bustanus Salatin*, written in the reign of Iskandar Thani, though the Kali Malik al-Adil was the first minister in the land, the Syaikh al-Islam Syams al-Din was the most prominent of all the Acehnese dignitaries. All of Aceh's shaikhs al-Islam in the seventeenth century exercised considerable religious and secular influence in the kingdom.[81]

Even the administrative divisions of the kingdom reflected Aceh's Islamic emphasis. There were four basic units: *gampong* (village), *mukim* (district or township), *nanggröe* (county), and *sagöe* (region). Of these four, only the mukim is a non-indigenous term. Its original meaning was a person living in an area with the requisite numbers of adult male Muslims to hold Friday congregational services. Later it came to mean the parish, including both the inhabitants and the area itself. One Dutch scholar, Van Langen, attributes this new administrative division to Iskandar Muda, who was also responsible for building many of Aceh's great mosques.[82] This innovation was yet another example of the attraction of the Islamic model to Aceh's rulers in the sixteenth and seventeenth centuries.

From the last quarter of the sixteenth century, Aceh became a major centre of Islamic studies in the archipelago with scholars coming from the Middle East and India, as well as from the archipelago itself. Among them were Shaikh Syams al-Din, Shaikh Ibrahim (whose expertise was Islamic law), Nur al-Din al-Raniri, and Abd al-Rauf. As advisors to the ruler they undoubtedly influenced the social and spiritual life of the Acehnese. Royal patronage was crucial in the strengthening of the Islamic aspects of Aceh society, and Sultan Iskandar Muda is credited by the *Bustan as-Salatin* with establishing the foundations for this transformation. He built the main mosque and saw to the construction of a mosque in each district. Islam was enforced throughout the land, and the people were made to observe Islamic practices such as the five daily prayers, the fast during *Ramadhan*, and the prohibition on drinking and gambling.[83] Sufi mysticism of the school of Ibn Arabi won favour in the court and became popular among the Acehnese. It is believed that Iskandar Muda himself became a devotee of Sufism early in his reign under the direction of his Syaikh al-Islam, Syams al-Din.[84]

Aceh was visited regularly by scholars on their way to and from the Holy Land, and many resided in Aceh for varying lengths of time before resuming their journeys back to their homes throughout the archipelago. Through writings of the influential shaikhs al-Islam and other religious scholars, Aceh came to be identified with the latest in Islamic learning. The Malay model offered by Aceh in the sixteenth and seventeenth centuries was one with a strongly Islamic flavour. It reflected its rulers' desire to demonstrate that their kingdom was indeed attuned to the latest fashions and ideas emanating from the heartland of Islam.

Conclusion

With the fall of Malay Melaka in 1511, Aceh became its *de facto* successor in the Straits for about 150 years from the reign of Sultan Ali Mughayat Syah (1514?-30) to that of Queen Safiyyat al-Din (1641-75). It dominated trade in the Straits of Melaka and beyond through its ability to attract the considerable traffic in Indian cloth to its port; its scholars produced Malay literary works of great quality in the court; it promoted Islam and was the leading centre for Islamic learning in the archipelago; and its institutions were modified to accord with the latest ideas from the illustrious empires of Islam. Aceh's model of a Malay court and kingdom owed much to the wider Islamic world, and in this it differed significantly from the Melaka-Johor model.

The Melaka court only embraced Islam in the mid-fifteenth century, and hence the new religion had to contend with a deeply embedded amalgam of Hindu-Buddhist and indigenous beliefs. The *Sejarah Melayu*, a document depicting the rise and fall of the Melaka kingdom, contains episodes which clearly demonstrate the co-existence and equality of indigenous, Indian, and Islamic ideas. It was a model which reflected the times, but it was not totally appropriate in the sixteenth and seventeenth centuries as Islam became the dominant world religion and made considerable inroads in the Malay world. Aceh's model, on the other hand, reflected this shift, and many throughout the archipelago looked to Aceh as the leader of the Malay world, as they had to Melaka in the fifteenth century. Aceh had become a Malay Muslim kingdom in which the role of Islam was central to its institutions. It was a model which was compatible with the times and one which appealed to other Malay kingdoms.

In the first half of the seventeenth century, Perak and Pahang acknowledged the overlordship of Aceh. Although Kedah was under the suzerainty of Ayudhya, it did not fail to offer allegiance to the Aceh ruler.[85] Areas on the north-east and north-west coasts of Sumatra were also counted among Aceh's territories. All of these lands conducted their affairs in the Acehnese manner by following Acehnese court protocol and by employing Acehnese titles and functions for their officials. They were also responsive to the royal seals dispatched from the Aceh court, and they regularly intermarried with the Aceh royal family.[86] Aceh's reputation as a centre for religious and secular learning would have also made it an attractive model for other Malay courts. In addition to religious tracts, many of which were either written in Malay or translated into Malay from the original Arabic or Persian, there was a considerable secular literature in Malay produced in the Aceh court.

The fateful decisions made by Johor to support and Aceh to remain non-committal toward the Dutch siege of Portuguese Melaka in 1641 quickly transformed the situation. Johor was rewarded by the Dutch for its stance and given trade and protection privileges which were denied other local kingdoms, including Aceh.[87] Dutch officials in Melaka persuaded their superiors in Batavia that Johor posed much more of a threat than Aceh and therefore should be favoured. They warned of the danger of the Orang Laut as pirates and of the threat that the surrounding Minangkabau settlements, who were Johor's subjects, could pose to the citadel of Melaka itself. A siege by Johor, they concluded, would be three times worse than one by Aceh.[88] Through continually harassing the Acehnese in their collection of pepper from west coast Sumatra, and by encouraging these Minangakabau pepper-producers to abandon Aceh, the Dutch succeeded in inciting a rebellion which led to the overthrow of Acehnese control on the west coast in 1664-5.[89]

With the loss of a major source of pepper, Aceh was no longer as attractive an entrepôt for Indian traders. Instead, much of the Indian traffic now began to go to Banten and Johor. By the last quarter of the seventeenth century, a combination of internal conflict in Aceh and a resurgent Johor under the leadership of the Laksamana family, saw Johor replace Aceh as the most prestigious kingdom in the Malay world.[90] Melaka traditions were resurrected and re-edited in the Johor court, and the theme of the unbroken line of Malay customs and history going 'as far back' as Melaka was born. In the process of asserting the Melaka-Johor model of Malayness, there was a conscious rejection of the Sumatran model represented by Aceh. This then signalled the end of Aceh's and Sumatra's claim of being part of 'Melayu.' Only in later centuries did the Aceh model emphasizing the centrality of Islam in the society regain favour. It is worthy of note that these ideas emerged once again in Sumatra at Palembang, one of the earliest homelands of the Malays.

NOTES

1. The term was coined by Hendrik Maier, 1988.
2. Leonard Y. Andaya and Barbara Watson Andaya, 1982, ch. 5.
3. The following account is from Leonard Y. Andaya, 'Origins of Melayu,' paper presented to the Conference on 'Contesting Malayness: Definitions of Alam Melayu,' Leiden 7-9 April 1998.
4. S.O. Robson, *Desawarnana*, pp. 33-4.
5. Wheatley (1961) was first to suggest that Melaka was *founded* and did not evolve into an international entrepôt.
6. O.W. Wolters, 1970.
7. Kassim Ahmad, *Hikayat Hang Tuah*, p. 175.
8. Bernd Nothofer, 1975, pp. 36-7.
9. Denys Lombard, 1967; M.C. Ricklefs, 1993, pp. 32-6.
10. 'Mughal' is the Indo-Persian form of the word 'Mongol.' The conquering armies which established the so-called Mughal dynasty, however, were not Mongols but Chaghatay Turks. As descendants of Timur, they should properly be referred to as Timuris, rather than Mughals. The correct name of the dynasty founded by Babur in 1526 is Timurid, acknowledging the ancestry of Timur. Those who came to serve the dynasty were a mixed group which should be called the 'Timuri' or 'Indo-Timuri.' But the term 'Mughal' came to be used incorrectly for the Chaghatay and others who served the Timurids. See Marshall G.S. Hodgson, 1974, p. 62. The name Mughal will be used in this paper, along with Timuri, to refer to this powerful Muslim kingdom and its subjects in India.
11. Arasaratnam, Sinnappah, 1994, pp. 40, 46, 59, 67-8, 72-3.
12. Sanjay Subrahmanyam, 1988, pp. 504-5.
13. Sinnappah Arasaratnam and Aniruddha Ray, 1994, p. 26.
14. Arasaratnam, *Maritime India*, pp. 119-22, 155-6.
15. Arasaratnam and Ray, *Masulipatnam and Cambay*, pp. 11, 26-9.
16. Arasaratnam, *Maritime India*, pp. 124, 128, 137.
17. VOC [Dutch East India Company Archives] 1229, Missive Malacca, 456r.
18. VOC 1143, Daghregister Pieter Willemsz., 559r.
19. VOC 1237, Verbael Balthasar Bort, 372v.
20. VOC 1157, Daghregister Arnold De Vlamingh van Outshoorn, 589r-v.
21. VOC 1221, Missive Malacca, 423r.
22. Anthony Reid, 1969, pp. 395-414; C.R. Boxer, 1964, pp. 109-21.
23. Leonard Y. Andaya, 1993, pp. 134-5.
24. Hodgson, *Venture*, p. 81.
25. Leonard Y. Andaya, 1995, pp. 133-41.

26 VOC 1240, Missive Malacca, 1142-3.
27 V.T. Braginsky, 1993, p. 71; Iskandar, Teuku, 1996; R.O. Winstedt, 1969.
28 Hodgson, *Venture*, p. 47.
29 Hodgson, *Venture*, p. 28.
30 For some examples see Anthony Reid, 1993, vol. 2, pp. 144, 146-7; and Leonard Y. Andaya, 1993, pp. 135-7.
31 Barbara Watson Andaya, 1997, pp. 391-409.
32 VOC 1157, Daghregister De Vlamingh v. Outshoorn, 554r.
33 R.O. Winstedt, 1961.
34 VOC 1144, Daghregister Soury, 668v, *passim;* Takeshi Ito, 1984, p. 42, fn. 92.
35 Barbara Watson Andaya, 1978.
36 VOC 1157, Relaas De Vlamingh van Outshoorn, 546v; VOC 1237, Verbael Bort, 346v, 366v.
37 VOC 1144, Daghregister Soury, 664v-665r-v; VOC 1155, Daghregister De Vlamingh van Outshoorn, 441r, 443r, 445v, *passim*.
38 John F. Richards, 1993, p. 58.
39 Hodgson. *Venture*, pp. 64, 99, 101-2.
40 VOC 1237, Verbael Bort, 340v.
41 VOC 1191, Truijtman,751r, 752v.
42 VOC 1241, Daghregister Groenewegen, 378v.
43 H.T. Colenbrander (ed.), 1919, p. 129, under date 22 October 1615.
44 Thomas Bowrey, 1905, pp. 299-300.
45 See, for example, Albert Howe Lybyer, 1913, p. 56.
46 R.J. Wilkinson, 1959, p. 1103; H.C. Klinkert, 1893, p. 418.
47 R.O. Winstedt, 1938, p. 115. Stuart Robson, in a personal communication, has suggested that it could refer to the fact that Tun Indera Segara may have come from a family which provided *sida-sida*.
48 Teuku Iskandar, 1970, p. 1103.
49 Hoesein Djajadiningrat, vol. 2, pp. 781-2.
50 Check Dewan Bahasa version of Sej. Mel.
51 Misa Melayu, 89:18--check
52 Peter Mundy, 1919; VOC 1143, 512r, 563r-v]
53 VOC 1237, Verbael Bort, 354r-v.
54 VOC 1143, Daghregister Willemsz., 503r; Memorie Willemsz.,594v; VOC 1157, Report De Vlamingh van Outshoorn, 546v; VOC 1157, Journal De Vlamingh van Outshoorn, 599r.
55 Richards, *Mughal*, p. 62.
56 H.A.R. Gibb and Harold Bowen, 1950, vol. 1, pt. 1, pp. 329-33; Albert Howe Lybyer, 1913, p. 57.
57 VOC 1226, Missive Thyssen, 592v.

58 Ramli Harun and Tjut Rahma M.A. Gani, 1985, pp. 45, 51.
59 Harun & Gani, *Adat Aceh*, p. 99, *passim*, ch. 4.
60 Harun & Gani, *Adat Aceh*, ch. 4.
61 VOC 1143, Daghregister Soury, 566v-567r.
62 VOC 1143, Daghregister Soury, 664r; VOC 1237, Verbael Bort, 354r-v; *passim*.
63 VOC 1157, Daghregister De Vlamingh van Outshoorn, 602v.
64 VOC 1237, Verbael Bort, 359v-360r, 369r-370v.
65 VOC 1143, Daghregister Soury, 565v.
66 VOC 1143, Daghregister Soury, 557v; VOC 1157, Daghregister De Vlamingh van Outshoorn, 581v, 597r.
67 John F. Richards, 1981, p. 256
68 VOC 1143, Daghregister Willemsz., 522v-523r.
69 VOC 1214, Missive Truijtman, 171v.
70 VOC 1214, Missive Truijtman, 171v; VOC 1177, Missive Perak, 82v.
71 VOC 1237, Verbael Bort, 354r-v; VOC 1157, Daghregister De Vlamingh van Outshoorn, 598r-v.
72 Harun and Gani, *Adat Aceh*, 73-4; Ito, *World*, pp. 287-8; M.A.P. Meilink-Roelofsz, 1962, ch. 3.
73 W.J.A. de Leeuw, 1926.
74 VOC 1200, Advijs De Vlamingh van Outshoorn, 225v; VOC 1214, Missive Thijssen, 126v; VOC 1237, Verbael Bort, 351r-v, 373r-v; VOC 1240, Memorie Thyssen, 1144v-1450v; VOC 1258, Missive, 2007.
75 VOC 1157, Relaas De Vlamingh van Outshoorn, 547r-548v; VOC 1157, Daghregister De Vlamingh van Outshoorn, 570v; VOC 1237, Verbael Bort, 345v, 350r-352v.
76 Hodgson, *Venture*, p. 47.
77 Leonard Y. Andaya, vol. 1, pp. 345-401.
78 VOC 1237, Verbael Bort, 354r-v.
79 Ito, *World*, pp. 153-4
80 Hodgson, *Venture*, pp. 65, 108.
81 Ito, *World*, pp. 164, 250, 259-60; C.A.O. van Nieuwenhuijze, 1945, pp. 360-1.
82 K.F.H. van Langen, 1888, pp. 390-1; C. Snouck Hurgronje, vol. 1, 1893, pp. 84-7.
83 Teuku Iskandar (ed.), 1966, p 36.
84 Ito, *World*, pp. 208, 249.
85 In a study of statecraft in Ayudhya, a Thai scholar has shown that it was common for a region to accept suzerainty from more than one overlord. This was particularly true for 'frontier' areas. Thongchai Winichakul, 1994, pp. 84-8. Kedah was a typical frontier area, being located

between two powerful cultural zones and loyalties: the Thai and the Malay.
86 VOC 1157, Relaas De Vlamingh van Outshoorn, 549v; VOC 1194, Missive Thyssen, 318r; VOC 1221, Daghregister Pitts, 451v; VOC 1229, Missive Keyser, 297r.
87 Leonard Y. Andaya, 1975, pp. 56-65.
88 VOC 1200, Advijs De Vlamingh van Outshoorn, 228v-229r.
89 VOC 1249, Rapport Cau, 139r-152r; De Leeuw, *Het Painansch Contract*.
90 See Andaya, *Kingdom of Johor*.

REFERENCES

Andaya, Leonard Y. (1975) *The Kingdom of Johor*. Kuala Lumpur: Oxford University Press.
--(1992) 'Interactions with the Outside World and Adaptation in Southeast Asian Society, 1500-1800,' in: Nicholas Tarling (ed.), *The Cambridge History of Southeast Asia*.
--(1993) *The World of Maluku: Eastern Indonesia in the Early Modern Period*. Honolulu: University of Hawai'i Press.
--(1995) 'Ayudhya and the Persian and Indian Muslim Connection,' *Proceedings of the International Workshop Ayudhya and Asia*. Bangkok: Thammasat University.
Andaya, Leonard Y. and Barbara Watson Andaya (1982) *History of Malaysia*. London: Macmillan.
Arasaratnam, Sinnappah (1994) *Maritime India in the Seventeenth Century*. Delhi: Oxford University Press.
Arasaratnam, Sinnappah and Aniruddha Ray (1994) *Masulipatnam and Cambay: A History of Two Port-towns 1500-1800*. New Delhi: Munshiram Manoharlal Publishers Pvt Ltd.
Bowrey, Thomas (1905) *A Geographical Account of Countries round the Bay of Bengal, 1669-1679*. Edited by Richard Carnac Temple. Cambridge: Hakluyt Society.
Boxer, C.R. (1964) 'The Achinese Attack on Malacca in 1629,' in: John Bastin and R. Roolvink (eds) *Malayan and Indonesian Studies*. Oxford: Clarendon Press.
Braginsky, V.T. (1993) *The System of Classical Malay Literature*. Leiden: KITLV Press.
Colenbrander, H.T. (ed.) (1919) *Jan Pietersz. Coen: Bescheiden omtrent zijn bedrijf in Indië*. vol. 1. (Brieven van Coen naar patria, 1614-1623). 's-Gravenhage: Martinus Nijhoff.

Djajadiningrat, Hoesein (1934) *Atjehsch-Nederlandsch Woordenboek*. Batavia: Landsdrukkerij.

Gibb, H.A.R. and Harold Bowen (1950) *Islamic Society and the West*. London/New York: Oxford University Press.

Harun, Ramli and Tjut Rahma M.A. Gani (1985) *Adat Aceh*. Jakarta: Departemen Pendidikan dan Kebudayaan.

Hodgson, Marshall G.S. (1974) *The Venture of Islam*. Chicago: Chicago University Press.

Iskandar, Teuku (1966) (ed.) *Nuru'd-din ar-Raniri, Bustanu's-Salatin*, bab 2, Fasal 13. Kuala Lumpur: Dewan Bahasa dan Pustaka.

--(1970) *Kamus Dewan*. Kuala Lumpur: Dewan Bahasa dan Pustaka, p. 1103.

--(1996) *Kesusasteraan Klasik Melayu Sepanjang Abad*. Jakarta: Penerbit LIBRA.

Ito, Takeshi (1982) 'The World of the Adat Aceh: A Historical Study of the Sultanate of Aceh.' PhD dissertation, The Australian National University.

Kassim, Ahmad, *Hikayat Hang Tuah*.

Klinkert, H.C. (1893) *Nieuw Maleisch-Nederlandsch Woordenboek*. Leiden: E.J. Brill.

Langen, K.F.H. van (1888) 'De inrigting van het Atjehsche Staatsbestuur onder het Sultanaat,' *Bijdragen tot de Taal-, Land- en Volkenkunde* 34.

Leeuw, W.J.A. de (1926) *Het Painansch Contract*. Amsterdam: H.J. Paris.

Lombard, Denys (1967) *Le Sultanat d'Atjeh au temps d'Iskandar Muda, 1607-1636*. Paris: Ecole Française d'Extreme Orient.

Lybyer, Albert Howe (1913) *The Government of the Ottoman Empire*, PhD dissertation, Harvard University.

Maier, Hendrik (1988) *In the Center of Authority*. Ithaca: Cornell Southeast Asia Program.

Meilink-Roelofsz, M.A.P. (1962) *Asian Trade and European Influence*. The Hague: Martinus Nijhoff.

Mundy, Peter (1919) *The Travels of Peter Mundy in Europe and Asia, 1608-1667*. Edited by Richard Carnac Temple. Cambridge: Hakluyt Society, vol. 3, pts 1 & 2.

Nieuwenhuijze, C.A.O. van (1945) *Samsu'-Din van Pasai*. Leiden: E.J. Brill.

Nothofer, Bernd (1975) *The Reconstruction of Proto-Malayo-Javanic*. 's-Gravenhage: Martinus Nijhoff.

Reid, Anthony (1969) 'Sixteenth Century Turkish Influence in Western Indonesia,' *Journal of Southeast Asian Studies* X, iii (Dec. 1969), pp. 395-414.

--(1993) *Southeast Asia in the Age of Commerce 1450-1680*. New Haven: Yale University Press, vol. 2.
Richards, John F. (1981) 'The Formulation of Imperial Authority under Akbar and Jahangir,' in: J.F. Richards (ed.) *Kingship and Authority in South Asia*, Madison: University of Wisconsin South Asian Studies.
--(1993) *The Mughal Empire. The New Cambridge History of India*. Cambridge: Cambridge University Press.
Ricklefs, M.C. (1993) *A History of Modern Indonesia since c. 1300*. Stanford: Stanford University Press.
Robson, S.O. (1995) *Desawarnana*. Leiden: KITLV Press.
Samad Ahmad A. (1979) *Sulalatus Salatin (Sejarah Melayu)*. Kuala Lumpur: Dewan Bahasa dan Pustaka.
Snouck Hurgronje, C. (1893) *De Atjèhers*. Leiden: E.J. Brill, vol. 1.
Subrahmanyam, Sanjay (1988) 'Persians, Pilgrims and Portuguese: The Travails of Masulipatnam Shipping in the Western Indian Ocean, 1590-1665,' *Modern Asian Studies* 22:2, 3.
Watson Andaya, Barbara (1978) 'The Indian "saudagar Raja" in Traditional Malay Courts,' *Journal of the Malaysian Branch of the Royal Asiatic Society* 51(i).
--(1997) 'Historicising 'Modernity' in Southeast Asia,' *Journal of the Economic and Social History of the Orient* 40(4), Nov. 1997.
Wheatley, Paul (1961) *Golden Khersonese*. Kuala Lumpur: University of Malaya Press.
Wilkinson, R.J. (1959) *A Malay-English Dictionary*. London: Macmillan & Co. Ltd, vol. 2.
Winichakul, Thongchai (1994) *Siam Mapped*. Honolulu: University of Hawai'i Press.
Winstedt, R.O. (1938) 'Raffles Ms. No. 18,' *Journal of the Malayan Branch of the Royal Asiatic Society* 16(3).
--(1961) *The Malay Magician: Being Shaman, Saiva and Sufi*. London: Routledge and Kegan Paul.
--(1969) *A History of Clasical Malay Literature*, Kuala Lumpur: Oxford University Press.
Wolters, O.W. (1970) *The Fall of Srivijaya in Malay History*. Ithaca: Cornell University Press.

CHAPTER 6

ACCUMULATION OF KNOWLEDGE:
PILGRIMAGE AS LEITMOTIF IN THE INDIAN OCEAN
IN THE ANCIENT PERIOD*

HIMANSHU PRABHA RAY

In the ancient period people travelled for a variety of reasons. Merchants and traders figure prominently in the Geniza papers which provide interesting details of transoceanic travel in the eleventh-twelfth centuries AD, and in early Buddhist sources dated to the beginning of the Christian era (*Jatakas*, Bk. I, no.4; Bk. X, no. 439; 442; Bk. XI, no. 463, Bk. XVI, no. 518). Also significant were peregrinations of wandering scholars, and pilgrims (Goitein, 1967:42-59). The seeking of knowledge in practically all major religions such as, Islam, Judaism, or Buddhism inspired extensive journeys. In the medieval period Palestine formed the spiritual centre of a diaspora extensively spread over the civilized world of the Mediterranean. Nor was language a barrier in these interchanges. 'Latin in western Europe, classical Arabic in the countries of Islam, and Hebrew in the Jewish houses of learning everywhere made it possible for foreigners to take part anywhere in classes or even to lead them' (ibid., p. 52).

In a similar way, the communities of South and Southeast Asia formed a part of what has been termed the *sasana* or Buddhist order (Obeyesekere, 1995:234). Buddhist monks and the laity travelled to centres of learning, as well as to spots associated with the Buddha's life in the Subcontinent. Fa Hsien returned from India to China by sea in the fifth century AD. About ten years later a famous Buddhist teacher, Prince Gunavarman of Kashmir, spent many years in Java before proceeding to China. A Buddhist monk from Gaudidvipa or Bengal is referred to in the Kelurak inscription from Indonesia dated to AD 782, while contemporary inscriptions of the Sailendras from Central Java mention a guru from Gujarat and learned monks from the Abhayagiri monastery in Sri Lanka.

These are some of the issues which will be addressed in this paper, in the context of voyages across the Bay of Bengal. The focus here is on the stupa of the Borobudur in Central Java and the paper will attempt to place its importance within the early Buddhist cultural sphere. At one level, this study highlights the story of Sudhana sculpted at Borobudur and its implicit message encouraging travel for the acquisition of knowledge; while at another level it focuses on the importance of pilgrimage and travel within the ancient realm of the Indian Ocean.

What makes the study of pilgrimage fascinating is that, while a pilgrim centre was often fixed in space, it was not fixed in significance, and pilgrims visiting the same place often engaged in 'a multiplicity of frequently incompatible interpretations' (Coleman and Elsner, 1995:202). The sacred landscape also varied over time; it was often authenticated by religious texts and by association with legendary events, but equally important was the legitimization provided by visitations from elite groups. Perhaps the most meaningful contribution of pilgrimage was its ability to link geographically dispersed groups and people and provide them with the opportunity to transcend parochial assumptions and concerns. Pilgrims also often acted as bearers of news, letters and cultural goods.

> The power of a shrine, therefore, derives in large part from its character almost as a religious void, a ritual space capable of accommodating diverse meanings and practices - though of course the shrine staff might attempt, with varying degrees of success, to impose a single, official discourse (Eade and Sallnow, 1991:15).

To what extent was this valid for Borobudur - a monument which first became known to Europeans in January 1814?[1] On the basis of the palaeography of the fragmentary inscriptions covering the base, the monument has been dated to the late eighth or ninth century AD. The 1,460 panels of sculptures have been studied by scholars and their attempts have largely been confined to identifying these with known Buddhist texts.[2] The scenes on the covered base of the stupa have been connected to the *Mahakarmavibhanga*, while the first and second galleries contain illustrations from the stories of the Jatakas and the Avadanas. Asvaghosa's *Lalitavistara*, in Sanskrit, covers the Buddha's life up to the First Sermon and has been depicted on 120 panels at Borobudur, but no other reliefs on this theme are known from Indonesia. At the time of the construction of Borobudur, the legend of the Buddha attracted very little interest in Indian sculpture and the only contemporary examples, those from Ajanta, are restricted to the four main events of his life: Birth, Enlightenment, the First Sermon, and Nirvana (Bernet Kempers, 1976:94).

Krom first suggested that the representations on the second gallery were based on the *Gandavyuhasutra* and this supposition was followed up by Bosch who maintained that the *Bhadracari* was used as the source of the carvings on the fourth gallery. Jan Fontein's study (1967) provides a comprehensive analysis of the figures on the third and fourth galleries and compares these with representations of the *Gandavyuhasutra* in Chinese and

Japanese art. There are frequent divergences between the text and the images and in fact none of the available literary sources exactly matches the sculpted panels. Short inscriptions survive on the figures on the base and it has often been assumed that these provided terse instructions to the sculptor, such as: heaven, *ghanta* or bell, gift of a sunshade and so on (Bernet Kempers, 1976:66). This explanation is considered unsatisfactory by other scholars who argue that, since the inscriptions were cut into stone rather than being painted on or written in chalk, their purpose was more permanent and was perhaps to provide indications to the pilgrim visiting the site (De Casparis, 1975:32).

In a recent study (1997), Dehejia raises the issue of 'discourse' in Early Buddhist art and argues that:

> Discourse itself has two important aspects: first is the selection of events from among those available in a story, and secondly, the ordering of the chosen events (p. 6).

The question then is one of choices, but the point is: who made the choice? Dehejia contends that it was the ancient artists who made deliberate decisions about the manner in which they wished to communicate their message (p. 7). This position may not be generally acceptable, especially since this does not take into account the role of the donor, but more than that, the part played by the clergy.[3] This has become even more pertinent since the image of early Buddhist monks and nuns as professional salvation seekers who distanced themselves from the world is being increasingly questioned (Schopen, 1988-9), particularly with regard to their role in innovation and social change.

This leads to the issue raised above, i.e. the question of choice and, in the case of Borobudur, the decision to base the illustrations on the text of the *Gandavyuhasutra*. Though the *Gandavyuha* enjoyed great prestige and popularity among the Buddhist communities of Indonesia, China, and Japan, unlike Borobudur, no works of art exist in either China or Japan which are based on the *Gandavyuha* and date from a period 'when *Avatamsaka* Buddhism was at the height of its spiritual influence.' All surviving examples date from a later period of revival in the tenth-eleventh centuries AD (Fontein, 1967:24). It is significant that the panels on Borobudur have little in common with the Chinese or Japanese illustrations, except the common scriptural source that they share. Among the many divergences between the two traditions, perhaps the most readily observable is that while the illustrators in China and Japan treated Sudhana's pilgrimage as if it had taken place in their own country, the portrayal on Borobudur has preserved a predominantly Indian cultural tradition (Sivaramamurti, 1961).

The active role of the Buddhist clergy in the propagation of certain texts is also gaining ground in scholarly circles. It is not known when and by whom the *Avatamsakasutra* was first composed, but it is thought to have been the product of the hands of various authors flourishing in the Indian cultural sphere in the first-second centuries AD. Comprehensive renditions of the text were made in China in the early fifth and late seventh centuries AD from versions of the text obtained from Khotan (Cleary, 1993:2). An autographed copy of the last section of the *Avatamsaka*, viz. the *Gandavyuha*, is said to have been presented to the Chinese emperor by an Orissan king of the Bhaumakara dynasty in 795. This text and a letter were entrusted to the monk, Prajna, who was instructed to supply a translation which was subsequently furnished between 786 and 798 (Levi, 1919-20:363-4). The *Avatamsakasutra* became one of the pillars of East Asian Buddhism and a major school of Buddhist philosophy developed on the basis of its teachings. It was propagated in at least three different versions all over the Far East and in the third and last translation, the *Gandavyuha* occurs as an individual text and not as a part of the *Avatamsakasutra*.

The *Gandavyuha* describes the attainment of Enlightenment through tales of pilgrimage - the primary aim of the scripture being to stress that constraints placed by fixed systems need to be overcome to attain full consciousness.

> It suggests that all views that are conditioned by cultural and personal history are by definition limiting, and there is a potential awareness that cuts through the boundaries imposed by conventional description based on accumulated mental habit. According to the scripture, it is the perennial task of certain people, by virtue of their own development, to assist others in overcoming arbitrary restrictions of consciousness so as to awaken to the full potential of mind (Cleary, 1993:47).

These enlightened people, according to the scripture, could come from all walks of life and from all regions, because 'the wisdom and virtues of Buddha are in all people, but people are unaware of it because of their preoccupations' (ibid.). Historicity is of little account in this Buddhist scripture as the discourse is presented by trans-historical, symbolic beings representing various aspects of universal enlightenment. This scripture thus became one of the pillars of East Asian Buddhism and led to the development of a major school of philosophy based on its teachings (Cleary, 1993:1). The enlightened beings, according to the *Gandhavyuha*, appear in a variety of forms from mendicants and ascetics to merchants, craftsmen, entertainers and doctors and are to be found in all communities, villages and towns. 'They live and work in the world without being controlled by fetters, bonds, propensities, or obsessions' (ibid., p. 47). It is not surprising then that this text should have been chosen for representation on the galleries at Borobudur constructed between AD 780 and 830 during the rule of the Sailendras in Central Java. The first inscription issued by a Sailendra king in Central Java dates from 778, while the last one dates from 824.

The secondary literature associating the monument at Borobudur with Tantric Buddhism has been recently reviewed and repudiated on the grounds that the earliest evidence of Tantric Buddhism in Java dates to a later period, namely the tenth century, whereas contemporary sources indicate that it was the Mahayana form of Buddhism that was prevalent at the time that the monument was built. This is further corroborated by the inscriptions of the Sailendras and the text of the *Pratityasamutpada* inscribed on eleven gold plates and dated on palaeographic grounds to between AD 600 and 850 (De Casparis, 1956:47-156; Klokke, 1996). Bronze, silver, and gold images from the mid or late ninth century onwards indicate a religious change, with increasing influence being exerted by Tantric Buddhism.

The texts illustrated in the reliefs at Borobudur such as the *Lalitavistara*, *Gandavyuha*, and the *Jatakamala* - all belong to the Mahayana school without any overt Tantric influences (De Casparis, 1981:53). But more than any other monument, Borobudur reflects 'successive stages in the accumulation of merit and wisdom' (ibid., p. 62). The lower terraces illustrating stories from the life of the Buddha cater admirably to different forms of bhakti, while the 'round terraces at the top with their hidden images demand advance forms of concentration' (ibid., p. 62). It has been argued that this is likewise true of the texts chosen for representation on the monument.

> A study of this aspect of the monument would require a careful analysis of the views on such fundamental points of doctrine as the Karmic Law of all texts which were illustrated on the Barabudur (Fontein, 1967:172).

More than that, this would also require knowledge of the meaning of the monument itself. Bosch explained the predominance of *Gandavyuha* reliefs by suggesting that it embodied the Indonesian ideal of the pious pilgrim who wandered from one teacher to another in search of supreme wisdom. De Casparis has extended the argument further by pointing out that since Borobudur had a close relationship with the Sailendra dynasty, there would also have been Sailendra princes among the pilgrims (De Casparis, 1981:72).

The monument itself 'must be attributed to the activity of the rulers of the Sailendra dynasty, first attested in Java in the Kalasan inscription of AD 778, still in full control at the time of the Karangtengah inscription of AD 824, disappearing from Java some time after that year, at the latest in AD 856' (ibid., p. 56). Contemporary inscriptions of the ninth century indicate that in some areas of Central Java, there must have been a continuous succession of villages surrounded by at least a number of large, cultivated rice-fields. An inscription dated AD 842 refers to the transfer of a village and its paddy fields to a *kamulan* or sanctuary called Bhumisambhara by Sri Kahulunan identified by De Casparis with a Sailendra princess, the sanctuary indicating the monument at Borobudur, though there is no unanimity on the latter view (ibid.).

The question is: what was the sacred geography of Buddhist pilgrim sites in the contemporary period in the Indian Subcontinent? Does the itinerary of Sudhana reflect this or is the preoccupation of the Indonesian traveller markedly different? It is significant that Sudhana's travels extended largely across peninsular India, though towards the end of his journey, Sudhana does travel to Magadha and Kapilavastu - regions hallowed by association with events from the Buddha's life. But by and large the trodden path traversed through regions south of the Vindhyas and along the coast - a path which was familiar through networks of trade and journeys across the Ocean. It was also a region that externalized the Buddhist *sasana* - the universal Buddhist community that transcended ethnic and regional boundaries (Obeyesekere, 1995:239). The itinerary itself reflects a sphere far wider than that involving a visit to pilgrimage sites, although by the Pala period, there is clear evidence of a popular cult, in the sense of a devotional practice, or soteriological method, connected with the eight major sites associated with the life of the Buddha (Huntington and Huntington, 1990:533).

This cult had earlier beginnings. References in the *Digha Nikaya* (Mahaparinibbana Sutanta, 5.8) indicate that the Buddha encouraged pilgrimage to centres associated with his life. While addressing Ananda, he states that four places that believing clansmen should visit are: where the Tathagata was born; where the Tathagata attained Enlightenment; where the Tathagata preached; and where the Tathagata attained *nibbana* (Rhys Davids, 1881:153-4). And those who die while performing *cetiya-carikam* (pilgrimage) will be reborn after death in heaven (*saggam lokam*). Perhaps the earliest pilgrim was the Mauryan ruler, Asoka, who visited the site of Buddha's birthplace at Lumbini, an event commemorated in his pillar inscription at the site. A legend in the *Divyavadana* (Cowell and Neil, 1886:389-90) states that this was undertaken in the twentieth regnal year of the king. Some of the pilgrimage sites, such as at Lumbini, Sarnath,

Bodhgaya, Samkasya and Vaisali are marked by Asokan pillars and there are several illustrations of visits to pilgrimage sites on the monuments at Sanchi and Bharhut. Of these, the site of Bodhgaya has perhaps received most attention in scholarly writings.

> As the place of the Buddha's enlightenment, Bodhgaya has long attracted attention. Venerated for centuries by Buddhist devotees, it has been a subject of scholarly interest since the nineteenth century when it was visited repeatedly and featured in various studies and drawings. Of special concern has been the history of the Mahabodhi temple which dominates the site and marks the place of the *bodhi* tree and the *vajrasana*, the seat on which enlightenment is obtained (Leoshko, 1995:45).

Gradually these pilgrimage sites became codified into a sub-cult leading to the emergence of an image of the *Astamahapratiharya*, known as the eight sacred locations, or *astamahacaitya* - an image type representing the eight events. The earliest extant representation of the cult of the *Astamahapratiharya* is the stele from Sarnath dated to the late fifth century AD. It depicts in detail the exact set of scenes from the Buddha's life that continued to appear in the Buddhist art of North India for the next six or seven hundred years (Huntington, 1987:62). These included the four primary scenes, viz. the Birth at Lumbini, the Enlightenment at Bodh Gaya, the First Sermon at Sarnath, and the *parinirvana* at Kusinagara, appended by the four secondary scenes: the Great Illusion at Sravasti; the Descent from Trayastimsa heaven at Sankasya; the Gift of Honey at Vaisali; and the Taming of Nalagiri at Rajagrha.

In contrast to this emphasis on sites associated with Buddha's life, there is a marked correlation between Sudhana's itinerary and the pilgrimage undertaken by Hsuan Tsang in the seventh century AD. Starting from Nalanda, where he spent fifteen months in the *vihara*, the Chinese monk travelled to the Ganjam coast and from there to Amaravati along the River Krishna. His subsequent halt was at Kanchi from where he hoped to visit Sri Lanka, but he then went back to Kashmir via Bharukaccha, from where he returned to China after sixteen years (Watters, 1904-5:335-42).

Sudhana's itinerary shows that his first stop was at Dhanyakara or Dhanyakataka, the sites of Dharanikota and Amaravati, located at the point up to which the River Krishna is navigable and which may be defined as landing places for maritime traffic. The Krishna takes a sharp turn at this spot and this link of Amaravati with the river is preserved in a stele discovered during a clearance of the site in 1958-9. Engraved on one of the faces is the legend: 'the *gosthi* called Vanda at Dhanyakataka' and the representation of waters enclosed by an embankment with a female figure shown drawing water from the river with a pitcher (Ghosh and Sarkar, 1964-5:175).

The finds of large numbers of stone and bronze images of the Buddha and Bodhisattvas such as Avalokitesvara, Cunda, Manjusri, Maitreya, Vajrapani, and Heruka from Amaravati suggest not only the continued prosperity of the site from the sixth to the eleventh centuries AD (Knox, 1992, plates 123-8), but they mark the gradual transformation of Buddhism into its Vajrayana form. There is little information on the physical characteristics of the shrines which housed these images or the settlements around the site. Elliot's drawings and sketches made during his work at Amaravati in 1845 would suggest the presence of a shrine complex, though its date seems uncertain, but certainly later than the fourteenth-century image house referred to in the Gadaladeniya record (ibid., Appendix I). A large inscription slab contains an elegantly engraved text in Sanskrit dealing with matters of Buddhist principles and has been dated to the seventh-eighth centuries or later (ibid., plate 130).

The Gadaladeniya rock inscription of AD 1344 records the restoration of a two-storey image house at Dhanyakataka by a *sthavira* named Dharmakirti (*Epigraphia Zeylanica* 4: 90), while the pillar inscription of AD 1182, during the rule of Keta II, refers to the presence of a Saiva temple of Amaresvara at the site and adjacent to it a very lofty caitya of Lord Buddha (*Epigraphia Indica*, 6, 1900-1:146-60). A second epigraph dated to AD 1234 mentions a grant to the Buddha 'who is pleased to reside at Sri Dhanyakataka' (ibid.). Another site which seems to have had ties with Sri Lanka is that of Nagarjunakonda where Sri Lanka Buddhists built a monastic establishment known as Sihala-vihara and an inscription records that it had its own shrine for a bodhi tree (Mitra, 1980:199).

That the lower Krishna valley owed its continued prosperity to trade is evident from an eighth-century copper plate grant from Arhadanagar or the present Nagaram near Repalle in Guntur district. The document records the delegation by the king of certain powers with regard to punishments and collection of taxes to traders (*Indian Antiquary* 13:185-7). In addition to the lower Krishna valley, Buddhism in its Vajrayana form continued to flourish at the sites of Sankaram, near Anekkapalle, fifty kilometres from Visakhapatnam on the highway to Vijayawada and Ramatirtham, fifteen kilometres north-east of Visakhapatnam. A ninth-century inscription from the site records gifts to the Buddhist monastic establishment. Bojjanakonda, the more eastern of the two hills at Sankaram is dotted with a series of rock-cut and occasionally brick-built stupas on different terraces. These undoubtedly represent the offerings to the site of pious pilgrims who came to worship at the apsidal shrine-cum-monastery to the east in the ancient period (Mitra, 1980:219).

Further north along the Andhra coast, the site of Salihundam is situated on a hill about eight kilometres from the ancient port of Kalingapatnam located on the seacoast. Images of Marici, Bhrkuti, Tara, and Manjusri have been found at the site indicating continuity of the Buddhist monastic establishment into the early medieval period and influence from the art and iconography of ancient Orissa (ibid., p. 222).

Kalingavana is mentioned in the *Gandavyuha* as one of the cities visited by Sudhana during his travels. Earlier, the region of Kalinga had been visited by Hsuan Tsang and has been described as a place where Buddhism was flourishing, the principal monastery being that of Pushpagiri. Archaeological excavations have brought to light extensive remains of the ninth-tenth century Buddhist monastic establishments on the two contiguous hills of Lalitagiri and Udayagiri, and also on Ratnagiri and Vajragiri - all in the district of Cuttack. These include the remains of an imposing stupa rebuilt at least once; two magnificent quadrangular monasteries; one single-winged monastery; eight temples; and a large number of small stupas, sculptures, and architectural pieces (Mitra, 1980:226).

The nucleus of the monastic settlement at Ratnagiri dates from about the fifth century AD and the earliest available Buddhist inscriptions, all of which record the text of the *Pratityasamutpada-sutra*, in some cases combined with the Buddhist creed, on palaeographic grounds can be assigned to the later part of the Gupta period. It was in the period from the seventh to the thirteenth century AD that the site witnessed a phenomenal growth, largely owing to the patronage provided by the Bhaumakaras. Two records found at Talcher provide evidence of the grant of two villages to meet the requirements of the temple of Buddha in the Jayasrama-vihara (ibid., p. 224).

More than seven hundred portable monolithic stupas were exposed in the area around the monastery at Ratnagiri and by their sheer numbers these indicate that the site competed with Bodh Gaya as a pilgrim centre (Mitra, 1981:31). The richest hoard of bronze images in Orissa, comprising of ninety-five figures, of which seventy-five were Buddhist, five Brahmanical and eight Jaina, however, came from Achutrajpur in the district of Puri. Some of these images carried the Buddhist creed inscribed in characters of the ninth, tenth, and eleventh centuries AD (ibid., p. 225).

A vivid account of the flourishing state of Buddhism and Jainism in Tamil Nadu is provided by the two Tamil epics, the *Manimekalai* and the *Cilappatikaram*. The author of *Cilappatikaram* was Ilanko Atikal, a Jaina ascetic and the central characters - Kannaki and Kovalan - were Jainas. The epics are set in the four major cities of South India: Kaveripumpattinam;

Madurai; Vanci; and Kancipuram - all major ports and mercantile centres. Puhar is praised as a wealthy river port where the famous ship captain, Manaikan, the father of Kannaki, lived (Danielou, 1993a:4).

The *Manimekalai* deals with the story of Madhavi's daughter and is outspokenly and polemically Buddhist. One of the main characters in the story is Aravana Adigal, a preacher of Mahayana Buddhism in South India (Danielou, 1993b:xi). Others, such as Kovalan and his family, were sea traders and had Manimekalai, the goddess of the sea, as their patron deity. There are references to Dharma Sravaka, the Preacher of Faith, who was sent on an embassy to the Cola king and who reached Puhar by sea after crossing the ocean (ibid., pp. 112-13). Punya Raja is said to have ruled over the rich kingdom in the island of Java and the narrative is interspersed with tales of merchants travelling across the ocean to make money through their trading activities (ibid., pp. 62-3), and voyages to the isle of Java (ibid., p. 58):

> songs of the boatmen on their ships anchored in the harbour, getting drunk on beer and other liquor to appease their boredom (ibid., p. 32).

On the island of Manipallavam was the temple of Lord Buddha. The island was:

> littered with the shells in which fishermen sow pearls to reap a harvest. Here and there the waves had left branches of coral and pieces of scented sandalwood (ibid., p. 35).

In the Cera country, a caitya of plaster was built on top of a mountain. Stone terraces were set aside in the garden for *dharmacaranas* who preached the Buddha's faith and who stopped there on 'returning from a pilgrimage consisting of encircling, from left to right, the holy mountain of Samanoli on the isle of Sri Lanka' (ibid., p. 145). The story of Aputra, the son of a brahmana born out of wedlock and abandoned by his mother, epitomizes the close interaction across the Bay of Bengal. For many years Aputra lived in the temple of Laksmi at Madurai and was famous for his acts of charity. He left his body on the isle of Manipallavam, one hundred and twenty leagues to the south of Puhar, taking with him his passion for feeding living beings. He was reborn straightaway of a cow of the king of Java, Bhumicandra, who reigned benevolently over his people (Danielou, 1993b:59-60).

There is abundant evidence to support the contention that Buddhism was in a flourishing state in South India from the eighth-ninth centuries onwards. Two *theras* from the Cola country, Buddhamitra and Mahakasyapa, were responsible for the composition of the two works the *Uttodaya* and the

Namarupapariccheda in Sri Lanka in the twelfth century. The Kalyani inscription of King Dhammaceti (AD 1472-92) of Pegu refers to Ananda *thera* (died in AD 1245), a native of Kinchipura identified with Kanchipuram, and versed in the Pali Tipitaka who went to Pagan in Burma. The record also refers to a group of *theras* who, having been shipwrecked on the way to Sri Lanka, trekked to the site of Nagapattana and worshipped an image of Buddha in a cave hewn on the orders of the king of Cinadesa (Mitra, 1980:194). King Parakramabahu IV (1302-26) is known to have appointed a learned monk from the Cola region to the office of the royal teacher (Paranavitana, 1960:773). Buddhism was strongest in the two coastal centres of Kanci and Nagapattinam and there was frequent intercourse between Buddhist communities of these areas and those in Sri Lanka.

No Buddhist monuments have survived at Kanchipuram, though several Buddhist images dated between seventh to fourteenth century AD have been discovered in and around the city. Buddha images have also been detected inside the enclosures of the Kamakshi and Ekamresvara temples at the site, indicating the possible earlier Buddhist affiliation of the monuments and subsequent appropriation by the Hindus (Mitra, 1980:194). Similarly no structural remains survive at Nagapattinam, though the epigraphs and finds of hoards of bronzes at the site indicate its earlier significance. About three hundred and fifty in number, the bronzes range from the early Cola to the Vijayanagara tradition and represent Buddha, Maitreya, Tara, Jambhala, Vasudhara, *arhats*, and votive stupas (ibid., p. 197).

In 1846 Sir Walter Elliot visited the monument at Nagapattinam and described it as a:

> four-sided tower of three stories, constructed of bricks closely fitted together without cement, the first and second stories divided by corniced mouldings, with an opening for a door or window in the middle of each side (1878:224).

In 1867 the building had been demolished at the insistence of French Jesuits who had settled near the tower and had subsequently petitioned the government for use of the land for construction of a college building (ibid.).

A Buddhist temple is said to have been erected at Nagapattinam specifically for Chinese Buddhists at the behest of a Chinese ruler during the reign of the Pallava ruler, Narasimhavarman II (c. AD 695-722). It is said to have been visited by the Chinese monk, Wu-hing, on his way to Sri Lanka (Ramachandran, 1954:14). Reference has been made earlier to the grant of a village in the eleventh century to the monastic establishment by the Cola ruler Rajaraja I and ratified by his son, Rajendra. On the basis of references in Buddhist texts from Sri Lanka, it would seem that, as late as the fourteenth century, the site of Nagapattinam was recognized as the point of departure for ships sailing to Sri Lanka from the Indian Subcontinent. The *Saddhamma sangaha* mentions this tradition in a discussion of the life and activities of the Pali commentator, Buddhaghosa - a native of north India who travelled to Sri Lanka. The author of the *Saddhamma sangaha*, Dhammakitti, was a native of Thailand, but received his ordination in Sri Lanka and studied in that island in the fourteenth century (Paranavitana, 1944:18).

A third Buddhist site on the Tamil coast was that of Kaveripumpattinam or Puhar located in the delta of the Kaveri River. The *Cilappatikaram* describes it as a 'wealthy river port':

> The riches of the Puhar ship owners made the kings of faraway lands envious. The most costly merchandise, the rarest foreign produce, reached the city by sea and caravans' (Danielou, 1993:6). 'Near the shore lighthouses had been built to show ships the way to the harbour. Far away one could see the tiny lights of the fishing boats laying their nets in the deep sea (ibid., p. 30).

The *Manimekhalai,* on the other hand, refers to the destruction of the city by the sea. Archaeological excavations at the site and at a series of villages in the vicinity have provided evidence of habitation from the third century BC to the twelfth century AD. A brick-built Buddhist *vihara* comprising of nine cells in a row and provided with a common veranda was unearthed at the village of Pallavanesvaram. Other finds included a Buddhapada of Palnad limestone, a miniature Buddha image in bronze and a gilded bronze Maitreya of the eighth-ninth centuries AD now housed in the Madras Museum. A Buddhist temple of more than one storey is known to have been built at the site. The plinth provides evidence of the presence of three flights of steps on the three sides (Soundara Rajan, 1994:26-40).

A major Buddhist site in the Deccan in the early medieval period was that of Kanheri on the west coast. The Konkan was one of the regions visited by Hsuan Tsang, and also by Sudhana who went to Bharukaccha to visit the goldsmith, Muktasara, and to Samudrapratisthana to the laywoman Prabhuta. Unlike most of the other Buddhist monastic establishments of the Deccan which were abandoned around the third-fourth centuries AD, rock-cutting activity continued at Kanheri, Aurangabad, Ajanta, and Ellora - at the last site, this activity being dated between the sixth to eighth centuries AD. Of these, the site of Kanheri survived the longest and figures prominently in the Cambridge University Library manuscript (no. Add. 1643) of AD 1015. In the fifth century AD, a resident of a village in the

Sindhu country, located perhaps in modern Pakistan, paid for the construction of a *caitya* at the site (Gokhale, 1991:17). A later inscription in Cave 11 dated AD 854, records a permanent endowment of one hundred *drammas* for the construction of a meditation room and clothing for monks by a resident of Gauda, identified with the region of Bengal (ibid., p. 70).

Cave 11 was also the largest *vihara*-cum-assembly hall located at the focal point on the hill at Kanheri. Unlike the *viharas* of the earlier phase which were meant primarily for housing monks, the cutting of this cave expresses a new concern and the inclusion of a place for worship. The cave comprises a broad courtyard with cistern niches at both ends and two benches occupying the central space, spanning much of its width. At the rear end is located a shrine chamber and within the chamber is a teaching Buddha in *pralambapadasana* (Leese, 1983:167).

A related development was the emergence of the cult of the Boddhisattva Avalokitesvara as a saviour of mariners and travellers in distress. This has generally been associated with Mahayana and the *Saddharma-pundarika-sutra* (Chapter XXIV), though an enumeration of dangers of travel is to be found in earlier texts such as the *Anguttara Nikaya* and the *Divyavadana* as well (Cowell and Neil, 1886:92, 25-8). The cult was prevalent at the time that the Chinese pilgrim Fa Hsien journeyed to India in the fourth century, though the first sculptural representations of the litany can be dated no earlier than the fifth century AD (Ray, 1994, chapter V). This theme is to be found in the Buddhist caves of Ajanta, Aurangabad, Ellora, and Badami, though nowhere is the composition so elaborate and the treatment so elegant as in Cave 90 at Kanheri (Mitra, 1980:165). For the first time around the sixth to eighth centuries AD, in the rock-cut sanctuaries at Ellora, the function of Avalokitesvara as the saviour from the eight perils is delegated to Tara (ibid., p. 185). This theme occurs prominently in the monastic establishment at Ratnagiri in Orissa. A standing image of *astamahabhaya* Tara dated to the eighth century AD is shown flanked by scenes of the eight perils depicted in two vertical rows of four panels each (Mitra, 1983:444-5). A second standing image is dated somewhat later to the eleventh century on the basis of a fragmentary inscription and graphically portrays the *jalarnava-bhaya* or fear of drowning in a sinking boat (ibid., p. 428).

Another feature of the second phase at Kanheri was the erection of votive stupas of brick. In Cave 87 on the south-western corner of the Kanheri hill, more than a hundred bases of brick stupas were found in a rock shelter. Archaeological excavations by West (1861:118) uncovered several sculptural elements from the cave and subsequent explorations in the area by Gokhale led to the recovery of a large number of well-cut stone slabs, with the names of Buddhist monks in whose memory the votive stupas had been donated (Gokhale, 1991:111-36).

On the evidence of the earlier archaeological excavations by Bird (1841:94-7), it is evident that these brick stupas were erected by pilgrims to Kanheri in memory of Buddhist monks. On excavating the largest brick stupa in front of Cave 3, Bird found a hollow in the centre covered by a piece of gypsum. Placed in the hollow were two small copper urns, in one of which were some ashes mixed with a ruby, a pearl, small pieces of gold, and a small box containing a piece of cloth; in the other, a silver box and some ashes were found. Two copper plates accompanied the urns. The smaller of the copper plates had an inscription, the last part of which contained the Buddhist creed, while the larger copper plate recorded the donation of a resident of the region of Sindhu. The same creed is also inscribed carved in relief beneath a stupa in Cave 3. While Cave 3 is dated to the second-third century AD, the relief was added later in the fifth century at the behest of a visitor to the site (Gokhale, 1991:56).

Archaeological excavations at Kanheri have yielded large numbers of sealings in various stages of baking. These oval sealings depict the figure of the Buddha seated on a low stool and in the upper register is shown the temple of Bodh Gaya. In the lower half of the sealings are three lines in the eight-ninth century script enshrining part of the Buddhist creed: *ye dharma hetu prabhava* ... (Tathagata, i.e. the Buddha, has revealed the cause of those phenomena which spring from a cause and also the means of its cessation) (Rao, 1971:46; West, 1861:13). These unbaked clay sealings or votive clay stupas were part of the Buddhist ritual of pilgrimage in the eighth-ninth centuries (Lawson, 1988). These have been found extensively at sites in South and Southeast Asia and some idea of the numbers involved from sites in Indonesia is evident from the following:

> Hundreds of these [tiny clay stupas] were found in 1924 at Pejeng on the island of Bali and in 1935 at Jongke in Java 7 km north of Jogjakarta while two have been reported from the neighbourhood of Palembang in Sumatra and over 1,200 were discovered during the restoration activities at Barabudur in 1974 (Lohuizen-de-Leeuw, 1980: 278).

Bronze moulds for making these have also been recovered during archaeological excavations.

It is evident then that a Buddhist visitor to peninsular India in the early medieval period would have found a familiar cultural ambience and a series of *viharas* and shrines to visit. What is also apparent is that these exchanges across the Bay of Bengal involved both the monastic community as well as the laity. Nor was travel across the ocean considered a deterrent - on the contrary, the sacred geography of Buddhism established an effective bond between the communities of South and South-East Asia. It is within this wider cultural sphere that the Buddhist monuments and sacred relics of the region need to be studied.

NOTES

* Research on the topic was made possible by the award of a Senior Visiting Fellowship by the International Institute for Asian Studies, Leiden. I am grateful to the Director, Prof. W. Stokhof for the opportunity and to the staff of IIAS for their generous support. This paper forms a part of the author's larger study under publication, titled 'Ethnohistory of the Boat: Early Maritime Communities of the Indian Ocean.'

1 It was at this time that Raffles sent an engineer, H.G. Cornelius to clear the monument of growth and to make plans of the structure. Though the drawings of the monument were published in 1873 in Leiden by C. Leemans, the photographic archive was made between 1907 and 1911 by Th. van Erp and published in three volumes of plates and two volumes of texts. N.J. Krom's text volume appeared in Dutch in 1920 and in a separate English version in 1927, while Van Erp's study on the architecture of the monument was published subsequently in 1931.

2 The total number of reliefs dedicated to the various texts is:
Lalitavistara (Ia): 120 reliefs
Jatakamala, jatakas and avadanas (Ib, Iba-b, IIB): 720 reliefs
Gandavyuha (II-III-IIIB-IVB): 388 reliefs
Bhadracari (IV): 72 reliefs

3 Similarly contentious is the multivalency theory propounded by Dehejia in which she proposes 'the need to recognize, accept, and even admire the multiplicity of meanings apparent in early Buddhist sculpture and painting' (1991:45). In contrast, Huntington (1992:114) maintains that it cannot be presumed that the same motif (or 'emblem') conveyed 'the same meanings throughout its history and in all of its usages. New layers of meanings may have been added over the course of centuries.' I am grateful to Prof. Karel van Kooij for this reference.

REFERENCES

Bernet Kempers, A.J. (1976) *Ageless Borobudur*. Wassenaar: Servire.

Bird, J. (1841) 'Opening of the Caves at Kanheri near Bombay and the relics found in them,' *Journal of the Asiatic Society of Bengal* 10, pp. 94-7.

Cleary, T. (1993) *The Flower Ornament Scripture*. Boston/London: Shambhala.

Coedes, G. (1968) *The Indianized States of Southeast Asia*. Honolulu: East-West Center Press.

Coleman, S. and J. Elsner (1995) *Pilgrimage: Past and Present*. British Museum Press.

Cowell, E.B. and R.A. Neil (1886) *The Divyavadana*. Cambridge University Press.

Cunningham, A. (1892) *Mahabodhi or the Great Buddhist Temple Under the Bodhi Tree an Buddha Gaya*. London: Allan.

Danielou, A. (1993a) *The Shilappadikaram*. Penguin Books.

--(1993b) *Manimekhalai*. Penguin Books.

De Casparis, J.G. (1956) *Selected Inscriptions from the 7th to the 9th century A.D.*. Bandung: Masa Baru.

--(1975) *Indonesian Palaeography*. Leiden: E.J. Brill.

--(1981) 'The Dual Nature of Barabudur,' in: L. Gomez and H.W. Woodward (eds) *Barabudur: History and Significance of a Buddhist Monument*. Berkeley Buddhist Studies Series, pp. 47-84.

Dehejia, V. (1997) *Discourse in Early Buddhist Art: Visual Narratives of India*. New Delhi: Munshiram Manoharlal Publishers.

Eade, J. and S. Sallnow (1991) *Contesting the Sacred: Anthropology of Christian Pilgrimage*. London: Routledge.

Elliot, Sir Walter (1878) 'The Edifice formerly known as the Chinese or Jaina Pagoda at Negapatam,' *Indian Antiquary* 7, pp. 224-7.

Fontein, J. (1967) *The Pilgrimage of Sudhana*. The Hague-Paris.

Ghosh, A. and H. Sarkar (1964-5) 'Beginnings of sculptural art in Southeast India: a stele from Amaravati,' *Ancient India* 20 & 21, pp. 168-77

Goitein, S.D. (1967) *A Mediterranean Society*, 1. University of California Press.

Gokhale, S. (1991) *Kanheri Inscriptions*. Pune.

Gomez, L. and H.W. Woodward (eds) (1981) *Barabudur: History and Significance of a Buddhist Monument*. Berkeley Buddhist Studies Series.

Huntington, J.C. (1987) Pilgrimage as Image: The Cult of the Astamahapratiharya, *Orientations* 18,4, April, pp. 55-63.

Huntington, Susan L. (1992) 'Aniconism and the Multivalence of Emblems: Another Look,' *Ars Orientalis* 22, pp. 111-56.

Huntington, Susan L. and John C. Huntington (1990) *Leaves from the Bodhi Tree*. Seattle and London: Dayton Art Institute.

Klokke, Marijke, J. (1996) 'Borobudur: A Mandala?,' in: P. van der Velde (ed.) *IIAS Yearbook 1995*. Leiden: IIAS, pp. 191-219.

Knox, J.R. (1992) *Amaravati: Buddhist Sculpture from the Great Stupa*. London: British Museum Press.

Lawson, S. (1988) 'Votive Objects from Bodhgaya,' in: J. Leoshko (ed.) *Bodhgaya: the site of enlightenment*. Bombay: Marg Publications.

Leese, Marilyn E. (1983) *The Traikutaka Dynasty and Kanheri's Second Phase of Buddhist Cave Excavation*. PhD Dissertation, University of Michigan.

Leoshko, J. (1995) 'Pilgrimage and the evidence of Bodhgaya's images,' in: K.R. van Kooij and H. van der Veere (eds) *Function and Meaning in Buddhist Art*. Groningen: Egbert Forsten, pp. 45-58.

Levi, S. (1919-20) 'King Subhakara of Orissa,' *Epigraphia Indica* 15, pp. 363-4.

Lohuizen-de Leeuw, J.E. van (1980) 'The stupa in Indonesia,' in: A.L. Dallapicola (ed.) *The Stupa - Its Religious, Historical and Architectural Significance*. Wiesbaden, pp. 277-300.

Mitra, D. (1980) *Buddhist Monuments*. Calcutta: Sahitya Samsad

--(1981) *Ratnagiri (1958-61)*. Memoirs of the Archaeological Survey of India 80(1), New Delhi.

--(1983) *Ratnagiri (1958-61)*. Memoirs of the Archaeological Survey of India 80(2), New Delhi.

Obeyesekere, G. (1995) 'Buddhism, Nationhood, and Cultural Identity: A Question of Fundamentals,' in: M.E. Marty and R.S. Appleby (eds) *Fundamentalisms Comprehended*. Chicago: University of Chicago Press, pp. 231-56.

Paranavitana, S. (1944) 'Negapatam and Theravada Buddhism in South India,' *Journal of the Greater India Society* XI, pp. 17-25.

--(1960) *History of Ceylon*. Colombo: University of Ceylon Press.

Ramachandran, T.N. (1954) 'The Nagapattinam and other Buddhist Bronzes in the Madras Museum,' *Bulletin of the Madras Museum* 7(1).

Rao, S.R. (1971) 'Excavations at Kanheri (1969),' in: S. Ritti and B.R. Gopal (eds) *Studies in Indian History and Culture*. Dharwad: Karnatak University, pp. 43-6.

Ray, H.P. (1994) *The Winds of Change: Buddhism and the Maritime Links of Early South Asia*. Oxford: Oxford University Press.

Rhys Davids, T. W. (trs.) (1881) *Mahaparinibbana Suttanta*. Oxford.

Salomon, R. (1990) 'Indian Tirthas in Southeast Asia,' in: H. Bakker (ed.) *The History of Sacred Places in India as Reflected in Traditional Literature*. Leiden: E.J. Brill, pp. 160-76.

Schopen, G. (1988-9) 'On Monks, Nuns and "Vulgar" Practices,' *Artibus Asiae* 49, pp. 153-68.

Sivaramamurti, C. (1961) *Le Stupa du Barabudur*. Paris: Presses Universitaires de France.

Soundara Rajan, K.V. (1994) *Kaveripattinam Excavations 1963-1973*. Archaeological Survey of India.

Stutterheim, W.F. (1934) 'A Newly Discovered pre-Nagari Inscription on Bali,' *Acta Orientalia* XII, pp. 126-32.

Watters, T. (1904-5) *On Yuan Chwang's Travels in India*. London: Royal Asiatic Society.

West, E.W. (1861) Copies of Inscriptions from the Buddhist Cave Temples at Kanheri, *Journal of the Bombay Branch of the Royal Asiatic Society* 6, pp. 1-14, 116-20.

CHAPTER 7

SCIENTIFIC FORESTRY: HISTORY, BOUNDARY
MAKING, AND POWER IN MALAYSIA[1]

FADZILAH MAJID COOKE

The major concern of this paper is to situate scientific forestry (the technical term for which is sustained yield management) as it is practised in Malaysia, within a historical context. In the contemporary period, scientific forestry (sometimes referred to as colonial forestry) has been criticized for the narrowness of its scope. Contemporary criticisms of sustained yield[2] management practices in Malaysia in many ways reflect a more generalized discontent with scientific forestry in the rest of the world. Since the contemporary critique of sustained yield management has been dealt with in more detail elsewhere,[3] a brief mention should suffice for the purpose of this paper. In a nutshell, debates about scientific forestry have centred on sustained yield practices, specifically the way they have privileged industrial production over subsistence and local use (Westoby, 1989); the manner in which the well-being of forests is treated as separate from (if not less deserving than) that of forest dwellers (United States Congressional Staff Study Mission to Malaysia, 1989); and the way complex tropical forests are regarded as resilient in the long term (Keto, Scott, and Olsen, 1990), (so that logging could proceed if the proper techniques were applied).

What is often overlooked in these criticisms is that most of the problems faced by contemporary forestry have been inherited from processes embedded in colonial forestry. Indubitably, some aspects of that inheritance have been appropriated and recuperated for purposes of national 'development' under post-colonial conditions. Only by going back into history has it been possible for us to analyse what processes and practices have been deleted, embellished, or remained the same.

The focus of this paper is on the institutionalization of sustained yield technology in Sarawak under the Brooke regime in 1919 to the colonial period, and in colonial Malaya up to the Second World War. Sarawak colonial forestry has a different history from that of peninsular Malaya. The decision to transpose similarities in approaches (to management of forest products, to shifting cultivation) onto different economic and political conditions therefore seemed remarkable. Pre-World War II conditions (the first forty years of colonial forestry) in Malaya are important for examining the institutionalization of scientific forestry given the context of demands for the opening up forests for large-scale plantation development and mining for tin. These were years when scientific forestry practices were contested. In contrast, sustained yield forestry in Sarawak did not have to contend with powerful state development goals, yet its practices were equally contested at least in the first thirty years of its formation. For Sarawak, the colonial period marked the beginning of rational planning in the Weberian sense and provides an excellent contrast for tracing the different ways in which certain issues (such as shifting cultivation) were treated.

During the nineteenth century, scientific forestry management practices in the colonies were associated with notions of 'progress,' industrial development, and the propagation of scientific knowledge. Scientific forestry had its beginnings in experiences originating in the nineteenth century forest management systems established in France and Germany and in the colonial sphere gained ascendance in Burma, India and from there passed on to Southeast Asia (Guha, 1989; Peluso, 1992; Bryant, 1997). Once established, the basic system of relations between key variables of the state, capital, technology, and certain institutions laid down by colonial forestry embraced a series of changes with the incorporation of new variables and new forms of operation and so forth. Moreover, specificities of history (of colonial trade, bureaucratic politics) and the biological characteristics of forests would affect the timing and implementation of certain management techniques, or the extent of the effectiveness of management systems in any one country. Despite all this, some fundamentals of that management system have remained more or less intact.

Three elements in scientific forestry that have remained constant are of concern to us here, namely: that 1) the state has the right to manage forests and sell their products; 2) industrial production (especially for export) takes priority over subsistence use such as shifting cultivation; and 3) swiddening or shifting cultivation is destructive. These elements are of concern because they illustrate our point that sustained yield discourse not only makes visible the physical conditions of forests, but in its professional practices incorporates judgements about social conditions, rights and needs under the umbrella of 'proper' or 'rational' use of forest resources. Given that there are other forms of management systems (such as 'indigenous ones,' of which swiddening is part), the institutionalization of scientific forestry practices in colonial situations was contested. In other words, resistance is not new to sustained yield management in many parts of the world in different historical periods (Guha, 1989; Peluso, 1992; Bryant, 1997).

FADZILAH MAJID COOKE

THE INSTITUTIONALIZATION OF SCIENTIFIC FORESTRY

Colonial Malaya in 1901 and Sarawak in 1919 were both endowed with scientific forestry with the establishment of Forestry Departments. Although formed under different historical (social, bureaucratic) conditions and confronted with differing forest types as well, both Departments shared the experiences of foresters trained in Europe, especially in Germany, at the Oxford Forestry School and at Dehra Dun in India, and in management practices implemented in the teak forests of Burma and Java in the 1850s (Kumar, 1986:67; editorial, Empire Forestry Journal, 1940:3).

Malaya's forest has a long history in Southeast Asia dating back to its important role of the trade in forest products during the Srivijaya period from the seventh to the eleventh centuries, in the Malacca period at the beginning of the fifteenth century, right through to the period of European intervention from the sixteenth to the nineteenth centuries (Dunn, 1975; Couillard, 1984). During these centuries product demands varied, but the much sought-after 'jungle products' included rattan, benzoin, camphor, sandalwood, bamboo and, in the nineteenth century especially *damar*, *jelutong*, and *gutta* (these three products will be discussed in more detail later). The central suppliers of forest products were the indigenous populations of Orang Asli and to some extent, Malays. The traders and middlemen varied over the centuries but included Malays, Chinese, Arabs, Indians and Europeans. During the Malacca period, before Islam had spread beyond the ruling elite and when their social links with Malay groups were relatively close (for example through marriage), Couillard (1984:98) suspects that there were Orang Asli middlemen who became rich through trade. So central were the Orang Asli that Dunn notes:

> In their absence (and in the absence of their counterparts in the forests of Sumatra, Borneo and elsewhere) there would have been no primary suppliers of forest products for a trade of ancient importance in the insular Southeast Asian area (1975:108).

Forest products were exchanged for imported goods which have now become part of much valued heirlooms (*pusaka*) including bronze-ware, ceramics, glass beads, textiles, and large jars in particular. In Sarawak, the Dayak of the interior featured prominently in the China trade (Chin, 1988; Lian, 1988).

In short, by the early nineteenth century there was a well-established network of suppliers and traders engaged in the trade of forest products. The trade was controlled by Southeast Asians where indigenous groups played a central role (Couillard, 1984).

SCIENTIFIC FORESTRY: HISTORY, BOUNDARY MAKING, AND POWER IN MALAYSIA

In contrast, colonial forest history in Malaya is of recent date, beginning in the nineteenth century. The then Malayan Forestry Service was heir to the Indian Forest Service; the first Malayan forest administrators were trained in that service (which included Burma). Its formation approximately eighty years after British first contact with the Malay Peninsula imbibed features that reflected the characteristics of fragmentation and ambivalence of the early British involvement in the country.[4] Thus the Malayan Forest Department was not a single department but consisted of many departments representing a merger between individual departments already established in the late 1890s in the Federated Malay States (Negri Sembilan, Pahang, Perak, and Selangor), and the earlier colonies known as the Straits Settlements (the Dindings located in the Perak coast, Penang or Pulau Pinang, Province Wellesley or Seberang Perai, Singapore, and Melaka). The Forest Departments of the Unfederated Malay States came into being at different stages in the first third of the twentieth century, namely: Johor and Kedah in 1920 and 1921, Kelantan and Trengganu in 1934 and 1936, and Perlis in 1946 (Wyatt-Smith, 1961:37). Given the terms of the agreement with Malay rulers at the onset of colonization which culminated in British residents and advisers being involved in indirect rule in the different states (which meant running all aspects of political and economic life of the country), land administration became an important basis for launching inroads into state (local) power (Emerson, 1979). As land became the basis for local power of British Residents and Advisers, forestry, like all other departments, had to comply with their decisions. This meant that in the states and at the local level, District Officers had power over land. The natural consequence was the subordination of forestry officers to land administration officers, especially District Officers (this point is dealt with in more detail later).[5] It is important to recall these features because these inherited characteristics marking the formation of forestry administration have remained an important factor in post-colonial practices.

The first Director of the Forest Department of Malaya, Burns-Murdoch, brought with him several years experience in Burma. Malayan legislation introduced by Burns-Murdoch was based on the Burma Forest Act and incorporated modifications to suit local needs (Troup, 1940:378; Watson, 1950:65). Mead, the first Conservator of Forests for Sarawak, had acquired some previous experience in Malaya (Flint and Richards, 1992:96) and returned to serve in Malaya upon completion of his years in Sarawak (Smythies, 1963:238). His career spanned service in Malaya, the Sudan, and Sarawak, with a short stint in Fiji (Cubitt, 1940:264-8).

According to Troup (1940:380-1), procedures for creating forest reserves were in place in Malaya by 1935. They were modelled on those which were in use in Burmese forests. Historically Sarawak reservation procedures were based on those of Malaya (Troup, 1940:393). What follows is the story of forest reserve creation in Malaya and Sarawak in the wake of the establishment of the various forest departments examining the social and political significance the process.

THE CONTESTED TERRAIN OF MAPS, SURVEYS, AND FOREST RESERVES[6]

Colonial forestry literature treats the creation of forest reserves as nothing more than the mechanical mapping of forest boundaries and territories into different forest types and categories, followed by specific procedures leading to announcements about their constitution being made in government Gazettes. Such technicalities occupied a prominent place and were well outlined in the manual written for foresters by E.C. Troup in 1940, entitled *Colonial Forest Administration.* Citing the example of Malaya, Troup described the procedure for reserving forests:

> 1) When it is proposed to constitute any land a reserved forest, the Resident publishes in the official Gazette a notification stating this fact and specifying the situation and extent of the land.
> 2) The District Officer then publishes locally a proclamation in English, Malay ... giving particulars of the Gazette notification ...
> 3) The District Officer conducts an enquiry into any objections and existing privileges, whether claimed or not, and considers any opinions expressed by the Deputy State Forest Officer ... Land within the proposed reserve may be acquired under the Land Acquisition Enactment, 1922.
> 4) After completion of the enquiry and the passing of all necessary orders the Resident, with the approval of the State Council, may publish in the Gazette a notification declaring the land specified to be a reserved forest ...
> 5) During the course of forest settlement proceedings, the Resident may at any time withdraw a proposal to constitute any land a reserved forest (1940:380-1).

Once categories (protection, commercial, domestic, and amenity) and boundaries have been arrived at, forests could be managed according to working plans.

> In a working plan, it is usual to lay down the general lines of treatment for a long period, ... and to prescribe detailed operations for a shorter

period, say 10 to 20 years ahead, at the end of which time the plan is revised. The area is divided into convenient units of working and a detailed description is made of the locality and growing stock, usually accompanied by an estimate of the latter based on enumerations ... the working plan then prescribes in systematic form the quantity of timber to be cut or the area to be felled each year or period, and the manner in which regeneration, tending, and other operations are to be carried out... A decision as to whether or not a working plan is justified will often depend on the result of a reconnaissance survey ... carried out with the object of ascertaining the composition of the forest and the quantity of timber available for extraction ... This work of stock-taking, ... may be regarded as one of the most important preliminaries to the introduction of organised forest working in the Colonies. (Troup, 1940:164-7)

Not much political underpinnings can be imputed to such practical attempts as categorizing forests involving such techniques as boundary mapping and reconnaissance surveys. Nevertheless, research on the history of mapping suggests that maps (as well as an array of seemingly innocuous new techniques such as censuses) contributed, as much as superior military force, to the colonial state's capacity to develop a profile of resources and peoples under its formal jurisdiction (Harley, 1992; Wood, 1992; Bryant, 1997). According to this view, maps exert a social influence through their omissions just as much as by the features they depict and emphasize. In colonial forestry, the contention is that maps were techniques of political control utilized to promote inclusion (through the legal and spatial definition of 'reserved forests') and exclusion (of popular access and local non-commercial production) (Bryant, 1997:16).

An examination of sustained yield forestry practices in colonial Malaya and Sarawak during the first half of the twentieth century suggests that a qualifier is much needed. Maps and boundaries, established initially by reconnaissance surveys and later, aerial photography, of themselves were only partial contributors because the kinds of information provided by these technologies was either patchy or fairly token. They provided minimal information (for example about general forest types) but they were useful in their time because they provided important groundwork for establishing boundaries of forest classes. Admittedly, once surveys and reconnaissances had been made procedures for the constitution of forest reserves could commence, but these technologies could not provide the detailed categorization and information required for 'scientific' management of specific patches (Majid Cooke, 1995). It is probably for this reason, reinforced by the foresters' unfamiliarity with the detailed characteristics of the forests themselves (Oliphant, 1934:49-50), that it took approximately thirty years or more of silvicultural experimentation before the Forest Department in Malaya was able to arrive at ways of creating an even-aged forest suitable for intensive timber production, and to come up with appropriate management technologies.

So, although important in the exercise of power, maps and techniques were an inadequate means of exercising control. What is often overlooked in the debate about power, mapping and boundaries is the importance of discourse.[7] Scientific forestry discourse, allied with specific management practices, legitimizes certain types of use and particular sets of rights above others in the context of specific socio-historical relations. Scientific forestry discourse in Malaya during the colonial period, and in Sarawak from the 1919 onwards, suggested that local practices (of shifting cultivation especially) were inferior and that the standards of measure for trade, production, and even for forest vegetation itself should be British.

These processes, although not sounding the death knell of the very active trade in forest products that had taken place in Southeast Asia, of which Malaya and Sarawak were very much part, meant that it was considered fairly unimportant and forest products relegated to the realm of 'minor.' By contrast, prior to the twentieth century, timber was an important product, but it formed only one of the array of products exported from Malaya (Dunn, 1975). Referring to this Dunn (1975:87) reminds us that "the major forest products of today have become 'major' only in the present century". With colonization, the nature and direction of trade changed, and hand in hand with this came the increasing use of synthetics so that the world demand for the so-called minor forest products shrank.

Not all forest products were exported and indeed the production of timber in colonial Malaya was largely meant for the internal market, especially for the provision of railway sleepers and for use as fuel in tin smelting (Flint and Richards, 1992:95-8). Nor indeed was there a large demand for Malayan timbers (Oliphant, 1934:56; 1937:36) and the unfamiliarity of foresters with the very diverse range of species available from its forests hindered any such development (Oliphant, 1934:49-50). The most highly prized market was the European one, which included that of North America (Oliphant, 1937:30). These were exacting markets demanding superfine quality timbers of a limited number of hardwood species. Although Malayan forests were well endowed with hardwoods, especially *chengal* (Balanocarpus spp.) and *balau* shoreas, they were not the hardwoods with which the European markets were familiar. Bereft of these narrow categories of desirable timbers, the forests of Malaya, up until WWII at least, were 'saved' from being exported.

The conditions that discouraged export prior to WWII, nevertheless failed to dampen enthusiasm for possible future export, for the time when Malayan timber would finally find a niche in the British market. To go 'local' had to be explained as a temporary measure; while the small demand from the local market relative to the expenses necessary to promote increased productivity, had to be properly justified. Today such justifications provide useful insights into fantasies nurtured about the 'white man's burden' in the colonies, about the role of the state and 'expert knowledge.'

The idea that mapping (and therefore classifying) forests may in fact have been a technique for exercising power, may be particularly unacceptable to foresters in government employ in the early twentieth century, who had to struggle constantly against an entrenched colonial attitude (which originated in late nineteenth century Malaya) that forests were valueless unless converted into something more productive such as agricultural plantations or (especially tin-)mines (Lim Teck Ghee, 1976:23). In 1891, a governor of the Straits Settlements and Protected Native States wrote:

> The great objective of government should be to get land taken up on almost any terms, for agriculture alone will bring about a settled thriving population. (Governor Cecil Clementi Smith, 1981 cited in Lim Teck Ghee, 1976:ix)

This particular perspective regarding the link between colonial development, well-being, and agriculture remained entrenched until roughly the 1930s. This view was in fact strengthened by the discovery of the wealth that rubber (Hevea brasiliensis) could bring to the colony. During this period, forests were opened up for rubber plantations without much heed being given to planning (Forest Research Institute of Malaya, 1959). Under such conditions, it could be assumed that colonial forest managers would have to struggle hard to keep any forest patch at all. Generally speaking reserved forests were regarded as forests 'locked up,' away from productive use (especially for mining and agriculture). Perhaps it is within this context that arguments about the potential of forests to contribute to the wealth of exports to Britain should be evaluated. Such arguments managed to pick up occasional support from the government, which was the case in 1929 when the Chief Secretary to the Government lent it his weight. Such support was actually a reflection of the concern about a possible timber shortage in England at the time, caused by the eventuality of dwindling supplies from its other colonies (Annual Report, Forest Department, Federated Malay States, 1929). By the late 1930s approximately 27 per cent of the land area of the Federated Malay States was designated forest reserves (Watson, 1939:148).

Generally speaking though, for as long as demand for hardwood in Britain before WWII was met from traditional sources such as from Africa, the case for managing forests for the local markets (with its financial and manpower implications) was hard to justify. Justification could be strengthened, up to a point, by moral arguments. This was clearly evident in much of the scientific forestry literature of the pre-WWII period and was most succinctly expressed in Oliphant (1937). In using these arguments, scientific forestry was engaging in implicit categorization of superiority and inferiority of cultures and needs.

The inhabitants of Malaya, according to Oliphant (1937:29), by virtue of their limited understanding of the protective value of forests could nevertheless be taught how to use them more fully. According to Oliphant, (1937:30-6), just as foresters could improve the primeval state of tropical forests by timber stocking, forest engineers, by their training, were capable of improving local sawmilling practices. Local sawmillers had the right attitude, he argued, but they needed engineering and governmental support (in the form of loans). Expenses incurred in strengthening the local sawmilling industry he felt would go a long way towards increasing the 'native' standard of housing. Profits kept in the country (rather than if sawmilling were conducted by multi-nationals) would create local employment and, ultimately, promote a higher standard of living. More importantly, localized production would ultimately expedite the process of converting forest to a quality required for export because production will be based on exploitation of forests yielding 'lower grade' timber scattered all over the country, for the time being sparing forests containing high quality hardwoods needed for the export market. So, in a long-winded way, improvement in the domestic market was justified because it was a stepping stone to the more important aim of production for the export market. Without access to Oliphant's inner thoughts, it would be difficult to gauge whether these arguments were clever bureaucratic ones designed to attract government support. However, one of the reasons given for the 'lack of development' in the production of high quality timber in Malaya, was 'the health factor, which makes technical supervision by experts from temperate climates difficult and costly' (Oliphant, 1937:30). Native use in the form of house-posts, rafters and other domestic usage he claimed, required only low quality unwrought wood, a higher standard of comfort and amenity not traditionally being 'the lot' of the native (Oliphant, 1937:30).[8]

Throughout this period the whole forestry enterprise was guided or reinforced by institutions in England, which were relied on for trained officers (from the Imperial Forestry Institute - IFI), for confirmation and verification of sample analysis of tree and vegetation species by the IFI, for testing timbers using methods recommended by the British Standards

Association, and for applying standards in conformity with those adopted by Princes Risborough and the forestry schools at Dehra Dun, Madison and elsewhere (Watson, 1934:224-30). The standard of measure therefore was the British one and this standard was extended to views about the actual forests themselves. Not endowed with the exact hardwood species that markets in Britain demanded, the complex Malayan forests were said to contain largely defective standing timber (Oliphant, 1937:35).[9]

In Sarawak, the Forestry Department's early attempts to create forest reserves was resisted by native peoples whose customary access to land would have been infringed upon were these to go ahead. In the 1920s and 1930s particularly, the Department will have encountered problems of funding shortage due to the Depression. Furthermore, overall the Forest Department would have to live with the effects of the general ambivalence shown by the Brooke governments in the area of native welfare. Needing native (especially Iban) support to uphold the very basis of its legitimacy (in the early years of the regime, most up-river Iban were opposed to the Brookes), successive regimes were accused of having exercised a form of paternalism in the area of native affairs. The conventional view among scholars is that the Brookes were averse to opening up Sarawak to foreign investment in order to maintain their domain in the tradition of British idealism (but see Kaur, 1995). To counter this it should be remembered that the Brookes had to shoulder the exacting demands of maintaining the regimes' economic viability without enjoying the advantages of Colonial Office support which Sarawak would have had had it been a colony (Reece, 1993). Without going into too much detail, the land regulations of the nineteenth century marked the beginnings of the erosion of native control over land (Kaur, 1998). By declaring all land to be state land, the nineteenth and twentieth century Land Codes enabled the state to grant lands to a few individuals and foreign companies for the purposes of establishing rubber plantations, or for logging or mining. Admittedly, in terms of area, the amount of land awarded to business concerns was small compared to that opened for plantation and mining in Malaya.

Similarly, exploration and demarcation of forests began after the gazettement of the Forest Reservation Order was passed in 1920. Constituting forest reserves began subsequent to the adoption of the 1924 Forest Ordinance. In these reserves 'Ibans were not allowed to farm, hunt and collect jungle produce' (Reece, 1993:56), without a licence. Given the Brooke administrations' overall attempt to curtail shifting cultivation (considered an unproductive and destructive activity), forestry control measures can therefore be viewed as part of an overall strategy of the exercise of power. However, in the absence of adequate enforcement staff, leading to insufficient mapping of forest boundaries, the exercise of power by domination could not have been altogether effective. It is in this context that the shrill rhetoric raised against shifting cultivators ought to be evaluated, namely, as an expression firstly of a lack of control and secondly of an attempt to garner more resources from government to support departmental projects.[10] Quite apart from this, antagonism towards shifting cultivation was buried in the traditions of colonial forestry at large, which incontrovertibly viewed this form of economic activity as 'unscientific' and destructive.[11]

Constituting forests into reserves followed certain strict procedures. As noted by Troup (1940:380-381), the gazettement procedures in Malaya (upon which the Sarawak procedures were based) were lengthy. More importantly, the procedures themselves suggested that real administrative power was in the hands of the land administrators, so that the requirement of examining complaints and appeals (should there be any) prior to the constitution of reserves was met by the land administration bureaucracy (specifically, District Officers), with the State Forest Officer acting in an advisory capacity.

The power hierarchy of administration in Sarawak involved the District Officer, the Resident and ultimately, the Chief Secretary. The Forest Department's role was again confined to one of protection. Objections to forest reservation were raised as often as those directed at Forest Departments in Malaya. The Sarawak Forest Department's Annual Report of 1938 (cited in Mead, 1938:323) included a response from a Senior Forest Officer to the accusation of 'land grabbing' by the Department and criticisms regarding the long delays surrounding the final constitution of the Melana protected forest in the Baram District:

> Responsibility for the delay does not lie with this department and the misunderstanding which caused it would have been avoided by a better understanding of the forest law. In this connection it does not seem to be sufficiently widely known that the Forest Department cannot constitute an area until all claimants to rights have had an opportunity of putting their case before the District Officer and that there is a further right of appeal to the resident if there is dissatisfaction with his ruling. It must be obvious, therefore, that there can be no high-handed land-grabbing ...

In the 1930s in Malaya, the ultimate power (to declare or rescind) reserves lay with the Residents in the Federated Malay States, the Governor in Council in the Straits Settlements, the State Secretary in Johor, and the State Council in Kedah (Troup, 1940:381). In other words, land was (and still is)[12] a state issue and is subject to local relations of power. At the local level,

District Officers' status and prestige were linked with land and its administration (Kumar, 1986:66); the Forest Department's role was mainly protective (Ashton, 1988:194). Malayan Forest Department Annual Reports of the period were full of records of excisions from forest reserves for agricultural and mining purposes.

Forest gazettement required considerable investment in detailed mapping and manpower. Being dependent on budget allocations which themselves varied enormously in concert with overall economic conditions and given the perception that reserved forests were not 'productive,' the required investment was often inadequate or in difficult times, simply not forthcoming. Mapping was made even more difficult because the instruments used were at best primitive. Trained staff who could undertake the mapping were often not available or fell far short of the required numbers (Menon, 1969:3). Progress was therefore slow. Poor survey capacity meant that boundaries were vague. In Sarawak, twenty years after the formation of the Department, only 4 per cent of the total land area was gazetted under forest reserves (Annual Report, Sarawak Forest Department, 1939).

Most indigenous inhabitants of the interior of Sarawak ignored the rules. In the 1920s, Sarawak Forest Departments Annual Reports contained many accounts of 'friction with the native population.' Continued antagonism from foot-dragging, avoidance of forestry rules, up to open rebellion, would have posed obstacles against the strict enforcement of forestry regulations. A good example of which was the protest movement led by the Iban leader Asun which lasted several years from 1929 (Reece, 1993:56) (to be discussed in more detail later). The problems must have been exacerbated by the administrative directive to stop the creation of further reserves in 1932 (Smythies, 1963:233). Nowhere was avoidance of Forest Department's rules more clearly marked than in the area of control over trade in forest products, especially *gutta percha* (Palaquium gutta) in Malaya and *jelutong* (Dyera costulata) in Sarawak.

THE STRUGGLE OVER FOREST PRODUCTS

Gutta percha and *jelutong* were two of a range of forest products that had been traded in Southeast Asia for centuries (Couillard, 1984; Dunn, 1974). The trade relied on a network of indigenous, usually inland, producers and middlemen linked by different forms of dependency relations, a relationship that was perceived to have become burdensome to the producers with the onset of colonization. In nineteenth century Malaya, for example, Orang Asli producers became dispensable to the Malay and Chinese middlemen, as colonization attracted other migrants (from Sumatra, Java and other parts of Indonesia - the 'foreign Malays') who became involved in the trade. By the early twentieth century Malay middlemen had largely been replaced by their Chinese counterparts. In nineteenth century Sarawak, Dayak collectors were the main suppliers of *gutta* to Chinese middlemen (Roff, 1968:242).

In the second half of the nineteenth century there was a boom in *gutta percha* because of rapid expansion of submarine telegraphy. Being one of the best known non-conductors of both heat and electricity at the time, *gutta* was used in the coating of submarine cables. But in the early twentieth century it was also used in electrical, surgical, and dental work, and in the manufacture of golf balls (Fyfe, 1949:26). In 1919 the price of *gutta* was at its highest for decades. Understandably, therefore, at no stage in the late nineteenth or early twentieth centuries were control regulations heeded by either collectors or traders. Controlled tapping methods introduced by the department made little impact on tappers.[13]

In 1900 *gutta percha* was an important export product for Malaya and provided a steady income for the state up until the 1920s (Watson and Cubitt, 1928:406). Possibly because of the tendency to emphasize the importance of timber in scientific forestry, the management of *gutta percha* was contested only from within the Department. This became clear in 1928 when forest officers wrote:

> The jungle produce enthusiast has probably done more to foster the spirit of distrust and antagonism than his opposite, who cannot be bothered with jungle produce, and frankly says so. Generally speaking, the tendency of Forest Department has been to try to work up a commercial interest in jungle produce without having made reasonably sure that it can be produced on a commercial scale. (Watson and Cubitt, 1928:408).

Broadly speaking, what Watson and Cubit were trying to do in their paper was venture a kind of apologia for the lack of commercial success experienced by the Department in marketing *gutta percha*. But the subtext was bureaucratic politics - namely the existence of contending views on the viability or otherwise of according resources (in terms of energy, time and finance) to a commodity that, in scientific forestry, has been relegated to the realm of 'minor forest products.'

In Sarawak, the position of the Forest Department in the hierarchy of power structure within government during the Brooke period was such that its decisions could be easily overturned, should the occasion required it. This was reflected in the area of managing *jelutong* (produced by large forest trees Dyera costulata, Dyera lowii, and Dyera boreensis). The latex from this tree was an important source of cash for native collectors. In the early twentieth century demand rose because *jelutong* was used in the manufacture of chewing gum. During 1923, 3,500 tons were exported (Mead, 1925:97). Because from the time of its establishment, Sarawak Forest Department's budget depended on direct revenue collection (as opposed to annual government estimates in Malaya) (Annual Report, Forest Department Sarawak, 1939 cited in Empire Forestry Journal, 1941:118; Troup, 1940:377), various attempts were made to control the trade and production of forest products. In trade, in view of the system established in Sarawak of charging royalties on forest produce exported (as opposed to those used within the country), the Department made several attempts to change the system. However, its efforts achieved little success. In its 1937 Annual Report, the Sarawak Forest Department expressed regret that despite repeated attempts it has been unsuccessful in exacting royalties on the 'minor forest products' used within the country (Mead, 1938:324).

Production procedures used to obtain *jelutong* in the 1920s and 1930s were considered destructive. The tapping of trees to extract latex, according to the Department, was carried out haphazardly. This form of tapping latex restricted the potential for the long-term survival of the revenue-generating trees. As part of management efforts, the Department formulated ways of tapping trees that were considered less harmful to their long-term survival, experimented with silviculture, and encouraged large-scale plantation production. (Similar rules were introduced in Malaya). Restrictions on extracting latex were met with hostility by native collectors so that the minimum girth limit prescribed for trees suitable for tapping was often disregarded (Annual Report, Forest Department Sarawak, 1932). Moreover, the Department's exhortation to protect *jelutong* and other forest products went unheeded by the Sarawak government (Mead, 1938:324). In 1931 the Department's '*Jelutong* Improvement Scheme' was abandoned when the officer appointed to head the project was retrenched because of budgetary cutbacks (Annual Report, Forest Department Sarawak, 1932). This decision was obviously amended some time later, because in 1939 the Forest Department reported that silvicultural treatment of *jelutong* 'continued' in the Setapok Forest Reserve near Kuching (Annual Report, Forest Department Sarawak, 1939).

The discussion above could easily provide support for the view that state ownership of forests does not necessarily mean effective control. Rangan (1997:74) suggests that the degree of control the state has over state-owned (as opposed to privately owned) forest resources does not result in automatic exclusion of common people (as claimed by populist critics of the state). According to Rangan (1997), the amount of control needs to be examined in the light of particular political and economic situations. An examination of forestry departments' practices in the first third of the twentieth century in Malaya and Sarawak certainly suggests that state ownership of forests does not imply total control. Policy practices were often contested by those upon whom technological control was exercised.

Native shifting cultivators negotiated forestry rules and often had an impact on policy. One example was the Asun rebellion in 1929. Already burdened by increased control through the tightening up of tax and fee collection (door tax, gun registration fees) and restricted from relatively free migration upriver for purposes of shifting cultivation or flight from war or disease, the added restrictions resulting from the imposition of forestry rules became too much to bear. Forestry rules curbed access rights to forests which led Asun and his followers to mount a rebellion. This uprising was not a nationalist or anti-Brooke movement, but was directed against specific Brooke officials (Reece, 1993:56), and it was an effective one. In the aftermath of this rebellion, in 1932, the effort to constitute forest reserves was frozen by government directive (see footnote 10). Another attempt at appeasing native discontent was the adoption of the 1934 legislation which paved the way for the constitution of 'protected' forests. The intention of that legislation was 'to protect a forest (sic) with the least inconvenience to the local inhabitants' (Annual Report, Forest Department Sarawak, 1934). In 'protected' forests, although shifting cultivation and commercial logging were prohibited, the 'taking of small quantities of forest produce for domestic use' was allowed.

In the extraction of *jelutong*, swidden farmers' actions affected management techniques in the 1920s and 1930s by the ignoring of rules or by outbursts of periodic agitation. The significance of such contestation can be glimpsed below:

> A girth limit of 6 feet for tapping in unreserved forests was originally introduced in 1920, the Conservator ... having complete control in reserves. Owing to agitation by native tappers, the girth limit was lowered to 4 1/4 feet in 1921 and this remained in force until 1926. In that year, most trees over 4 1/2 feet having been killed, there was renewed agitation for a further reduction to 3 feet in spite of the protests of the Conservator. In 1930, owing to the continued wholesale destruction of trees, the limit was restored to 4 1/2 feet, but before the year was out the Government again decided to put it back to 3 feet from 1st January, 1931. ... During 1934, ... the limit was again raised to 4 1/2 feet. Unrestricted tapping has been allowed in unreserved forests since 1933, and the girth limit now applies only to reserves, in

which the head of the department should have full control. (J.P.M.,[14] 1935:109)

As noted, *jelutong* was an important source of cash income to native groups, who in turn possessed the power to affect policy practices. What is also clear in the case of *jelutong* management is that the Brooke administration in the 1930s, either through relative disorganization, disinterest, or both, was a relatively effective medium for taking up native grievances.

The examples of *gutta percha* and *jelutong* management point to the bureaucratic obstacles in the way of exercising control. The situation was made worse by the imprecise nature of maps and surveys especially in such complex terrain as tropical forests and the inadequacy of trained staff which called into question the accuracy of information which managers used to manage forests. As Stoler (1997) reminds us, hegemonic projects may be pushed but success is not often guaranteed.

British foresters in colonial Malaya and those in Sarawak were aware of the importance of this trade. Far from wanting to destroy it, they wanted their respective administrations to be involved in it. This explains the early attempts made at managing *gutta percha* and *jelutong* by less destructive tapping or extraction methods, by trying to extricate control from middlemen (Malaya), and by advancing strategies for more rigorous revenue collection (Sarawak).

The attempts to participate in the trade in forest products generally failed. As far as can be gleaned from the various annual reports from the 1920s and 1940s, there was a reluctance among Malay suppliers[15] and Orang Asli collectors to sell products directly to the government. Chinese dealers or middlemen often made small cash advances to Malays in expectation of supply. These advances were probably made at rates favourable to the dealers, and could therefore be viewed as exploitative as they provided a useful hold on the latter. However, the advances were often viewed by the borrowers as loans that might or might not be repaid (Watson and Cubitt, 1928:305). The Forest Department frowned on such arrangements (Watson and Cubbitt, 1928:305) and, in any case could not follow suit as it could not afford to risk using departmental funds. It would only provide cash upon the supply of the product (Watson and Cubbitt, 1928:305).

Among the Orang Asli, Chinese middlemen were known to provide *ex gratia* payment in addition to the estimated value of the product, but the value was often determined by the latter and did not reflect the amount of labour and risk involved in collecting the products or the time it took in transporting them from the interior (Dunn, 1975:94).[16] Therefore, the relationship was not necessarily an equal one.

In the case of *damar*[17] production, there were additional problems. In the 1920s, unable to acquire sufficient support for supervised *damar* collecting, Sumatran labourers, largely from Mandahiling, were imported expressly for the purpose of developing the *damar* industry (Annual Report, Forest Department of the Federated Malay States, 1926 and 1930). They were employed (as were a few Orang Asli, the traditional collectors) in forest reserves in the state of Negri Sembilan. Within a year the number of tappers dwindled from 333 in 1925 to 278 in 1926 (Annual Report, Forest Department of the Federated Malay States, 1926). In the long run, the industry failed to thrive because of falling world demand (Watson and Cubitt, 1928) and labour shortage. Another contributing factor may have been the strict no cash advance policy that was adopted towards collectors by the Department. Dunn (1975:96, citing Cairns, 1947-8) points out that most of the Sumatran immigrants brought out to Negri Sembilan, abandoned tapping as soon as they could in favour of agriculture and animal husbandry. He concludes that despite government involvement, immigrant agriculturists could not be turned into forest collectors (Dunn, 1975:96).

The analysis thus far has presented one major problem. Drawing attention to inter-departmental rivalry, strategic obstacles in enforcing rules, and other problems of management obscures certain macro effects or fundamental changes in the management structure of Malayan and Sarawak forests. As noted earlier, the so-called minor forest products were in fact major products in Malaya and Sarawak up until the early twentieth century. With the advent of scientific forestry, the scales were turned and forests were seen in terms of their timber value and trees valued primarily for their pulp. Discourses about needs and wants now centred on the needs for timber production or timber potentials, reflecting the requirements of colonial governments for obtaining railway sleepers and fuel for use in tin-mines. The implementation of conservation was first and foremost about useful products, especially timber (including future supply for the export trade with England), with concerns for watersheds and wildlife a close second. These may or may not have been the concern of the Orang Asli or Malays, be they the older or the more recent settlers. The latter may have required timber for housing and were known to engage in the timber trade, especially in Pahang early in the twentieth century (Dunn, 1975), but timber was only one of the many forests products being exported out of the Peninsula at the beginning of colonial rule.[18]

Early management practices did take account of other non-timber forest products especially *gutta percha*, *jelutong*, and *damar*. In the end, it was the inexperience with the complexity of markets, the forests themselves, and the social and political power networks built around the trade in forest products that stifled management interest. Against this backdrop, the argument in favour of greater investment in timber management (as opposed to that of forest products) became stronger than ever before.

Modern accounting practices helped to reinforce forestry discourses of 'minor status.' Dunn (1975:95-7) shows how, in terms of Forest Department revenue, many non-timber forest products of value were not accounted for in Malayan government's annual external trade statistics in the 1950s. Excluded was a range of products including *gutta percha, jelutong, damar* (of the superior and 'other' categories), bamboos, and wood oils (Dunn, 1975:97, tables 7.3 and 7.4).

In Sarawak, where the Forest Department had to compete for control over resources with native shifting cultivators, discourses on needs regarding timber supply led to the creation of forest reserves. This was a slow process as already noted. Nevertheless, the discourse about timber needs and timber potentials made other equally legitimate needs less important. The needs of subsistence being local, possessing no industrial (especially export) potential, implicitly enjoyed secondary status. The position was not helped by the view that management can only be 'scientific' if conducted by 'experts,' which automatically rendered management systems of non-experts, such as native peoples 'unscientific.'

After World War II, Sarawak officially became a Crown Colony. Viewing forests as a source of revenue for funding the development process, the colonial government encouraged the cutting down of forests to generate funds for financing other sectors of the economy such as transport (Kaur, 1998). The Forest Law (Forest Ordinance 1953), which came into effect in 1954 had four objectives; one was concerned with protection and conservation; the other three with raising revenue from forests as efficiently as possible, including through trade. To implement state development plans, surveillance and mapping intensified, as monopoly concessions and greater capital investment in the economy, especially in the timber sector, were encouraged.

At this juncture in Sarawak's history, once again the arguments centring on the 'primitiveness' of shifting cultivation proved useful. Upon moving the second reading of the 1954 Forest Bill, the Sarawak Conservator of Forests presented several arguments to explain why the Forest Ordinance was important. He observed that forests were being degraded by many causes, including primitive logging methods. However, he argued that at that time 'only the most primitive (sic) logging methods were used, and exploitation of the forests rarely extended far from the banks of floating streams.' This was bad enough, but in his view the destruction of forests by shifting cultivation was a bigger worry, especially so since stands of Sarawak's most valuable kind of timber, *belian*, was being destroyed (cited in Browne, 1954:32-5). In the 1950s, a time in which plans were drawn up for the opening up of Sarawak's forests on a larger scale than has been done during the Brooke era, the Forest Department was allowed more staff to survey, categorize, and constitute permanent forests as well as prepare and enforce working plans (Kaur, 1998:132). The Forest Ordinance of 1953 has remained the basic foundation on which scientific forestry is practised today, except that in the post-colonial era surveillance has been tightened even more through various amendments in order to promote and safeguard the timber industry (Majid Cooke, 1997).

The struggle over forest policy in general and within scientific forestry in particular in the post-colonial period in Malaysia is one in which specific elements inherited from the colonial period are recuperated, embellished, deleted, or have remained the same. These have been discussed elsewhere (Majid Cooke, 1995).

Notes

1. I wish to thank three institutions that made the completion of this paper possible. The Royal Melbourne Institute of Technology for a post-doctoral fellowship, the Australian National University for a fellowship that enabled travel and work in the Netherlands and the International Institute for Asian Studies, Leiden University, for assistance in time and resources that made the writing of this paper possible. This paper is part of a larger project of writing on contemporary forest resource policy in Malaysia which was published in August 1999 by Allen & Unwin Sydney, in conjunction with the University of Hawai'i Press. It is entitled: *The Challenge of Sustainable Forests, Forest Resource Policy in Malaysia, 1970-1995.*
2. The definition of sustained yield is highly contested. At a very general level, in forestry parlance, it applies to timber production. But as a principle it may not be confined to timber but has to include non-timber forest products such as wildlife, water, and recreation. In wildlife management sustained yield appears as bag limits and, in wilderness and recreation management as carrying capacity (Behan, 1990:13).
3. See Majid Cooke (1995)
4. See Emerson (1979) for a history of the colonization of the Straits Settlements, Federated, and Unfederated Malay States.
5. The Hill Report of 1900, which recommended the formation of the Forest Deparment, must have taken this aspect of administrative and colonial politics into account (Kumar, 1986:82, footnote 2).
6. This section of the paper is my interpretation of processes in colonial forestry that is based on an examination of Forest Department annual

reports for Sarawak (from 1919 to the 1950s) and Malaya (from 1920s to 1939). Also analysed were exchanges among foresters in the Empire Forestry Journal of the same period discussing certain issues of concern at the time. Examples included the concern raised surrounding the decision of the Brooke regime to prevent any more forests from being reserved in 1932; and excisions in Malaya of forests already constituted as reserves for large-scale rubber plantation or tin-mining.

7   The term discourse is used in combination with the term practice (Sivamarakhrishnan, 1995; Keeley, 1990). In this perspective, discourses are not merely theoretical constructs, but are forms of 'ordering' with implicit sets of norms and prescriptions.

8   In the 1990s, a feature of Malaysian tourism is to enjoy the woodwork of old Malay houses. Some of them were built before WWII, and have become models of the sophisticated use of high-class timber.

9   The issue of 'defective' timber stands was used by Oliphant (1937) to argue for the need to develop simpler sawmilling technology to meet local market demands.

10 The stand against shifting cultivation may be seen in the debates surrounding the new law for the creation of 'protected forest' introduced in Sarawak in 1934. This law allowed native peoples access to reserved forests for the purpose of collecting forest products for their own use but not for swiddening. It caused such great consternation among foresters that the editorial page of the Empire Forestry Journal in 1935 exclaimed that: 'This (1934) legislation seems superfluous, as privileges to take forest produce for domestic use could be conceded in a reserved forest under the previously existing forest law. The unlimited privileges granted under the new law would seem rather dangerous and in any case, it is the agitation of shifting cultivators against any form of forest protection that is to be feared ...' (J.P.M., 1935:108). In contrast, in colonial Malaya, the rhetoric against shifting cultivation was more controlled. After all, the introduction of land legislations in Perak and other Federated Malay States in the second half of the nineteenth century and earlier parts of the twentieth century was partly aimed at controlling shifting cultivation (*ladang*) activities of both Malay and Orang Asli groups (Lim Teck Ghee, 1976). By the time of formation of the Forest Department in Malaya in 1901 and the subsequent reservation works that followed, much shifting cultivation by Malays has been abandoned. Those Malay groups who did not totally abandon their *ladang* were persuaded by various government incentive schemes to engage in more remunerative ways of production, namely wet rice. The colonial government also encouraged wet rice cultivation as an attempt to meet increased food demand from the expanding and largely

imported labour force. Only a few Orang Asli groups persisted with shifting cultivation but this was undertaken in combination with other forms of wage work, cash-crop production, and forest product collection. However, this did not necessarily mean that the colonial perception of 'destructive' shifting cultivation was non-existent which could be glimpsed from the way in which Forest Departments' annual reports of the 1920s and 1930s begrudged excisions from forest reserves for Orang Asli use. The Report on Forest Administration in Malaya for 1937 provides a good example. In that year, several excisions from forest reserves were conceded by the department including the one made for the use of an *Orang Asli* community. The Department's comment on p.3 was illuminating:

'The aboriginal tribes need protection and assistance, but hardly to the extent of settling them in localities where there is a real danger of a timber famine, to the neglect of other places where the destruction of a few trees is not a matter of great moment.'

What is being attempted here is the establishing of a hierarchy of use rights. As far as the Department was concerned, sustaining timber supply is a priority right. Industrial production has higher importance than production for Orang Asli subsistence, especially if the latter activity perceived to be associated with 'destruction.'

11 This position can be gleaned from any quick glance at opinions published in forestry journals of the period. A clear example was outlined in the editorial notes of the Empire Forestry Journal, 1941 vol. 20:124-5 and is reproduced in part here. The editor cited an unnamed review of a forest administration in the colony: 'The problem of the defense of the three great natural resources - soil, vegetation and climate - against the menace of shifting cultivation extends over the greater part of the colonial Empire; and little has yet been done to grapple with it ... Yet, if there is to be any hope of remedy, someone must be so responsible ... there should be some technical organization on which the Government can devolve this special task of preventing the abuse of land ... Generally speaking, the crops grown in shifting cultivation give a bare maintenance to the cultivator and lead to so rapid an impoverishment of the soil that cultivators are always poor and live from hand to mouth and have constantly to be running to fresh localities where more forests, or potential forests are destroyed ... .'

12 In Majid Cooke (1994) I examined the issue of federalism and how it affects forest management practices in contemporary Malaysia.

13 This puts a qualifier on the popularly held view that forest products, other than timber, were of little interest to colonial forestry. The first attempts at managing *gutta percha* was made in 1889 upon instruction

of the British Resident of Perak, Hugh Low, who wanted production restricted (Fyfe, 1949:27). In the early twentieth century the Forest Department attempted to manage *gutta percha* by formulating new ways of extracting the latex without damaging the *taban* trees or felling them altogether which was the practice among collectors. It also attempted to manage *gutta percha* by reserving forests rich in the product (Wyatt-Smith, 1961:37), and by promoting its growth in natural forests as well as in plantations (Fyfe, 1949). In fact, the Forest Department's first attempt at forest management was in the management of *gutta percha* (Fyfe, 1949).

14 Read: 'J.P. Mead.' Mead, the first Conservator of Forests in Sarawak, took up his post in 1919 and left in 1928 to resume service in Malaya, where he felt freer to criticize policy than when he was in Sarawak. During his time in Sarawak he was able to establish 'the soundest of foundations on which his successors may build, and a high example of personal, energy and ability' (Calver, 1929 cited in Smythies, 1963:238). However, it was clear from his subsequent reactions to policy changes in Sarawak management that he perceived the Sarawak government as recalcitrant and altogether 'soft' on native demands. Significantly, the push for reserving forests during his time in Sarawak and in the subsequent years was done in such a way and invited so much 'friction' from native swidden farmers that in 1940 Carson (cited in Smythies, 1963:239) described the forest department as 'the oak tree in the fable ... stood unbending,' so that when the 1932 orders arrived for stoppage of all reservation work, they were regarded as 'the anti-reservation hurricane' interpreted by Carson as an expected outcome of an uncompromising stance.

15 By the twentieth century because of the influx of 'new Malay' migrants especially Minangkabau, Bugis, and Javanese, Malay control over the forest product trade weakened. This prompted a dual effect; first, enhanced exploitation of the Orang Asli by Malay middlemen or secondary traders and, second, a change of allegiance by the Orang Asli from Malay to Chinese middlemen (Couillard, 1984; Dunn, 1975). In the first third of the twentieth century therefore Malay middlemen had largely been replaced by Chinese ones. However, in some areas there were still a few Malays who were middlemen but who would not have had the export network (especially in Singapore where much of forest products were exported from) that the Chinese had.

16 In one account of an Orang Asli sale of *jelutong* to a Chinese dealer in 1968 in Ulu Kelantan, Dunn (1975:94) estimated 40 per cent of the sale value went to the dealer, 20 per cent to transport, and other miscellaneous costs for exporting to Singapore, the rest to the Orang

Asli. For the latter, however, the sale represented six months work involving 150 collectors.

17 There are many types of damar including: *damar minyak* (copal) - Agathis alba - used in varnish, sealing wax, etc.; *damar penak* - Balanocarpus heimii - varnish resin; and other *damars*. However, the Forest Department was mainly concerned with *damar penak*.

18 Dunn (1975:111) provides an indication of the range of forest products exported from the Southern Malay Peninsula from the fifth to nineteenth centuries.

REFERENCES

Ashton, Peter (1988) 'A Question of Sustainable Use,' in: J.S. Denslow, and C. Padoch (eds) *People of the Tropical Rainforest*. Berkeley and Los Angeles: University of California Press.

Behan, R.W. (1990) 'Multiresource Forest Management: A Paradigmatic Challenge to Professional Forestry,' *Journal of Forestry* 88(4), pp. 12-18.

Browne, F.G. (1954) 'Regional Notes: Sarawak,' *Malayan Forester* 17(1), pp. 32-5.

Bryant, R.L. (1997) *The Political Ecology of Forestry in Burma, 1824-1994*.

Chin, S.C. (1988) 'Trade Objects: Their Impact on the Cultures of Indigenous Peoples of Sarawak, Borneo,' *Expedition* v.30(1), pp. 59-64.

Couillard, M.A. (1984) 'The Malays and the 'Sakai': Some Comments on their Social Relations in the Malay Peninsula,' *Kajian Malaysia* 2(1), pp. 106-7,

Cubitt, E. (1940) 'Forest Administration in Malaya,' *Empire Forestry Journal* 19, pp. 264-8.

Dunn, F.L. (1975) *Rainforest Collectors and Traders: A Study of Resource Utilization in Modern and Ancient Malaya*. Monographs of the Malaysian Branch of the Royal Asiatic Society, No. 5.

Emerson, R. (1979) *Malaysia: A Study in Direct and Indirect Rule*. Kuala Lumpur: University of Malaya Press, 4th edition.

Empire Forestry Journal (1940) *'The Last of Coopers Hill,'* Editorial Notes and Miscellanea *19,* pp. 3-5.

--(1941) Shifting Cultivation. *Editorial Notes and Miscellanea* 20, p. 124-5.

Flint, E.P. and J.F. Richards (1992) 'Contrasting Patterns of Shorea Exploitation in India and Malaysia in the Nineteenth and Twentieth Centuries,' in: J. Dargavel and R. Tucker (eds) *Changing Pacific Forests: Historical Perspectives*. Durham, N.C.: Forest History Society.

Forest Research Institute of Malaya (1959) Research Pamphlet No. 25.
Fyfe, A.J. (1949) 'Gutta Percha,' *Malayan Forester* 12, pp. 25-7.
Guha, R. (1989) *The Unquiet Woods: Ecological change and Peasant Resistance in the Himalaya.* New Delhi: Oxford University Press.
Harley, J.B. (1992) *History of Cartography.* Vol. 1. Chicago: University of Chicago Press.
J.P.M. (1935) Sarawak Annual Report. *Empire Forestry Journal* 14, pp. 107-8.
Kaur, A. (1995) 'The Babbling Brookes: Economic Change in Sarawak 1841-1941,' *Modern Asian Studies* 29(1), pp. 65-109.
--(1998) 'A History of Forestry in Sarawak,' *Modern Asian Studies* 32(1), pp. 117-47.
Keeley, J.F. (1990) 'Toward a Foucaldian Analysis of International Regimes,' *International Organisation* 44 (1), pp. 83-105.
Keto, A., K. Scott, and M. Olsen (1990) *Sustainable Harvesting of Tropical Rainforests: A Reassessment.* Paper presented at the Eighth Session of the International Tropical Timber Council, Bali, Indonesia, 16-23 May.
Kumar, R. (1986) *The Forest Resources of Malaysia: Their Economics and Development.* Singapore: Oxford University Press.
Lian, F.J. (1988) 'The Economics and Ecology of the Production of the Tropical Rainforest Resources by Tribal Groups of Sarawak, Borneo,' in: J. Dargavel et al. (eds) *Changing Tropical Forests: Historical Perspectives on Today's Changes in Asia, Australasia and Oceania.* Canberra Australian National University, Centre for Resource and Environmental Studies.
Lim Teck Ghee (1976) *Origins of a Colonial Economy: Land and Agriculture in Perak 1874-1897.* Penang: Penerbit Universiti Sains Malaysia.
Majid Cooke, F. (1994) 'The Politics of Regulation: Enforcing Forestry Rules in Pahang,' *Journal of Contemporary Asia* 24(4), pp. 425-40.
--(1995) 'The Politics of Sustained Yield Forest Management in Malaysia: Constructing the Boundaries of Time, Control and Consent,' *Geoforum* 26(4), pp. 445-58.
--(1996) The Politics of 'Sustainability" in Sarawak. Journal of Contemporary Asia, 27(2), pp. 217-41.
--(1998) *The Challenge of Sustainable Forest. Forest Resource Policy in Malaysia 1970-1995.* Sydney: Allen & Unwin/University of Hawaii Press.
Mead, J.P. (1925) 'Forestry in Sarawak,' *Empire Forestry Journal* 4(1), pp. 91-9.
--(1938) 'Sarawak: Annual Report of the Forest Department, 1937. Commentary,' *Empire Forestry Journal* 17, pp. 322-4.

Menon, K.D. (1969) 'A Brief History of Forest Research in Malaya,' *Malayan Forester* 32(1), pp. 3-13.

Oliphant, J.N. (1934) 'Some Aspects of Timber Production in Malaya,' *Empire Forestry Journal* 14, pp. 45-57.

--(1937) 'The Development of More Intensive Use of Mixed Tropical Forest,' *Empire Forestry Journal* 16, pp. 29-38.

Peluso, N. (1992) *Rich Forests, Poor People: Resource Control and Resistance in Java.* Berkeley: University of California Press.

Rangan, H. (1997) 'Property vs. Control: The State and Forest Management in the Indian Himalaya,' *Development and Change* 28(1), pp. 71-94.

Reece, R.H. (1993) *The Name of Brooke: The End of White Rajah Rule in Sarawak.* Persatuan Kesusasteraan Sarawak, Second edition.

Roff, H.L. (1968) *The Natives of Sarawak and British North Borneo.* Kuala Lumpur: University of Malaya Press, v.II.

Sivaramakrishnan, K. (1995) 'Colonialism and Forestry in India: Imagining the Past in Present Politics,' *Comparative Studies in Society and History* 37(1), pp. 3-40.

Smythies, B.E. (1963) 'History of Forestry in Sarawak,' *Malayan Forester* 26(4), pp. 232-50.

Stoler, A.L. (1997) *Tensions of Empire.* Berkeley: University of California Press.

Troup, E.C. (1940) *Colonial Forest Administration.* London: Oxford University Press.

United States (1989) Report of the Congressional Staff Study Mission to Malaysia to the Committee on Foreign Affairs. US House of Representatives. Government Printing Office, Washington.

Watson, J.G. (1934) 'Forest Research in Malaya,' *Empire Forestry Journal* 13, pp. 222-31.

--(1939) 'Forestry and Tin Mining,' *Malayan Forester* 8(3), pp. 145-8.

--(1950) 'Some Materials for a Forest History of Malaya,' *Malayan Forester* 13, pp. 63-72.

Watson, J.G. and G.E.S. Cubitt (1928) *The Minor Forest Products of Malaya.* Third British Empire Forestry Conference, Summary Report, Resolutions, Reports of Committees.

Westoby, J. (1989) Introduction to World Forestry, People and Trees, Basil Blackwell, Oxford.

Wood, D. (1992) *The Power of Maps.* New York: Guilford Press.

Wyatt-Smith, J. (1961) 'The Malayan Forest Department and Conservation,' Conservation in Malaysia. *Malayan Nature Journal* 21st Anniversary, Special Issue.

ANNUAL REPORTS
Forest Department, Federated Malay States, 1926-32.
Forest Administration, Malaya including Brunei, 1935 and 1939.
Forest Department, Sarawak, 1933-9.

CHAPTER 8

PROVIDENCE AND POWER:
KOREAN PROTESTANT RESPONSES
TO JAPANESE IMPERIALISM

KENNETH M. WELLS

Nationalism, pronounced an historian several decades ago, is 'first and foremost a state of mind.'[1] In much of the historiography on Korea, this state of mind is manifested in an almost undeviating use of a politically and ethnically defined nation as interpretative framework, evaluative standard, and ultimate meaning, in any exploration of human experience on the peninsula. Nowhere is this more apparent than in the comparative treatment of two Protestant leaders, Yun Ch'iho (1864-1945) and Kim Kyoshin (1901-45), in which the former is judged a collaborator and the latter a good nationalist. I shall argue that the nation-centred approach taken to these men has led to serious misstatements of both men's positions and that an understanding of them is better reached through an examination of the Christian beliefs on which they explicitly based their decisions. It is my contention that the germane issue is not their view of imperialism but their understanding of the doctrine of divine providence.

The notion of general providence is itself a view of the world that precludes adoption of the nation as the central category of interpretation and meaning. It does not do so by denying the existence or, perhaps, validity of nations, any more than of families, political parties, or individuals, but by placing God's purposes at the centre. The chief implication for nations is that they become one among a large number of categories that surround the divine centre, and as such their status as a category and the status of any one nation is entirely relative to the purposes of that divine centre. The issue is complicated by the doctrine of the new dispensation, that is, the transition from Old to New Testaments, from Israel before Christ to the church after Christ. If the purposes of God were formerly revealed through his relation to Israel, are they now revealed through his relation to the church? If the identity of believers was formerly a matter of their membership in Israel, is it now a matter of their membership in the church? Does the nation, political or cultural, now have any spiritual significance at all?

When the fate of a nation is in question, there has been a tendency among its Christian members to appeal to a doctrine of special providence, according to which God has a specific purpose for that nation which is tied to its particular historical situation. In such instances, such as Thomas More's belief that God had a unique mission for England at the time of the Reformation,[2] the Dutch Calvinists' identification of the Netherlands with Ancient Israel in the sixteenth century,[3] and the claim, repeated at various times since its founding, that God created the United States in order to extend his rule throughout the world,[4] the idea of a special providence may garner considerable power, but it is regarded as a theological aberration. No official Protestant, Roman Catholic, or Orthodox doctrine supports the idea. For the most part, God's specific purposes are believed now to be pursued through the church and believers. For the rest, nations may be considered to reap the rewards of their own good or bad behaviour, a position that is liable to very fluid interpretation.

Unless these issues are understood, it is difficult to see how a proper historical study could be made of Yun Ch'iho and Kim Kyoshin, or of any of the Korean Protestants who attempted to view their nation's situation in terms of providence. To the degree that they placed the doctrines of providence, evil, and God's rule at the centre of their interpretations of Korea's colonial subjection to Japan, their positions were incompatible with the dominant nationalist identification of Japan as the exclusive or even principal source of Korea's ills. Nor were the problems of evil and power disposable of, as in Leninism and the kind of Confucianism that had informed Korea's intelligentsia, by recourse to cut-and dried judgements concerning righteous or winning causes. Instead, evil was considered present in all regimes to relative degrees, and rather more so in colonial regimes. But even here there was some doubt, as we shall see. For Yun, who lived under it, the pre-colonial Korean regime was marred in his eyes by a rather high concentration of evil, while for Kim the stresses of colonial rule served equally to expose the seriousness of the evils afflicting the Korean people.

PATRIOT OR TURNCOAT?

'Did Christianity plant in modern Korea a servile ethos of spontaneously submitting to imperialism? Or did it play the role of restructuring national identity?'[5] The reason Yang Hyônhye raises this question in her recent and thoughtful work on Yun and Kim is the fact that whereas after a twelve-month term in jail in 1942 for his publishing activities Kim spent the two years remaining till his death from typhus working in a factory in Hamhûng, without implicating himself in the imperialist activities of the Japanese, Yun in the 1940s made a number of speeches on behalf of Japan's war effort, after himself being interrogated in 1938 and manoeuvred into a 'political settlement,' and possibly committed suicide soon after Japan's surrender in 1945.

Yang introduces her discussion with a statement that reasonably clearly defines her starting-point: 'Probably no other period so clearly distinguishes light from darkness in historical figures as one where national identity has been destroyed and its form is being sought after again.'[6] Hence, the subject of inquiry is 'how Christianity related to the reconstitution of national identity' in a critical historical period.[7] Although Yang points out that the question is a matter of the tension inherent between transcendent and immanent modes of a Christian's life, I would like to step back and question the question. The question appears to assume that there is no important or legitimate history other than national history; and that Christianity is to be evaluated according to its relation to national identity. The nation is thus given a special ontological status, something that exists there all the time and *is* history, and a category within and for which Christianity is required to work if it is to have any place in history. While it seems as though Christianity is given an active role, in fact there is no room allowed here for the idea that Christianity might have its own historical agenda quite separate from the 'nation,' and which might perhaps involve the eradication of a nation-centred history and even of nations themselves.

The fact that Christianity spread to other places in direct or indirect company of Western imperialisms makes this question more momentous.[8] Historically, this is undebatable: European, North American, and Australian missions were imbued with a sense of connection between Christianity, nation, and civilization, and in one way or other some of them encouraged the Korean Christians to think of nation as a basic category for Christian thought and action. Quite apart from the critical political situation in Korea from the latter half of the nineteenth century, the possibility of Christian nationalism was learned also through reading Western literature and history. Furthermore, it should be added, Japanese nationalism reinforced Korean nationalism and by basing its presence and policies in Korea on nationalism, Japan made it very difficult indeed for Koreans to respond other than in kind.

CHRISTIAN CIVILIZATION AND NATIONAL INDEPENDENCE

In his search for a new understanding of the fortunes of peoples and the foundations of civilization, Yun Ch'iho, politician, leader of the Independence Club (1896-8), and intellectual, had to grapple with the seemingly endless history of imperialism, invasion, and colonization. As far as appearances were concerned, might was right.[9] But beneath the appearances, Yun claimed God's work in history followed a principle of what we might call the balance of morality: '[W]hat seems to be a triumph of might over right is but a triumph of comparative - I do not say absolute - right over comparative wrong.'[10] In some ways this reflected Yun's need at the end of the nineteenth century to find a Christian position *vis-à-vis* social darwinism. The moral for Koreans was that they had better learn to be good stewards of the territory over which they were responsible, or lose it. It followed, then, that certain peoples could exercise better stewardship than others and thereby create something like a Christian civilization.

Since Uchimura Kanzō, founder of the non-church movement in Japan, had such a powerful influence on both Yun Ch'iho and Kim Kyoshin, it is worth considering what Uchimura had to say about providence in relation to nations. On 5 December 1886 he confided to his diary:

> Much impressed by the thought that God's providence must be in my nation.... God does not want our national characters attained by the discipline of twenty centuries to be wholly supplanted by American and European ideas. The beauty of Christianity is that it can sanctify all the peculiar traits that God gave to each nation. A blessed and encouraging thought that J - too is God's nation.[11]

But what did the spread of Christianity in Japan foreshadow? 'One characteristic of Truth is that it makes the bad worse and the good better. ... We may reasonably expect therefore the worst badness in Christendom.'[12] From this he draws the moral that no earthly state is ultimate or approximates God's kingdom: 'This Earth ... was meant as a school to prepare us for some other places. This educational value of the Earth must not be lost sight of in our poor attempts to make it what it should be.[13] His disciple, Kim Kyoshin, likewise noted, five decades later, that since 'our real country is Heaven, this world is just a house for travellers.'[14] There is in this respect no great difference between the positions of Uchimura, Kim and Yun, although Yun took a more positive approach than Kim to the task of approximating a 'Christian civilization' through political and social activism beyond the personal level. In this respect he was closer to Uchimura than was Kim.

Yun's subscription to the possibility of a Christian civilization derived in part from his neo-Confucian training, which predisposed him to the view that a civilization must be founded on an ideal, and the best civilization on the truest ideal. Again, Confucian training inclined him to the view that knowledge and wisdom are mutually necessary and mutually supportive. 'The rise and decline of a nation depends on the wisdom and nature of its people,' he wrote.[15] So too Uchimura Kanzō: 'With us we make no distinctions between moral and intellectual training. School is our church, and we are expected to bring up our whole beings in it.'[16] Uchimura initially used this idea against Western concepts of the church, and later against any institutional church form. Yun had no argument with the church as such, but he certainly viewed it in terms of increasing knowledge. Indeed, he saw in this institution the hope for Korea's independence.[17]

There was a difference between the two men's perspectives on independence, however, which in terms of responses to concrete historical situations could lead to considerable divergence. Yun did not regard national independence as a right guaranteed by God: it was always dependent on stewardship and the overall purposes of God in the world. Uchimura, however, and Kim Kyoshin followed him here with regard to Korea, stated that '[Japan's] existence as a nation was decreed by Heaven Itself, and its mission to the world and human race was, and is being, distinctly announced.'[18] For Yun, not only was the idea that providence fixed the inviolability of each nation for all time disproven by history, but also the fact that God allowed political violation of nations by other nations required an explanation. Following his principles of stewardship and the 'rights' of comparative good over comparative bad, Yun asked whether God could be blamed if he delivered Korea into the hands of another nation, although he did add that he had to be 'desperate' to wonder whether it would be better to fall under the dominion of England or Japan.[19]

The root of divergence at this point, then, is a difference of opinion over the implication for national independence of their shared belief in providence. It might also be added that Yun's notoriously critical and even contemptuous attitude towards the behaviour and qualities of his fellow Koreans possibly made it easier for him to accept the possibility of God delivering Korea to imperialism. But his contemplation of this possibility, against the background of his readings of history and the realities of Korea at the time, was certainly an attempt to understand the issue Christianly. In any case, when the Japanese did take over his nation in November 1905, Yun immediately resigned from his political post, refused Japan's offer of appointment as Minister of Foreign Affairs, and decided to devote himself to education and Christian endeavour through the church and YMCA. The church's mission was universal and Christians were obliged to pursue it first, whatever the temporal situation.[20] In 1911 Yun was imprisoned on trumped-up charges of heading a conspiracy to assassinate the governor-general, and upon his release in 1915 he continued his educational and church activities. After sustained pressure on him from the Government-General from the early 1930s to join the Privy Council, Yun finally yielded in 1942 and in this capacity was obliged to support Japan's war effort.

KIM KYOSHIN AND PATRIOTISM

Kim Kyoshin was born in 1901, nearly forty years later than Yun Ch'iho. His first memories were of the Russo-Japanese war, through which Japan gained control over the peninsula; he was nine when Japan formally annexed Korea. Growing up in Hamhŭng, he was far removed from the centre of events, however, and soon after the nation-wide March First uprising in 1919 he went to Japan to further his education. He returned to Korea in 1927, became a schoolteacher, and devoted himself to the cause of the non-church movement in Korea. Unlike Yun Ch'iho, he had no personal experience of the transition of Korea from independent to colonial status nor of the frustrations of a Christian politician wrestling with the cause of national independence amidst a divided monarchy and an ineffective succession of reforms, coups and revolts. Kim's only experience of his nation was as a colony under the heavy and exploitative hand of Japan. There were fewer external inhibitions to his sympathy for Koreans. Contrary to Yun, who had dedicated himself to a strenuous struggle to preserve Korea's independence for twenty years before Kim's birth, only to see all efforts fail, Kim's world was one in which recovery of national independence was the focus.

The impact of Uchimura Kanzō on Kim, who studied under him for seven years and remained devoted to him till his death, was extraordinary. It was through Uchimura that he and Ham Sŏkhŏn met and organised together the non-Church movement in Korea. Uchimura's view of providence as God's affirmation of each nation is very clear in Ham's thought. Ham defined providence as the operation of God's *agape* (divine love) in history, and believed Christians were duty-bound to share in the embodiment of that *agape* in their given historical condition. Kim followed much the same understanding. According to Yang Hyŏnhye, Kim believed that if he sundered his connection with Korea, or the connection between the Christian faith and Korea, this would prevent the attainment of universal truth in Korea. Colonial Korea was the location for realization of *agape* love, and the Bible was the most precious gift he could give to 'Chosŏn, the greatest object of my love.'[21] Hence the name of his serial publication: Sôngsô Chosŏn (Bible Korea).

This identification of the Bible with the nation is not self-explanatory, however. Kim's influence in present-day South Korea, for example, ranges from the conservative, evangelical, politically quietist Student Bible Fellowship which takes 'Sôngsô Chosŏn' as its motto, to the anti-government activists who value him - or Ham Sôkhôn perhaps more so - for the notion of national responsibility. The argument continues over whether a nationalist and political use of Kim is appropriate. In 1947 Ham Sôkhôn, founder with Kim Kyoshin of the Korean non-church movement in Korea, remarked that in any case, Kim's love for his country 'was not the so-called patriotism that is generally fashionable in the world.'[22]

That Kim was a founder of the non-church movement is of course crucial to the issue of identity. If they have no church, what is the collective identity of Christians? Kim taught that there was only one basis for Christian identity: the Bible. Nor did he want to substitute identity with the non-church movement for identity with the church: 'What I have learnt from Uchimura is not non-churchism but the truth of the Bible.'[23] But in fact, Kim substituted race for church. A race and their country, he argued, have a character just as does an individual, and positing the existence of a 'Korean soul,' Kim avowed that it was his mission to find this soul rather than so-called 'Christian believers.'[24] Some Koreans have queried whether Kim took this to the point of dissipating religious identity before racial identity, since he was prepared to admit any religious or other viewpoint into the national soul: 'If it is another Korean, whoever it is, we must be in harmony with that Korean.'[25]

In their pursuit of the Korean soul, Kim and Ham Sôkhôn laid down a particular providential view of Korean history and geography that affirmed Korean tradition and history and asserted a God-given national mission. Thus the Korean ethical tradition's *chi* (knowledge or wisdom), *chông* (affection), and *ûi* (will) corresponded to the Bible's faith, hope and charity, and it was Korea's destiny to spread these conceptions.[26] This pursuit involved also idealization of Confucian prescriptions for the family, specifically the distinct nature and function of male and female whereby Korean women were to be prized for their position in the home as preservers of piety and custom, a model for the world to emulate.[27] In 1935 Kim reiterated that 'What I desire is to disseminate teaching that will form the power of Christianity in Korea, and to build an eternal, immortal Korea on the basis of biblical truth.'[28] 'Korea' and the 'Bible' were to become identified as Two Persons in One Body; national history was the expression of the race's soul and the key to its development was providence.[29] Since all Korean history was equally under the same divine direction, a complete identification of Christianity and the nation was apparently effected.

But Kim Kyoshin was too strict a biblical fundamentalist to allow this to rob Christianity of its universalist essence: the Bible remained the standard and the nation was to achieve its historical fulfilment through conformity to it. What Kim Kyoshin did do, however, was to answer the question whether God privileges the 'nation' over other categories in his providential purposes very firmly in the positive. One may legitimately expect that if Kim urged his readers to read the whole Bible from the perspective of the non-church movement's deconstruction of the structure and authority of an organization so important to the experience and history of Christianity as the church, he might then urge also a similar deconstruction of the structure and authority of the nation-state, a phenomenon several centuries more recent than the birth of the church itself. The common explanation for this uncritical position on the nation-state is that the use by Korea's Christians during the colonial period of certain Old Testament passages concerning Israel under foreign occupation encouraged both spiritual and political identification of Korea with Ancient Israel.

PROVIDENCE: THE OLD TESTAMENT AS SOURCE BOOK

If we widen the purview of our inquiry for a moment, we discover that there was a rather general tendency among Korean Christians throughout the colonial experience to draw hope and inspiration from the Old Testament accounts of the exodus of the Israelites from their bondage in Egypt and from the rebuilding of Jerusalem by Nehemiah. This was not a politically naive tendency, and the Japanese saw enough of its point to proscribe at times use of symbolism surrounding Moses and the restoration of Israel's fortunes at different times. While some missionaries thought the Japanese read more into these symbols than was there, accounts by Korean Christians confirm some degree of political intention.[30] There is little reason to believe that this proclivity for Old Testament symbolism did not owe a great deal to Korean hopes for restored political independence. Certainly the precarious state of the nation prompted intense contemplation of the Old Testament, and the use of the Old Testament as the source of an understanding of divine providence had an important impact on the view of their nation among many Korean Christians, including Kim Kyoshin who was encouraged in this by Uchimura's example.[31]

The obvious problem is that whereas in the Old Testament era only one nation was 'Israel,' such a restriction in the era of nation-states is repugnant - as Kim's own negative reaction to the very idea confirms.[32] Is then every nation 'Israel'? On Uchimura's showing, Russia certainly was not; and to Koreans, it was hard to see how Japan could possibly qualify. Yet this difficulty does not appear to have worried either Kim or his and Yun's later critics. But then, it did not worry the Dutch Calvinists either when they were locked in war against Cromwell's Puritans: on the contrary, when shortly after the war Cromwell proposed an Anglo-Dutch alliance on the basis of their common faith, this otherwise consistent idea was greeted with astonishment.[33] For his part, Kim observed to one of his fellow Korean non-church members that Uchimura was every inch a patriot, and he prided himself on possessing the same quality.[34] He followed Uchimura in his identification of the nation - but of course his own nation! - with Israel to such a degree and imputed to it such a special place in providence that even one of his closest non-church movement colleagues, Song Tuyong, was moved to observe: 'Kim loved the Chosôn of his ancestors more than Jesus.'[35]

When employing the Old Testament for lessons on nationhood, Uchimura, Kim, and the Christians in Korea generally, appealed most to Exodus, Daniel, Nehemiah, and Jeremiah. However, it is difficult to see how these could serve the purpose, if the purpose is the nationalistic one attributed to Kim Kyoshin and the 'patriotic' Christians. If one reads these prophetic books on their own terms, two aspects stand out: the message that providence is concerned with the exclusivity of Jehovah's divinity, honour and power; and the lesson that a seeming traitor to the Israelites might be a servant of Jehovah's providential rule.

The first thing the Book of Daniel tells the reader is that Jehovah delivered Judah into the hands of the Babylonians. In secular terms, the Babylonian empire invaded and annexed Judah. The Babylonian king, Nebuchadnezzar, immediately ordered the finest young men of Israel to be taught 'the letters and language of the Chaldeans [i.e. the language of Babylon]' and how to 'serve in the King's palace.' Daniel was deemed the best student and was given the Chaldean name of Balteshazzar, while his deputies were given the Chaldean names of Meshach, Shadrach, and Abednego, the names by which they are known to posterity. From the outset, then, we learn that the colonization of Judah by Babylon was part of God's providential activity in history, and that this hero of Christian patriots in Korea was schooled in both the language and the arts of administration of the invader in order to rule over the Israelites on behalf of the empire.

Some historical vicissitudes later, Judah is subjected to another non-Hebrew empire, that of the Medes and Persians. Under Darius, Daniel is made the senior of the three presidents and pleases the king so well in his implementation of imperial rule that even the Mede officials become jealous and plot against Daniel. It is here that Daniel is used as a model nationalist. But again, a reading of the incident on its own terms suggests that using him this way obfuscates the essential point of the whole drama. The only way the officials can get Daniel off-side with Darius is not by getting him to resist imperial rule over the Israelites but to refuse an order he has to regard as blasphemous: worship of the king as God. It is thus not the independence of Israel that is put at the centre of providence but the exclusive divinity and honour of the one God.

Daniel is trapped by the order, and there follows the famous incident of his deliverance unscathed from the den of lions. There is, certainly, an analogy to be drawn here, about how God will deliver the faithful, which in Old Testament terms could be applied to a whole nation. However, the reward for Daniel's faithfulness was not the deliverance of Israel in any political sense. The offending law was rescinded, Daniel was restored to his high office in the colonial administration, and imperial rule continued. Daniel, we read, 'prospered in the reign of Darius, and in the reign of Cyrus the Persian.' (Daniel 6:28. This and all other biblical references are taken from the New International Version.) The important point is that Darius was converted to the Israelite religion and made it the official religion of the whole empire. And lest, even in the Old Testament scheme of providence, we be left under any illusion that God's providence could be identified with any particular political order on earth, we read: 'For he is the living God and he endures forever; his kingdom will not be destroyed, his dominion will never end.' (Daniel 6:26)

Yun Ch'iho's conception of providence does appear close to this reading, since he recognized that being under God's providence was actually a politically (and therefore culturally) very risky matter indeed. Even on Old Testament terms, his position that the Japanese invasion might be a matter of providence is more genuinely Christian than the common presumption that providence means that God is on one's own nation's side against another or that national independence is an inviolable part of God's purposes. Kim Kyoshin, too, was torn between recognition of the biblical warrant for Yun's understanding and his own strong race-nation instincts. Kim was perfectly aware that the issue at stake in both incidents in Daniel was the spiritual issue of honouring only one God, and commented: '[Daniel's] continuation as ever of praying three times every day did not stem from a spirit of resistance but was a natural disclosure of his faith.'[36] However, neither Kim nor the great majority of Korean Christians considered the establishment of Japanese rule over Korea as an opportunity given by God to convert the Japanese to Christianity and thereby spread it throughout the Japanese empire, a possibility that is explicit in the Book of Daniel. Nor would this idea have been particularly foreign to East Asian tradition, where the Chinese for example prided themselves on 'sinifying' both the Mongol Yüan and Manchu Ch'ing empires.

If we turn to the Book of Jeremiah, the question of providence in relation to Korean nationalism becomes acute. Here we read of Jeremiah counselling the Hebrew king, Zedekiah, to submit to Babylon. But he goes even further and urges the Israelite people to go over to the Chaldeans and give themselves up, so that they will escape death as a kind of war booty: 'Do not listen to [those who counsel resistance]. Serve the king of Babylon, and you will live. Why should this city become a ruin?' he asked (Jeremiah 27:17). It is hardly surprising that Jeremiah was branded a traitor and thrown into prison. Tradition has it that he was eventually executed by being sawn in half. A similar fate awaited Koreans who advised that their compatriots should submit to the yoke of Japan. It is not necessarily the case that these Koreans did so out of altruistic or purely religious motives, but given Yun's and Kim's views on providence the question should surely be raised.

It is evident that the Old Testament doctrine of providence does not itself provide a rationale for nationalism, and is only construed as such after nationalism has already been adopted uncritically and relies on selective use of the Old Testament imagery. By the same token, it is also a belief in divine justice that justifies religious nationalisms, a sense that nations that put other peoples in chains will receive their just deserts and that Christians have a duty to oppose injustice. This, however, is always the case and not necessarily more so under colonial regimes than under oppressive indigenous regimes. And while it is historically evident that oppressing nations often do not get their come-uppance in any event, for Christians there is no guarantee this will happen in history rather than at the 'Final Judgement.' In short, it is not a nationalist issue.

An examination of Kim Kyoshin's exegeses of the relevant Old Testament passages suggest that he, too, saw the issue not so much as a nationalist one as a matter of the spiritual regeneration of national character. In his commentary on the Book of Exodus, he wrote: '[O]ne is simply astonished at how closely it resembles the present features of the Korean race, even more clearly than if looking in a mirror.' But this did not draw from his pen any promise of independence. Rather, we are treated to a dismal catalogue of Israelites' and Koreans' common failings, followed by this lament: 'Oh, how is it that the national character of the ancient Israelites is so closely reflected in the fighting today among Korean coolies, and the fighting over the dissolution of the Shin'ganhoe [the national front, 1927-31], and the fighting among the Presbyterians and the [Methodist] Assembly!'[37] Further, although he chose not to elaborate on the reasons for Jeremiah's persecution, it is clear that Kim recognized that Jehovah's mission for Jeremiah put him fatally at odds with the Israelite leadership and people. When Jeremiah had to tell the people that according to God's revelation to him they must both repent and submit to Babylon, Kim commented, he was not only a lone voice but was in a very painful situation 'which we Koreans should find no difficulty in surmising.'[38]

Kim was, to be sure, ambivalent in some of his asides. Commenting on the Book of Nehemiah he observed that 'patriotic sentiment is also found in exiled peoples, as in Nehemiah's case - and in fact it burns even hotter in such cases. ... Don't laugh at the patriotic sentiment of a ruined race! Only a people in the same position as Nehemiah can properly penetrate Nehemiah's heart.'[39] But the core message and the proper form of patriotism, in his view, was Nehemiah's response to this national situation, which was not to lament over his people's incapacity, or express resentment over the foreign power's oppression and violence, or to devise a great plan, but to counsel repentance and prayer: 'Since he knew that the rise and fall of a country did not depend on the number of its soldiers or the quality of its diplomacy, he attended to the fundamental issue. Thus his patriotism was true patriotism.'[40]

In his writings in Sôngsô Chosôn, Kim frequently contrasted the way of the secular nationalists and many of the religious activists, who resorted to militarist, diplomatic, reformist and generally political means, to the 'true' Christian mission of establishing individual and national life on the sure foundations of scriptural knowledge. His criticism of those who lamented over the Koreans' incapacities, however, was a barb directed at the likes of Yun Ch'iho, whose emphasis on the doctrine of stewardship - making responsible use of one's talents and resources - led him to think of national independence in terms of how deserving of it the Koreans were. Nevertheless, Kim himself levied a great deal of criticism against the supposed 'national' traits of the Koreans, and attributed the failure of the Korean university movement in the mid-1920s to the fact that 'out of 20 million Koreans not a single person had one yen's worth of sincerity.'[41] Likewise, he construed Jehovah's deliverance of Judah to the Babylonians as an exercise in divine discipline of the nation,[42] a position very close indeed to Yun Ch'iho's views of the late 1930s and early 1940s concerning Korea's tutelage under Japanese rule, for which he earned censure as a collaborator.[43] The complexity of the question is revealed further by an examination of the developments that led to Kim Kyoshin's imprisonment.

THE SÔNGSÔ CHOSÔN INCIDENT

In 1942, Kim Kyoshin and many other members of his non-church movement were arrested on account of an article published in Kim's journal, Sôngsô Chosôn, which the Japanese government-general considered inflamed Korean sentiment against the Japanese. Trouble had been brewing since the late 1930s, when Japan began invading China and attempted to focus Koreans' loyalty on the Japanese emperor. This attempt involved compulsory obeisances at Shintō shrines dedicated to the emperor and the printing of a pledge of allegiance at the head of all publications.

Faced with this situation, Kim advised his followers in May 1937 that there is one object for non-Church members to resist. That being 'declaring [the fact] to those who walk contrary to the truth,' the objects of resistance differ according to time and place. Today that which has taken on the role of disobeying the truth before us Christians and which we must resist, is a very powerful beast. The whole company of believers, whether inside the church or outside it, who would while worshipping Jehovah render what is Caesar's unto Caesar and what is God's unto God alone, are faced with times in which they must join their strength together and fight.[44]

The context is important. Kim was anxious to defend his decision to co-operate with the churches, something which seemed to violate the non-church movement's charter. Kim asks his readers not to accuse him of going against the great leaders of the faith, particularly Uchimura Kanzō,[45] and he does so not, as Yang suggests, because he saw Korea as a nationalist whereas the Japanese non-church members did not, but because he believed solidarity with the organized Korean churches was demanded by the times.

In January 1938 Kim announced his decision to cease publication of Sôngsô Chosôn in a letter to Katayama, a leader of the Japanese non-church movement after Uchimura's death in 1937. Upon submitting issue No.108 to the Government-General Police Bureau as required of all publishers in Korea, Kim explained, he was informed that he had to print the pledge at the top of the first page. His immediate impulse was not to publish, but 'on second thought, in light of the fact that it was the only Bible journal in Chosôn, I decided to contain myself and print the pledge as ordered.'[46] Some days later, however, he learned the issue had been denied publication and that further changes were required. This was too much.

We too pray for the emperor in our hearts and as citizens try voluntarily to follow the state laws, but we can't adorn the heads of our publications with these words as the condition of publishing.... I am not suspending Sôngsô Chosôn because I cannot promote anti-war and pro-peace doctrines as I please. If there is any 'injury to the public peace' through conflict over political issues, I will voluntarily withdraw from it and exercise caution. But since I cannot tolerate, or dissemble under, instructions by officials to print certain words and forced flattery, praise, and Biblical testimony for present politics, I have chosen rather to accept an 'honourable death.' I feel deeply heart-broken that the only Bible journal in Korea is thus hidden from view. But God will lead things forward in some other way even better than before. My Elder Brother, please pray for the Korean peninsula too. I pray for your emperor and the true mission of your country.[47]

This heart-rending letter was followed two weeks later by another, in response to a missive from Katayama. Kim had changed his mind and reported that the issue was printed with the required amendments and the pledge.

> This far have I retreated. And from Brother Yamamoto's New Year message I learned that in order to render under God what is His one must be all the more particular to render unto Caesar what is Caesar's. I've resolved as far as possible voluntarily to refrain from outbursts over social and political questions. ...

> As we enter the new year the attitude of the officials is softening somewhat. If there is no active interference beyond wording, things can probably carry on as they are. ...
> In any case, I intend not to write any articles that might excite the officials unduly, and thankfully regard the fact that I can speak according to the Bible as the greatest freedom. Should it happen that we are forced to praise or give Biblical support to the war, Shintō shrine obeisance, or the present politics of the government-general, we will have to cease publication or choose some other means such as changing publisher.[48]

There is little warrant to draw from these particular words evidence of a nationalistic motive behind Kim's decision to join forces with the Christian churches in Korea in their struggle against orders to worship at Shintō shrines. Opposing orders to render unto Caesar what was God's was hardly a contended Christian duty by anyone at the time or since. This puts the issue into the same category as the fate of early Christians under the Romans, and has little to do, except incidentally, with race, let alone nation or nationalism, but rather with human power become, in Christian terms, blasphemous.

The journal thus remained in publication for four more years, until Kim's arrest. Following his release from jail in 1943, Kim Kyoshin returned to his home area of Hamhŭng and found employment in an important Japanese munitions factory, where he enjoyed very cordial relations with the Japanese foremen. From there, he sought to persuade other non-church members to join him at the factory, on the basis that workers in munitions factories were exempt from military service, since they were deemed to be working on behalf of the war effort already. It was in Kim's mind that non-church members should take advantage of this situation so that they would be in a strategic position together to continue their mission once Japan was, as Kim thought likely, defeated in the war. Kim was unsuccessful in attracting members, however, and shortly before Japan was defeated, he himself contracted and succumbed to typhus.

CONCLUSION

If the nation is taken as the starting-point and the principles that politics is the highest human activity and political action on behalf of the country is the highest virtue are accepted, naturally Christians will be expected to justify themselves according to these criteria. But in terms of a Christian definition of fundamental identity, Christ seemed more interested in whether a Roman had faith than whether he were a centurion posted to enforce Roman rule over Judea. It is not a different question whether it is justifiable to base resistance to a colonial oppressor on ethnic antipathies. This was central to Yun's, Kim's, and Uchimura's understanding of the Christian faith, and it can be queried whether any of them would have been wholly happy with the nationalistic framework within which their positions and actions have often been viewed. Kim did not base his decisions in the late 1930s and early 1940s on identity as a Korean nationalist who was impelled thereby to resist the Japanese nation, so much as on Christian grounds which would have applied equally had the rulers been Korean.

But the problem runs even deeper. In his meditations in June 1938 on the 'Way of the Cross,' Kim criticizes the tendency for Christians to talk about Christianity as a path, not to the cross, but to health and material well-being. To this he contrasts the uncompromising words of Jesus in Mark 8:32-38 and Luke 12:49-53.[49] In the former, Christ calls Peter 'Satan' for urging him to follow worldly conceptions of power and says, 'Whoever would save his life will lose it; and whoever loses his life for my sake and the gospel's will save it.' It is problematic to hold up as a paragon of nationalism one whose thinking amounts to a rejection of the secular framework within which the nation-state operates and through which nationalism gains its power.

As for Yun Ch'iho, I am not sure we can get to the bottom of his motives in agreeing to speak on behalf of the government-general's policies. But there are some factors already alluded to that one might put forward as partial explanation. First, Yun had quite different experiences and memories than Kim, having been active in Korea's national affairs well before the Japanese invasion. His potential political influence was well known to the Japanese rulers and he was thus subjected to greater political pressures - and temptations - than Kim. According to his diary, Yun made certain decisions to submit to colonial pressure in order to protect the work among the Korean people through educational and Christian institutions that he believed were central to his Christian calling. But then, much the same reasons lay behind Kim's decision to submit to invidious publication laws. It is also curious that Kim's voluntarily employment at a Japanese munitions factory is not readily deemed to be working on behalf of Japan's war effort, although Yang Hyônhûi's disguising of this fact might indicate some misgivings.[50]

Second, Yun's idea of providence was bound up closely to the phenomenon of the nation-state and attendant international system. He sought to see God's hand and a Christianly supportable logic in the political vicissitudes that surrounded him and had such concrete consequences for his country. Yun's view of providence in which God appears to order international affairs partly with regard to the degree of stewardship a people exercises, coupled with his increasing impatience with the alleged failure of Koreans to improve at all in this regard, moved him to consider the positive ways in which Japan might be disciplining Korea and to allow that he and other Koreans ought perhaps to take a more active part in this. In a sense, Kim was less well placed to work out the relation between faith and nation than Yun, both because he had no political experience and because of the incipient Manichean streak in the non-church movement's position: it is easy to understand his legacy of political quietism in contemporary South Korea.

Third, Kim was a committed pacifist whereas Yun was definitely not. While this makes Kim's employment in the munitions factory even more intriguing and perplexing, it does clarify Yun's willingness to perceive the purposes of providence in the military march of empires over the world, much as did the Old Testament prophets cited above.

Whatever the case, in relation to the mainstream nationalist thinking of the time, both Yun and Kim can only be found wanting. It was, after all, not until 1938, and then over the question of blasphemy and idolatry, that Kim considered direct defiance, and not until 1942 that he actually did defy the government-general, not through his own words but by publishing those of another. Both men were conscious of the gulf that separated their views of the world, its nations and history from secular nationalism. The most uncompromising expression of this gulf issued from the pen of Kim in his commentary on the books of Ezra and Nehemiah, with which words it seems fitting to conclude this discussion:

> It is possible to attribute the fact that Babylon conquered because Israel was weak and then Babylon was invaded because Persia was stronger, to the principle of the survival of the fittest. But if one sees how Jehovah God had already a definite plan which he publicised in advance through the mouth of his prophet and then steadily brought to pass, then this is an extremely important matter for believer and non-believer regardless. If it be the case that in order to discipline Israel God delivered them into Babylon's captivity and then in order to save them out of his mercy he caused Cyrus king of Persia to destroy Babylon, then both Babylon and Persia were the means, the materials, that God employed to fulfil his fixed objective. One views the world and the universe in entirely different ways according to whether one affirms or denies this fact. For our belief in Christianity entails a conversion that is founded on the view of world history and the universe that is taught in the Bible.[51]

NOTES

1   Hans Kohn, 1965, p. 9.

2   See Alistair Fox, 1982.
3   See Simon Schama, 1991, chapter 2.
4   See John F. Berens, 1978.
5   *Yang Hyônhye. Yun Ch'ihowa Kim Kyoshin: Kûndae Chosôn e issôsô minjokchôk aident'it'iwa kidokkyo*, Seoul: Hanul, 1994. From the blurb.
6   Yang, p. 6.
7   Yang, p. 14.
8   Yang, p. 15.
9   Wells, pp. 51-2.
10 Wells, p. 52.
11 Uchimura Kanzō, 1895, p. 147.
12 Uchimura, p. 181.
13 Uchimura, p. 187.
14 Kim Kyoshin's diary entry for 25 March 1937, in *Kim Kyoshin Chônjip* (7 volumes), Seoul: Cheil ch'ulp'ansa, 1991, vol. 5. Hereafter: *Collected Works*.
15 Wells, p. 51.
16 Uchimura, p. 166.
17 Wells, p. 51.
18 Uchimura, p. 108.
19 Yun Ch'iho Diary, 18 May 1890.
20 See Yun Ch'iho's diary entries for 1905-7.
21 Yang, p. 107.
22 Ham Sôkhôn's forward to the 1947 edition of Kim Kyoshin's *Collected Works*, reprinted in *Collected Works*, 1991, vol. 1, pp. 5-7.
23 Quoted in 'Min Kyôngbae. 'Kim Kyoshin no mukyokaishugi to 'Chōsenteki' kurisutokyo,' in Kan, vol. 8, no. 2, February 1979, p. 24.
24 Kim Tuhwan, 1979, pp. 56-8.
25 Ibid., p. 66.
26 Ibid., p. 61. Cf. No P'yônggu, 'Naega saengakhanûn Kim sônsaeng,' in: *Collected Works*, supplementary volume, pp. 69-83.
27 Ibid., pp. 77ff.
28 Ibid., p. 25.
29 Ibid., p. 37; Kim Tuhwan, 1979, p. 82.
30 Compare, for example, H.H. Underwood's observations of Japanese censorship in his book *Modern Education in Korea* (N.Y. 1926), with the books of Christians such as Henry Chung, Hugh Heung-Woo Cynn, and Yim Louise. Some exaggeration by the latter must be allowed for, however.

31 According to his own testimony, Uchimura Kanzō was criticized by fellow-Christians for over-emphasizing the place of the Old Testament in the Christian faith. Uchimura, p. 128.
32 See Kim Kyoshin's response in 'Isûrael chôndo e kukhan iyu,' August 1936, *Collected Works*, vol. 1, pp. 71-3.
33 Simon Schama, 1991, p. 96. See also pp. 104-5.
34 No P'yônggu, 'Naega saengakhanûn Kim sônsaeng,' in *Collected Works*, supplementary volume, p. 72.
35 Min Kyôngbae, 'Kim Kyoshin no mukyokaishugi to 'Chōsenteki' kurisutokyo,' p. 36.
36 Kim Kyoshin, *Collected Works*, vol. 3, pp. 184-5.
37 *Collected Works*, vol. 3, pp. 21-2.
38 *Collected Works*, vol. 3, p. 157.
39 *Collected Works*, vol. 3, p. 94.
40 *Collected Works*, vol. 3, p. 95.
41 Min Kyôngbae, 'Kim Kyoshin no mukyokaishugi to 'Chōsenteki' Kurisutokyo,' pp. 32, 34, and 37.
42 *Collected Works*, vol.3, p. 94.
43 See for example Yun Ch'iho's article, 'Naesôn Ilch'e e taehan soshin,' published in the Japanese journal Tōyō shi kō, April 1939, of which a Korean translation is provided in Pak Chongguk (comp.). *Ch'in-Il Nonsôl Sônjip*, Seoul: Silch'ôn munhaksa, 1987, pp. 112-15.
44 *Collected Works*, vol. 1, pp. 202-3.
45 *Collected Works*, vol. 2, p. 363.
46 *Collected Works*, vol. 6, pp. 531-2.
47 *Collected Works*, vol. 6, pp. 533-4.
48 *Collected Works*, vol. 6, pp. 534-5.
49 *Collected Works*, vol. 1, pp. 62-5.
50 Yang simply says that Kim entered employment in a fertilizer factory. This might be an oversight, or attributable to confusion over the conversion of such factories into munitions plants, but since the details of the case are clearly stated in the *Collected Works*, vol. 6, pp. 524-5, there is room for doubt.
51 *Collected Works*, vol. 3, pp. 92-3.

REFERENCES

Berens, John F. (1978) *Providence and Patriotism in Early America: 1640-1815*, Charlottesville: University Press of Virginia.

Fox, Alistair (1982) *Thomas More: History and Providence*, Oxford: Basil Blackwell.

Kim Tuhwan (1979) 'Kim Kyoshin no minzoku seishinshiteki isan,' *Kan* 8(2), February 1979.

Kohn, Hans (1965) *Nationalism: Its meaning and history*, rev. ed., Princeton, New Jersey: D. van Nostrand Co., Inc.

Schama, Simon (1991) *The Embarrassment of Riches: An Interpretation of Dutch Culture in the Golden Age*, London: Fontana.

Uchimura, Kanzō (1895) *How I Became a Christian: Out of My Diary*, Tokyo: Keiseisha.

CHAPTER 9

THE CENTRAL-EUROPEAN JEWISH COMMUNITY IN SHANGHAI 1937-45

PAN GUANG

Half a century ago, more than 25,000 Jewish refugees from Central Europe, endeavouring to escape from Nazi persecution, travelled all the way to Shanghai seeking a safe haven. They suffered many tribulations, but almost all of them miraculously survived the holocaust and the war. Why did Shanghai - the largest metropolis of the Far East - the only big city available to them at that time, become an ideal haven for Central-European Jewish refugees? How did these refugees flee the Nazi-controlled areas and reach Shanghai? How did they settle down in the city and spend the long and hard days of the Pacific War? Why could they survive under the Japanese occupation authorities, theoretically Hitler's allies? These questions still arouse strong interest in international academic circles even more than fifty years later.

WHY DID SHANGHAI BECOME AN IDEAL HAVEN FOR JEWISH REFUGEES?

The accepted historical account is that Jews came to China as early as the Tang Dynasty. Some scholars think that the date could be extended back to the Han or Zhou Dynasty about 2,000 years ago. Whatever the actual date, the Jewish community in Kaifeng, which took shape during the Song Dynasty, was known to all.[1] In modern times, Shanghai, Tianjin, and Harbin had become the places where Jews chose to live, usually to close-knit communities. Shanghai, in particular, had a Jewish community of about 5,000 souls in the early part of 1930s, comprised of Sephardic Jews who came to the city from British-ruled Baghdad, Bombay, and Hong Kong in the second half of the nineteenth century and a large number of Russian Jews who came to make a living in the city via Siberia and Harbin after the pogroms and revolutions in Russia at the beginning of the twentieth century. The community had its own communal association, synagogues, schools, hospitals, clubs, cemeteries, a chamber of commerce, political groups, newspapers, magazines, and a small fighting unit (a Jewish company belonging to the Shanghai Volunteer Corps).² Several notable families such as the Sassoons, the Hardoons, the Kadoories, the Ezras, the Toegs, and the Abrahams became an economic power and not just in Shanghai but they even made their presence felt throughout the whole of China. The important point is that although many Jews have inhabited China from ancient to modern times, no indigenous anti-Semitic activity has ever taken place on Chinese soil. While anti-Jewish movements flooded over Western Europe between the eleventh and fifteenth centuries, the Jewish community in Kaifeng prospered. Again, when pogroms occurred in Eastern Europe and Russia, the Jewish community in Shanghai remained secure. That is why European Jewish people retain a friendly and affectionate feeling towards Chinese people and Chinese cities such as Kaifeng and Shanghai. I use the word 'indigenous' because there had been some anti-Semitic activities in Shanghai and Harbin in 1920s, 1930s and 1940s, but they were all committed by White Russian and Japanese anti-Semitists, and later by Nazis. I call this 'imported' or 'imposed' anti-Semitism. No such sentiment has ever emerged naturally and spontaneously on Chinese soil, or has it exerted any substantial influence on Chinese lives.

Viewed culturally, most Chinese are influenced by Confucianism, Buddhism, and Taoism rather than Christianity, and Chinese and Jewish cultures share a great deal in common. For example, both lay great stress on family ties and educational values, and although both have absorbed various exotic cultures, their central core has never changed. On a stone monument erected in 1489, the Kaifeng Jews wrote: 'Our religion and Confucianism differ only in minor details. In mind and deed both respect Heaven's Way, venerate ancestors, are loyal to sovereigns and ministers, and filial to parents. Both call for harmony with wives and children, respect for rank, and for making friends.'³ For this reason, the ideological roots of anti-Semitism which lie in religious prejudice and racial discrimination against Jews do not exist in China, and never have. Therefore, Jewish people living in China enjoyed a sense of security. No doubt, this environment was strongly appealing to Central-European Jews who had suffered untold tribulations. As the most Europeanized city in China, Shanghai above all other places in China combined Chinese tradition with Western civilization and provided the most favourable conditions in which the European Jews could settle down and make a livelihood.

The international environment of that time also accounted for Shanghai's popularity among Jews. In the wake of the global economic Depression and imminent threat of war, many countries refused to accept immigrants. This made it very difficult for Jewish refugees from Europe to find a haven. In May of 1939, the British government issued the 'White Paper' which imposed strict restrictions on the entry of Jewish immigrants into Palestine.[4] The United States, which has the world's largest Jewish community, also set a limit on the entry of Jewish refugees.[5] Meanwhile, many neutral states, afraid to bring troubles upon themselves, also refused to take Jewish refugees. It was in these desperate days that the European Jews found Shanghai. There is little doubt that their decision was related to the special open status which then existed in Shanghai. After the concessions of 1843, Shanghai opened its door to foreigners and became a so-called 'Adventurers' Paradise.' In what was very nearly one century between 1843 and 1941, all kinds of immigrants and refugees found no difficulty in seeking their living space in Shanghai, especially in the Western-held sector. After the August 13 Incident in 1937, Japanese troops occupied most parts of Shanghai and the regions around it so that the city's International Settlement and French Concession were transformed into 'isolated islands' in a Japanese controlled area. The Chinese government was powerless to continue its control of the Shanghai region, while the Japanese occupation forces, pressing westwards in pursuit of the Chinese troops, did not have enough time to set up a puppet regime in the city. As a consequence, Shanghai was the only metropolis in the world which foreigners could enter without visas and financial guarantees in the two years between the autumn of 1937 and the fall of 1939. These advantages were particularly important to Central-European Jewish refugees, most of whom were penniless and some of whom had just escaped from concentration camps.

All these factors conspired to turn Shanghai, a Far Eastern metropolis, into an ideal haven for Central-European Jews, adding a bitter but memorable chapter to the history of Shanghai.

ROUTES, TIME OF ARRIVAL, AND NUMBER OF CENTRAL-EUROPEAN JEWS IN SHANGHAI

Different works express different opinions about the routes, times of arrival, and the number of Jewish refugees in Shanghai. Based on several years' research, I have come to the following conclusions which I shall approach chronologically.

The first period involved the five years between 1933, when Hitler began his campaign against Jews, and August of 1937, when Japanese troops invaded Shanghai. During these years, the conditions of German Jews, though unpleasant, were not as atrocious as those they were to suffer later. Many of them had enough insight to sense that imminent disaster was at hand, and, while they still had a chance, left their homes. Not many of these

German Jews came to Shanghai because many countries had not yet closed their doors to Jews. In 1933, the first group of German Jews who arrived in Shanghai was composed of twelve families consisting in all of about 100 people.[6] It is hard to know exactly how many German Jews had arrived in the city by the summer of 1937, because some of them moved on to other places from Shanghai. I have estimated the number at 1,000 to 1,500, excluding those who later moved on. Strictly speaking, the Jews who came to the city during this period should be considered immigrants and not refugees. Because there were no major wars in Europe and Asia at that time, these German Jews made their way directly from Germany to Shanghai via the normal sea routes.

The second period extended from August 1937 to August 1939 when the Shanghai authorities began to set a limit to the entry of Jewish refugees into the city. These two years were peak years in which Jewish refugees from Germany and other Central European countries swarmed into Shanghai. This great influx was a response to the aggravated persecution by Nazi Germany and its propagation in other parts of Europe following the German annexation of Austria and Czechoslovakia. It was also affected by the strict restraints many countries had imposed on the entry of Jewish refugees by that time. In contrast to these countries, Shanghai remained open to Jews because of its special position in the war.

Jewish refugees who had left the areas occupied by Nazi Germany for Shanghai suffered indescribable tribulations. Some of those who arrived in Shanghai in December 1938 said: 'Many of our 187 refugees were wealthy local merchants with millions in capital. But when we were expelled from Germany, each of us was allowed to take only 10 marks, not counting our passage money. The rest was confiscated.'[7] The routes they could take to Shanghai were three: most of them went first to Italy, and from there travelled to Shanghai by sea; some of them first entered France, Holland, or Belgium, then took ships for Shanghai at the Atlantic ports; a small number of Jewish refugees travelled by ship to the Balkan states, from where they found vessels to get to the Far East. Opinions about the number of Jewish refugees who arrived in Shanghai during this period differ. Some say it may have reached 15,000. Others have estimated the figure at 17,000 to 19,000. Based on an analysis of comprehensive data, I would argue that the two figures, which are derived mainly from the statistics of refugee settlements, are incomplete, because large numbers of refugees did not go to the refugee camps, but either moved in with relatives or rented houses in which to settle down. If the numbers of these refugees are added as well, the total number could reach as high as 20,000.

The third period lasted from August of 1939 to June 1940 when Italy proclaimed war against Britain and France. In August 1939, the authorities in the Shanghai International Settlement and the French Concession reached an agreement with the Japanese occupation forces concerning the entry of Jewish refugees, declaring that the European Jewish refugees holding a 'J'-passport had to ask for permission before setting foot on Shanghai soil. The conditions for obtaining permission were that each person pay a bond of US$ 400 (US$ 100 for children under 13); the applicant should either have a close relative resident in Shanghai or have work in the city or plan to marry a local resident.[8] When the regulation was put into effect, shipping companies in Europe began to refuse to sell tickets for Shanghai to Jewish refugees who did not have such permission. The implementation of the regulation put refugees halfway on the voyage to Shanghai in a difficult position. Undeterred, many refugees still found ways to enter Shanghai with the aid of Jewish organizations throughout the world. At this point in time, after declaring war against Germany Britain began to expell German nationals from its territories and possessions. Falling victim to this expulsion, more than 100 Jews with German nationality came to Shanghai from Hong Kong and Singapore, despite the fact that these expelled Jews had already been deprived of their German nationality in accordance with Hitler's decrees. Though the number was falling, it is estimated that the city still accepted 2,000 to 3,000 refugees from Germany, Austria, Poland, Czechoslovakia, Hungary, Romania, and the three Baltic States. The routes Jewish refugees took to Shanghai during this period were similar to those they had taken in the previous period.

The fourth period covers just one year, from June of 1940 to June of 1941 when Germany invaded the Soviet Union. This year should be counted as a separate period, because after June 1940 the routes Jewish refugees would take to Shanghai changed greatly. In June 1940, Italy proclaimed war against Britain and France. Soon afterwards, France was defeated and surrendered. Britain continued to carry on a fierce sea and air war against Germany and Italy in the Atlantic and the Mediterranean. The upshot was that the regular sea routes taken to Shanghai by European Jewish refugees were completely cut off. This critical time was marked by a last, agitated tide of European Jews desperate to escape Europe, because West European countries such as France, Holland, Belgium, and the Balkan states like Yugoslavia and Greece had fallen into the hands of the Nazis, because the three Baltic states were then being confronted with the Nazi threat and were later merged into the Soviet Union, and because the German Occupation meant that the anti-Jewish movement had systematically begun to operate in the Central European coutries. By now, the rate of success of these refugees in their efforts to escape persecution was rapidly declining. During this period some Jewish refugees still wanted to come to Shanghai but this meant they had to cross the Soviet Union, then reach their destination by way of Manchuria, Korea, or Japan. The journey usually took several months, during which they braved numerous dangers and hazards to reach Shanghai. Lack of material means it is very hard to determine the exact number of Jewish refugees who arrived in Shanghai during this period, but I estimate the figure at about 2,000 persons.

The fifth period lasted the six months from June to December 8 1941 when the Pacific War broke out. Because the war between the Soviet Union and Germany erupted in June 1941, the land routes available to European Jewish refugees were completely cut off. The German invasion of Russia meant it was no longer possible for Jewish refugees to leave Europe for Shanghai. However, some Jewish refugees, who had left Europe before the war and had settled in the far eastern part of the Soviet Union, Manchuria, or Japan still continued to seek a haven in Shanghai, for the flames of the world war left them little other choice, in the face of the strict limits set by most countries. Therefore, over 2,000 Jewish refugees set foot in Shanghai during this period, most of whom came from Poland and Lithuania. The tortuous journey on the way to Shanghai, experienced by over 1,100 Polish Jews, including about 400 teachers and students from Mir Yeshiva and some other Yeshivas, is particularly worthy of note. They fled to Lithuania in 1939 when Germany invaded Poland. Driven to the wall, they thought up a way to escape from Europe by acquiring Japanese transit visas on the excuse that they were going to the Dutch colony of Curacao, then by trying their best to go to the United States from Japan. Their unremitting efforts were rewarded when they were unexpectedly granted transit visas by Chinue Sugihara, the Japanese consul in Kovno, and then were able to obtain exit permits from the Soviet government (by that time Lithuania had been merged into the Soviet Union). When all was in order, as arranged by the Soviet Travel Service (each had to pay US$ 200), they went across Siberia by train and arrived at Vladivostok, from where they reached Kobe, Japan, by ship. They remained there about half a year. Since they felt there was no hope of obtaining entry visas from the American government, during the second half of 1941 they decided to go to Shanghai.[9] It was the last big group of Central European Jewish refugees to get into Shanghai in wartime.

After the outbreak of the Pacific War, it became impossible for Jewish refugees to enter Shanghai either by sea or by land. In total, Shanghai accepted almost 30,000 Central European Jews who came in successive waves from 1933 to December of 1941. Excluding those who left Shanghai for other countries, the city contained a total of 25,000 Jewish refugees at the time of the outbreak of the Pacific War. This means that Shanghai accepted more Jewish refugees than those taken in by Canada, Australia, New Zealand, South Africa, and India combined.[10]

MAKE A LIVING IN SHANGHAI 1937-43

After escaping the Nazi concentration camps and arriving in Shanghai, Central European Jewish refugees were faced with the problem of making a living in a completely strange environment. Before the middle of 1937, most newcomers found it easy to find jobs in pre-war Shanghai. Eking out their existence with some savings, most of them resided in the International Settlement and French Concession living what was considered a fairly average life in the Jewish community in Shanghai. Then the situation deteriorated because of the onset of the anti-Japanese war and the continued influx of a growing stream of Jewish refugees from Europe. By the beginning of 1938, almost all newcomers to war-torn Shanghai were virtually penniless. They had no relatives or friends waiting for them; they did not speak Chinese or even English; they knew nothing of the city or its inhabitants. Uprooted and bewildered, many of them had decided to go to Shanghai on the spur of the moment.

The Jewish community in Shanghai made great efforts to help their own compatriots settle in. The Committee for the Assistance of European Refugees in Shanghai (CFA) and the International Committee for Granting Relief to European Refugees (IC) were established in 1938 mainly by Sephardic Jews and Russian Jews. The wealthy Sephadic Jews played a particularly big role in aiding Jewish refugees. The Kadoorie family donated a large amount of money to help Jewish refugees settle down and also set up the Shanghai Jewish Youth Association School which accepted the children of penniless refugees free of charge.[11] The Sassoon family did not lag behind in the granting of assistance. At the beginning of 1939, Sir Victor Sassoon contributed US$ 150,000 for the settlement of Jewish refugees.[12] Russian Jews were not as rich as the Sephadic Jews, but there were many of them with considerable influence. They were brimming with initiative and worked assiduously in all sorts of ways to help their Ashkenazi compatriots. The Committee for the Assistance of Jewish Refugees from Eastern Europe (EASTJEWCOM) was set up in 1941 by Ashkenazi Jews especially for helping Jewish refugees from Poland and Lithuania.[13] Meanwhile, Jews all over the world offered financial and material assistance to the Jewish refugees in Shanghai. The JDC (American Jewish Joint Distribution Committee) contributed more money than any of the others. And the

HICEM-HIAS (Hebrew Immigrant Aid Society) also made a great contribution in this respect. After the Pacific War broke out, Jewish residents with British and American nationalities were interned by the Japanese as 'enemy nationals,' but Russian Jews still enjoyed treatment as 'neutral nationals' because there was no war between Japan and the Soviet Union. This meant that the Russian Jews shouldered the burden of aiding Central European Jewish refugees until the end of war.[14]

LOCATION AND HOUSING

At first, an attempt was made to find individual rooms and apartments for the refugees in various parts of the city, but there was not much room for newcomers in the International Settlement or in the French Concession. Therefore, the bulk of the refugees was obliged to settle in Hongkew, an intersectional district wedged between the International Settlement, the Japanese-held sector, and the Chinese area. There had been heavy fighting in Hongkew in 1937. Suffering from the slump in the market caused by chaos of war, Hongkew offered cheap prices for consumer goods, 20 per cent less than other districts, and lower rent for accommodation, 75 per cent less than in the International Settlement or the French Concession. At the beginning of 1940, 11,000 refugees were living in Hongkew with another 1,500 in the International Settlement and 4,000 in the French Concession.[15] Two types of dwellings were made available in Hongkew: shelter camps and what was known as Lane Housing. Shelter camps were improvised by the local committees from hastily converted and reconstructed schools, warehouses, army barracks, and similar edifices. Upon their arrival, many refugees lived in these camps with thirty to fifty people, sometimes as many as 100-200, sharing one big room or hall. There was no privacy whatsoever, with men, women, and children in the same room. Each family staked out a few square feet for itself and its belongings, and of course, human nature being as it is, there were constant boundary disputes. Ward Road Camp, which also housed the kitchen, was the headquarters for all the camps in Hongkew. Although the living conditions were so bad, the camps were still called 'home' by refugees, taken from the German 'heim.' Lane Housing consisted of either single-storey or two-storey houses situated on either side of a narrow lane or alley leading off from the main thoroughfare. The houses were flimsily built, airless, and dark. Each house had up to ten rooms, with primitive sanitary facilities which everyone had to share. Most of the houses were owned by foreign or Chinese companies and were rented to the refugees. If a family had two rooms, it was considered to be well off, for most lived in one room and sublet a second room to other families. By the end of 1940, about 3,000 to 4,000 refugees lived in the camps; about 10,000 refugees had settled in the lane houses.[16]

OCCUPATION AND BUSINESS

Although few refugees who could speak English well or had friends in Shanghai were lucky and did find jobs, most Central European Jews found it so difficult to get professional or even regular work, and of course they were in no position to compete with Chinese coolie labour. Turning to their own resources, the vast majority of refugees began to set up their own domestic businesses. They reconstructed dozens of shattered streets, using the rubble to erect the new building and shops, and Hongkew soon began to take on the appearance of a small German or Austrian city. Chusan Road, once a small, dingy, typically Chinese lane, now looked like a street in Vienna. Hundreds of business establishments were opened, catering mostly to refugee customers. There were groceries, pharmacies, bakeries, plumbers, locksmiths, barbers, tailors, milliners, cobblers - and, of course, there were the inevitable Viennese 'coffee-houses,' without which the average native Viennese would find it difficult to exist. A few enterprising souls even established small factories, turning out such products as soap, candles, knitwear, leatherwear, and especially European-type food products like sausages, confections, soft drinks and the like. Many of these products also found a ready market among the Chinese, since they had previously been unknown or had to be imported from abroad.[17]

There was a large number of medically trained personnel among refugees, including 200 physicians. These doctors, dentists, and nurses soon set up little clinics in Hongkew. They even established the first hospital for refugees, with 120 beds, and the Association of Central European Physicians.[18] Although doctors did a fairly good business, most former high-level intellectuals had a much more difficult time. Engineers and architects encountered greater difficulties in finding work, although they aided in the reconstruction of Hongkew. Lawyers, economists, university professors, and the like, found no outlets for their abilities. Some of them became door-to-door salesmen or peddlers; others sold newspapers; many engaged only in local politics and helped in arranging the affairs of the community.[19] Despite the enforced closeness and intermingling, many of them managed to retain the old social stratifications and insisted on retaining their old titles. Ragged newspaper vendors were respectfully addressed as Herr Doktor; one shabbily-dressed old man insisted on being called Herr Oberlandesgerichtstar.[20]

By the end of 1941, Central European Jews had succeeded in establishing a flourishing communal economy or had managed to find jobs in local businesses. After Pearl Harbour, however, conditions deteriorated rapidly. Those refugees who had found employment with British and American firms found themselves out of work when the firms came under Japanese management and their former employers were interned. Subsequently the economic situation in Hongkew was made desperate again because all assistance from abroad, indeed all connections with the outside world, was cut off.

Social Organization and Religion

In the midst of the utter confusion of wartime, it was only natural for the Central European Jewish community to adopt a certain amount of self-government. The various relief committees formed the nuclei of all social organization and were often treated as the official representatives of the community by the Japanese authorities. Each shelter camp had its own elected officials, in addition to an administrative staff which supervised all camp activities. The refugees living outside the camps usually formed small social units of their own. The inhabitants of a certain lane or building elected committees to run the lane or building. Although the traditional Jewish Communal Association was established in the summer of 1939 by Central European Jews in Shanghai, in general, there was no single overall community government. The Japanese were content to let the refugees run their own affairs, so long as these did not interfere with any Japanese plans. The only step they took was to select certain prominent community leaders and hold them responsible for the actions of the entire group. There was a considerable amount of internal friction, but almost all normal personal quarrels and fights, which can be found in even the best-run community, were settled by refugee arbitration courts without recourse to the Japanese or Chinese authorities. The majority of refugees bore up very well.[21]

It was quite natural that the Central European Jewish community should feel the need to organize its own religious establishments. Most of the refugees who originated from Germany and Austria were Reform Jews and accustomed to the liberal or reform type of service, with an organ and a mixed choir. Up until November 1941, the Reformist Congregations held their services in such places as school auditoriums, meeting halls, and rented theatres. Then, in November, the 'Juedische Gemeinde' dedicated its own synagogue on MacGregor Road. In some camps, the services were conservative, the more orthodox Jews made use of a small Russian Jewish temple, the Ohel Moshe synagogue, on Ward Road. On the whole, religion did not seem to play a prominent role in the community.[22] One exception that must be noted was the Polish Jews. Most of them remained completely orthodox and maintained several Yeshivas and Talmud Thoras. Four hundred rabbinical students and their teachers from the Mir Yeshiva and some other Yeshivas had come all the way from Poland as a unit, and had reached Shanghai without a single student, teacher, or book being lost or even a lesson missed. Upon arrival they set up their school in the Beth Ahron synagogue in Museum Road and continued with their studies, refusing to be deflected by all the difficulties.[23] There seems little doubt that the influx of Central European Jews gave a tremendous impetus to the religious life of the Sephardic and Ashkenazi communities. A new sense of friendship, responsibility, and unity developed among the older settlers and they discovered that their own, rather neglected religious traditions, were worthy of being revived

EDUCATION AND RECREATION

In 1938 Shanghai had a number of British, French, and American schools and universities. One of these was the Shanghai Jewish School, which had been first founded in 1900 by D.E.J. Abraham and then rebuilt in Seymour Road in 1932 by Horace Kadoorie. The first German-speaking refugees to arrive in Shanghai sent their children to the SJS, which was run strictly along British lines, for non-religious training. But as thousands of Central European Jews began to pour into Hongkew, it became obvious that they would need a school of their own. Again, with the aid of Mr Horace Kadoorie, the Shanghai Jewish Youth Association School was opened in Hongkew in November 1939. Even during the war, the SJYA School operated exceedingly efficiently and served some 700 students.[24] Another 150 students attended the Freysinger Jewish Elementary and Middle School, which was set up in April 1941. Five hundred adults, who took English courses in the evenings, also attended the FJEM School.[25] Caring for the needs of adults, the ORT (the Society for Promotion of Handicrafts and Agriculture among Jews) played an important role in providing occupational training in a variety of skills and cultural lessons for adults.[26] In addition to the afore-said Mir Yeshiva, Rabbi Meir Ashkenazi, the spiritual leader of Russian Jewish community, started Hebrew schools in two camps for about 120 boys and established a Beth Jacob School for girls.[27] There is no doubt that all these educational institutions were necessary for and vital to the continuation of Jewish studies and survival.

One of the chief factors which made life bearable for refugees was the amount and variety of recreation they could enjoy. There were many cinemas in Shanghai, which specialized in American films, and these were quickly patronized by refugees - eager not only for entertainment, but also for an opportunity to learn English. During the war, American films were forbidden, but old German, French, Italian, and Russian movies helped to provide fairly entertaining filmfare. Among the refugees, there were many professional, as well as amateur, entertainers and they quickly swung into action. Actors and actresses organized drama groups, even a Yiddish theatre; musicians set up bands and orchestras; several singers even formed a light opera company, which put on some highly successful operettas.[28] In Hongkew, there were, of course, the ubiquitous coffeehouses and bridge clubs, and even a few nightclubs, including a very pleasant roof-terrace on one of the neighbourhood's tallest buildings. As was to be expected in a closely-knit community of this type, there was a good deal of home entertaining and the art of conversation reached an all-time high. Because of the scarcity of food, the hostess usually provided hot water, while the guests brought their own coffee or coffee substitute, tea, and sugar or saccharin.[29] Shortly after their arrival, refugees set up soccer teams and, within a few months, they had succeeded in establishing a three-division amateur soccer league, which played annual tournaments before thousands of enthusiastic spectators, and whose teams even competed against Chinese and other foreign squads. Other popular sports included boxing, ping-pong, a little tennis, and even some baseball.[30] Although the community did not have any public libraries, several enterprising refugees rounded up small stocks of books and established highly successful circulating libraries. From 1938 to 1943, editors and journalists among refugees ran more than ten German publications, and several Polish and Yiddish ones. They included Shanghai Jewish Chronicle (Shanghai Echo), Shanghai Woche, Acht Uhr Abendblatt, Die Gelbe Post, Yeddish Almanach, Unser Wort, In Weg, Das Wort, Die Tribune, Medizinisch Monatshefte, Unser Weg and so on.[31]

THE STRUGGLE FOR SURVIVAL IN THE HONGKEW GHETTO 1943-45

THE PRESSURE OF NAZI GERMANY AND THE CAPRICE OF JAPANESE POLICY

As Japan had declared war against the United States in December 1941, Germany assumed that Japan would be certain to begin implementing

German-type anti-Semitic policies. In July 1942, eight months after the Pacific War broke out, Colonel Josef Meisinger, chief representative of the Nazi Gestapo in Japan, arrived in Shanghai and put forward a plan for 'the Jewish Solution in Shanghai' to the Japanese authorities. It was designed to be implemented in two steps. Step one was to arrest all Jews in Shanghai in a surprise attack as they were spending the Jewish New Year with families. Step two was to 'deal with' the problem they were assumed to create in a decisive manner. The plan suggested three ways of 'dealing with' these Jews. They could be placed in old ships and set a drift on the East China Sea, so that they would eventually die of hunger; they could be forced to toil themselves to death in the abandoned salt-mines on the upper reaches of the Huangpu River; or the Japanese could set up a concentration camp on Chongming Island, where the Jews would be subjected to medical experiments and die of their sufferings.[32] Although the 'Meisinger Plan' was not put into effect, the Japanese authorities proclaimed 'the Designated Area for Stateless Refugees,' ordering all Jewish refugees from Central Europe to move into the area.[33] The whole operation was similar to setting up a concentration camp.

Why did the Japanese not carry out the 'Meisinger Plan'? I think that there are four main reasons, which are: First, the lobby within Japan which advocated peace with the United States still considered the Jews in China to be a means by which good relations with the United States could be restored and exerted their limited influence over the Japanese leadership to this end.; secondly, at that time Japanese leaders were still hoping to maintain non-belligerent relations with the Soviet Union. If the Jews in Shanghai were to be slaughtered as Germany demanded, no doubt this barbarism would involve Russian Jews and would have an adverse influence on relations between the two countries; thirdly, the Jews in Harbin and Japan, who spoke up for the Jewish community in Shanghai with Japanese senior officials in an attempt to persuade Japan not to carry out the 'Meisinger Plan,' also exerted some influence, and lastly, as a result of the Confucian cultural tradition, East Asia did not foster the same religious, racial, and cultural prejudices against Jews which were prevalent in Christian Europe. Even the Japanese and the puppet officials at the middle and lower levels in Shanghai found it hard to accept the 'Meisinger Plan' both intellectually and emotionally. For example, Mr Shibata, Japanese Vice-Consul in Shanghai, was arrested because he secretly supported the Jews. All the factors mentioned above notwithstanding, the Japanese were still Hitler's allies, and the probability that Japanese fascists would take sudden action against Jews in Shanghai was an ever-present threat. The pressure and the capriciousness of Japanese policy towards the Jews put them in a difficult, unpredictable, and sometimes dangerous position for nearly four years.

VITAL STRUGGLE AND MUTUAL AID

The move to the ghetto imposed tremendous economic, physical, and above all psychological burdens on the Central European Jewish community. But it also moulded the earlier heterogeneous group of refugees into a genuine community, living together in close proximity in a real Jewish atmosphere.

Although few refugees, who were lucky enough to keep their jobs and business out of 'The Designated Area,' were permitted to leave the ghetto during the daytime, most people lost their jobs and business when they were moved to the ghetto. During this time the situation in Hongkew continued to deteriorate drastically as the economy continued to shrink. Some of the more physically robust members of the community began to compete with Chinese coolie labourers to earn a few pennies. A few of the more desperate ones resorted to begging.[34] Approximately 6,000 refugees were dependent upon relief from the Kitchen Fund by the beginning of 1944. Malnutrition and disease brought the total mortality figures for 1943 to 311.[35] Everybody waged a vital, dire struggle to survive.

Despite such difficult conditions, on the whole the community showed a surprising amount of solidarity. The majority of refugees maintained a remarkable degree of stability and equilibrium. They did their best to help each other. There were so many outstanding intellectuals and professionals among the Jewish refugees from Central Europe, it was a relatively simple matter for them to turn their knowledge and skills to supporting each other. One symbolic development was that, after entering the ghetto, three German-speaking refugees' Zionist groups were merged into one organization called the Zionist Organization Shanghai. Since the ZOS was well organized with a fixed membership and strong leadership core, it played an important role in organizing recreational and sports activities among refugees which served to reinforce the unity of the Central European Jewish community.[36] On July 17, 1945, American aircraft accidentally bombed the refugees area in Hongkew, causing the death of thirty-one refugees and leaving 250 refugees injured. At this moment of tragedy, the moral, physical, and mental resources of the refugee community were marshalled very quickly and effectively. Almost all the refugees rushed from where they happened to be to the nearest medical offices and other emergency stations to offer help. The refugee air-raid wardens and stretcher-bearers proved their worth.[37] This bombing was to be the last blow the

Central European Jewish community suffered during the war years. One month later, Japan surrendered.

SUPPORT FROM OVERSEAS JEWISH COMMUNITIES

In the bleak ghetto period, various international organizations, especially Jewish communities and organizations all over the world, gave great support to Central European Jewish refugees in Shanghai. The unremitting rescue efforts undertaken by the JDC (American Jewish Joint Distribution Committee) should certainly be mentioned. The JDC set up its office with a resident representative in Shanghai in 1938. At regular intervals it wrote a report detailing the situation of Shanghai Jewish refugees and collected donations in the States for Jewish refugees in Shanghai with monthly donations averaging US$ 30,000. After the outburst of the Pacific War, fearing reproaches from the American government, the JDC headquarters in New York had to discontinue posting money to Shanghai in May 1942. This was just at the time the JDC's resident representative, Laura Margolies, was put into a concentration camp by the Japanese.[38] Thanks to the efforts of Rabbi A. Kalmanowitz and Ms Margolies, who was later released and returned to the States by the end of 1943, the US government granted permission for the resumption of communication with enemy-occupied Shanghai. In March 1944, the JDC was able to transfer the equivalent of US$ 25,000 to Shanghai through Switzerland. Because of the steadily rising inflation in Shanghai during 1944, the rate of relief sent by the JDC soon increased. Starting with US$ 35,000 per month, it reached a sum of US$ 100,000 by January 1945, a rate which continued until the end of the war.[39]

Some other organizations and communities, which also played important role in rescuing and aiding Jewish refugees in Shanghai, should also not be overlooked. They include: the Jewish Agency in Jerusalem, the World Jewish Congress in New York, the Va'ad ha-Hazalah, Hebrew Immigrant Aid Society, the Polish Relief Committee for War Victims, the Jewish community in Kobe, Jewish community in Harbin, Arbeitsauschuss zur Hilfeleistung für Europäische Juden in Stockholm, and the Comite Comunidade Israelita de Lisboa. Of course, they are too many to be listed in their entirety.

MEMORABLE FRIENDSHIP BETWEEN CHINESE AND JEWS

Throughout history, Chinese people have experienced untold sufferings just as the Jewish people have done. Over thirty-five million Chinese were killed and wounded by Japanese Fascists during the Sino-Japanese war and the World War. This shared experience engendered in the Chinese people a deep respect and sympathy for the Jewish people. Soon after Hitler's anti-Jewish campaign commenced, Madame Sun Yet-sen headed a delegation in which she met the German Consul in Shanghai, and lodged a strong protest condemning Nazi atrocities. Her delegation included all the important leaders of the China League for Civil Rights: Dr Tsai Yuan-pei, Mr Lo Shun, Dr Lin Yu-tang to mention only a few.[40] Just when thousands of Jewish refugees were arriving in Shanghai, millions of Shanghai residents were themselves becoming refugees in the wake of the Japanese occupation of Shanghai. Despite their own very real troubles, the Shanghainese tried their best to help Jewish refugees in various ways. Chinese residents in Hongkew overcame all kinds of difficulties to vacate some of their own rooms to put up refugees. Before the hospitals for Jewish refugees was set up, Chinese hospitals treated a great number of Jewish refugees and saved many lives.[41]

I should emphasize here that Jewish refugees also did their best to support the Chinese national-democratic movement and joined in the resistance against Japanese aggression. Some Jews participated in the anti-Japanese war or co-operated with the Chinese Underground. They even gave their lives for the cause of the liberation of the Chinese people. I could mention many names here with deep respect: Jacob Rosenfeld, Hans Shippe, Wilhelm Mainzer, Gunter Nobel, Wilhelm Mann, Frank Theyleg, among them. Hans Shippe, a writer and reporter from Germany, was the first Jewish volunteer to fall in battle on Chinese soil during that country's war against the Japanese aggressor. He left Shanghai and joined the Chinese Army in 1939. On November 30, 1941, several days before Pearl Harbour, he died with a gun in his hand in an engagement with Japanese troops in Yinan county, Shandong province. Chinese people erected a monument for him near the battlefield.[42] Dr Jacob Rosenfeld arrived in Shanghai as a Jewish refugee from Austria in 1939 and left Shanghai to join the anti-Japanese war in 1941. He served in the ranks of the Chinese army for ten years, as a foreigner obtaining the highest rank of Commander of the Medical Corps.[43] Had he not died suddenly of a heart attack in Tel Aviv in 1951, it was speculated he would have been appointed Vice-Minister of Health of the PRC. Wilhelm Mainzer, another Jewish doctor from Germany, also became a high medical officer in the Chinese army.[44] Frank Theyleg, a Jewish engineer from Germany, was forced to make grenades for the Japanese military, but he found a way to make all the weapons he made ineffective.[45] Most of these heroic chapters in wartime Shanghai have yet to be written.

In the hardest days in Hongkew from 1943 to 1945, Jewish refugees and their Chinese neighbours enjoyed mutual help and shared weal and woe. Though largely separated by linguistic and cultural barriers, they found themselves bound together by mutual suffering. Wang Faliang, 78, who lived in Hongkew throughout the war, said: 'The Japanese persecuted us; Hitler persecuted the Jews, we were all subjected to great hardship.'[46] William Schurtman recalled that relations with the Chinese were pretty good, on the whole; a few refugees learned to speak a little Chinese, but many Chinese learned to speak fluent German.[47] Lilli Finkelstein wrote: 'We noticed that the Chinese in the neighbourhood behaved very well towards us. They knew how precarious our situation was, and they did not take advantage of it. They let us live our life unmolested. One should not overlook the fact that these people were among of the poorest and least educated. I even formed a kind of friendship with one or two of those women. Once a family invited us to their festive meal at their New Year celebration.'[48] Especially worthy of note is the close co-operation between Chinese and Jews on July 17, 1945, when American aircraft accidentally bombed the refugee area in Hongkew. Some memoirs described how Jewish refugees were ripping up the last of their treasured table and bed linen to make bandages, how Chinese helped carry the wounded through rubble, and offered to transport heavy loads of cots, mattresses, and buckets of water to the clinics, and how the poor Chinese in Hongkew brought food and even money to the emergency clinics.[49] I am especially touched by Rena Krasno's description of her friend Max's call from Hongkew on July 17. After describing the mutual aid between Chinese and Jews during the bombing, Max cried with youthful enthusiasm: 'Now we are all brothers!' When Rena repeated Max's words to her family, her father brightened visibly. He said 'Wonderful! Hitler has not been able to destroy the Jewish spirit nor have centuries of repression killed the inherent goodness of the Chinese!'[50]

Viewing what happened sixty years ago in retrospect, we, the people of Shanghai, are proud of the fact that when all the civilized world closed its doors to Jewish refugees, Shanghai provided a vital haven and every possible relief for them. Rabbi Arthur Schneier, one of leaders of the Jewish community in New York, said: 'Schindler's list saved a thousand lives but Shanghai saved a whole community of many thousands.'[51] On behalf of the Israeli people, when he visited Shanghai in 1993, the late Yitzhak Rabin expressed his heartfelt thanks to Shanghai for providing a haven for Jewish refugees from Nazi Europe. During his visit to Shanghai in 1995, the Austrian president paid a special visit to Hongkew to lay a wreath in memory of the Holocaust victims from Austria. Just like 'Schindler,' 'Wallenberg,' and 'Sugihara,' 'Shanghai' has now become a synonym of 'rescue' and 'haven' in the annals of the Holocaust. Former refugees have never forgotten Shanghai; Shanghai also does not forget its former refugees. In 1994, the Shanghai Municipality and Hongkou government erected the Monument for Holocaust Survivors in Huoshan Park, the heart of the former ghetto. Recently, Shanghai authorities decided to establish a museum in memory of the wartime Jewish refugees in Shanghai. As scholars, my colleagues and I have been doing our best to preserve the stories and write the historical chapter for the future generations, and make them keep the historical lesson firmly in their minds.

NOTES

1. There are a great number of books about Kaifeng Jews. For a general picture, see Sidney Shapiro (ed.), 1984.
2. See Pan Guang (ed.), 1995.
3. Chen Yuan and Ye Han, 1923, p. 2.
4. H.H. Ben-Sasson (ed.), 1976, p. 1034
5. Alex Grobman and Daniel Landes (ed.), 1983, p. 299.
6. A. Mars: 'A Note on the Jewish Refugees in Shanghai,' *Jewish Social Studies* Vol. 31 (October 1969), p. 286.
7. *Shanghai Journal*, December 5, 1938
8. A. Mars, 1969, p. 291.
9. See Rabbi Elchonon Yosef Hertzman, 1984.
10. Alex Grobman and Daniel Landes (ed.), 1983, p. 299.
11. Interview with Lord Lawrence Kadoorie, Hong Kong, April 19, 1989. See also Kadoorie 1985, pp. 80-99.
12. *North China Herald*, January 25, 1939.
13. Herman Dicker, 1962, p. 102. See also the name list of leading board of EASTJEWCOM.
14. Interview with Rena Krasno, Sankt Augustin, Germany, September 23, 1997.
15. Comprehensive statistics according to materials from interviews and The International Red Cross's report (1940) about Jewish refugees in Shanghai.
16. Interviews with Horst Eisfelder, Fred Freud, Egon Kornblum, Berlin, August 20-2, 1997.
17. Interviews with Horst Eisfelder, Fred Freud, Egon Kornblum, Berlin, August 20-2, 1997.
18. Annual Report of Shanghai Municipal Council, 1940, p. 472.

19 Interviews with Horst Eisfelder, Fred Freud, Egon Kornblum, Berlin, August 20-2, 1997.
20 Interview with William Schurtman, New York, January 17, 1989.
21 Interviews with Horst Eisfelder, Fred Freud, Egon Kornblum, Berlin, August 20-2, 1997.
22 Interview with William Schurtman, New York, January 17, 1989.
23 See Rabbi Elchonon Yosef Hertzman, 1984.
24 Interview with Lord Lawrence Kadoorie, Hong Kong, April 19, 1989. See also Kadoorie, 1985, pp. 80-99.
25 Interview with William Schurtman, New York, January 17, 1989.
26 Pan Guang (ed.), 1995, pp. 3, 39, 67, 78.
27 See Commemorative Anthology for the 40th anniversary of Beth Rivkah Schools Lubavitch. New York, 1981
28 Interviews with Schurtman and with Heinz Grunberg, Berlin, August 20-2, 1997.
29 Interviews with Schurtman and with Heinz Grunberg, Berlin, August 20-2, 1997.
30 Interviews with Schurtman and with Heinz Grunberg, Berlin, August 20-2, 1997.
31 See Rena Krasno, 1991. See also Abraham Kaufman, 1991.
32 Marvin Tokayer and Mary Swartz, 1979, p. 223.
33 David Kranzler, 1976, p. 489-90.
34 Interviews with Schurtman, Freud, Eisfelder (Berlin August 20-2, 1997).
35 Comprehensive statistics according to materials from oral interviews and the International Red Cross's report (1943) about Jewish refugees in Shanghai.
36 Interviews with Kornblum and with Leon Ilutovich, New York, October 12, 1992.
37 Interviews with Schurtman, Freud, Eisfelder (Berlin August 20-2, 1997).
38 Laura Margolis, 1995, pp. 18-34.
39 Interview with Laura Margolis, New Jersey, February 24, 1989.
40 *Israel's Messenger*, June 2, 1933.
41 Interview with Wang Faliang, Shanghai, May 5, 1997.
42 Wang Huo, 1979, pp. 17-19.
43 See Gerd Kaminski, 1993.
44 Pan Guang (ed.), 1995, p. 67.
45 Frank Theyleg, 1995, pp. 150-1.
46 Interview with Wang Faliang, Shanghai, May 5, 1997.
47 Interview with William Schurtman, New York, January 17, 1989.

48 Lilli Finkelstein, 1995, p. 163.
49 Interviews with Schurtman, Wang Faliang, Freud, and with Michael Blumenthal, New York, June 17, 1996.
50 See Rena Krasno, 1992.
51 Pan Guang (ed.), 1995, pp. 3, 39, 67, 78.

REFERENCES

Ben-Sasson, H.H. (ed.) (1976) *A History of the Jewish People*. Cambridge, Mass: Harvard University Press.

Dicker, Herman (1962) *Wanderers and Settlers in the Far East: A Century of Jewish Life in China and Japan*. New York: Twayne.

Finkelstein, Lilli (1995) 'Four Decades of My Life,' in: Pan Guang (ed.) *Shanghai Jews Memoirs*. Shanghai.

Grobman, Alex and Daniel Landes (ed.) (1983) *Genocide, Critical Issues of the Holocaust*. Los Angeles: Simon Wiesenthal Centre: Chappagua, N.Y. Rossel Books.

Guang, Pan (ed.) (1995) *Youtai ren pai Shanghai* (The Jews in Shanghai). Shanghai: Shanghai hua ban chu ban che.

Hertzman, Rabbi Elchonon Yosef (1984) *Escape to Shanghai*. Translated from Hebrew by Rabbi Dr Chaim U. Lipschitz, New York & Jerusalem.

Huo, Wang (1979) 'He Died on China's Soil, the Story of Hans Shippe,' *China Reconstructs*, Beijing, December 1979.

Kadoorie, Lord Lawrence (1985) 'The Kadoorie Memoir of 1979,' *Monographs of the Jewish Historical Society of Hong Kong* 1, Hong Kong.

Kaminski, Gerd (1993) *General Luo Genannt Langnase, Das abenteuerliche Leben des Dr med. Jacob Rosenfeld*. Wien: Löcker.

Kaufman, Abraham (1991) 'Jewish Journalism in the Far East,' *Our Press* 8, Tel-Aviv, World Federation of Jewish Journalists.

Kranzler, David (1976) *Japanese, Nazis and Jews. The Jewish Refugee Community of Shanghai 1938-1945*. New York: Yeshiva University Press.

Krasno, Rena (1991) 'Jewish Publications in Shanghai during First Half of 20th Century,' *Points East* 6(1), Seattle.

--(1992) *Strangers Always, A Jewish Family in Wartime Shanghai*. Berkeley.

Margolis, Laura (1995) 'Report of Activities in Shanghai, China, from December 8, 1941 to September 1943,' in: Pan Guang (ed.) *Shanghai Jews Memoirs*. Shanghai.

Mars, A. (1969) 'A Note on the Jewish Refugees in Shanghai,' *Jewish Social Studies* 31 (October 1969).

Shapiro, Sidney (ed.) (1984) *Jews in Old China*. New York: Hippocrene Books.

Theyleg, Frank (1995) 'The History of My Life,' in: Pan Guang (ed.) *Shanghai Jews Memoirs*. Shanghai.

Tokayer, Marvin and Mary Swartz (1979) *The Fugu Plan. The Untold Story of the Japanese and Jews during World War II*. New York and London: Weatherhill.

Yuan, Chen and Ye Han (1923) *Study on the Israelite Religion in Kaifeng - Commentaries on the Stone Inscription of the Israelites*. Shanghai.

Part Three

Performance and Presentation

CHAPTER 10

READING FOR PERFORMANCE:
A CIREBONESE ROMANCE
AS A NARRATIVE MODEL FOR WAYANG

MATTHEW ISAAC COHEN

I

E ana sing duwe! 'Hey, someone else is taking charge!' A crowd. Some people sitting, some milling about. *Ana, ana.* 'I'm here, I'm here.' Voices, music, stylized movement. Selling and buying. Food and hot drinks circulated and consumed. *Sing ditembangi Mama Kuwu...* 'Mr. Headman is being sung to...' The odour of stale perspiration mixed with the sweet aroma of clove cigarettes. Dim lights. A sequined dress. *Kocapa ingkang wonten dhateng negari wau.* 'Let us speak of the conditions in the aforementioned kingdom.' Tightly packed-in bodies and jostling elbows. The high-pitched shriek of feedback from an audio speaker.

A theatrical event involves an observer-participant with a overwhelming potpourri of sensations. The scholarly mind demands order. A trained researcher at such an event, whether for the first time or on any number of subsequent occasions, is inclined to be *conditioned* to see with certain basic analytical ideas or assumptions previously established in her mind's eye. 'An aesthetically marked and heightened mode of communication, framed in a special way and put on display for an audience' is a definition for performance suggested by Richard Bauman (1989:262). Even in such a minimal definition, assumptions surface in the relation of observer to observed phenomenon that are problematic in their cultural specificity.

The adjectival use of aesthetic is intended to signal the artistic quality of performances. 'Aesthetics,' however, involves more than just art: it is a systematic approach to reception, grounded in figurations of taste and relative value. (The relative value component of aesthetics is linked as well to Bauman's use of the word 'heightened.') Any such system is not universal, but worked out *vis à vis* particular contingencies of markets, generic histories, and individual affectations and sympathies.

The metaphor of framing, derived from Gregory Bateson (1972) and Erving Goffman (1974), might also be problematized. Framing an oil painting not only demarcates a canvas from the space of the wall around it, it also commodifies the object: placed in a frame, a painting is 'put on display,' with the implicit message of 'hands off: this is a completed work of art that is to be preserved and appreciated *as it is.*' Oil paintings can be rigidly marked from the observer because they are artifacts of the past. While in fact subject to the rigours of time (decay, vandalism), paintings are meant to be viewed as atemporal. It is this illusion which allows them to maintain their value, both aesthetic and economic. The European stage of the late nineteenth century, with the elimination of the apron in front of the proscenium arch, consciously replicated the framing of oil paintings. Lights projected into the eyes of the actor prevented interactive eye-contact and the establishment of a direct audience-performer relationship. Audiences became quieter and texts sacrosanct. Performances were no longer tied to performative interaction: a 'paranoid' (Feldman, 1991:66-7) realist theatre developed in which actors pretended they were not on display. A 'framed' model is a legitimate way of understanding certain performances, but it is clearly exceptional, not a comprehensive approach to the gamut of performance events. It is *normally* the case that performances are experienced as a moment in social life, not 'framed' outside of it.

And who or what constitutes 'an audience,' so facilely incorporated into Bauman's definition, anyway? Is an audience always distinct from performers? Did not Chinese *q'in* players perform their music primarily for themselves? Were not Roman emperors watching events, whether gladiator contests or classical tragedies, at least as much 'on display' as the goings-on in the arena?

My point in focusing attention on Bauman's definition of performance, which is really no worse than many others, is to indicate some of the *pitfalls* of universalizing the concept, as well as the *usefulness* of putting forward the idea of performance in such general terms so as to sensitize ourselves to how fixed our own perceptions are. Simple exposure to other *forms* of artistic production and reception will not necessarily unfix or dissolve imposed categories such as audience, performer, event, frame, or aesthetics, all derived from normative, 'high' performing arts of Europe and America (Bauman himself has studied many sorts of performances, primarily 'folk'). I suggest that to accomplish such a creative dissolution (a necessary prelude to creative re-integration), it is necessary to go further, and examine non-Western *critical models* for understanding performance intensely.

In many non-Western and particularly Asian cultures, sophisticated models of performance have been codified in aesthetic writings, formulated independently of Western traditions of performance writing originating in Aristotle's *Poetics*. The much studied *Natya Sastra* on the Sanskrit drama of ancient India is perhaps the most celebrated, but there are many additional stimulating examples to be encountered by the persistent student of cross-cultural aesthetics, such as the inspired treatises of Zeami on *noh* drama and the deeply spiritual *Dharma Pawayangan* on Balinese shadow puppet theatre. However, not all literate cultures appear to have been interested in codifying the aesthetics of performance in such philosophical terms, at least not before encountering European values and norms. For such cultures, it is incumbent upon the scholar to look at other materials, particularly at narrative representations of performance events and genres.

Narrative representations of performances have commonly been used as 'sources' for the historical study of a particular art form. 'Biases' in representation have consequently been viewed as something to be filtered out by the historian. Exemplary of this move is the cultural historical approach of Peter Burke, who recommends a strategy of 'oblique reading' of Early Modern European writings on folk performances. Burke writes: 'We want to know about performances, but what have survived are texts; we want to see these performances through the eyes of the craftsmen and peasants themselves, but we are forced to see them through the eyes of literate outsiders' (Burke, 1978:65). Another approach is possible, however: to use textual representations of performance to see the eyes of the *seer*. Some of these seers may indeed be 'literate outsiders,' in Burke's terms, to the traditions they describe. But others are more aptly characterized as well-informed 'insiders.' In any case, the line between scholar-observer and performer-participant, like many other lines, must not be taken for granted.

II

Understanding narrative performance theory means looking at particular texts. These texts tend to be unruly; they are not ordered in terms of theses and theories, but by principles of poetry and drama. As such, they must be read inter-textually, not only in terms of how they serve to represent live performance analogues, but how they are enmeshed in particular literary genres.

The Cirebon region of north coastal West Java, Indonesia, where I have been conducting anthropological fieldwork on theatrical cultures since 1993, yields many rich examples of such texts. Read as theory, they can allow one to understand the constitution of live performances more aptly. I would like to turn to one of these texts, *Jaka Menyawak*, which contains a narrative model of the performance of *wayang kulit* (shadow puppet theatre; henceforth referred to as *wayang*) strikingly different from ones set out in the scholarly (largely ethnographic and philological) literature on *wayang* written by both Indonesians and non-Indonesians. These differences are partially attributable to the fact that most of these performance models concern implicitly or explicitly Java's 'normative' *wayang*, associated with the princely courts of south Central Java.¹ But the *Jaka Menyawak* model, I believe, is also applicable to Javanese performance in general. More than that, it challenges the dominance of any 'universal' performance study model claiming the power to explain all performative processes.

First, briefly, the text and its provenance. Sudibjo (1985:2) has described *Jaka Menyawak* as a 'folktale' (*cerita rakyat*) and the text refers to itself as a *kandha* or 'tale,' although from the point of view of European genre theory, the tale could well be classified as a romance conforming to a classic pattern in which a disadvantaged youth gains the hand of a beautiful princess. The romance of Jaka Menyawak is one of the most famous of the stories from the Cirebon cultural area. It was one of the six most popular stories performed by *wayang wong* or *topeng dhalang* masked-dance-drama troupes during the 1930s and early 1940s (cf. Harja Somantri, 1978-9:19). The popularity of the tale in the late colonial period is indicated as well by the fact that the renowned Gegesik painter, Sitisiwan (c. 1865-1948), created at least two large cloth paintings illustrating the tale.² The story of *Jaka Menyawak* remains a staple of the 'rod puppet theatre' (*wayang golek cepak*) repertoire and is well-known to 'professional story-tellers' (*dhalang kandha*) and cultural aficionados in the Cirebon region today.³

In contrast, the poetic telling of the tale, at least judging from the public collections of Javanese manuscripts in Leiden, Jakarta, and Yogyakarta, appears to be not widely distributed within the Cirebon area itself and entirely unknown outside of it. One version of this text, from the sub-district of Ciwaringin written on 'thin bark paper that was in a state of extreme decay due to its antiquity,' has been published (cf. Sudibjo, 1980, 1985).⁴ I encountered another inscription of the text in this same sub-district, differing in some particulars, in the course of my field research in the Cirebon region (1993-5). The paper of the manuscript on which the published version is based, and certain internal cultural referents, indicate a *terminus post quem* date for the published inscription of the second half of the nineteenth century.⁵

Both of these inscriptions of *Jaka Menyawak* were or are part of the collections of professional singers of literature, known in Cirebon as *dhalang maca* or *dhalang bujangga*. It is performed on occasion at all-night vigils in conjunction with rites of passage and at *unjungan* ritual events held in cemeteries in honour of the ancestors.⁶ Many literary works from the Cirebon area are composed entirely in the work-horse *dhandhanggula* metre that can be sung easily by non-professionals. In contrast, *Jaka Menyawak* is composed in a variety of metres, suggesting that the text was originally written to be sung by professional reader-singers of literature. These reader-singers are accompanied antiphonally by small choruses of *panjak* who provided 'sung responses' (*senggakan*) - repeating final line endings or entire lines, singing nonsense syllables, shouting out brief explications and comments (*adhuh!*), and beating out rhythms with whatever percussive instruments are around (spoons against glasses, lighters against the floor). The performance practice of this text, as described by Sudibjo (1980:7-8; 1985:5-6) and confirmed by Arps (1992:26), bears upon the written inscription: certain words and phrases are repeated in particular positions where one would expect reduplication from accompanying *panjak*.

The romance of *Jaka Menyawak* tells the story of Jaka Pekik, a son of the king of Madenda, who is cursed by his father and becomes a *menyawak* (monitor lizard) as he refuses to accede to his father's demand for him to get married. Thus does Jaka Pekik become known as Jaka Menyawak. After being exiled by his father from Madenda, Jaka Menyawak studies the mystical sciences with his grandfather, *Ki Ajar* (Honourable Anchorite) Mustakim, and another guru named *Ki Ajar* Kismayajati. He is adopted by a poor fisherwoman named *Nyi Rangdha* (Honourable Widow) Kasiyan. Finally, after many adventures, Jaka Menyawak decides that the time has come for him to get married, anticipating his re-entrance into human society.

The object of the young hero's desire is none other than a daughter of the king of Majapait.[7] It takes a bit of convincing, but he is able to persuade his adopted mother, the Widow Kasiyan, to go to the palace of Majapait to present his suit. The Widow tells the king of Majapait that she has a son who has the form of a lizard but can speak like a human being. Her son wants nothing more than to marry the daughter of a king, namely the daughter of the king of Majapait. Jaka Menyawak's offer is flatly refused by the king's three eldest daughters, but finally accepted by the beautiful Dewi Pata, his youngest daughter. The king of Majapait tries to persuade his daughter to reconsider, but she will not listen. Finally, in desperation, the king tells the Widow that he will accept her lizard son as a son-in-law, but that he has some conditions which must first be fulfilled. To be considered as a son-in-law, Jaka Menyawak must present the king with a set of betel nut equipment made from gold and a farm filled with many different sorts of animals. Not only that, before the king gives his consent, Jaka Menyawak must already rule a nation as powerful and large as Majapait, 'densely inhabited by a multi-ethnic populace' (*pepek sakehing jalmi*), including people of Chinese, Dutch, and Javanese descent.

The bridal procession, the king states, must include a variety of art forms, likewise multicultural.

Diiring tetanggapan iki /
wayang topeng berokan /
genjring trebangipun /
mesthine lawan musikan
Kudu pepek reyog lan berdangsa iki /
Galaganjur neng ngarsa.

It should be accompanied by these hired entertainments:
Wayang, *topeng* [mask-dance], *berokan* [animal-mask-dance],
A single-headed drum ensemble of *genjring* and *trebang*.
There must be *musikan* [European music].
The *reyog* ensemble and ballroom dancing must be complete.
[A *gamelan* playing] *Galaganjur* should be at the front.

The Widow Kasiyan goes home to Jaka Menyawak with a heavy heart to report to her beloved adopted son the king's arduous demands. But Jaka Menyawak is unperturbed. That night, he changes back to his human form and uses magical objects given to him by his *gurus* to fulfill the king's demands. He then returns to his lizard form. The king of Majapait has no choice but to agree to accept Jaka Menyawak, now the king of the nation of Gebangtinatar, as his son-in-law. A date and time is set for Jaka Menyawak to arrive at the capital of Majapait to procure his bride, accompanied by all the requisite entertainments.

Several forms of cultural performance are subsequently enacted in the palace courtyard in the days preceding the wedding. One is *ujungan* (also known as *sampyong*), a sort of fencing competition-*cum*-musical accompaniment, in which representatives from the kingdoms of Majapait and Gebangtinatar strike each other with strips of rattan. This is won by Gebangtinatar. Then follows the main 'hired entertainment' (*tetanggapan*), a troupe which enacts *topeng* (mask dance) in the day and shadow puppet theatre at night. The troupe performs consecutively over several days and nights. It is apparently so appealing that Jaka Menyawak transforms himself into his human form once again and surreptitiously slips out of the royal court of Majapait, for he 'desires to watch this shadow puppet performance' (*arsa nongton wayang iki*).

Wancinipun tengah dalu /
Jaka Menyawak umijil /
medal saking pedaleman /
arsa ningali ringgit /
karsa anggenteni ngendhang./
Wong nongton padha ningali.//

In the middle of the night,
Jaka Menyawak goes out,
Exiting from the inner quarters of the palace.
He desires to see the shadow puppet show.
He intends to play drum, replacing the drummer.
The spectators all stare at him.

Sakabe wong nongton iku /
netrane pating pucicil /
ningali pangendhang anyar /
ora kathik kethip-kethip /
kenang lamuk tan denrasa /
keringete nurut wentis.//

All the spectators,
Their eyes bulging in-amazement,
Stare at the new drummer
Without blinking.
Bitten by mosquitoes, they feel not a thing.
Sweat trickles down the calves of their legs.

Sakabe wong nonton ibur /
ake wadon dentempiling /
dening iku lakinira /
sabab lali adang iki /
pijer sira nongton wayang /
ana nguma boca nangis.//

All the spectators are in a commotion.
Many women end up getting slapped
By their husbands
For forgetting to cook rice.
'You're always out watching *wayang*.
But our child is at home crying!'

Papireng dening sang ayu /
putri ratu Majapait /
sakabe anongton wayang /
sekawan panganten istri /
ingkang aran Dewi Pata /
titiga sadherekneki.//

When word reaches the beautiful
Daughters of the king of Majapait,
All go to watch the *wayang* performance.
Four young women:
The one named Dewi Pata
And her three sisters.

Sakabe pan samya wuyung /
ing pangendhang wayang iki /
nanging sang Jaka Menyawak /
ningali garwane muli /
nuli balik ingkang ngendhang /
andhingini garwaneki .//

All swoon over
The drummer of the *wayang*.
But when the honourable Jaka Menyawak
Sees that his fiancée has gone home,
The drummer then returns,
Arriving before his fiancée.

Menyawak ngandika arum /
maring garwanira iki /
rayi padha nongton apa? /
Mangsuli garwanireki /
kula anongton pangendhang /
pangendhange dhalang ringgit.

Menyawak speaks sweetly
To his fiancée now.
'What were you watching, little one?'
His fiancée answers him.
'I was watching a drummer.
The drummer of the *wayang* puppeteer.'

When Jaka Pekik asks her where his 'clothes' are (that is the skin he shed when he transmogrified back into his human form), Dewi Pata says that she has no idea. She does admit to having found the skin of a crocodile in a pot, which she disposed of by burning. The clever Dewi Pata has apparently known all along that Jaka Menyawak was in fact a human in disguise.

Complications then arise. Pata is discovered by her elder sisters in the company of Jaka Menyawak, whom they do not recognize because of his transformation. Each of them vies for the hand of the handsome drummer. Pata's sisters do not know or will not believe that the drummer is the same individual as Dewi Pata's fiancée, Jaka Menyawak. But as usual in tales of this sort, Dewi Pata and Jaka Menyawak end up marrying, with the blessings of the king of Majapait and his hope that Jaka Pekik 'in the future will desire to fulfil the commands of the Messenger of God' (*ing mbesuke kudu gelem anglampahi/ dhawuhe Rasululla*) that is to say, Muhammad.

III

Jaka Menyawak is allegedly set in the time of the pre-Islamic kingdom of Majapait. But it in fact represents very much a colonial Cirebonese world, filled with 'anachronisms,' including the king's Islamic blessing and the Dutch cultural performances alluded to above (ballroom dancing, European music). The anachronisms are knowing, and often comic, as when the Widow Kasiyan, upon hearing of her adopted son's return from a sailing expedition, rushes to greet the boat, forgetting in her motherly enthusiasm first to put on a *tapih* skirt. Jaka Menyawak takes some time in emerging from the boat, and the Widow frets and worries that Jaka Menyawak has been sold to a Chinese trader. The text does not intend itself to be taken seriously as 'history,' but as a tale. This being said, *Jaka Menyawak* is not simply a work of escapist fiction. It is meant to be instructive. The narrative poem yields vital insights into how performances are viewed, and sets out with particular strength a narrative model of participant roles. It is somewhat hyperbolic in some ways, but in others absolutely realistic. That is a characteristic of models, in general.

I would like to open up *Jaka Menyawak*, reading it as narrative performance theory, by looking at it through terms which the text ultimately subverts and overturns: *genre, event, sponsorship, performers, audiences*, and *meanings*. Each of these aspects of performance can be read intertextually *vis à vis* the scholarly literature on performance in Java and my own observations from the field about contemporary performance practice in the Cirebon region.

GENRE

One of the basic axioms of performance studies, and particularly the study of Asian performance, is that it is possible to classify events according to their generic constituencies. '*This* is a performance of *wayang kulit*, *that* is a performance of pop music, and *that* - well, *that* is social dance.' Such classifications allow for the development of disciplinary discussions, but also maintain the 'minority status' of the study of Asian performance as a discipline, prevent the diversity of so-called variants from being studied on the grounds that such-and-such has 'already been described,' and impose a fixity and unity upon a performative field that might be heterogeneous in orientation or hybrid in composition as well as historically in flux. Contemporary Cirebonese *wayang* performances are simultaneously shadow puppet plays, popular music concerts, social dances, and much more.

Jaka Menyawak refers explicitly and repeatedly to numerous artistic genres. Eight distinct art forms are requested by name by the king of Majapait for the *mapag penganten* (collecting the bride) procession from Majapait to Gebangtinatar. *Wayang*, *topeng*, and *berokan* - three art forms mentioned in a single line - are three of the four Javanese performing arts (along with *ronggeng*, or social dance) which are symbolic of the different stages on the Sufic path to enlightenment (Zoetmulder, 1995). Each of these four is seen as quintessentially Javanese.[8] *Genjring* and *trebang* designate single-headed frame drums, instruments associated with Islamic chant forms, Arabic texts, and Middle-Eastern style melodies and rhythms (Linck, 1921; Endo Suanda, 1993). These instruments are said to be *mestine lawan*, literally 'necessarily juxtaposed with,' *musikan* or European music, typically referring to either a string ensemble or brass band (Sumarsam, 1995). *Reyog* refers not to the well-known *Reog Ponorogo*, the lion-dance of East Java, but rather to a West Javanese form of folk music-theatre featuring clowns, single-headed frame drums, and a shawm. This theatre is typically associated with Sundanese culture by Cirebonese observers and participants, although the Cirebonese variant has many distinctive features, such as dramatic elements (Kasim Achmad, 1975; Tisna Sopandi, 1980). *Berdangsa* refers to ballroom dancing, a favoured pass time of Europeans in colonial Java, but an art that few Javanese practised. Finally, the procession is to be headed by a classical *gamelan* ensemble tuned to the pentatonic *prawa* scale playing the processional melody *Galaganjur* (Pikes), a piece in the repertoire of the gamelan ensemble of the royal court of Kacerbonan when Jaap Kunst conducted his investigations circa 1920 (Kunst and Kunst-van Wely, 1924).

In the enactment of the procession, however, the distinct identities of these art forms breaks down.

Ana ingkang nabu bedhug /
ana ingkang nabu suling /
ana ingkang nabu trebang /
reyog topeng lan gong beri. //

There was someone playing a *bedhug* [bass drum]
There was someone playing a *suling* [bamboo flute]
There was someone playing a *trebang* [single-headed frame drum],
Reyog, *topeng*, and *gong beri* [small gong].

It is not clear who is playing what. Is the *bedhug*, a bass drum used for the Islamic call to prayer but also a part of some Cirebonese musical ensembles, a part of the *wayang* musical ensemble? What is the *suling* accompanying? Is the *trebang* player a part of the *reyog* group, or is he playing with the *genjring* drummers? *Reyog*, *topeng*, and *gong beri* are mentioned on a single line, despite their different 'ethnic' orientations: *reyog* being characteristically Sundanese, *topeng* Javanese, and the *gong beri* a part of a hybrid European-Javanese marching band.

The rather wild mixing of the procession is suggestive of a hybrid colonial cultural form referred to alternately in Malay as a *pasar malam* or 'night market' and in Dutch as a *jaarmarkt* (fair). These combined trade exhibitions, fairs, and cultural festivals enjoyed enormous popularity in late colonial urban Cirebon, appealing to mixed audiences of Europeans, Chinese, Sundanese, and Javanese, and drawing selectively on cultural features and forms of all of the above. Particularly of interest to Javanese spectators was the participatory ballroom dancing. Admission to a dance hall usually required purchasing food or beverages at an adjacent European restaurant, but less affluent Javanese spectators who could not afford the price of a drink would crowd around to get a peek at the dancers. For the many visitors unaccustomed to seeing men and women dancing cheek-to-cheek, it was the most interesting *tontonan* (spectacle) of a fair.[9] The influence of these *pasar malam* was not limited to urban Cirebon. They provided a model as well for communal celebrations throughout the countryside that is still intact. The otherwise bizarre presence of ballroom dancing in a wedding procession might be explicable by the influence of such *jaarmarkt*.

Following the procession, the generic mixing seems to resolve itself into a series of cultural performances: *ujungan* (fencing with strips of rattan), followed by a hired entertainment or entertainments described initially as *wayang topeng*, performed day and night. Subsequently, only '*wayang*' is mentioned. It seems reasonable, at least at first glance, to assume that *wayang* and *topeng* refer to different art forms, shadow puppet theatre and mask-dance, likely performed by the same troupe. '*Topeng*' usually refers to Cirebon's famous *tari topeng*, also known as *topeng kecil, topeng Cirebon*, or *topeng babakan* (Endo Suanda, 1983; Rodgers-Aguiniga, 1986; Westerkamp, 1987:33-6). In this dance form, usually performed during the daytime, a solo dancer known as the *dhalang topeng* enacts a series of masked impersonations of contrasting dramatic characters, including Samba (also sometimes called Pamindho) and Klana (also referred to as Rahwana). These dances are interspersed with comedy provided by *bodhor* (clowns). It remains a common practice in the Cirebonese area that a single troupe will perform a *topeng* show in the day and a shadow puppet play at night. At least until the recent past, many puppeteers (*dhalang wayang*) were also competent mask-dancers (*dhalang topeng*), and would dance during the day and perform puppetry in the night. Shadow puppet theatre has long been absolutely the cultural performance *de rigueur* for the celebration of royal rites of passage, including circumcisions and weddings.

The supposition that '*wayang*' refers to *wayang kulit* is a normative reading, but not the only one possible, for '*wayang*' in the Cirebon area does not only refer to shadow puppet theatre: Cirebonese rod puppet theatre, or *wayang cepak*, is also referred to commonly as '*wayang*.' According to Foley

(1989:65), both rod and shadow puppeteers commonly performed in the recent past as *dhalang topeng* during the day and as puppeteers at night. There is also a form of mask-dance theatre that was performed in the Cirebon region up through the 1980s, in which masked dancers enacted stories from the shadow puppet and rod puppet theatre repertoires. This form has been given many alternate designations in the literature: *topeng dhalang*, *wayang urang*, and *topeng besar* (Westerkamp, 1987:36-43), *wayang wong* and *wayang topeng* (Endo Suanda, 1973). This may also have been called '*wayang*' for short.

The text does not clarify to which form of *wayang* it refers by indicating the performing objects used. The description of the performance focuses solely on one musical instrument, the *kendhang*, a type of drum that is part of the musical ensemble of *wayang kulit*, *wayang cepak*, and *wayang wong* alike. I read 'shadow puppet theatre' for *wayang* for I know that this is the preferential form for Cirebonese royal court performances (the model for the 'Majapait' performances of the text) and that the phrase *wayang topeng* normally refers to 'shadow puppet theatre [at night] and mask-dance [during the day],' but in fact what precisely is enacted is textually unresolved.

Event

Performances of *wayang* are occasioned. It is possible, in theory, for a puppeteer to sponsor him or herself. Such a performance is referred to as *babar-babar wade*, and are put on primarily by beginning puppeteers for the sake of publicity. However, the vast majority of *wayang* performances are sponsored by either communities in association with communal celebratory rites or by families in connection with rites of passage, above all wedding celebrations.

The *wayang* performance of *Jaka Menyawak* is related to an intricate system of exchange around the celebration of a wedding. It is in a sense a by-product of one of the *jalukan* or 'demands' of the bride's father, the king of Majapait. Before his mother approaches the king, Jaka Menyawak imparts the following advice.

Lamun wis katampa /
mbok ana jajalukan /
Aja ora den sanggupi /
karsaneng nata. //

Once you have been received,
There will possibly be demands made.
Don't refuse to fulfill
The wishes of the king.

True to form, the king insists that the bridal procession be accompanied by a vast array of cultural entertainments, including *wayang*. If the Widow Kasiyan cannot fulfill this and his other demands, the king threatens that he will break her neck. The anticipation of the king's demands by Jaka Menyawak demonstrates that they are part of an implicit model of courtship, involving *prestations*, in the sense developed by Marcel Mauss (1990) in his classic essay, *The Gift*. For with 'acquiring a son-in-law' (*olih mantu*), as marriage is referred to in virilocal Cirebon, it is expected that a father-in-law will also acquire material wealth and prestige items, including performances.

No mention is made among the king's demands of a need to have performances *following* the bridal procession, however. This might be taken as an implicit necessity. *Of course* one will have the *wayang* troupe that participated in the bridal parade perform afterwards for the public. However, the *wayang* and *topeng* performances are referred to distinctly in the text as *tanggapan*, 'hired entertainments.' This classification doubly distinguishes the *wayang* and *topeng* performances from the demand performances insisted upon by the king as *jalukan* and the communally enacted *ujungan* which immediately precedes them. The classification of the *wayang* and *topeng* shows, as *tanggapan* strongly suggests, that a distinct effort was made to ensure that the combined *wayang-topeng* troupe not only participated in the procession, but performed afterwards. (None of the other entertainments featured in the parade are described as *tanggapan*.)

SPONSORSHIP
The text leaves wide open the question of who the sponsor of the *wayang* is. Surely, for a *tanggapan* to happen, someone must perform the act of *nanggap* (hiring). But the act of hiring is never described, nor is the patron or sponsor of the troop named. Again, one might assume: it was Jaka Menyawak who provided the cultural entertainments for the bridal procession, so it *must* have been the same party who provided for the post-procession hired entertainments. Yet this idea finds no explicit textual support. The text in this and other ways exemplifies a particular type of audience experience of *wayang*. It is written 'from below,' from the perspective of spectators who are apathetic to who the sponsoring agent might be.

Wayang performances are part of daily social life in many parts of rural Java. In the town of Gegesik (some thirty kilometres outside of the city of Cirebon), where I have been living since 1994, some forty *wayang* performances occur annually within an easy walking distance of the town square. In the past, I have been assured, performances were even more frequent. Many spectators simply assume that performances will happen, without worrying overmuch whether a certain performance is sponsored by a town ward in association with an agrarian rite, held as part of a *wayang* festival self-sponsored by puppeteers, or enacted in conjunction with a wedding. A person may well think deeply about the sponsoring agent if the institution or person has a particular relation to herself - her brother, neighbour, or own town ward. But such direct sponsor-audience ties, I have found, are discernible for fewer spectators than one might assume.

The absence of a visible sponsor is in a sense a comic inversion or even *parody* of the model of performance outlined by Ward Keeler (1987) for south Central Javanese *wayang*, which is written from the vantage-point of sponsorship. Sponsors, in Keeler's influential depiction, purposefully and methodically attempt to 'dissemble and enhance' their authority through hiring a *wayang* troupe to perform. A puppeteer, in capturing the attention of an audience, represents the power of a dissembled sponsor to exert control over audience-guests and a community at large. Keeler presents in essence an elaborate defence of why someone would go to the trouble of sponsoring a *wayang* performance. In our text, Jaka Menyawak sheds his lizard disguise in order to perform himself. The king's daughters all fall shamelessly in love with a drummer. Afterwards, Dewi Pata is castigated by her elder sister, Indrawati:

ngiseni dhayang dedalan /
cok nelembuk pantes rupanira iki /
grejeg ing panongtonan. //

You bring shame, base woman.
Your appearance befits a prostitute,
Creating an uproar like you did at a spectacle.

Keeler's categories are turned upside-down. The performance brings shame, not enhanced authority, to the king of Majapait. Jaka Menyawak makes himself known and visible at the performance by becoming a performer, not dissembling himself behind one. The text essentially mocks any attempt to appropriate *wayang* for instrumental purposes. In *Jaka Menyawak*, *wayang* is a spectacle, a *penongtonan*, not a contest to win an audience's submission.

PERFORMERS

As a *tanggapan*, the *wayang* troupe is by definition professional. It is formally engaged by a sponsor for a predetermined fee. *Jaka Menyawak* treats only one performer, the drummer, in any detail, for reasons to be discussed below. But the type of treatment afforded the drummer is indexical of a generalized model of performance.

It is assumed by spectators, represented by the princesses of Majapait, that the troupe's status as a *tanggapan* necessarily entails that all the troupe members are professional as well. Dewi Pata tells her fiancée, 'I was watching a drummer./The drummer of the *wayang* puppeteer.' The doubling indicates that it was not *any* drummer that Dewi Pata believed she was watching, but the drummer belonging to the troupe directed by the puppeteer. This illusion, that the drummer is a regular troupe member, is actively supported by Jaka Menyawak. He makes it a point to return to the palace only after Dewi Pata leaves so that she cannot possibly know that the drummer was only a temporary substitute.

Jaka Menyawak's dramatic portrayal of a professional drummer is dead on. It is an important characteristic of Cirebonese *wayang* that musicians not only play their instrumental parts, but also act out dramatic roles and perform as a puppeteer's interlocutors. Charles O. van der Plas (1937:655), in a description of a 1935 *wayang* performance by a Cirebonese puppeteer, describes the musicians as a puppeteer's *tegenspelers*, or 'opposites,' in the sense that a female star plays opposite a male star in a film. Part of the role of a musician is to act as a puppeteer's interlocutor. 'The play was extremely lively after the Cirbonese style, Van der Plas notes. The indefatigable puppeteer performed opposite his noisy *tegenspelers*, the musicians. In contrast with the puppeteer's sober yet splendid discourse, [...] the musicians responded with exclamations, questions, contradictions...' Musicians also inhabit certain *dramatis personae*. This is also the case for musicians in a European orchestra, where flautists are stereotypically flighty, trumpeters loud-mouthed and obnoxious, and so on. But in Cirebonese *wayang*, musicians actively highlight these *personae* in performances, presenting staged, professional selves in Goffman's sense. 'The individual typically infuses his activity with signs which dramatically highlight and portray confirmatory facts that might otherwise remain unapparent or obscure' (Goffman 1959:30).

A drummer in Cirebonese *wayang* is not only the 'conductor' of the *gamelan* orchestra (under the general supervision of the puppeteer), the battery of drums he must play also demands the highest degree of physical exertion. Many other *gamelan* instruments can and are played by women, but drum is always played by a man. Drum-players must have great physical endurance and also must endure a degree of physical pain, for a drummer must strike hide drum heads with his open hands repeatedly during performances. Some drummers obtain the necessary strength and insensitivity to pain by drink, others through implanting *susuk* or magical slivers into their hands or arms.

Drummers dramatically highlight their prowess through costume, gesture, and speech. It is typical for a drummer to take off his shirt part way into a performance, displaying his well-developed upper body, or wrap a strip of cloth around his heads as a sweatband. Drummers strike dramatic poses during performances, lunging for a distant *bedhug* bass drum or playing a small *ketipung* drum with his shoulders up and elbows cocked at a striking angle to his torso. Many drummers establish and maintain eye contact with audience members during performances and may be sex idols for female audience members. Comments made by drummers in performances tend to be shouted with bravura and comments made *about* drummers by other musicians in a group frequently allude to their salaciousness. A reference to a character whose eyes role in pain prompts a musician to say about a drummer, '*His* eyes roles, when he looks at a *woman.*' In a performance of the ritual drama *Murwakala* (The Origin of Kala), Divine Guru asks his monstrous son, Divine Kala, a riddle. 'Do you know of something with four penises?' Kala answers, 'Nah, there is nothing like that.' A musician promptly shouts out, 'There is, the drummer!'

For reasons related to musicality, dramatic presence, and sex appeal, drum-players can develop reputations independent of the ensembles of which they are part, and are sometimes specially requested by sponsors. Drumming is not the only part of a *wayang* performance, but for many spectators it is one of the most important aspects.

Jaka Menyawak's impersonation of the role of drummer is so complete that it carries over to the post-performance domain. Dewi Pata's three elder siblings are not looking for their little sister after the show, but rather for the drummer.

kocapa putri titiga /
angilari pangendhange dhalang ringgit /
mlebet ing dalem pura. //

Let us describe the three princesses.
Looking for the drummer of the *wayang* puppeteer,
They enter the inner quarters of the palace.

The three princesses clearly *expect* to find the drummer in the midst of an arranged rendezvous with Dewi Pata. This is what handsome young drummers do: they seduce female spectators on stage, and arrange to meet them afterwards.

The boundaries of life and art become increasingly indistinct and porous. Roles established on stage become transferred to real life.

AUDIENCES

Jaka Menyawak's first question to his wife after she returns to the palace is what she had been watching. Her answer is not *wayang*, but rather the drummer of the *wayang*.

Focal points of audience interest in *wayang* are multiple. Any attempt to 'read' a performance means situating oneself or empathizing with a certain participant position. Keeler's position, elucidated above, is primarily that of a sponsor of a *wayang*. A.L. Becker (1979), in a classic article on *wayang* 'text-building,' draws a picture of *wayang* from a puppeteer's point of view, informed by his own puppetry studies in East Java. *Jaka Menyawak*, in contrast, takes an audience point of view, and more particularly a *female* audience point of view. I have found, from the direct experience of seeing perhaps three hundred *wayang* performances in the Cirebon area and performing myself as a puppeteer perhaps fifty additional times, that the constitution of *wayang* audiences varies considerably from place to place. In some areas, *wayang* audiences are primarily made up of young men. But in certain villages and hamlets, such as the village of Srombyong, audiences are predominately female. *Jaka Menyawak* attempts to suggest what makes a *wayang* attractive to a woman, to interpret a gendered gaze.

The radical circumscription of the focus of the text on one particular performance element, the drummer, is highly intentional. No mention is made of the puppeteer's name or performance style, the story performed, or any *wayang* characters depicted at the screen. All energies are focused upon the drummer. Eyes bulge, physical discomfort goes unnoticed. Familial responsibilities are forgotten and proprietal norms not heeded. The text represents the flip side of what Richard Schechner (1988) has characterized as 'selective inattention' - a phenomenon we might call 'selective fixation.'

With this single-minded focus on the drummer, the text also subverts status differentiations. Laurie Sears (1996:x) writes that 'Javanese of a certain status would never consider going to a ritual celebration uninvited; only foreigners and *wong cilik* (little people, village people) can get away with such behaviour.' This is an elite point of view, not far from the ideology of sponsorship described by Keeler. In contrast, the princesses of Majapait depart for the performance not as invited guests, but because they have *kapireng* or 'heard by chance' about the drummer. Once present at the performance, the princesses are no longer distinguished as subjects. The text does not state explicitly that it is they who swoon over the drummer; the princesses are part of the collective subject of *sakabeh* (all). Hearing from a distance, the princesses are still distinct subjects; but seeing the performance is a collective experience. The gaze, in Barbara Feldman's terms, is staged (Feldman, 1991).

MEANINGS

What lessons do participants in *Jaka Menyawak*'s *wayang* performance take home with them? What are the enduring effects of the experience?

These are difficult questions to answer. There are Cirebonese texts on *wayang*, including the earliest Cirebonese text referring to *wayang*, the *Suluk Wujil* (Poerbatjaraka, 1938), which dwell at length on post-performance interpretations and discursive reactions. In such texts, characters watching the performance discuss their opinions of the art form, and draw symbolic meanings, often related to Islamic themes, from the play of shadows upon the *wayang* screen. Nothing comparable happens in *Jaka Menyawak*. This text is driven by action, not by reflection.

What does happen is that Jaka Menyawak's substitution as drummer causes conflict between Dewi Pata and her sisters. Judging from what Jaka Menyawak tells Dewi Pata immediately before her sisters enter in search of the drummer, he is aware of the repercussions of his performance.

iku rayi wis jangjinira /
tangtu sira bakal jogol /
tukar klawan sedulur /
tangtu bae la iku yayi. //

You shall certainly fight and
Argue with your sisters.
That is certain, dear.

Again, the text shifts our attention away from what is depicted at the screen and to the audience experience. It is common at Cirebonese *wayang* performances, and all such mass gatherings, for spectators to get into fights. A threat of violence is imminent. Recall the mention of crying babies and wives getting slapped by their husbands. The window of opportunity of *wayang* allows Dewi Pata to destroy Jaka Menyawak's lizard skin, directly assaulting his assumed identity as a monitor lizard. *Wayang* drama does not transport spectators into a sublime alternate dimension, rather it intensifies worldly conflicts. The submerged rises to the social surface.

IV

Theorists of theatre, going back at least as far as the Prague School, commonly stress the multi-dimensionality of drama in performance, and the complexity of theatre semiotics. The difficulty of 'understanding' a theatrical event is consequently related to the conceptual difficulty of integrating the many different channels, modalities, or domains that compose such an event in an abstract model. Such models tend to be constructed as 'views from nowhere.' Visceral and social factors that have profound effects upon what one takes in of a performance and how one experiences it - uncomfortable seats, obstructed sight lines, too much to drink beforehand, an upset stomach, sooty spectacles, the company of a friend or loved one - all are ignored or swept under the rug.

Jaka Menyawak takes a different approach, writing strongly from a spectator point of view, the opposite of a 'view from nowhere.' Its spectators - mosquito-bitten, sweating profusely, with crying babies at home - have a visceral reality that is much more concrete than even that of the title character. Jaka Menyawak lives a fantasy life, able to change into a monitor lizard at will (as long as his 'clothing' remains intact) and plays the most technically demanding instrument of the *gamelan*, the drum, without any apparent difficulty or prior experience.[10] In contrast, the spectators, and particularly female spectators, are not fantasized, but *sampled* from social reality.

The text is a narrative model of and for performance. It describes and prescribes performance through telling a story about it. People watching performances focus intently upon one and only one performative aspect: selective fixation. The puppeteer, the other *gamelan* musicians, the puppets, the play, the sponsor, the performance arena, even the performance genre - all disappear in the text, as spectators stare without blinking, with bulging eyes, at Jaka Menyawak, the drummer. Clearly defined performance roles, distinctions between participant and observer, become of secondary or negligible importance to the staged gaze. This gaze, we have seen, and the act of spectating more generally, cannot be detached from social practice. So this poetic tale tells us. So it importunes.

NOTES

1 *Wayang* as practised in the Cirebon region of north-coastal West Java differs in so many respects from the well-studied *wayang* forms of south Central Java that it would be a mistake to think of them as being simply different variants of the 'same' art form. Hardly a single musical piece is common between Cirebon and south Central Java. Dramaturgical structures also differ radically. Characterizations and puppet voices are incommensurable. Puppet iconography and design differ recognizably. There is an additional complication. Properly speaking, there is no single 'Cirebonese *wayang*' as within Cirebon, there are many different local styles, associated with particular villages or sub-regions. For an overview of one of the major local styles of Cirbonese *wayang*, see Cohen 1997.

2 The painter Sitisiwan is the subject of a forthcoming essay, written in collaboration with T.E. Behrend and T.L. Cooper.

3 Rod puppet theatre is known in the Cirebonese area as *wayang cepak*, *wayang pepak*, or *wayang golek*. It is also referred to (in a kind of short hand) as either *wayang* or *golek*. In this essay, references to *wayang*, unless stated explicitly, are to *wayang kulit* or 'shadow puppet theatre.' On Cirebonese rod puppet theatre, see Foley 1986.

4 Sudibjo titles the text *Jaka Pekik*, but it is more commonly referred to as *Jaka Menyawk* by Cirebonese artists, including professional singers of

literature. I follow the latter usage.
5 One of these internal referents is to batik cloth from Pekalongan, which began to be mass-marketed only in the mid nineteenth-century.
6 One copy of the text, more complete than the one published by Sudibjo, is in the possession of Marsita, a *dhalang maca* from the village of Ujunggebang. Other *dhalang maca* are familiar with the text as well.
7 As Supomo (1979) describes, Majapait (also known as Majapahit) figures prominently in folk-tales, legends, and chronicles of Islamic Java. Frequently, the kingdom is used figuratively as a large, classical kingdom.
8 *Berokan*, also known as *bangberokan*, is probably the least familiar of these three art forms outside of Cirebon. But in the recent past, it was a highly popular children's entertainment throughout the Cirebon area. For a brief description, see Ghulam-Sarwar Yousof, 1994, pp. 12-13.
9 Period newspaper reports describe how disappointed Javanese spectators were at a 1926 *pasar malam* that the dance floor was roped-off because of fears of a bomb attack, preventing non-paying customers from watching the ballroom dancing. See '2e Jaarmark' in *Teradjoe* 1 November 1926, p. 2. and 'Karewelan dalem Gemeente Cheribon (oorzaak, gevolg en slachtoffers)' in *Teradjoe* 7 March 1927, p. 2.
10 The character of Jaka Menyawak might be said to be emblematic of the 'professional dream' side of Javanese literature identified by Ben Anderson (1990), in his remarkable range of abilities.

REFERENCES

Anderson, Benedict R. O'G. (1990) 'Professional dreams: reflections on two Javanese classics,' in: *Language and Power: Exploring Political Cultures in Indonesia*. Ithaca: Cornell University Press, pp. 271-98.

Arps, Bernard (1992) *Tembang in Two Traditions: Performance and Interpretation of Javanese Literature*. London: School of Oriental and African Studies, University of London.

Bateson, Gregory (1972) *Steps to an Ecology of Mind*. New York: Ballantine Books.

Bauman, Richard (1989) 'Performance,' in: E. Barmouw (ed.) *International Encyclopedia of Communications* 3. New York: Oxford University Press, pp. 262-6.

Becker, A.L. (1979) 'Text-building, epistemology, and aesthetics in Javanese shadow theatre,' in: A.L. Becker and Aram Yengoyan (eds) *The Imagination of Reality*. Norwood, New Jersey: Ablex Publishing, pp. 211-43.

Burke, Peter (1978) *Popular Culture in Early Modern Europe*. New York:

Harper and Row.

Cohen, Matthew Isaac (1997) *An Inheritance from the Friends of God: The Southern Shadow Puppet Theatre of West Java, Indonesia*. Ann Arbor: UMI.

Endo Suanda (1973) *Wayang Wong di Desa Suranenggala-Lor Cirebon*. Unpublished thesis, Akademi Seni Tari Indonesia Bandung.

--(1983) *Topeng Cirebon: In Its Social Context*. Unpublished thesis, Wesleyan University.

--(1993) 'Islamic musical of Cirebon,' *Scope* 2, pp. 49-56.

Feldman, Barbara (1991) *Staging the Gaze: Postmodernism, Psychoanalysis, and Shakespearean Comedy*. Ithaca: Cornell University Press.

Foley, Kathy (1986) 'At the graves of the ancestors: chronicle plays in Indonesia,' in: James Redmong (ed.) *Themes in Drama 8: Historical Drama*. Cambridge: Cambridge University Press, pp. 31-49.

--(1989) 'My bodies: the performer in West Java,' *TDR* 34 (2), pp. 62-80.

Ghulam-Sarwar Yousof (1994) *Dictionary of Traditional South-East Asian Theatre*. Singapore: Oxford University Press.

Goffman, Erving (1959) *The Presentation of Self in Everyday Life*. New York: Anchor Books.

--(1974) *Frame Analysis*. New York: Harper & Row.

Harja Somantri, Gaos (1978) *Topeng Cirebon*. Translated by Sardinah. Bandung: Proyek Pengembangan Institut Kesenian Indonesia.

Kasim Achmad, A. (1975) Teater tradisionil di Indonesia. *Buletin Kebudayaan Jawa Barat* 4:, pp. 20-6.

Keeler, Ward (1987) *Javanese Shadow Plays, Javanese Selves*. Princeton: Princeton University Press.

Kunst, J. and C.J.A. Kunst-van Wely (1924) Over toonschalen en instrumenten van West-Java. *Djawa* 3, pp. 24-40.

Linck, A.A.C. (1921) 'Een overblijfsel in Cheribon van ouderwetsche kettersche mystiek: de Birahi's,' *Notulen van de Algemeene en Directievergaderingen van het Bataviaasch Genootschap van Kunsten en Wetenschappen* 59, pp. 163-76.

Mauss, Marcel (1990) The Gift. Translated by W.D. Hall. New York: Norton.

Plas, Charles O. van der (1937) 'Een desa-wajangvertooning in 1935,' *Koloniaal Tijdschrift* 26, pp. 654-58.

Poerbatjaraka (1938) 'De geheime leer van Soenan Bonang,' *Djåwå* 18, pp. 145-81.

Rodgers-Aguiniga, Pamela (1986) *Topeng Cirebon: The Masked Dance Theatre of West Java as Performed in the Village of Slangit*. Unpublished thesis, University of California at Los Angeles.

Schechner, Richard (1988) *Performance Theory*. New York: Routledge.

Sears, Laurie Jo (1996) *Shadows of Empire: Colonial Discourse and Javanese Tales*. Durham: Duke University Press.
Sudibjo Z. Hadisutjipto (1980) *Jaka Pekik*. Jakarta: Department of Education and Culture.
Sudibjo (1985) *Sastra Cirebon Selayang Pandang*. Yogyakarta: Javanologi.
Sumarsam (1995) *Gamelan: Cultural Interaction and Musical Development in Central Java*. Chicago: University of Chicago Press.
Supomo, S. (1979) 'The image of Majapahit in later Javanese and Indonesian writing,' in: Anthony Reid and David Marr (eds) *Perceptions of the Past in Southeast Asia*. Singapore: Heinemann Education Books, pp. 171-85.
Tisna Sopandi (1980) 'Teater rakyat,' *Kawit* 22, pp. 14-19.
Westerkamp, Willem (1987) *Javaanse Maskers en Maskervertoningen in Cerbon en de Vorstenlanden*. Unpublished MA thesis, University of Amsterdam.
Zoetmulder, P.J. (1995) *Pantheism and Monism in Javanese Suluk Literature*. Translated by M.C. Ricklefs. Leiden: KITLV Press.

Chapter 11

Modelling and Measuring the Parametres of Performance[1]

Hae-Kyung Um

In this paper I will attempt to illustrate the interrelationships between what performance practice is, the processes of performance, a model for studying the performing arts and its associated methodological instruments by focusing on my own research on *p'ansori,* a form of traditional Korean musical drama.

This will be done by reviewing some of the different concepts of performance practice found in ethnomusicology and then by describing a theoretical model comprised of a set of concentric circles that bring together these various concepts.

When this has been done, I will describe a particular *p'ansori* performance in detail in order to illustrate the artistic processes of composition, performance, and transmission, their associated aesthetic values and the historical, social, cultural, and political forces that all help to give shape to the performance. These include, for example, the personal and artistic background of the performer, the performance setting, social institutions associated with the recruitment and training of artists, various systems of patronage, and questions of identity.

In the penultimate step, by employing the analytical framework of the theoretical model all aspects of the creative process will be related through the model from a specific *p'ansori* performance to the broadest of historical events by moving from the centre to the periphery and back.

Finally, I will review the various research methods and instruments that are required to describe each element in the model as used in my own analysis of *p'ansori* and address some of the methodological and practical questions that arose from my own research in Korea and the Korean migrant communities in the former Soviet Union and China.

CONCEPTS OF PERFORMANCE PRACTICE

The term 'practice' in ethnomusicology has several different meanings. Firstly, 'practice' refers to 'performance practice' of music in contrast to theories about musical systems. It is the way, or ways, in which musicians make use of given technical devices, such as melodies, rhythms, texts, bodily movements, and the like, in their composition and performance. The artistic creativity and technical competence of the artist is thus realized in performance practice. However, performance practice is located in and identified with the music system of the given genre or form of which it is a part.

'Practice' is also related to the concept of 'bi-musicality' which was put forward by Mantle Hood in the 1960s. As a theory, this 'bi-musicality' advocated a study of music 'in its own terms' (Hood, 1960). As a methodology it emphasized the importance of learning to perform as a student and musician rather than as a simple observer. This approach to music stands in contrast to Alan Merriam's anthropology of music (Merriam, 1964), which views music as culture. The method of participant observation was to be employed, but learning to perform was not always necessary.[2] These two different approaches, which are now over three decades old, can be understood in terms of a dialectic relationship rather than as being in opposition, just as much as the dichotomy of emic versus etic or subjective versus objective is similarly understood (also see Rice, 1997 for his discussion of 'dialectic strategy'). In fact, many ethnomusicologists, especially those who are anthropologically trained, set out with the music-as-culture metaphor and often participate in musical performance and composition, or one or the other, in the field, for example, Steven Feld (1982), Anthony Seeger (1987), and Timothy Rice (1997) to name a few.

The dialectic nature of music and of the study of music is defined in even more detail by John Blacking who argued that:

> 'Music' is not only reflexive; it is also generative, both as cultural system and as human capability and an important task of musicology is to find out how people make sense of 'music' in a variety of social situations and in different cultural contexts, and to distinguish between the innate human capabilities that individuals use in the process of making sense of 'music' and the cultural conventions that guide their actions (Blacking, 1995:223).

A Model for an Analysis of Performance

All these concepts of performance practice can be analysed using a theoretical model comprised of concentric circles as illustrated below.

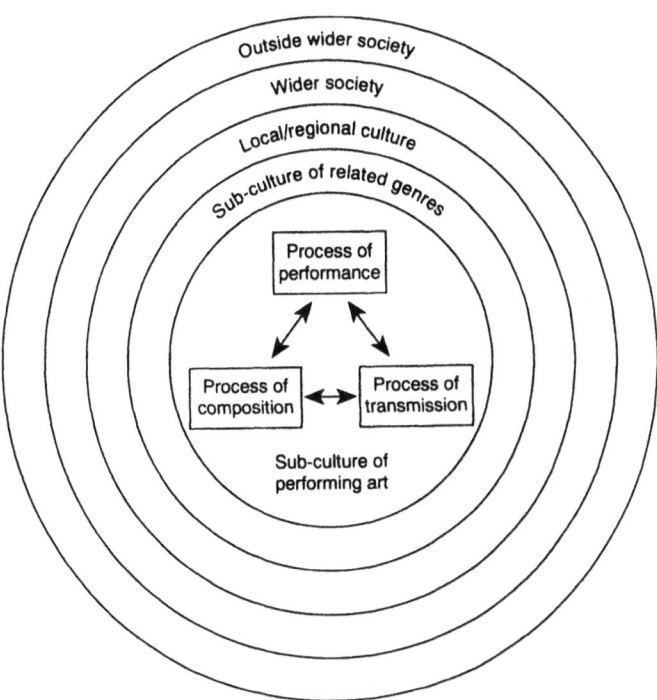

Processes of Performing Arts-Making

In the diagram, the '*sub-culture of performing art*' refers to the arena of interacting individuals involved directly in the creative process of performing art in a particular genre or form. The '*sub-cultures of related genres*' indicate any other cultural arenas that are associated with the given genre or form, for example, literature, music, dance, theatre, ritual, and the like.[3] The '*local/regional culture*,' here, represents any regional variation within the geopolitical boundary of the given country or culture under examination. '*Wider society*' refers to social institutions in general, social and cultural systems, and their historical context in the appropriate period. Finally, *'outside wider society'* in the diagram relates to any external influence on the cultural and social life of the given country or culture (Um, 1992, 1994, 1996).

These social and cultural forces that give shape to the performing arts are represented by concentric circles with the more distant and less direct elements on the outside and the more direct and interpersonal elements on the inside to create a spectrum of influences equivalent to Hood's 'G-S line' (Hood, 1982:56) which range from the general to the specific.

The model is necessarily inclusive of individuals and social institutions, such as performers, audiences, mediator and patrons, education system, and so on, whose various contexts also generate systems of aesthetics and values. In this sense the whole set of concentric cycles represents what Bourdieu termed 'social space,' or a series of fields of forces, whereas each circle in the model corresponds to Bourdieu's concept of a 'field' of dynamic forces (Mahar et al., 1990:8-9).

However, I do not wish to suggest that each circle in the model is self-contained or that its boundaries with the adjacent circles are fixed. On the contrary, they are flexible and interrelated with each other, producing the subsequent dynamics. Furthermore, the symbolic or material power relationships between the inner and outer circles are not necessarily hierarchical in their position because 'power,' as Foucault (1981) defines it, is a 'discursive field' in which the 'multiplicity of force relations' are confronted by a 'multiplicity of points of resistance.'

I would also like to suggest that within the *'sub-culture of performing art,'* there are three interrelated processes of performing art-making, namely, the *process of composition, process of performance,* and *process of transmission.* The operational mechanism of these processes are similar to Bourdieu's concept of *'habitus'* (Mahar et al. 1990:10), or a set of dispositions.

DESCRIPTION OF A *P'ANSORI* PERFORMANCE

P'ansori is a form of traditional Korean musical drama which has been developed by professional folk musicians[4] since the beginning of the eighteenth century. At that time *p'ansori* musicians were itinerant entertainers who generally performed in an open space such as a market place or the courtyard of a wealthy patron, in association with other entertainers such as acrobats, tumblers, clowns, and tight-rope-walkers, or sometimes in the sitting room of a wealthy patron. *P'ansori* slowly became independent of these other forms of entertainment, and from the turn of this century it was brought onto a stage in indoor settings such as a concert hall or auditorium (Yi Po-hyông, 1982a:245-6).

The prefix '*p'an-*' refers to a place where people gather together and the suffix '*-sori*' means a sound indicative of a singing voice or song. It is performed by a solo singer, either male or female,[5] accompanied by a barrel drummer. The singer presents a dramatic story through songs or *sori*, narrations or *aniri*, and gestures or *pallim* using a fan and handkerchief as symbolic props. Before the start of the *p'ansori* proper, which may take several hours, or as much as eight or ten, the singer sings an introductory song with a lyrical text or *tan'ga* as a warm-up exercise. In performance, both the drummer and audience give calls of encouragement or *ch'uimsae* at appropriate phrase endings. The role of the audience in *p'ansori* performance is so indispensable that the traditional saying 'First comes the drummer and second the singer' is sometimes rephrased as 'First comes the audience, second the drummer, and third the singer' (Um 1992:310).

In this paper I will describe a *p'ansori* performance from the gala concert 'Sound of Millennia.' This concert was performed in Los Angeles and New York City, USA, in September 1991 in celebration of Korea's entry to the membership of the United Nations. Both traditional and contemporary Korean music and dance were presented by various performing arts groups. In this gala concert a few excerpts from the two best known *p'ansori* pieces were performed. They were: 'the song of the secret royal inspector's appearance' and 'the love song' from *Ch'unhyang-ga* or the Song of Ch'unhyang[6] and 'the boat song' from *Simch'ông-ga* or the Song of Simch'ông.[7]

The first piece, *Ch'unhyang-ga*, was presented in the traditional *p'ansori* style. The performers were the male singer, Cho Sang-hyôn (b. 1939), who is best known for his dynamic 'gifted voice' or *ch'ôn'gusông* and the female singer, An Suk-sôn (b. 1949), who is currently the most popular female *p'ansori* singer in South Korea. Their singing was accompanied by the drummer, Chông Hwa-yông (b. 1943). The second *p'ansori* story, *Simch'ông-ga*, was presented by the National Theatre Troupe with a large cast of chorus and dancers. This theatrical version, which included scenery, is a relatively new style and is called *ch'anggûk*.

The gala concerts from the two different venues were filmed and edited into a fifty-nine minute video programme with an English introduction and titles. The production of this audio-visual material was sponsored by the Korea Foundation which has distributed the tape to various overseas academic and cultural institutions in order to introduce Korean culture to Western audiences.

AN ANALYSIS OF A *P'ANSORI* PERFORMANCE

I will focus my description and analysis of *p'ansori* on the first two excerpts from *Ch'unhyang-ga* and my analysis of this particular recorded performance, in relation to the model, will begin from the centre of the model as follows.

'SUB-CULTURE OF PERFORMING ART'

The *process of composition* is interrelated to the *process of transmission* insofar as the different stylistic conventions of various *p'ansori* schools prescribe the text, music, and dramatic gestures used by the two singers. For example, the male singer, Cho Sang-hyôn, learnt from Chông Ung-min (1894-1961) who transmitted *Ch'unhyang-ga* in the style of Kim Se-jong (the late nineteenth century) from the Eastern School which is known for its majestic and energetic singing style. This stylistic convention of the Eastern *p'ansori* School developed in contrast to the elegant and elaborate style of the Western *p'ansori* School.

Cogently the re-interpretation and re-creation of the compositional elements of *p'ansori*, such as melodies, rhythms and textual content, also takes place during the process of transmission. For example, the female singer An Suk-sôn learnt from Kim So-hûi (1917-1995) who had combined the two different traditions of the Eastern and Western Schools in her *Ch'unhyang-ga* singing (Um, 1992:199, 203).[8]

This *process of composition* is related to the *process of performance* in the sense that the *process of composition* can only be fully realized in a *p'ansori* performance, either live or recorded, because the singers have the final control over composition. At the same time the gender of the singer, setting, time limit, and type of audience also give shape to the outcome of the performance. For example, in this performance the male and female singers had to adjust to each other's vocal range - especially when singing in duet. The two excerpts from *Ch'unhyang-ga*, namely, the energetic and powerful 'song of the royal secret inspector's appearance' and the lyrical and romantic 'love song,' were probably chosen because of the effectiveness of their contrasting dramatic and musical contents. However, these two highlights were presented in a reverse order. The first excerpt, sung by the male singer, Cho Sang-hyôn, was, in fact, from the finale whereas the second excerpt, sung in duet, was taken from the beginning of the original story as it is normally performed. The narrations and dialogues from each scene were entirely omitted, while a greater emphasis was given to the dramatic gestures by the two singers. This was done because of the time limit and the fact that many members of the audience would not understand the Korean language. Finally melodies were also added between the two songs by the female singer, An Suk-sôn, in order to create a musical bridge between the two dramatically unconnected songs.

In the model the *process of performance* is also interrelated to the *process of transmission*. This relationship is illustrated in our example by the fact that the different stylistic conventions from which the two singers came prescribed their own singing style which, in turn, influence each other's style as the two singers perform together. Pertinently this performance may become a model or point of reference for other *p'ansori* singers and students and so influence their performance in practice.

'*SUB-CULTURES OF RELATED GENRES*'

These three interrelated processes are linked to the '*sub-cultures of related genres*,' such as literature, dance, and theatre. In fact, the origins of *p'ansori* cannot be explained without including its relationship with other genres (Kim Tong-uk, 1976; Chông No-sik, 1940; Yi Hye-gu, 1955; Yi Po-hyông, 1982b). The shamanist chant from the southwestern province of Korea is known to be a predecessor of *p'ansori*, and *p'ansori*, in turn, influenced shamanist chants in the late nineteenth century (Walraven, 1985). With regard to the textual material, both oral and written Korean literature and Chinese classical literature influenced *p'ansori* (Kim Tong-uk, 1976).[9] Some of the musical sources were also taken from other musical genres, such as Korean classical vocal genres (Han Man-yông, 1972) and folksongs from various regions (Yi Po-hyông, 1971, 1972).

This type of interaction with '*sub-cultures of related genres*' often results in changes within the given genre or even in the creation of a new genre. For example, the new genre, *kayagûm pyôngch'ang*-singing, accompanied by a twelve-stringed zither developed at the turn of the twentieth century as a result of a 'marriage' between *p'ansori* and instrumental music.[10] The theatrical adaptation of *p'ansori* gave rise to a new genre called *ch'anggûk* at the beginning of the twentieth century. Whereas *p'ansori* focuses on a lineal representation of the story delivered by a solo singer, *ch'anggûk* emphases a realistic representation of the story through a multiple cast of singers and dancers acting with costumes and stage settings as well as an elaboration of the musical medium with an orchestral accompaniment and chorus. Conversely the visual performance style of *ch'anggûk* is sometimes introduced into *p'ansori* performances, as was done in this concert by the two singers who performed with more elaborate dramatic gestures characteristic of *ch'anggûk*.

'LOCAL/REGIONAL CULTURE'
These interrelated processes are also influenced by and are a product of *'local/regional culture,'* or perhaps one or the other. For example, although *p'ansori* is now performed all over Korea, this genre has always been associated with the regional culture and identity of the southwestern province where it originated. Most *p'ansori* artists, including the two singers in this gala concert, are from the southwestern province. The language used in *p'ansori* is an archaic form of the southwestern dialect and the majority of *p'ansori* melodies are also composed in the folk-song style of the region.

'WIDER SOCIETY'
All these interactions take place in contact with the *'wider society.'* Social institutions, such as the system of patronage, recruitment, and training of musicians, the role of mediators and modern technology (Wolff, 1981), all influence *p'ansori*. This is particularly true of the new system of state patronage, namely, the scheme of 'Preservation and Promotion of Cultural Assets' which is closely related to the construction of national identity in modern Korean society. Distinguished artists have been designated by the Ministry of Culture as the 'holders of the artistry of Korean intangible cultural assets,' also known as 'human cultural treasures.' In return for this official acclamation, these artists are expected to transmit their artistic skills to a privileged and select number of students. In fact, the professional careers of the two singers, namely, Cho Sang-hyôn and An Suk-sôn, have been closely associated with this official patronage. This state cultural scheme has also created new types of mediators. For example, the academics specializing in Korean arts who provide their expertise in the procedure of the selection, evaluation, and recommendation of the genre to be 'cultural assets' and artists to be designated 'human cultural treasures.'

In addition to the contemporary influences of changing institutions, the social and cultural system of Korean society associated with patronage and the flow of economic and political power throughout Korean history has also influenced *p'ansori* (Cho Tong-il, 1969; Kim Hûng-gyu, 1974, 1978). For example, in the second half of the nineteenth century, upper class patrons, who held economic and political power, had considerable control over the text and repertoire of *p'ansori*. Their preoccupation with 'appropriate' *p'ansori* texts contributed to the refinement of the literary content of *p'ansori*, sometimes clashing with the interests of lower class audiences and *p'ansori* musicians. Unfortunately this process led to a decrease in the *p'ansori* repertoire: those pieces of *p'ansori* with obscene and vulgar texts and themes did not survive Confucian censorship. The main themes of the five remaining traditional *p'ansori* pieces coincide with the five ethical codes derived from Confucian ideology, namely, loyalty to the king,' 'filial piety to parents,' 'fidelity to husband,' 'brotherhood,' and 'sincerity to friends.'[11] Amongst the five *p'ansori* pieces *Ch'unhyang-ga* has been most highly esteemed because it touches on nearly all of these themes (Um, 1992:108-9, 1993a).

The cultural values of Korean society permeate both the text and music of *p'ansori*. For example, various style registers (Giles and Powesland, 1975:15-23, 36-146), which are found in both *p'ansori* texts and the modern Korean language, may be examples of a socio-linguistic expression of a hierarchical social structure. Some musical elements in *p'ansori*, for example, *cho* (mode or melodic type), have been developed in association with socially and culturally defined concepts (Um, 1993b). For example, *cho* derived from the classical genres tend to be related to domains such as male, the upper class, power, majesty, elegance, imperturbability, and the like; whereas the folk counterparts tend to be linked with their opposites, such as female, the lower class, provinciality, vulgarity, and cheerfulness.[12] These associations have probably been constructed by a process, which Barthes calls 'the second order semiotic system' (Hawkes, 1977:130-2).

'*OUTSIDE WIDER SOCIETY*'

Sometimes the influences on *p'ansori* come from '*outside* [the] *wider society*' of Korea. For example, the rise of *ch'anggûk*, or *p'ansori* theatre, is related to the internal and external socio-political change at the turn of the century. With the Japanese occupation of Korea in 1910 the Chosôn dynasty disintegrated and *p'ansori* musicians had to adapt to a change of patronage from the upper classes in traditional society to the middle class in modern society. The influences of Chinese opera and Western-style theatre on the rise and development of *ch'anggûk* also came about as a result of contacts with the outside world.

The gala concerts described in this paper were presented to promote Korean culture and to celebrate Korean nationhood associated with Korea's entry to the United Nations. Shortly after the gala concerts in the United States, one of the performers wrote a travelogue. According to her description (Yi Chi-yông 1991:30) these concerts were successful in several ways. The performers and other staff (about 150 of them) felt that through the concerts the essence of the cultural and artistic heritage of Korea was presented to a wide range of audiences, both Americans and American Koreans. She also reports that after the gala concert, in New York city, a Korean American woman came up to the cast to express her appreciation on the successful performances, her sense of national identity evoked by the concert, and her pride in being Korean. Cogently, modern technology and globalization now make it possible for anyone to view a recording of the performance at anytime anywhere in the world.

RESEARCH METHODS AND INSTRUMENTS

All the data reviewed in this example were analysed using various methods and theoretical perspectives developed by scholars in various disciplines such as ethnomusicology, musicology, sociology, comparative literature, linguistics, semiotics and social linguistics, which, in turn, were combined in the context of the theoretical model. More specifically the research methods and instruments which I employed in my fieldwork include learning by performing, participant observation, recordings, structured and open interviews, archival research and historical scholarship. Each of these methods has had a role to play in describing the *p'ansori* performance. In practice I can illustrate how this was relevant to the development of the analysis using the concentric circle model for each method as follows.

LEARNING BY PERFORMING

I took private voice lessons from a female singer, Sông U-hyang (b.1935), and group voice lessons from a male singer, Cho Sang-hyôn (b. 1939). Both of these artists studied *p'ansori* with Chông Ung-min from the Eastern School. I also took drumming lessons from the master drummer, Kim Myông-hwan (1913-89), who used to perform with Chông Ung-min, the teacher of the two singers who taught me. I was first introduced to the master drummer, Kim Myông-hwan, in 1987 by the Korean musicologist Yi Po-hyông. After a month of basic training in voice and drumming, Kim Myông-hwan introduced me to Sông U-hyang for private voice lessons. I also joined in public *p'ansori* classes given by Cho Sang-hyôn at the Institute for Preservation and Promotion of Korean Intangible Cultural Assets. In addition to my daily voice lessons with Sông U-hyang I also spent many hours at her studio listening and practising *p'ansori* and sharing food and household chores with other students. By contrast, the group lessons given by Cho Sang-hyôn were held weekly for two hours in a more formal classroom setting with a strong focus on theory as well as practice.

By learning *p'ansori* from two singers with the same musical genealogy and a drummer who knew both singers and their teacher, I was able to study a number of important issues associated with the creative processes of composition, performance, and transmission. For example, from my lessons I learned various techniques of vocalization and ornamentation, rhythmic patterns and their variations, *p'ansori* terminology and the relationships between *p'ansori* text and music. My formal background in Korean musicology and performance of Korean music, including the twelve-stringed zither, *kayagûm*, and classical lyric songs, *kagok*, also helped me to understand the relationships that exist between *p'ansori* and other genres of the Korean performing arts. My *p'ansori* teachers also demonstrated how different performing and teaching strategies could be employed to match various settings, audiences, and students and how they developed their own individual style within the convention of the *p'ansori* school to which they subscribed.

Participant Observation

In addition to my own voice and drumming lessons, I also attended many of the lessons of other students at different levels of technical ability and from various backgrounds. The students whose lessons I attended included both professional and amateur ranging from *p'ansori* singers to actors, pop singers, housewives, and businessmen who were learning *p'ansori* for different reasons. For example, actors were sent by their theatre company to complete an intensive voice-training course for their theatre production. Popular singers took up *p'ansori* to improve their vocal techniques, whereas university students joined in the classes as part of their extra curricular activities. Housewives and businessmen came to *p'ansori* lessons simply because they loved to sing. This type of indirect learning, which is also encouraged by many *p'ansori* teachers, provided me with opportunities to observe and record the different teaching strategies of the teachers, the learning processes of the students, and the instructional content of the lessons all of which are critically important to the process of transmission of *p'ansori*.

Various *p'ansori* clubs provided me with important information about social and regional network of *p'ansori* musicians, their audiences, and patrons. For example, *p'ansori* clubs are usually organized through personal contacts and regional affiliations between *p'ansori* artists and club members. These clubs often function as an organizing body for various meetings and formal and informal *p'ansori* concerts. They finance these functions themselves or bring in sponsorship through their social network. Some *p'ansori* clubs have several academics specializing in *p'ansori* whose membership enhances the profile of the club and the status of the *p'ansori* artists. In return these academics gain the full co-operation and support for their *p'ansori* research from the *p'ansori* musicians and the club.

P'ansori singing competitions and *p'ansori* seminars which I attended also provided me with valuable opportunities to study the dynamic relationships which exist between 'the sub-culture of *p'ansori* and other related genres,' 'local/regional culture' and the 'wider society' of Korea. For example, these *p'ansori* competitions and seminars were often held in Chôlla province where *p'ansori* and many genres of Korean music originated. These events were attended by a variety of individuals and organizations such as musicians, academics, connoisseurs, competition organizers and sponsors, regional and national mass media, civil servants from the Ministry of Culture, *p'ansori* club members, general audiences and so on. I was, therefore, able to observe musical and social networks of musicians, symbiotic relationships between musicians, academics and the mass media and regional and national cultural politics.

RECORDINGS

During my fieldwork in Korea from 1987 to 1988 I made extensive recordings of various *p'ansori* singers from different schools. This was done in an attempt to identify and compare the stylistic characteristics of various *p'ansori* singing traditions. These recordings were made using a Sony TCD-5M cassette tape-recorder and two AGE microphones. Recording levels and the balance of the two microphones often had to be adjusted to match the physical distance between the singer and the drummer and their respective volumes. However, no original video recordings were made during my fieldwork in 1987 and 1988.

These original sound materials were collected at various *p'ansori* singing competitions, formal and informal concerts, and voice and drumming lessons. Many audio and visual materials, especially those recorded before 1987, were collected from public archives and private collections as well as from commercial distributors. Some of the other sound materials collected were made by *p'ansori* students who recorded their teacher's demonstrations and verbal instructions during their own voice lessons.[13]

By collecting and analysing original, archival, and commercial recordings of *p'ansori*, I was able to compare the singing styles of various *p'ansori* schools and the different individual styles of singers from the same school. I was also able to study how different technology (for example, short-play records, long-play records, audio and video cassettes and CDs) and various recording purposes (for example, historical and archival collection, domestic or overseas distribution, commercial or educational distribution, TV and radio broadcasting or teaching aid) influence *p'ansori* in its creative processes of composition, performance and transmission and how these various recordings play different roles in the construction of the 'authenticity' of *p'ansori* amongst both the *p'ansori* musicians and the 'wider society.'

STRUCTURED AND OPEN INTERVIEWS

In addition to my lessons given by the three musicians mentioned above, and frequent interviews with them, I also interviewed and recorded singers who subscribed to other schools and styles of the *p'ansori* tradition.[14] In these interviews a wide range of topics was covered including the personal history of individual singers, the musical genealogy of different *p'ansori* schools, *p'ansori* terminology, aesthetics, and musicians perspectives on theories and the performance practice of *p'ansori* all of which shape the subculture of *p'ansori*.

Korean specialists in *p'ansori*, sponsors, and organizers of *p'ansori* competitions and concerts were also subjects for structured study. My interviews with them were arranged through both formal appointments and chance meetings at *p'ansori* seminars, concerts, singing competitions, and associated social gatherings held in a variety of locations. Through these interviews and meetings I was able to examine the ways in which different individuals and institutions influence *p'ansori* through the exercise of power across the fields of the model at its points of social and political interaction.

ARCHIVAL RESEARCH AND HISTORICAL SCHOLARSHIP

Those publications and copies of handwritten and printed *p'ansori* texts not commercially available in Korean book stores were examined in the public libraries in Korea. Additional texts were also made available to me from private collections of various Korean and non-Korean scholars. These historical and written *p'ansori* texts were valuable to my research for several reasons. Firstly it was possible to study historical changes in *p'ansori* texts and their social and cultural contexts (see Chapters Two and Six in Um 1992). Secondly it was also possible to compare both the overall structure and details of different *p'ansori* texts employed by various *p'ansori* schools (see Chapter Four in Um 1992). Thirdly, these written texts, or 'literary *p'ansori*,' also provided a point of comparison with 'performed *p'ansori*' for my analysis of the relationships that exist between the literacy and orality of this performing art (see Chapters Four and Five in Um 1992).

Historical and contemporary academic and popular writings on the topic of *p'ansori* were all reviewed in an attempt to analyse both scholarly and public discourse associated with this genre. Writings on *p'ansori* by Confucian scholars from the middle of the eighteenth to the end of the nineteenth centuries informed of conservative but changing attitudes toward *p'ansori* amongst the upper classes. Studies of *p'ansori* by contemporary Korean scholars from various disciplines such as Korean literature, musicology, and folklore provide a foundation upon which my analysis of *p'ansori* history, text, music, and aesthetics was built. It should be noted that the trend in modern *p'ansori* scholarship in the twentieth century has passed through a number of different stages.[15] Especially since the 1970s when a great number of popular writings on *p'ansori* have were published by both academics and non-academics in Seoul and Chôlla Province (see Introduction in Um 1992). This trend in national and regional cultural revivalism has been supported by state nationalism which, in turn, promotes *p'ansori* as a national heritage at home and abroad.

At the institutional level, the cultural policy of the Korean government and mass media have also created a new role for academics as the mediators of traditional Korean performing arts. My archival and historical research suggests that all types of writings on the topic of *p'ansori* by different individuals create both academic and public discourse which, in turn, influences the creative process of *p'ansori* making across the model from the sub-culture of *p'ansori* to other related genres to local/regional cultures to the wider society and even outside the world.

DISCUSSION

In the example selected here the model is used to illustrate my study of *p'ansori*, *Ch'unhyang-ga* in particular, in relation to the full spectrum of influences that range from the specific to the general. It included detailed descriptions and analysis of *p'ansori* texts, music, *p'ansori* terminology, individual styles, schools, various performance settings, aesthetics, and relationships with other related genres. It also covered a variety of wider contexts such as social institutions associated with various systems of patronage and education, political, social, and historical changes and cross-cultural influences. This was done in an attempt to understand the relationships between the processes of 'making music' and 'making sense of music' in different social situations and cultural and historical contexts (Um 1992).

Mantle Hood's theory of 'bi-musicality' is a useful methodological tool in the study of music. However, the notion of 'practice' is not limited only to the performers who make use of their technical devices and artistic knowledge in their creation of a particular performance. It is, likewise, found in the audiences who participate in this performance event because the audience also 'performs,' as noted by Blacking (1987:35). It follows, therefore, that theories of practice posited by Bourdieu and De Certeau could also be used as one of the methods and analytical tools for studying the performing arts of Asia - or anywhere else in the world. Moreover, as illustrated in my analysis of a *p'ansori* performance, practice can be located in all the mediums of expression such as music, text and bodily movements as well as various agents and contexts such as musicians, dancers, audiences, mediators, social institutions, the wider society and outside world. These mediums, agents, and contexts associated with the processes of production and consumption of performing arts interact, appropriate, compete, and negotiate with each other, producing multiple layers of practice.

However, some questions still remain to be addressed. How is practice associated with the performing arts different from everyday practice as understood by Bourdieu and De Certeau? And if there is a difference, are there certain specific patterns to be found in practice associated with the performing arts that distinguish them from everyday practice? And if there are differences - why?

It is also important to note that researchers, either as outsiders or insiders, can never place themselves completely outside of the dialectic processes. Ethnomusicologists and anthropologists often become a part of the processes of composition, performance, and transmission. For example, Steven Feld (1982) composed and performed Kaluli songs which he studied. Kay Kaufman Shelemay (1997) also reports that her academic research and recordings of music from the Syrian Jewish community in New York city were often used by this migrant community to transmit their music to their younger generations. *P'ansori* scholars are also part of the processes which they study. During my fieldwork in the Korean communities in the former Soviet Union and China, I was often asked to perform traditional Korean music by these Korean migrants. I have given lectures on traditional and contemporary Korean music to the students and teachers of the College of Arts in Yanbian where I undertook fieldwork in

1998. So I have become their informant who performs and transmits my cultural knowledge of Korea and other Korean migrant communities in the former Soviet Union and the United States.

CONCLUSION

In this paper I have described and analysed a *p'ansori* performance using a theoretical model that illustrates how the process of performance is related to all aspects of a performing art from a particular performance to the broadest of historical events. By employing various research methods and instruments it was possible to understand the complex nature of performance and its associated contexts. The concept of practice, either as a theory or as a method, is both a useful perspective and research tool. However, it is important to note that practice associated with the performing arts must also be located in relation to a variety of mediums, individuals, institutions, and their contexts. A performance is built upon these multiple layers of practice with various aims and purposes, whose interactions, in turn, produce different meanings, values, and identities.

All too frequently the processes of data collection and analysis are limited to different techniques which are required by the nature of the discipline and topic of investigation. In the case of the performing arts, a comprehensive understanding of the research topic demands both a broad perspective and intimate knowledge of the minutest technical details of the genre or form under examination. However, as James Clifford (1986:7) pointed out, ethnographic truths are 'inherently partial.' In this sense our own descriptions and analysis are subject to 'blind spots' which may even include ourselves as we are very much part of the processes of 'making' and 'making sense' of the performing arts which we study. However, by using a theoretical and methodological framework that spans all of the disciplines, these gaps in our knowledge can hopefully be identified and become the focus of future research with a view to achieving a better understanding of the relationship that exists between performance and artistic creativity in the human context.

NOTES

1. This is an extended version of my paper 'Food for Body and Soul: Measuring the Dialectics of Performance' first presented at the ICAS Conference and subsequently published in the electronic journal

Oideion. In this version greater attention is given to questions of methodology.
2. Merriam makes the argument that: 'The ethnomusicologist is not the creator or the music he studies, nor is his basic aim to participate aesthetically in that music (though he may seek to do so through re-creation). Rather his position is always that of the outsider who seeks to understand what he hears through analysis of structure and behavior, and to reduce this understanding to terms which will allow him to compare and generalize his results for music as a universal phenomenon of man's existence. The ethnomusicologist is sciencing about music' (Merriam, 1964:25).
3. It should be noted that 'sub-culture' as it is used here does not imply any notion of marginalization that is sometimes associated with the term and its use in Cultural Studies.
4. They were also called *kwangdae*, which refers to folk performing artist(s) in general including *p'ansori* singers, acrobats, actors, jugglers, tight-rope-walkers, and the like.
5. *P'ansori* was performed exclusively by male singers until the second half of the nineteenth century. The first female singer was Chin Ch'ae-sôn [1847-?] (Chông No-sik, 1940:234). Since then progressively more female singers have joined in this performing art. Currently female singers outnumber male singers.
6. The Song of Ch'unhyang is a love story of a young maiden, Ch'unhyang, the daughter of a retired female entertainer and a young man, Mongyong, the son of the magistrate of Namwôn prefecture, Chôlla province. The outline of the story is as follows although some details may vary depending on the version used. On a beautiful spring day Mongyong meets Ch'unhyang at the Kwanghan Pavilion and falls in love with her. They are unofficially married by Ch'unhyang's mother, Wôlmae, since the legal marriage procedure of the time did not allow the daughter of a female entertainer to become the wife of an aristocrat's son. Their happiness is shattered when Mongyong's father is summoned to the capital Seoul and Mongyong has no choice but to follow his own family leaving Ch'unhyang behind in Namwôn. The new magistrate, Pyôn Hakto, refuses to recognize Ch'unhyang's marriage to Mongyong and demands that Ch'unhyang be his concubine. Ch'unhyang refuses and is cast into prison after brutal torture. In the meantime, Mongyong passes the highest civil examination in Seoul and is appointed a royal secret inspector. He returns to Namwôn in the disguise of a poor man. After discovering the situation he punishes the wicked magistrate and rescues Ch'unhyang.

7. The Song of Simch'ông is a story about a young girl, Sim Ch'ông, and her blind father, Sim Hakkyu. Sim Ch'ông's mother died in childbirth and Sim Ch'ông is brought up by her blind father. As soon as Sim Ch'ông is old enough she looks after her father with the greatest sincerity and devotion. One day Sim Hakkyu falls into a ditch and is rescued by a Buddhist monk who tells him that Buddha would restore his sight if he donates three hundred bags of rice to the temple. When Sim Ch'ông learns that some sailors are looking for a virgin sacrifice to the Dragon King at any price she offers herself for three hundred bags of rice. After being tossed into the sea Sim Ch'ông finds herself in the underwater palace of the Dragon King who is deeply moved by Sim Ch'ông's filial piety. He puts her inside a lotus flower and sends it to the pond of the royal palace. The emperor finds Sim Ch'ông in the lotus flower, falls in love with her, and makes her his empress. The empress later holds a great banquet for all blind men and women in the country in the hope of finding her father. When Sim Hakkyu arrives at the banquet and learns that his daughter is alive and is also the empress he suddenly regains his sight because of the shock and joy.
8. Kim So-hûi's style is a combination of several styles including those of Kim Se-jong and Song Man-gap from the Eastern School and that of Chông Chông-nyôl from the Western School (Um, 1992:182).
9. For example, the Song of Ch'unhyang or *Ch'unhyang-ga* has borrowed from various legends and stories for its thematic resources. These include the legend of the ghost of Maiden Ch'unhyang from Namwôn, and other tales about revengeful ghosts, legendary stories about royal secret inspectors, the legends of virtuous woman from the lower classes, and love stories of female entertainers (Kim Tong-uk, 1976:33-68). A number of quotations from Chinese and some Korean classical poetry are also found in the *p'ansori* texts. These quotations have often been used as a device to elaborate the text (Ch'oe Tong-hyôn, 1983:77-88).
10. The female singer, An Suk-sôn, is also a well known *kayagûm pyôngch'ang* performer.
11. The five existing traditional *p'ansori* pieces are: the Song of the Underwater Place (*Sugung-ga*), the Song of Simch'ông (*Simch'ông-ga*), the Song of Ch'uhyang (*Ch'unhyang-ga*), the Song of Hûngbo (*Hûngbo-ga*), and the Song of the Red Cliff (*Chôkpyôk-ka*).
12. For a further discussion see Chapter Three, 'Music and Text' in Um Hae-kyung (1992).
13. Some *p'ansori* teachers even provide a tape-recorder in their studio for the students to record the lessons. Later the students replay the tape when practising on their own. This type of recording as teaching aid

plays an important role in *p'ansori* transmission in contemporary Korea as a supplement to the traditional apprenticeship.

14. Among these singers some of the major figures include: Chông Kwang-su (b. 1919), who sings *Ch'unhyang-ga* in the style of Kim Ch'ang-hwan (1854-1927) from the Western School; Ch'oe Sûng-hûi (b. 1937), who performs *Ch'unhyang-ga* in the style of Chông Chông-nyôl from the Western School; the late Pak Pong-sul (1922-89), who sang *Ch'unhyang-ga* in the style of Song Man-gap from the Eastern School; and Kang To-gûn (b. 1918), who learnt *Ch'unhyang-ga* from Kim Chông-mun (1887-1935), a student of Song Man-gap (1865-1939) from the Eastern School.

15. For example, up to the middle of the 1960s, this scholarship was led by those from Korean literature, who were mainly interested in the historical and philological aspects of *p'ansori*. From the mid-1960s to the end of the 1970s, scholars from Korean literature, musicology and other disciplines have studied *p'ansori* using an increasing number of perspectives and methodologies associated with psychology, sociology, history, criticism and ethnography rendering the distinctions between these disciplines increasingly less important (Um, 1992).

REFERENCES

Blacking, John (1987) '*A Commonsense View of All Music.*' Cambridge: Cambridge University Press.

--(1995) 'Music, Culture, and Experience,' in: Reginald Byron (ed.) *Music, Culture, and Experience: Selected Papers of John Blacking*. Chicago: Chicago University Press, pp. 223-42.

Cho, Tong-il (1969) '*Hûngbu-jôn ûi Yangmyônsông* (A Duality in the Tale of Hûngbu),' *Kyemyông Nonch'ong* 5, pp. 71-123.

Ch'oe, Tong-hyôn (1983) '*P'ansori ûi Hanmun Sasôl e Kwanhan Sogo* (A Study of Chinese Characters in the Text of *P'ansori*),' *Inmun Nonch'ong* 12, pp. 75-88.

Chông, No-sik (1940) *Chosôn Ch'anggûksa (History of Korean Vocal Theatre)*. Keijo (Seoul): The Chosôn Daily Newspaper Press.

Clifford, James (1986) 'Introduction: Partial Truth,' in: James Clifford and George E. Marcus (eds) *Writing Culture*. Berkeley: University of California Press, pp, 1-26.

de Certeau, Michel (1984) *The Practice of Everyday Life*. Translated by Seven Rendall. Berkeley: University of California Press.

Feld, Steven (1982) *Sound and Sentiment: Birds, Weeping, Poetic, and song in Kaluli Expression*. Philadelphia: University of Pennsylvania Press.
Foucault, Michel (1981) *The History of Sexuality*. Vol. 1. Harmondsworth: Penguin.
Giles, H. and P.F. Powesland (1975) *Speech Style of Social Evaluation*. London: Academic Press.
Han, Man-yông (1972) 'P'ansori ûi Ujo (Ujo mode in P'ansori),' *Han'guk Umak Yôn'gu (Studies of Korean Music)* 2, pp. 67-88.
Hawkes, Terrence (1977) *Structuralism and Semiotics*. Berkeley: University of California Press.
Hood, Mantle (1960) 'The Challenge of "Bi-Musicality",' *Ethnomusicology* 4 (1), pp. 55-9.
--(1982) *The Ethnomusicologist*. Kent: Kent University Press.
Kim, Hûng-gyu (1974) 'P'ansori ûi Iwônsông kwa Sahoesa chôk Paegyông (A Duality in P'ansori and Its Socio-historical Background),' *Ch'angjak kwa Pip'yông* 31, pp. 69-100.
--(1978) 'P'ansori ûi Sahoe chôk Sôngkyôk kwa Kû Pyônmo (Social Characteristics of P'ansori and Their Changes),' *Segye ûi Munhak* 10, pp. 70-99.
Kim, Tong-uk (1976) *Chûngbo p'an Ch'unhyang-jôn Yôn'gu (A Study of the Tale of Ch'unhyang, Revised Edition)*. Seoul: Yônse University Press.
Mahar, Cheleen et al. (1990) 'The Basic Theoretical Position,' in: Richard Harker et al. (eds) *An Introduction to the Work of Pierre Bourdieu: The Practice of Theory*. London: The Macmillan Press, pp. 1-25.
Merriam, Alan (1964) *The Anthropology of Music*. Evanston: Northwestern University Press.
Rice, Timothy (1997) 'Toward a Mediation of Field Methods and Field Experience,' in: Gregory Barz and Timothy J. Cooley (eds) *Shadows in the Field: New Perspectives for Fieldwork in Ethnomusicology*. Oxford, New York: Oxford University Press, pp. 101-21.
Seeger, Anthony (1987) *Why Suya Sing?: A Musical Anthropology of Amazonian People*. Cambridge: Cambridge University Press.
Shelemay, Kay Kaufman (1997) 'The Ethnomusicologist, Ethnographic Method, and the Transmission of Tradition,' in: Gregory Barz and Timothy J. Cooley (eds) *Shadows in the Field: New Perspectives for Fieldwork in Ethnomusicology*. Oxford, New York: Oxford University Press, pp. 189-204.
Um, Hae-kyung (1992) *Making P'ansori, Korean Musical Drama*. Unpublished PhD thesis. The Queen's University of Belfast.

--(1993a) 'Changing Views on the Aesthetics of *P'ansori*, Korean Narrative Music with Reference to *Ch'unhyang-ga* (The Song of Ch'unhyang),' in: Max Peter Baumann, Artur Simon and Ulrich Wegner (eds) *European Studies in Ethnomusicology: Historical Developments and Recent Trends*. Wilhelmshaven: Folorian Noetzel Verlag, pp. 189-98.

--(1993b) 'Mode (*Cho*) in: *P'ansori*, Korean Narrative Music,' in: Giovanni Giuriati (ed.) *Ethnomusicologica II: Atti Del VI European Seminar in Ethnomusicology Siena 17-21 Agosto 1989. Quaderni dell'Accademia Chigiana XLV*. Siena: Accademia Musicale Chigiana, pp. 135-52.

--(1994) 'Socio-Historical Context and Creative Process in the Construction of Korean Dramatic Narrative,' *Lore and Language* 12, pp. 253-75.

--(1996) 'The Korean Diaspora in Uzbekistan and Kazakhstan: Social Change, Identity and Music-Making' in: Kirsten Schultze, Martin Stokes and Colm Campbell (eds) *Nationalism, Minorities and Diasporas: Identities and Rights in: the Middle East*. London: I.B. Tauris, pp. 217-32.

Walraven, Boudewijn C.A. (1985) *Muga: The Song of Korean Shamanism*. PhD thesis, University of Leiden. Dordrecht: ICG Printing.

Wolff, Janet (1981) *The Social Production of Art*. London: Macmillan.

Yi, Chi-yông (1991) 'The Gala Concert Tour to the United States,' *Korean Music Newsletter* 17, p. 30.

Yi, Hye-gu (1955) '*Song Man-jae ûi Kwanuhûi* (Viewing Folk Entertainers' Performance, [the Poem] by Song Man-jae),' in: *Chungangdae Samsipchunyôn Kinyôm Nonmunjip*. Seoul: Chungang University Press, pp. 93-119.

Yi, Po-hyông (1971) '*P'ansori Kyôngdûrûm e Kwanhan Yôn'gu* (A Study of the *Kyôngdûrûm* Melodic Type in *P'ansori*),' *Sônangdang* 1, pp. 11-33.

--(1972) '*Menarijo* (The *Menarijo* Melodic Type),' *Han'guk Umak Yôn'gu (Studies of Korean Music)* 2, pp. 111-29.

--(1982a) '*P'ansori ran Muôsinya* (What is *P'ansori?*),' '*Tan'ga ran Muôsinya* (What is *Tan'ga?*),' in: *P'ansori Tasôn Madang: Haesôl kwa Chusôk ûl Tan Sasôljip, Purok-Yôngmun Haesôl* (Five Pieces of *P'ansori*: Annotated *P'ansori* Text with English Introductions). Seoul: Korea Britannica Corporation. Korean text: pp. 7-16, 29-231. English text (translated by Song Pang-song): pp. 245- 66, 267-71.

--(1982b) '*P'ansori Che e Kwanhan Yôn'gu* (A Study of *Che* in *P'ansori*),' in: Yesul Yôn'gusil (ed.) *Han'guk Umakhak Nonmunjip* (Anthology of Articles in Korean Musicology). Seoul: Academy of Korean Studies, pp. 61-104.

CHAPTER 12

THE MAITHILI LANGUAGE[1]

YOGENDRA P. YADAVA

Maithili, sometimes also referred to as *Maitli, Tirhutiyā, Dehāti* or even *Bihāri*, is a language spoken in the two adjoining South Asian countries, India and Nepāl. As its name implies, Maithili is, properly speaking, the language of *Mithilā*, an ancient kingdom. It was once ruled by King Janak and was the birth place of Jānaki or Sitā (Lord Rām's consort). As a seat of learning, this kingdom attracted scholars from all over India eager to receive the rigorous training in logic and philosophy available during the period and also hosted some highly intellectual deliberations in the history of human thought. This region was also called *Tairabhukti*, the ancient name of Tirhut comprising both Darbhanga and Muzzaffarpur districts of Bihār, India. Modern Mithilā is, however, politically split into the adjacent parts of the two different nations - Nepāl and India - and yet it exists as an inalienable cultural entity mainly owing to the proximity of and regular interaction between the Maithili-speaking communities of the two nations.

The Maithili language is spoken by about 30 million people mainly in the north-eastern part of Indian state of Bihār and the eastern part of Nepalese terai region. It is also used marginally in neighbouring Indian states like West Bengal, Maharashtra, and Madhya Pradesh. In Nepāl, it is the language of approximately 12 per cent (approximately 2.3 million) of the total population and figures second in terms of the number of speakers - second only to Nepāli, the language of the nation, spoken by a little over fifty per cent of the population (CBS, 1991).

In both Nepāl and India, Maithili has been taught as a subject of study from school to university levels of education. Especially in India, however, it has been hampered by the lack of official recognition as a medium of instruction. In Nepāl, a constitutional provision has been recently made for introducing all the mother tongues spoken in Nepāl, including Maithili, as a medium of instruction at the primary level of education (HMG, 1991). This is, no doubt, a welcome step for their promotion, but in spite of its speakers' zeal there has not been much headway made in this regard hampered by the dearth of official initiatives and the lack of provisions of basic requirements like teaching and reading materials, not to mention trained manpower. Both the P.E.N. (Poets, Essayists, Novelists) club and Sāhitya Akādemī have recognized Maithili as the sixteenth largest language of India, though it has not yet been included in the Eighth Schedule of the Indian Constitution despite the unceasing efforts to achieve this made by Maithili-speaking community in India.

Maithili is a distinct Indo-Aryan language; unlike Hindi, which is a part of the central group of Indo-Aryan languages, it belongs to its eastern group (Masica, 1991:436-7).[2] It forms a sub-group with Bhojpuri and Magahi and is linguistically closer to Assamese, Bengāli, and Oriyā than to its more contiguous languages, namely, Hindi and Nepāli. It is, therefore, a misnomer conceived by foreign linguists like Hoernle (1880) and recently propagated also by some Hindi-speaking zealots to treat it as a Bihāri or eastern dialect of Hindi.

Formerly, Maithili had its own script, called Mithilākshar or Tirhutā, which is derived from Brahmi (of the third century BC Asokan inscriptions) via proto-Bengāli script and is fairly similar to modern Bengāli and Oriyā writing systems.[3] It was used in earlier written texts. Besides Mithilākshar, Kaithi script was also used by Kāyasthas (belonging to a caste of writers and clerks), especially for keeping written records at government and private levels. These two scripts have now been virtually abandoned. For the sake of convenience if education and printing (and also perhaps under the influence of Hindi writing system), they have gradually been replaced by Devanāgari script used for writing Hindi, Nepāli and some other languages of both Indo-Aryan and Tibeto-Burman stocks spoken in adjoining areas. Note, however, that all the alphabets in this script are not distinctive and phonemic. For example, Devanāgari alphabet makes short/long vowel contrasts, but they are not pertinent at the phonological level of the Maithili language; that is to say, Maithili has only short vowels and no long ones (see Table 2 below for the inventory of Maithili vowels).

LITERATURE

Maithili has had a long, rich tradition of written literature in both India and Nepāl. The earliest written record is the Verṇa-Ratnākar, the oldest text in Maithili, written by Jyotiriśvara Kaviśekharāchārya in the fourteenth century. The most famous Maithili writer is Vidyāpati Ṭhakur, popularly known as Mahākavi Vidyāpati. Apart from being a great Sanskrit writer, he composed melodious poems in Maithili entitled Vidyāpati Padāvali, of which the main theme is the love between Radhā and Kriṣṇa. It is this anthology of poems which has made him popular to the present day and ensured him of immortality among its speakers.

Maithili also flourished as a court language in the Kāṭhmāndu valley during the Malla period. Several literary works (especially dramas and songs) and inscriptions in Maithili are still preserved at the National Archives in Kāṭhmāndu.

In the contemporary context there have been works in Maithili in all literary genres, especially poetry, plays, and fiction, from both Indian and Nepalese writers. Apart from literature, Maithili writers have also been contributing to other fields like culture, history, journalism, and linguistics.

In addition to written texts, Maithili has an enormous stock of oral literature in the forms of folk tales in prose and verse, ballads, and songs. Of them, the ballads of Rās Lilā (expressing the love between Radhā and Kriṣṇa) and Salhes (a prehistoric king) are well-known examples.

A SURVEY OF LINGUISTIC STUDIES

Linguistic studies available on the Maithili language have been pursued for a little more than a century. We find the earliest reference to Maithili (or Tirhutiya) in Amaduzzi's preface to Beligatti's *Alphabetum Brammhanicum* (1771), which gives a list of Indian languages. It was followed by Celebrooke (1801), who was the first to identify Maithili as a separate language. The studies so far carried on the Maithili language may be conveniently discussed in terms of its grammar, phonology, lexicography, historical/ comparative linguistics, and sociolinguistics/pragmatics.

The tradition of Maithili grammar may be traced to Hoernle (1880), who treated Maithili as a dialect distinct from Hindi on the basis of some examples of its grammatical forms. It was, however, with the publication of Grierson (1881) that the study of Maithili grammar was undertaken seriously. In his book, he presented a comprehensive grammar of the existing standard dialect of Maithili.[4] Other major works in this field completed during this period include two more works by Grierson (1883, 1903) and Kellog (1893).

The earliest grammar of Maithili by a native grammarian was written by D. Jha (c. 1946) in Maithili. In this study the grammatical rules are presented in the form of *sutra*s in the Pāninian style of Sanskrit grammar. This was followed by G. Jha's Maithili grammar (1979) which attempts to analyse the language using modern linguistic insights.

In their studies, Davis (1973) and Williams (1973) have collected Maithili sentences during their fieldwork in the Nepāl terai and analysed their patterns within the tagmemic model. Recently, attempts have also been made to present Maithili syntax within the framework of transformational-generative grammar. The first work of this nature is that by Singh (1979), who has presented an account of Maithili sentences within the model of relational grammar, a version of transformational-generative grammar. In addition, Yadava (1983, forthcoming) has tried to investigate the syntactic phenomena of Maithili and to explore their bearings on a more recent version of transformational-generative grammar, namely, Government-Binding theory proposed by Noam Chomsky. Mention must be made of Burghart (1992), who has presented a comprehensive description of the spoken Maithili in social context mainly for the use of foreigners who want to learn the language, but also with linguists in mind. More recently, R. Yadav (1996) has produced a detailed description of the Maithili language which deals extensively with its phonology, morphology, and syntax, and several other related issues. S. Jha (1941) was the first to study the Maithili sound system also taking into account its historical development. G. Jha's (1974) work has been done in almost the same vein. R. Yadav's (1984) work is the first study of Maithili sound system and phonology within the framework of generative phonology. His work has been pursued a step further by S.K. Jha (1984) and more recently, by M. Mishra (1996).

Lexicography or dictionary-making in Maithili has had a very long tradition. The earliest attempt in this field can be traced back to *Verṅa-Ratnākar*, which is not only the first lexicon but also the oldest text in Maithili written by Jyotiriṣvara Kaviṣekharāchārya in the fourteenth century.

After a long gap, the lexicography in Maithili was resumed by Grierson, who published the chrestomathy and vocabulary of the language in 1882. He pursued this enterprise further and brought out *Bihār Peasant Life* (1885), a list of names used in daily life by Bihār peasants. It was followed by Hoernle and Grierson (1885, 1889), who collaborated to produce *A Comparative Dictionary of the Bihāri Language,* only two parts of which are published.

The Maithili monolingual dictionary by D. Jha (1950) has been a major contribution in this field. In 1973, two attempts were made to compile Maithili dictionaries. The first is a comparative word list including Maithili words by Trail (1973). Another work is by J. Mishra (1973), who undertook the ambitious task of producing an etymological and historical dictionary of the language on the model of *Oxford English Dictionary*; so far only two volumes of the dictionary have come out. Mention must also be made of Davis's (1984) basic Maithili dictionary with Nepāli and English equivalents. Recently, a monolingual Maithili dictionary has been published in two volumes. Finally, a Maithili-Nepali-English dictionary has been undertaken by Yadava (in progress) at Royal Nepāl Academy.

We find a comprehensive account of the development of the Maithili language through time in S. Jha (1958). In this significant study using an ample number of specimens from both spoken and written texts he shows how the language has evolved from the old Indo-Aryan period up to the present. Another important work in this respect is G. Jha's (1968) study on the history of the Maithili language.

The first reference to Maithili in comparison to other Indo-Aryan languages was made by Colebrooke (1801). Apart from being synchronic in general framework, *The Indo-Aryan Languages* by Masica (1991) is a major contribution to the field of synchronic as well as diachronic study of Maithili in relation to other languages of the Indo-Aryan subfamily.

Bickel and Yadava (forthcoming) is the most recent attempt to investigate the typology of grammatical relations (such as subject, direct and indirect object) in some selected Indo-Aryan languages including Maithili.

There have been very few sociolinguistic studies in the Maithili language. In an article Singh (1989) has schematically demonstrated how the choice of verb agreement forms in Maithili is constrained by the addresser-addressee relationship and their social status. In an another study S.K. Yadav (1989) has dealt with the use of some major languages of Nepāl, including Maithili in various domains and suggested a viable language policy for the Nepalese context. In addition, Burghart (1992) is a major contribution in understanding the Maithili language in relation to its social contexts.

In their paper Bickel et al. (forthcoming) demonstrate that the complex paradigm structure of Maithili verb agreement is far from arbitrary, but can be predicted by two pragmatic principles of human interaction in Maithil society: a principle of social hierarchy underlying the evaluation of people's 'face' (Brown and Levinson, 1987), and a principle of social solidarity defining degrees of 'empathy' (Kuno, 1987) which people identify with others. Maithili verb agreement not only reflects a specific style of social cognition but it also constitutes a prime means of maintaining this style by requiring constant attention to its defining parametres.

MAJOR GRAMMATICAL FEATURES

This section aims to highlight the major characteristics of the Maithili language at different linguistic levels. These characteristics are often presented in comparison to other languages, especially Indo-Aryan ones, in order to show how Maithili converge with and diverge from them.

PHONOLOGY

There are twenty-six consonants and eight oral vowels in Maithili. They are listed in the following table:

Tabel 1: Maithili Consonants (Yadav, 1984, 1996)

Place→ Manner↓	Bilabial	Dental	Retroflex	Palatal	Velar	Glottal
Stops	p pʰ b bʰ	t tʰ d dʰ	ʈ ʈʰ ɖ ɖʰ		k kʰ g gʰ	
Affricates				c cʰ j jʰ		
Nasals	m	n				
Tap		r				
Fricatives		s				h
Lateral		l				
Approximants	(w)			(y)		

Table 2: Maithili Vowels (Yadav, 1984, 1996)

Parts of the tongue→ Heights of the tongue↓	Front	Central	Back
High	I		u
Mid	e	ə	o
Low	æ	a	ɔ

Note that the vowel length which is maintained in Devanāgari script is not distinctive in Maithili. In this respect, Maithili behaves like Nepāli but is divergent from Hindi. Besides, in principle, all the oral vowels in Table 2 can be nasalized; so there are eight nasalized vowels. Taken together, there are forty-two phonemes in the language. There are also some diphthongs and tripthongs in the language, which are not discussed here.[5]

MORPHOLOGY
The most striking feature of Maithili grammar is the extremely complex verbal system. Like other Indo-Aryan languages, Maithili has a

polymorphomic verb paradigm. It consists of several elements normally to the right of the verb stem (Masica, 1991:257). Its structure may be expressed as follows:

(1)
V→Stem (Asp) (Suff be) (Asp Suff)(Aux) Tns Agr_1 (Agr_2) (Agr_3)
This structure is illustrated in the following sentence:
(2)
hari-ji daur-ait rah-ait cha-l- āh.
Hari-3h run-IP be- IP AUX-PT-3h
'Hari had been running.'

Unlike most of the Indo-Aryan languages, however, Maithili encodes one of the most complex agreement systems of Indo-Aryan languages. In this language, not only nominative and non-nominative subjects, but also objects, other core arguments, and even non-arguments are cross-referenced, allowing for a maximum of three participants encoded by the verb desinences. Examples in (3a-c) illustrate single, double, and triple agreement, respectively:

(3)
a. ham sut-l-aũ(h).
   1N sleep-PT-1N
   'I slept.'
b. ham hun-kā madat kar-l-i-ainh.
   1N 3h-ACC help do-PT-1N-3hACC
   'I helped him.'
c. ham to-rā hun-ak kitāb de-l-i-au-nh.
   1N 2mh-ACC 3h-GEN book give-PT-1N-2mhACC-3hGEN
   'I gave his book to you.'

The controllers of verb agreement in all the three types of verb agreement include not only the arguments of a predicate and the possessors (as shown in (3a-c)) but also non-arguments like nominals in postpositional phrases and possessors therein as well as deictic referents in a discourse. Examples are given below:

(4)
a. tõ hun-kā-lel kāj kai-l-ah-unh. (*agreement with non argument*)
   2mhN 3h-OBL-for work do-PT-2mhN-3hOBL
   'You worked for him.'

b. ham toh-ar ghar-par ge-l ch-al-i-ah. *(agreement with the posses*
sor in a non-argument)
1N 2mh-GEN house-at go-pcl Aux-PT-1N-2mhGEN
'I had been to your house.'
c. ham o-krā mār-l-i-ah. *(agreement with a deictic referent)*
1N 3nh-ACC beat-PT-1N-2mh
'I beat him (who is related to you, etc.).'[6]

However, it has been found that the system is partly reduced by lower caste speakers, who are least interested in maintaining this style, especially its emphasis on hierarchy.

The categories reflected in the morphology are three persons with four honorific degrees and, in the case of third persons only, masculine vs. feminine gender, proximate vs. remote spatial distance, and in focus vs. out of focus reference. However, not all combinations of category choices are equally represented, and there are many cases of neutralization.

A related issue in Maithili grammar is pro-drop phenomenon, in which we mean that a pronoun in a clause can be optionally dropped. Like several Indo-Aryan and Tibeto-Burman (especially Kirānti) languages, Maithili is a pro-drop language. Note, however, that in Maithili, it is not only the pronominal subject but also the pronominal direct object and possessive within the direct object, which can be (optionally) dropped. The reason is (as mentioned earlier) that agreement in Maithili contains the grammatical features not only of the subject but also of the direct object, possessor within the direct object and even missing referents. As an illustration of pro-drop in Maithili, consider the following examples:[7]

(5)
a. ham torā mār-b-au.
   I-[1] you-[2nh] beat-FUT-$_{1SUB+2nhDO}$
   'I will beat you.'
b. pro torā mār-b-au.
c. ham pro mār-b-au.
d. pro pro ṇār)b-au.

(6)
a. I hunak ghar chi-I-ainh.
   This hi-[3h] house be–PRES-$_{3h.POSS}$
   'This is his house.'
b. i pro ghar ch-i-ainh.

Like Hindi, but unlike Nepāli, a verb in Maithili employs two types of causative verbs, e.g. *kaṭā-/kaṭbā-* 'have cut by someone/cause someone to have cut by someone.' Furthermore, the first causative is derived from its transitive counterpart *kāṭ-* 'cut something,' which is further derived from its intransitive form *kaṭ-* 'cut' (as in 'The tree is cutting well').

A verb in Maithili, as in other South Asian languages, can be expanded in another way, namely, in the form of a serial verb construction (often referred to as 'compound verb') which involves a sequence of two verbs. The first of these verbs is in the form of conjunctive participle and may be referred to as a 'host,' while the second one is in the finite form and may be called a 'light verb,' e.g.

(7)
hari-ji   kitāb   paidh   le-l-aith.
Hari-h   book   readCP   take-PT-3h
'Hari completed the reading of the book.'

Apart from aspectual functions in (7), serial verbs in Maithili also express other semantic functions, e.g. volitional and control of the action by the agent as well as the speaker's attitude.

In addition to causativization and verb serialization, there are other types of complex predicates in Maithili. For example, a verb can combine with a noun or adjective to form a complex verb, e.g.:

(8)
rām   cor-ak   pichā   kai-l-ak. (Noun+Verb)
Ram   thief-GEN   pursuitNdoIP-PT-3nh
'Ram chased the thief.'
(9)
rām   ghar   sāph   kai-l-ak. (Adjective+ Verb)
Ram   house   clean   do-PT-3nh
'Ram cleaned the house.'

	Nominative	Dative	Genitive
1	*ham*	*hamrā*	*hamar*
2nh	*tū̃*	*torā*	*tohar*
2mh	*tõ*	*torā*	*tohar*
2h	*ahā̃*	*ahā̃-kẽ*	*ahaā̃-k*
2hh (indirect)	*apne*	*apne-kẽ*	*apne-k*
3nh proximate	*I*	*ekrā*	*ekar*
3nh remote	*u*	*okrā*	*okar*
3h/hh proximate	*i*	*hinkāl*	*hinak*
3h/hh remote	*o*	*hunkā*	*hunak*

Table 3: Maithili Personal Pronouns
Like the agreement morphology, the pronouns of Maithili distinguish person, honorificity, proximity, and case. They are summarized in Table 3.

With regard to most categories, pronouns are equally or less differentiated than verbal inflections. They are less specific with regard to the 'honorific' vs. 'high-honorific' distinction among third persons which are registered as -*aith* and -*ath-inh*, respectively, on the verb. In either case, the pronoun is *o*. Moreover, if third person reference is proximate, all honorificity distinctions are neutralized to *i*. Among second persons, pronouns are just as discriminatory as verb forms. However, the distinction between honorific *ahã* and high-honorific *apne* is not encoded synthetically. Rather, *apne* combines with a periphrastic passive-like construction that contrasts with the active form agreeing with *ahã*.

(10)
a. apne padḮh-alge-l-aik.
 2hhN read-P PASS.AUX-PT-3
 'You^{hh} were reading.'
b. ahã padḮh-ait cha-l-ãuh.
 2hN read-IP AUX-PT-2hN
 'You^h were reading.'

Mid and non-honorific second person are differentiated by *tu)* vs. *to)*, respectively, but this contrast is not always maintained. It can be neutralized especially among lower caste speakers.

The distinction between honorific degrees is not limited to pronouns. Proper nouns can also be marked by an honorific (-*ji*) or a non-honorific (-*yā, -bā, -mā*) suffix, triggering corresponding verb inflection.

(11)
a. Hari-ji bhajan gab-ait ch-aith.
 h religious.song sing-IP AUX-3hN
 'Hari^h is singing a *bhajan*.'
b. Hari-yā bhajan   gab-ait ai-ch.
 H.-nh religious.song sing-IP 3-AUX
 'Hari^{nh} is singing a *bhajan*.'

Without such marking, a name has a neutral to mid-honorific value. Common nouns sometimes differentiate an honorific and a non-honorific lexical form, such as *bauā* 'boy^h' vs. *chaurā* 'boy^{nh},' or *daiyā* 'girl^h' vs. *chauri* 'girl^{nh}.'

Another feature that is restricted to nominals is number. This category, however, is not fully grammaticalized with nominals either. It is expressed by the suffix *-sabh* or, with honorific reference only, the suffix *-lokain* (cf. Singh, 1989:88). Notice that *-sabh* also occurs as a free word in the sense of 'all,' which attests to a low degree of grammaticalization (cf. R. Yadav, 1996:69). In verb agreement, no number distinctions are made. This fact, which makes Maithili quite different from other Indo-Aryan languages such as Hindi or Nepāli, is the result of reanalysing inherited number differentiation into honorificity distinctions.

Grammatical gender in Maithili nouns is rather very much restricted both as a morphological category and as a syntactic category. There are declensions like *-i (chaurā* 'boy'/*chauri* 'girl') and *-āin (guru/guruāin* 'teacher masculine/feminine'). These gender markers are, however, confined to a limited number of nouns and do not apply across the board. Maithili pronominals do not encode gender distinctions at all. But in highly formal speech, Maithili verbs encode, as a syntactic category, the feminine gender associated with third person honorific nouns and pronouns in past and future tenses:

(12)
a. o daur-l-ih   daur-t-ih.
   3h run-PT-3hN:FEM run-FUT-3hN:FEM
   'She ran / will run.'
b. o daur-l-aith   daur-t-aah.
   3h run-PT-3hN   run-FUT- 3hN
   'He ran / will run.'

It should to be noted that unlike Hindi and Nepāli, possessive modifiers do not agree with their nominal heads in gender:

(13)
okar   pati/patni
'his/her husband/wife'

However, if the modifier is an adjective it does agree with its human head noun in gender:

(14)
okar pahilkā betā/okar pahilki beti
'his/her first son/his/her first daughter'

Like other South Asian languages, Maithili nominals involve a rich case system. They encode three types of case markings: zero-marking, clitics and -(a)k +postpositions. This is shown in the examples below:

(1) Zero-marking

There are two cases in Maithili which are zero-marked, viz. nominative and accusative with non-human nouns, as shown in (15) and (16), repectively:

(i) Nominative

(15)
u-Ø   daur-l-ak.
he-NOM   run-PT-3nh
'He ran.'

(ii) Accusative

(16)
u-Ø   kitāb-Ø   kin-l-ak.
he-NOM   book-ACC   buy-PT-3nh
'He bought a book.'

(2) Clitics

(i) Accusative/Dative- -ke)

(17)
a. rām chaurā-k   mār-l-ak.
   Ram boy-ACC   beat-PT-3nh
   'Ram beat the boy.'
b. hari-ke   bhukh   lāg-al.
   Hari-DAT   hunger feel-PT
   'Hari felt hungry.'

(ii) Genitive: A. -(a)k (with nouns and honorific pronouns)

(18)
a. ham   rām-ak   ghar   dekh-l-i-ainh.
   I   Ram-GEN   house   see-PT-1-3h
   'I saw Ram's house.'

b. ham   ahã-k   ghar   dekh-l-au①h.
   I   2h-GEN   house   see-PT-1
   'I saw your^h house.'

B. *-ar* (with pronouns other than honorific ones)

(19)
ham-ar   ghar   dur   ai-ch.
my-GEN   house   far   3-AUX
'My house is far away.'

        (iii) Instrumental/ Source: *-sã*

(20)
a. hari   pensil-   sãlikh-l-ak.
   Hari   pencil-INS   write-PT-3nh
   'Hari wrote with a pencil.'
b. hari-ji   apan   gãm-sã ai-l-ãh.
   Hari-h   self   village-SRC come-PT-3h
   'Hari came from his village.'

(iv) Locative: *-me/-par*

(21)
a. hari-ji   kothari-me   ch-aith.
   Hari-h   room-LOC   AUX-3h
   'Hari is in the room.'
b. hari-ji   ghar-par   ch-aith.
   Hari-h   home-LOC   AUX-3h
   'Hari is at home.'

It should be noted that, in contrast to many other Indo-Aryan languages including Hindi and Maithili, Maithili has no ergative case marking; that is, the subject is always zero-marked and never takes an overt case marker.

(3) *-(a)k* + postposition

(22)
ham   kitãb-ak-lel/bãste ae-l   ch-i.
I   book-GEN-P   come-PCL   AUX-1
'I have come for the book.'

Case and verb agreement are, no doubt, related in the languages of the world. What is striking about Maithili verb agreement is the fact that it makes binary contrast of nominative and non-nominative agreement. That is to say, there are two sets of verb agreement in Maithili: the nominative set for the subjects in nominative case and the non-nominative set for the subjects and non-subjects in non-nominative cases shown in (23a-f). Thus, nominals are differentiated more than verb agreement with regard to case.

Like Nepāli, Hindi, and several other South Asian languages, there is no one-to-one correspondence between cases and grammatical relations in Maithili. For example, the subject of a clause need not necessarily be the nominals in the nominative case (as shown in (22)), but also the nominals in non-nominative cases like dative(DAT), instrumental(INS), genitive(GEN) and locative(LOC) as well as logical subject in a passive construction. Examples are given in (23a-f), respectively:

(23)
a. hunkā   bhukh   lag-l-ain(h).
   3h-DAT   hunger   feel-PT-3h
   'He felt hungry'
b. hunkā   cithi   likhai-kẽ   cha-l-ain(h).
   3h-DAT   letter   to write   be-Pt-3hNN
   'He had to write a letter.'
c. hunkā-sã i kitāb padh-al nahi bhe-l-ain(h).
   3h-Ins this book read-PCL not become-PT-3hNN
   'He couldn't read this book.'
d. hunak   paisā   harā   ge-l-ain(h).
   3h-GEN   money   lose   go-PT-3hNN
   'He lost his money.'
e. hunkā-me sāphe   dayā   nahi   ch-ain(h).
   3h-LOC   at all   mercy   not   be-Pres3hNN
   'He has no mercy at all.'
f. hunkā-sã i   cithi   likh-al   ge-l-ain(h).
   3h-by   this letter   write-PCL   go-PT-3hNN
   'This letter was written by him.'

SYNTAX
The normal order of constituents in a Maithili sentence is S(ubject) V(erb) O(bject), e.g.:

(24)
rām kitāb   kinat.   -SOV
Ram book   will buy
'Ram will buy a book.'

However, these constituents can be permuted in any order. For instance, the transitive construction like (1) can have any permutation of S, O and V:

(25)
a. kitāb rām kinat.   -OSV
b. kitāb kinat rām.   -OVS
c. kinat rām kitāb.   -VSO
d. kinat kitāb rām.   -VOS
e. rām kinat kitāb.   -SVO

The order SOV in (1) is unmarked and stylistically neutral, whereas the various permuted orders in (i-v) are generally accompanied by phonological and semantic effects like topicalization, focusing, afterthought, definiteness, and the like.

The freedom of word order also extends to Indirect Object and adverbials of various types. What is more interesting about Maithili word order is that even elements like adjectives within NPs (as in (26a)) and auxiliaries within verbal sequences (as in (27a)) can be permuted with other elements of the sentence:

(26)
a. geetā [$_{NP}$ [$_A$ hariyar] sāri] pahirne a-ich.
   Geeta green sari wearing AUX-PRES3
   'Geeta is wearing a green sari.'
b. geetā hariyar pahirne aich sāri.
c. geetā sāri pahirne aich hariyar.

(27)
a. rām khā-it ai-ch.
   Ram eat-IP PRES3-AUX
   'Ram is eating.'
b. khā-it ai-ch rām.
c. rām ai-ch khā-it.
d. ai-ch rām khā-it.

The change in word order is not only restricted to simple sentences and phrases in Maithili but also extends to complex sentences. Consider the unmarked order of the constituents in the complex sentence in (28a) and how the elements of both main and subordinate clauses can be juxtaposed with one another:

(28)
a. rām   hari-kẽ   kitāb padh-bāk-lel kah-l-ak.
   Ram   Hari-ACC   book   read- INF   tell-PT-3nh
   'Ram told Hari to read the book.'
b. hari-kẽ rām padh-bāk-lel kitāb kah-l-ak, etc.

Taking the unmarked order into consideration, Maithili, like all languages of South Asia *sprachbund* ('linguistic area'), is a head-final language, by which we mean that the head of a phrase follows its complement. Thus, the head of a verb phrase (VP) is a verb (V) and it follows its complement (object NP); the head of a postpositional phrase (PP) is a postposition (P) and it follows it complement (object NP); and the head of a noun phrase (NP) is a noun (N) and it follows its complement (genitive marker -*ak*), as shown in (29a-c), respectively:

(29)
a. rām [$_{VP}$ hari-kẽ mār-l-ak].
   Ram3nhN Hari-Acc beat-PT-3nhN
   'Ram beat Hari.'
b. [$_{PP}$ nepāl me]
   Nepāl in
   'in Nepāl'
c. [$_{NP}$ rām-ak kitāb]
   Ram-GEN book
   'Ram's book'

These examples show that Maithili is a head-final language and chooses the 'follows' (rather than 'precedes,' as in English-type languages) value of parameter.

Maithili has an interesting rule which is analogous to the Raising-to-Subject rule of English. We refer to this rule as Subject-to-Subject Raising. The rule in question has the following unusual property. This Maithili rule raises the subject of a *tensed* embedded clause, whereas the English Raising-to-Subject rule raises to the matrix subject position the subject of a *tenseless* embedded clause:

(30)
a. lagait aich   je   ahã   āi   ghar   nahi
   seems   that   you   today   home   not
   jā sakab.
   go can
   'It seems that you cannot go home today.'

b. ahã lagait chi je āi ghar nahi jā sakab.
   'You seem not to be able to go home today.'
   (Literally: *'You seem that cannot go home today.')

In (30), the rule takes structure (a) as its input and derives structure (b) by preposing the embedded subject *ahã* to the empty subject position in the matrix clause. The rule applies only if the matrix predicate is a member of the class known as 'raising predicates,' e.g., *seem*-type verbs. Such verbs in Maithili include *lagnāi*, *bujhenāi*, *pratit honāi*, and the like, all of which mean 'to seem.' The structure in (b) is, however, not permitted in English. It should be noted that this phenomenon is rare not only in South Asian languages but also in other languages of the world.[9]

CONCLUSION

As noted above, Maithili possesses a rich heritage of both literary writings and linguistic studies and has sufficient potential for further growth and development. Coupled with this, it has a large number of speakers with strong sense of language loyalty, which is essential for language maintenance. Maithili speech communities in both India and Nepāl have been active in promoting the cause of their mother tongue. For example, several initiatives have been taken to include Maithili in the Eighth Schedule of the Indian Constitution. Similarly, Maithili speakers in Nepāl, in collaboration with speakers of other indigenous languages, have recently launched a concerted effort to introduce their languages as official languages, at least at the level of local administration. It must be, however, admitted that there are quite a few factors stand in the way of the promotion of Maithili; they include relatively low level of literacy, competition with Hindi/Nepāli as medium of education and administration, and sometimes identification of the language with a particular group or caste, to name just a few.[9]

From linguistic perspective, it may be noted that the presentation of the facts about Maithili grammar in this article is just descriptive in its approach and no attempt has been made to analyse them within the framework of language typology or any linguistic theory; it is hoped, however, that these data will be of interest to further linguistic research in this field.

NOTES

1   I would like to express my gratitude to International Institute for Asian Studies (IIAS), Leiden, The Netherlands, for providing me a Senior

Visiting Fellowship to carry out research on the Maithili language from May till July, 1998, during which I completed this article apart from working on other related issues of the language. A part of this article was also presented on the Institute's lecture day, June 4, 1998.

2   For details, see Grierson (1881a:2) for treating Maithili as a distinct language and not as a dialect of Hindi.
3   As noted in Masica (1991:143), the proto-Bengali is the source of Maithili and Oriya as well as of Manipuri and Newari scripts.
4   For Grierson (1881), Maithili spoken in Madhubani district and its adjoining areas was its standard dialect.
5   See R. Yadav, 1984, 1996; S. Jha. 1958; S.K. Jha. 1984; and Mishra. 1994 for further details.
6   For a detailed discussion of this issue, see Grierson, 1909; S. Jha, 1958; Williams, 1973; Singh, 1979; R. Yadav, 1996; and Yadava (forthcoming), besides others; for a pragmatic account of this phenomenon, see Bickel et al. (forthcoming). (Note: We demonstrate that the paradigm structure of Maithili verb agreement is far from arbitrary but can be predicted by two general principles of human interaction in Maithil society: a principle of social hierarchy underlying the evaluation of people's 'face' (Brown and Levinson, 1987), and a principle of social solidarity defining degrees of 'empathy' (Kuno, 1987) to which people identify with others. Maithili verb agreement not only reflects a specific style of social cognition but it also constitutes a prime means to maintain this style by requiring constant attention to its defining parameters.)
7   For comprehensive treatment of this issue within the Government-Binding framework, see Yadava, 1983.
8   Note that such a construction has not yet been accounted for in linguistic theory, especially Chomskyan theory.

REFERENCES

Amaduzzi (1771) 'Preface' to Beligatti's *Alphabetum Brammhanicum*.

Bickel, Balthasar, Walter Bisang and Yogendra P. Yadava (1997) 'Face vs. Empathy: the Social Foundation of Maithili Verb Agreement,' a paper presented at Himalayan Languages Conference, Paris and Conference on Agreement, University of Delhi.

Bickel, B. and Y.P. Yadava 'Grammatical Relations in Indo-Aryan Languages'Ms. Johannes-Guttenberg Universität, Mainz

Brass, P.R. (1974) *Language, Religion and Politics in North India*. Cambridge: Cambridge University Press.

Brown, Penelope and S.C. Levinson (1987[1978]) *Politeness: some Universals in Language Use*. Cambridge: Cambridge University Press.

Burghart, R. (1992) *Introduction to Spoken Maithili in Social Context* Parts 1-3, Universität Heidelberg, Südasien-Institut Abteilung für Ethnologue, MS.

CBS (1991) *Population Report*. Kāṭhmāndu: Central Bureau of Statistics, HMG/Nepāl.

Colebrooke, H.T. (1801) 'On the Sanskrit and Prácit Languages,' *Asiatic Researches* 7, pp. 199-231.

Davis, A.I. (1973) 'Maithili Sentences,' in: A. Hale (ed.) *Clause, Sentences and Discourse Patterns*, Vol. 1. Kāṭhmāndu: SIL Tribhuvan University Press.

--(1984) *Basic Colloquial Maithili - A Maithili-Nepali- English Dictionary*. Delhi: Motilal Banarsidass.

Grierson, G.A. (1881) *An Introduction to the Maithili Dialect of the Bihāri Language as Spoken in Bihār Part I: Grammar*. Calcutta: The Asiatic Society of Bengal [Reprinted in 1909].

--(1885) *Bihār Peasant Life*. [second and revised edition 1926] Patna: Superintendent, Government Printing, Bihār and Orissa

--(1903) *A Linguistic Survey of India 5/2* [reprinted 1968]. Delhi: Motilal Banarsidass.

HMG (1991) *The Constitution of the Kingdom of Nepal*. Kāṭhmāndu: HMG/Nepāl.

Hoernle, A.F.R. (1880) *A Comparative Grammar of the Gaudian Languages*. London: Trübner and Company.

Hoernle, A.F.R. and G. A. Grierson (1885) *A Comparative Dictionary of the Bihāri Language* 1. Calcutta, Bengal Secretariat Press.

--(1889)*A Comparative Dictionary of the Bihāri Language* 2. Calcutta: Bengal Secretariat Press.

Jha, D. (1946) *Maithili-bhāṣā Vidyotana* ('Maithili Grammar'). Darbhanga: Maithili Sahitya Parishad.

--(1950) *Maithili Bhāṣā Koṣ* ('Dictionary of the Maithili language'). Patna: Sri Rambhajan Press.

Jha, G. (1968) *Maithili Udgam o Vikās* ('The Origin and Development of Maithili'). Calcutta: Maithili Prakashan Samiti.

--(1979) *Uccatara Maithili Vyākaraṇ* ('Higher Maithili Grammar'). Patna: Maithili Academy.

Jha, S. (1958) *The Formation of the Maithili Language*, London: Luzac and Co.

--(1965) 'Maithili Phonetics,' *Indian Linguistics* 2, pp. 435-59.

Jha, S.K. (1984) 'A Study of some Phonetic and Phonological Aspects of

Maithili,' unpublished doctoral dissertation, University of Essex.
Kellog, S.H. (1893) *A Grammar of the Hindi Language* [Second edition]. London: Routledge and Kegan Paul.
Kuno, Susumo (1987) *Functional Grammar*. Chicago: University of Chicago Press.
Masica, C.P. (1991) *The Indo-Aryan Languages*. London: Cambridge University Press.
Mishra, J. (1973) *Bṛhat Maithili Sabdkoṣa* ('A Comprehensive Maithili Dictionary'). Simla: Indian Institute of Advanced Study.
Mishra, M. (1996) 'Aspects of Maithili Phonology,' unpublished doctoral dissertation. Urbana, Illinois: University of Illinois.
Singh, U.N. (1979) 'Some Aspects of Maithili Syntax: a Transformational-Generative Approach,' unpublished doctoral dissertation. Delhi: University of Delhi.
--(1989) 'How to Honor someone in Maithili,' *International Journal of the Sociology of Language* 75, pp. 87-107.
Trail, R.L. (1973) *Word Lists*. Kāṭhmāndu: SIL Tribhuvan University Press.
Williams, J. (1973) 'Clause Patterns in Maithili,' in: Trail (ed.) *Patterns in Clause, Sentence, and Discourse in Selected Languages of Nepal and India*. Oklahoma: SIL.
Yadav, R. (1984) *Maithili Phonetics and Phonology*. Mainz: Selden and Tamm.
--(1996) *A Reference Grammar of Maithili*. Berlin and New York: Mouton de Gruyter.
Yadav, S.K. (1989) 'Language Use in Nepal,' unpublished doctoral dissertation. Jaipur: University of Jaipur.
Yadava, Y.P. (1982) 'Maithili Sentences: a Transformational Analysis,' *Indian Linguistics* 7-28.
--(1983) 'Movement Rules in Maithili and English: their Implications for the Theory of Government and Binding,' unpublished doctoral dissertation. Hyderabad: Central Institute of English and Foreign Languages.
--(1996) 'Verb Agreement in Maithili,' *Journal of Nepalese Studies* 1.1, pp. 109-21.
--(Forth.) 'The Complexity of Maithili Verb Agreement,' in: R. Singh (ed.) *The Yearbook of South Asian Languages and Linguistics* 2. Delhi: The Sage Publications.

ABBREVIATIONS

A	=	adjective	N	=	noun/nominative
ACC	=	accusative			
Agr	=	agreement	nh	=	non-honorific
Asp	=	aspect	NN	=	non-nominative
Aux/AUX	=	auxiliary	NP	=	noun phrase
CBS	=	Central Bureau of Statistics	O	=	object
			OBL	=	oblique
CP	=	conjunctive participle	P	=	postposition
			pcl	=	participle
DAT	=	dative	PP	=	postpositional phrase
FEM	=	feminine			
FUT	=	future	PRES	=	present
GEN	=	genitive	pro	=	pronominals (dropped in a clause)
h	=	honorific			
hh	=	high honorific	PT	=	past tense
HMG	=	His Majesty's Government	S	=	sentence
			Suff	=	suffix
INF	=	infinitive	Tns	=	tense
INS	=	instrumental	V	=	verb
IP	=	imperfect	1	=	first person
LOC	=	locative	2	=	second person
mh	=	mid-honorific	3	=	third person

CHAPTER 13

A NEW APPROACH TO AN OLD PROBLEM: ON CHINESE DISCOURSE *LE*

GUO WU

The particle *le* is one of the more frequently used and discussed, but least understood, elements in Chinese grammar. The NWO (Netherlands Organization for Scientific Research) research project 'On Chinese Discourse *LE*,' undertaken collaboratively by Marinus van den Berg, Chinese Department, Leiden University, and Guo Wu, School of Marketing, International Business, and Asian Studies, The University of Western Sydney, Nepean, Australia, is an effort to approach this old problem from a new (discourse) perspective. The overall goal of the project is to develop a pragmatic functional framework that will allow for the description and explanation of the various functions of the particle *le* in an interactive context. The approach can then be extended to other particles and various grammatical processes employed by the Chinese language so as to produce 'A Chinese Discourse Grammar.'

During the six-month period from July to December 1998 we first focused on issues of the historical development of the discourse particle and thereafter constructed a discourse model that incorporated social interaction and the cognitive constructions underlying the understanding of discourse. The model was also based on earlier joint research and on recent studies in mental space theories. It was inspired by many hours of discussions of a large number of interactive examples of the use of *le* and tested on a wider data set including ten children stories, two plays, several short stories published in Chinese literary journals, and examples of everyday conversations. This paper is a brief account of our research on the particle, relevant historical data, the theoretical framework, and the way the particle is handled within that framework.

Previous Studies

It is generally accepted that the Chinese particle *le* indicates a change. While the particle regularly features in everyday discourse, traditional studies have mainly focused on its role in the sentence without paying adequate attention to the interactive social context in which it is used. Among various approaches to the functions of *le*, the two most influential ones up to now have been 'changes in a situation' (Lü, 1991) and 'currently relevant state' (Li and Thompson, 1981; Li, Thompson and Thompson, 1982). The former catches the essence of the particle's semantics, but falls short when explaining its functions in everyday interactions. The latter acknowledges some basic discourse functions of *le*, but fails to specify what is exactly relevant in different situations. According to Li and Thompson (1981, p. 240-1), the 'currently relevant state' is relevant to the situation indicated by the time expression in the sentence (if there is one) rather than to the present interaction, or the immediate situation. Moreover, both approaches focus more on what is expressed in linguistic forms than on the implications for the interlocutors' actions.

The Historical Development of the Particle *Le*

There are two *LE*'s in Chinese: one is the particle that most frequently occurs at the end of a sentence, the other is a verb suffix that marks perfectivity (hereafter *-le*). One of the controversies in Chinese linguistics is whether the particle *le* has the same origin as the verb *-le*. The different-origin approach (Chao, 1968; Sun, 1996) hypothesizes that the particle *le* originates from the phonological reduction of the lexical verb *lai* (to come), a development that took place between the twelfth and eighteenth centuries. The same origin hypothesis (Wang, 1947; Mei, 1994) assumes that both the particle *le* and verbal *-le* developed from the lexical verb *liao* meaning to finish, complete, or accomplish. The project traced the path of grammaticalization of the two grams through a variety of historical texts and supports the same origin hypothesis. Both *le* and *-le* originated from the lexical verb *liao*.

The various uses of the particle *le* are in essence the signalling of inchoativity, i.e. indicating the beginning or occurrence of a situation as a result of some change. This inchoative use of *liao* is found in texts from the tenth century onwards, and *liao* had developed functions similar to its modern use as a particle by the thirteenth century. The development of *le* from *liao* is supported by evidence from some living dialects. In Shantou dialect, for example, the Chinese character *LE* has retained various uses of the Middle Chinese and Early Mandarin *liao* but also has the functions of the modern particle *le* and the verb suffix *-le* (Shi, 1996, p. 47). The synchronic uses of *LE* in Shantou dialect reveal the path of the diachronic development from the verb *liao* in Middle Chinese to the modern particle *le*.

In historical perspective, the modern particle *le* is a combination of *liao* and *ye*, a particle indicating assertion. During its development to *le*, the verb *liao* first became a completive indicating the end of a dynamic situation in the clause-final position; then it started to occur with stative situations signalling inchoativity and with *ye* in sentence-final positions. Gradually, *liao* merged with *ye* and became the particle *le* (Liu, 1985). This development is supported by the co-existence of the sentence-final *ye*, *LEye* and *le* in the sixteenth century Korean textbook of Mandarin Chinese (Kim, 1998). Assuming the particle *le* to be an historical merger of *liao* and *ye* helped the project to focus on the two essential aspects of the particle *le*: new situation and assertion.

THEORETICAL FRAMEWORK

Given the essence of situation and assertion, the project then proceeded by investigating these concepts and building them into a general theoretical framework. Earlier work by Van den Berg (1998a;b) focused on the necessity for understanding the nature of reality framing and the creation of social context (Goffman, 1974; Van Dijk, 1997), and tried to make clear that verbal messages are highly dependent on cognitive constructs. Continuing to work along these lines, we realized that to understand a piece of discourse, the linguistic forms alone are not enough and these forms only make sense when the social interaction involved is taken into account as well. It is in this sense that we reject sentence logic and strongly agree with Chafe's (1994, p. 8) view 'that there are many important things about language that can never be understood by constructing sequences of words that begin with John and end with a period, and asking oneself whether or not they are sentences...'

The framework we accepted also incorporated recent developments in cognitive linguistics, especially those in the study of mental spaces, which has lead to a re-examination of the role of language in communication. Owing to the fact that we have taken too much of the backstage cognitive processing for granted, language has traditionally been assigned a greater role than it really plays in our understanding of discourse. As pointed out by Fauconnier (1997, p. 187), what language does is to 'to prompt the cognitive constructions by means of very partial, but contextually very efficient, clues and cues.' That is to say, contrary to our common-sense view that we say what we mean, linguistic expressions do not really have meaning; it is we who construct the meaning in a certain context with the words as cues on the basis of our knowledge about the world. It is in this sense that 'the words themselves say nothing independent of the richly detailed knowledge and powerful cognitive processes we bring to bear' (Turner, 1991, p. 206). Therefore, to understand a piece of discourse is to apply in context the partial grammatical instructions provided by its linguistic forms to construct the situation, and make appropriate response to it. And in order to reconstruct the situation one needs to activate selectively his/her knowledge on the typifications of everyday situations to fill in the gaps between the linguistic clues and cues.

KNOWLEDGE AND SITUATION

Being conscious implies the mental construction of a situation (cf. Chafe, 1994; Goffman, 1974). Situation therefore is an essential concept in our theoretical framework and we work from the assumption that our knowledge of situations is the essential key to discourse understanding. A situation is seen as an incidence of reality framing (Goffman, 1974), as the mental representation (cf. Fauconnier, 1994) of the immediate situation. Situations are never single, monolithic entities, they are perceived interactions of time, locality, participants, and scenes. Situations can be immediate (occurring now), remembered (happened before), or envisaged as happening in the near or not too distant future. A framed immediate situation is dynamic and develops continuously along its time axis. Participants in that situation act upon this knowledge and can signal to each other their awareness of this ongoing change and the time frame they are in. At a party, for instance, a participant can say either (1) or (2) to signal to a relevant audience that he intends to leave the scene:

(1)
Bu   zao   le.
Not   early   *LE*
It's already late.

(2)
Wo   zou   le.
I   leave *LE*
I need to leave now.

Both remarks signal efficiently that the speaker wants to leave. In example (1) this is done by pointing to the perceived time frame, in example (2) by hinting to an intended near future action.

Situations as remembered events are also often normative. In a restaurant, we expect a waiter to arrive to take our order, unless we are aware that the situation we are in is that of a self-service restaurant and we realize that we need to act ourselves to answer our needs. This normativity can be used by a speaker either to orient the other participant to changes that have reportedly taken place and created a new situation, or make clear to a responsible person within the audience that an intended norm was not met, implying that there is some deviation from an expected situation and that it would be appreciated if a corrective act could take place. *Le* in example (3) draws the attention of the audience to the fact that a guest has arrived and expects the audience to take note of that announced change and act upon this information appropriately.

(3)
Zhang taitai   lai   le!
Zhang madam   come   *LE*
Mrs Zhang is here!

These examples illustrate the various forms of changes that can take place within a situation. The status in an event of a participant can change (somebody leaving the scene and thereby potentially changing the nature of the event), or the situation can change because of the arrival of some new participant (arrival on the scene).

LE AND DISCOURSE TYPES

The framed immediate situation forces participants to act (transactional interactions), whereas remembered situations are less forceful and often form the content of conversations. Narrated events, in contrast, can be presented as if they are immediate, thereby bringing the audience as a spectator into the narrated event and involving him fully into the developing scene.

In transactional interactions participants have clearly defined roles (salesperson, customer) and discourse *le* typically signals a situation change on which the other interactant needs to act. In conversations, the discourse participants, as a rule, know each other well and the situation is constructed by the interactants (either remembered or projected into the near or not too distant future), the addressee is typically not requested to act upon the conversational remarks. Narratives are similar to conversations in this respect, with the difference that the audience is not requested to respond other than through ritual applause or other approval or disapproval signs. Narratives (and plays) are presented in the immediate situation but the event sequences are in a different time frame. Even though there is only an indirect relation with the immediate situation, the audience takes the events portrayed as real and immediate. The rhetorical purpose of narratives and plays is universe construction and universe maintenance (Berger and Luckmann, 1967; Goffman, 1974). The audience processes the events as they develop and urgency is used as a technique for developing a plot and constructing suspense.

These three interaction types are listed below:

1. Transactional interactions: the immediate situation involves participants with clearly defined roles and an obligation to respond and act according to social rules;
2. Conversation: rhetorical goal is mainly universe maintenance; interactants have a high degree of familiarity; turn taking and responding are the main activities; no obligation to act;
3. Story-telling/reading/plays: rhetorical goal is entertainment, audience is spectator; no need to respond or to act
    The particle *le* has different functions in each of these discourse types.

An illustration:

(4)
a. setting: home roles: daughter to mother who told her to take her medicine
Yaowan   qia   zai   sangzili   le!
pill   stuck   in   throat inside   LE
It's stuck in my throat! [Appeal to mother for help.]

(4)
b. conversation; narrated event; friends interacting
Yaowan   qia   zai   sangzili   le!
Pill   stuck   in   throat inside   LE
It was stuck in my throat! [Report of event.] [Further questions allowed.}

(4)
c. narrated event; story read by participant
Yaowan   qia   zai   sangzili   le!
Pill   stuck   in   throat inside   LE
It was stuck in his throat! [Report of event.] [Audience awaits further developments.]

We decided to approach the use of discourse *le* following these distinctions and to start with an analysis of the use of *le* in transactional situations.

LE AND SPEECH ACTS

The function of *le* also varies with the type of speech act. Searle (1975) put forward a speech act typology of five major acts: representatives, commissives, directives, expressives, and declaratives. While *le* has similar functions within these categories, the illocutionary force of the message varies between assertion, reminder, and warning, among other modes. Example (4) above illustrates that a representative can be an appeal for help. The establishment of a new situation in declaratives can be illustrated with the declaration of the People's Republic of China in 1949 by Mao Zedong:

(5)
formal setting: Tian Anmen square
Zhonghua   Renmin   Gongheguo   chengli   le!
China   People   Republic   establish   LE
I herewith declare the People's Republic of China established!

The study of the interaction between the function of *le* and speech acts is not yet completed and will be continued in the second part of the project.

LE AS A DISCOURSE MARKER

To account for the use of the particle *le* in transactional interactions, we propose the following eight-step process:

1. P1 perceives present situation as not according to [expected] normal make-up;
2. Projection [through the grammar] of situation aspect that can guide P2 toward realization of what P1 has perceived as not normal or new;
3. Project grammatical pointer [*le*] to flag the externalized situation cue;
4. The flagging indicating that according to P1 (the speaker), a new situation holds as of that moment;
5. The adding of the pointer [*le*] to the message signals some urgency;
6. The expressed urgency is an appeal to P2 [Audience] to update the situation, and;
7. A request to P2 to calculate the implications of the update, and;
8. Act upon it

This process is based on our world knowledge of the typification of everyday situations involving participants, circumstances, scenes, and events and interacts with discourse types and speech acts. For instance,

(6)
Chi   fan   le.
Eat   meal LE
a. It's time to eat.
b. (Someone) has started to eat his meal.
c. (Someone who could not/refused to eat meals before) has started to eat meals.
d. (I) have had my meal.

What is specified in (6) is some change about the eating event; it is up to the addressee to fill in the participant and the circumstances of the situation and deduce the appropriate meaning. The different interpretations of (6) are the result of this cognitive operation involving different participants, circumstances, and speech acts. The various stages of the eating event in these interpretations are: people are going to eat in (6a), someone is eating in (6b), someone may or may not be eating in (6c), and I have finished eating in (6d). This seems contradictory and confusing, but is appropriate in each specific context.

(6a) is a directive used as an initiative move to call for the start of a meal. It occurs typically in a household scene at about dinner (or some other meal) time: someone, e.g. mother, is preparing the meal while the rest of the family are doing different things, most likely anticipating the dinner. When dinner is ready, the mother would say (6) to call the family members to the dinner table and start the eating event. As a family member in the home setting at dinnertime, probably waiting for dinner, one would unmistakably pick up the message as a directive. In (6) the directive *le* indicates the change from a non-eating situation to an eating situation, and signals to the family members to update their perception of the situation and come to the dinner table accordingly.

(6b) is a statement used as a reactive move to indicate someone is not available at the moment. It could occur in a family scene at dinnertime: the telephone rings, and the father picks up the phone. When the caller asks whether it is convenient to talk to the mother, the father could say (6) and tells the caller that the mother will call back in half of an hour or so. The caller, then, would understand that the mother is now engaged in eating. Thus the change *le* indicates in (6) is the mother's having entered into the eating event, signals to the caller to update the situation in which the mother will not be available for about half an hour, and act accordingly: to wait for her call in half an hour's time.

(6c) can be used as a report in both initiative and reactive moves either to answer a question or report about someone. In this case, the person concerned could typically be a hospitalized patient, who could has not been able to eat for some time, and the setting could be either the hospital or home. The participants in the conversation are the doctor or nurse and family members, relatives or friends, and the time is evening. When the son of the patient comes to the ward, the father is sleeping, and the son asks the nurse whether his father is getting better. The nurse then says (6) to the son, the son will follow the cue provided by *le* to update the condition of his father's health on the basis of his knowledge about his father's illness. He will interpret the change as that from not being able to eat to being able to eat, and conclude that the latter is certainly getting better. He would then go home and tell (6) other family members or friends, who will also update their perception of the patient's situation and act upon it accordingly - next time they go to the hospital, in addition to flowers, they might take some tempting food with them as well.

(6d) is typically a reactive move to answer the question about whether one has had his/her meal, or to turn down an invitation for a meal at that moment. As having one's meal is an experience so common that one rarely declares it unless it is made significant in the situation. One could be asked directly whether one has had one's meal, e.g. when one drops in a friend's place at about dinnertime. If the answer is no, they will probably ask him/her to join them. Or one needs to volunteer the information, e.g. when one meets friends in the street and is asked to join them for dinner. In either case, *le* signals the change of the speaker's situation from not having had his/her meal to having had his/her meal, direct the addressees to update the situation, and act accordingly, i.e. to enjoy the meal themselves without the speaker.

From the above, it is clear that what *le* contributes to the message is the cue of a change and the necessity for updating the situation according to the change; as for what in the situation is to be updated, it is up to the addressee to work that out on the basis of his/her knowledge of the typifications of the situations in the real world. Once the situation is constructed, there is no confusion as to the specific change involved, the way one's perception should be updated and the action to be taken accordingly. Like any other grammatical marking, the *le*-marking is contextually efficient.

LE AND NEW SITUATIONS

A new situation may be an actual change of a previous situation, or a deviation from the norm or from an existing belief or assumption in the immediate situation. The former is related to changes in the scene, circumstances, or participants, including physical, conceptual, or emotional changes, while the latter asserts one's opinion opposing a conventional norm or other assumptions or claims in the situation, either expressed or implied. What is important here is that either a change or a deviation makes situation-updating necessary, hence the use of *le*.

Traditionally, the use of *le* is discussed in terms of changes without specifying what change is involved. The discourse model developed by the project can now pinpoint the change to specific perceived elements in the situation: circumstances, participants, or scenes or whatever else. Furthermore, the concept of situation-updating includes 'deviation' as a feature of *le*, which was unaccounted for in traditional studies, and explains why under certain circumstances *le* can be used in structures that are incompatible with *le* in traditional terms.

For example, copula *shi* is normally incompatible with *le* when the relationship is an existential one. However, (7) can be used in a situation where the speaker was initially not sure about the addressee's identity and probably went through a list of possible candidates in his/her mind, and finally reached the conclusion that the person concerned must be Madam

Li. It involves a judgement on a situation which is not a straightforward one, but emerges as a result of a mental process of hypothesizing, verifying through a list of candidates, thus representing a new realization of the situation, i.e. situation-updating. This use of *le* does not involve any possible changes in the candidate concerned. What is presented as changed is the final settlement of the speaker's judgement on the candidate that 'It has just occurred to me that X is A.' In other words, *le* signals that the speaker has just updated the situation and urges the addressee to do so, or to confirm it when the speaker is certain that the addressee knows the answer as in (7).

(7)
Ni   yiding shi Li   taitai le.
You   must   be   surname Mrs   LE
You must be Madam Li.

(8)
Zhe   yiding shi konglong dan le.
This must   be   dinosaur egg LE
This must be a dinosaur egg.

Similarly, (8) suggests that the speaker, after a process of examining the object concerned and excluding other possible candidates, has finally updated his judgement on the identity of the object and appeals to the addressee to do so.

The concept of situation-updating also throws light on what Chao (1968) calls the excessive use of *le* as exemplified in (9):

(9)
Tang xian   le.
Soup salty LE
It's too salty.

In our view, this so-called excessive meaning does not come from *le*, but from the meaning of Chinese adjectives, whose unmarked form is comparative in nature. What is responsible for the excessive meaning is the comparison between the saltiness of the soup and a certain standard in the speaker's mind, i.e. his/her desired degree of saltiness. *Le* simply signals the update of the situation that the soup is saltier than the expected norm as perceived by the speaker, and does not express a separate excessive meaning.

Similarly, *tai* (too) or *zui* (most) plus adjectives indicate that the quality concerned is perceived by the speaker as reaching the end/extreme of the scale and away from the norm, therefore *le* is naturally used with such words, and the whole expressions function as idioms.

(10)
tai/zui hao   le
too/most good   LE
Excellent! /Extremely good!

The particle *le* is also often used to update the deviation from what is believed or assumed in the situation. If there are views, assumptions or expectations in the situation, whether existing as conventions, or expressed explicitly or only implied, that are different from the speaker's view of the situation, the speaker feels the need to update the addressee with his/her view and thus the use of *le* is warranted. For instance, when a host saying (11) to a guest:

(11)
Bu   song   le.
Not   see-to-the-door   LE
I won't see you to the door.

What triggers the use of *le* can be an observable change, e.g. the host stops seeing the guest off to answer the telephone. However, the use of *le* does not have to be based on any such changes in situation, but purely on the convention or the guest's expectation that the host should see guests to the door. The use of *le* in this case is based on the deviation of the speaker's practice from the guest's assumption or expectation. Since no changes can be observed in such situations, this use of *le* is hardly recognized in the literature. For example, Chao (1968) thinks a similar use of *le* in (12) is to express obviousness.

(12)
Zhege ni   dangran dong   le.
This you   of course understand LE
You are well aware of this, of course.

In fact, the obviousness is expressed by *dangran* (of course), not by *le*. What *le* does is to update the deviation of the speaker's opinion from the addressee's assumptions. From an interactive point of view, (12) is reactive and occurs only in a context where someone claims either that s/he may/does not understand this or that s/he understands it. The use of *le* is here to update the situation with the speaker's opinion which contradicts the first claim or dismisses the need for the second claim, meaning 'of course, you understand it and you do not need to tell me that.'

To sum up, while real changes typically involve situations in different time points in reality, deviations, in general, reflect the differences between a situation in reality and that in the speaker's mental world. The extended use of the particle *le* from indicating changes to deviation reflects the tendencies of semantic changes: from external to internal situations, and becoming increasingly based on the speaker's subjective belief state (Traugott, 1982; 1989).

LE AND UPDATING

Obviously 'updating' is not directed to the speaker but to the addressee or audience. As a matter of urgency the speaker wants the audience to update the situation they hold as actual as of that moment. This is a very crucial element of interpersonal communication and most likely the most powerful explanation for understanding the force of *le* as a conversational particle. Conversation can only proceed smoothly when the interlocutors can assume that both hold the same or similar framings (Goffman, 1974) of reality. 'Updating' implies a signalling by the speaker that it is time to adjust the situation the interactants are in. The conversation will then proceed from the conception that the new situation is perceived and activated by both (or all) interactants.

Li, Thompson & Thompson (1982) propose that the currently relevant state expressed by *le* means that the state of affairs is current to the time indicated by the time expression in the sentence if there is one. Our view is that the particle *le* in conversations, in general, marks situation-updating at the speech time, though the content of the assertion may be related to different times. For example, as an initiative move, (13) introduces a past event as a discourse topic, opening a space for elaboration; as a reactive move, it answers the question 'What did you do yesterday?' or provides reason for the speaker's absence somewhere else. In any case, *le* signals to the addressee: update the situation now. In (14), although her turning twenty-one will not happen until next month, it is exactly her going to be twenty-one that is what the speaker wants the addressee to update. What is in the speaker's mind may well be 'we should decide on the birthday present now.'

(13)
Zuotian   wo   qu   Zhang   jia   le.
Yesterday   I   go   surname   home   LE
Yesterday I went to Zhang's home.

(14)
Xiage   yue   ta   jiu   ershi   yi   sui   le.
Next   month s/he   then   twenty-one   years old   LE
S/he'll be twenty-one years old next month.

It is this link with the speech time and the present scene of interaction that enables the particle *le* to play an important role in the discourse development.

THE OPENING AND CLOSING FUNCTION OF *LE*

The project claims that the particle *le*, as a cue for situation-updating, has a line-development function in discourse, i.e. it may initiate or conclude a sequence of discourse acts (Dik, 1997). This function is the result of the interaction between the pointing function of *le* and the information of the message *le* points to (Wu, 1997).

A *le*-sentence may open a line, i.e. it may initiate a sequence of discourse acts by drawing the addressee's attention to a certain change in the situation. An opening *le*-sentence necessarily carries new information that is somewhat incomplete for a satisfactory update: either its relevance to the present situation is unclear and needs to be spelt out or the information is too sketchy and needs to be elaborated. In both cases, the situation-updating calls for the addressee's attention to what follows. The opening update has different implications for the addressee in his/her immediate situation in different discourse types. In verbal interactions it urges the addressee to react accordingly to the new situation by doing something. In such cases a *le*-update often functions as a directive or is combined with one. For example, when it starts to rain and the mother wants the son to collect the washing on the clothes-line. She might say:

(15)
a. *Xiayu le!*
   Rain LE
   It's raining!

(15)
b. *Xiayu   le!   Kuai   qu   shou   yifu!*
   Rain   LE   hurry go   collect clothes
   It's raining! Go and bring the washing in!

(15a) might be enough to achieve the purpose if the washing on the clothes-line is active in the situation, whether they just hung the clothes there or are talking about it, or the son is a very understanding one. In that case (15a) would be enough for the son to work out what to do. However, since the rain is a natural phenomenon affecting a wide range of things at the scene, more often than not the son probably cannot figure out its relevance to the immediate situation, as least not as fast as the mother expects. Therefore (15b) is used to guarantee a quick response, in which the rain situation is updated first opening the space for the following directive and the directive about what to do under the updated circumstances is then spelt out for the addressee. This pattern typically reflects the Chinese way of thinking from general to specific as exemplified by the ordering of year-month-day in the expression of dates. It represents a major discourse strategy in the use of the particle.

In conversations the situation-updating signalled by *le* is mainly for universe maintenance - a continual updating of the common ground between the interactants. The only thing to be acted upon is probably turn-taking. or signalling to the addressee to hold his/her turn to wait for the speaker to further specify or elaborate on the new situation just introduced as a discourse topic. For example, when one hears:

(16)
Xiao Wang chushi   le!
Name have an accident LE
Xiao Wang has had an accident!

S/he will have to hold his/her turn and wait for what follows, or solicit further information by saying something to the effect of 'What?' or 'Really?.' Thus the use of *le* effectively creates the space for the speaker to go on to make his/her point or elaborate on how the accident happened or what friends can do to help now.

A *le*-sentence may close a line, i.e. it may close a sequence of discourse acts. A closing *le*-sentence carries information that is somewhat more complete for an update in the context of the previous discourse. It may be a concluding remark on the situation just described, or a scene already active in the situation, or a scene indicating a temporal closure of activities according to our world knowledge such as *jiu huijia/shuijiao le* (then (I) went home/to bed). By concluding the previous discourse, or by bringing the discourse back to the present scene or a scene of non-actions, the speaker effectively winds up his turn on the current topic and signals to the addressee that it is time for him/her to take his/her turn in the conversation, or expect a topic shift.

The opening and closing functions of *le* lie in its function as a cue for situation-updating, which links the situation to the speech (or a reference) time. By relating a certain scene to the speech time, *le* brings the discourse back to the present interaction, or the speech theatre, effectively closing the established discourse world. The closure of the previous discourse world where some change happened, meanwhile, marks the inception of the new situation resulting from that change. The two functions are, in fact, two sides of the same coin. The closing function of *le* is mainly 'backward looking' and reacts to the foregoing discourse, creating the space for turn taking or topic shift, while the opening function of *le* is 'forward looking,' allowing the space for elaboration or the addressee's reaction.

SIGNIFICANCE

The project 'On Chinese Discourse *LE*' has so far developed a discourse model that draws strength from both functional and cognitive grammar. From a new perspective provided by the discourse model, the project has made a number of findings concerning the core meaning of the particle and its discourse functions as well as the path of its grammaticalization in history. These findings lead to a better understanding of how the Chinese particle *le* operates: when, how, and under what circumstances it is used and its implications and social functions when used in specific situations. The same approach may be applied to the analysis of other particles in Chinese to explore their functions in social interactions, and the results of these studies will provide more data for situation-marking in Chinese. A systematic treatment of such markings would not only advance our understanding of Chinese, but also contribute to typological studies of languages in general. Furthermore, the approach adopted in the project allows grammar and pragmatics to work harmoniously by recognizing the role of our knowledge and cognitive operations in discourse processing. It is of far-reaching significance beyond the studies of the particle *le*, or of Chinese grammar, with methodological implications.

REFERENCES

Berger, Peter L and Thomas Luckmann (1967) *The Social Construction of Reality*. Harmondsworth: Penguin.

Chafe, Wallace (1994) *Discourse, consciousness, and time*. Chicago: University of Chicago Press.

Chao, Yuenren (1968) *A grammar of spoken Chinese*. Berkeley: University of California Press.

Dik, Simon (1997) *The Theory of Functional grammar. Part I: The Structure of the Clause, Part 2: Complex and Derived Constructions*. Amsterdam: John Benjamins Press.

Fauconnier, Gilles (1994) *Mental spaces*. Cambridge: Cambridge University Press

--(1997) *Mappings in thought and language*. Cambridge: Cambridge University Press.

Goffman, E. (1974) Frame analysis. An essay on the organization of experience. New York: Harper & Row.

Hopper, Paul J. (ed.) (1982) *Tense and aspect: between semantics & pragmatics*. Amsterdam: John Benjamins Press.

Kim, Kwangjo (1998) '*On the usage of the linguistic signs LE, LAI, YE in the Ponyok Nogoltae*,' paper presented at the IACL-7 and NACCL-10, Stanford University.

Li, Charles N. and Sandra A. Thompson (1981) *Mandarin Chinese: A Functional Reference Grammar*. Berkeley & Los Angeles: University of California Press.

Li, Charles N., Sandra A. Thompson and R. McMillan Thompson (1982) 'The discourse motivation for the perfect aspect: the Mandarin particle *LE*,' in: Hopper, Paul J. (ed.) *Tense and aspect: between semantics & pragmatics*. Amsterdam: John Benjamins Press, pp. 19-44.

Liu, Xunning (1985) '*Xiandai Hanyu juwei LE de laiyuan*' (The origin of the sentence-final *le* in modern Chinese). *Fangyan* 2, pp. 128-33.

Lü Shuxiang (1991) *Xiandai Hanyu babai ci* (Eight hundred words in Modern Mandarin). Beijing: Commercial Press.

Searle, J. (1975) 'A classification of illocutionary acts,' *Language in Society* 5/1, pp. 1-24.

Shi, Qisheng (1996)'*Shantou fangyan de LE ji qi yuyuan guanxi*' (The uses of Shantou dialect *LE* and their origin). *Yuwen Yanjiu* 3, pp. 43-7.

Sun, Chaofen (1996) *Word-Order Change and Grammaticalization in the History of Chinese*. Stanford: Stanford University Press.

Traugott, E.C. (1982) 'From propositional to textual and expressive meanings: some semantic-pragmatic aspects of grammaticalisation,' in: W.P. Lehmann and Y. Malkiel (eds) *Perspectives on historical linguistics*. Amsterdam: John Benjamins Press, pp. 245-71.

--(1989) 'On the rise of epistemic meaning in English,' *Language*. 65, pp. 31-55.

Turner, M.
1991 *Reading minds*. Princeton: Princeton University Press

Van den Berg, Marinus (1998a)'An outline of a pragmatic functional grammar,' in: Mike Hannay, and A. Machtelt Bolkestein (eds) *Functional Grammar and Verbal Interaction*. Amsterdam: John Benjamins.

--(1998b) *Making a Move: The Social Construction of Discourse. First International Conference of Discourse Analysis*. May 20 to 22, 1998, Universidad Complutense de Madrid. CD ROM.

Van Dijk, T. (ed.) (1997) *Discourse as social interaction*. Amsterdam: John Benjamins Press.

Mei Tsulin (1994) '*Tangdai, Songdai gongtongyu de yufa he xiandai fangyan de yufa*' (The grammar of the common language in Tang and Song and the grammar of modern dialects). *Zhongguo jinnei yuyan ji yuyanxue* (Languges and linguistics within China) 2, pp. 61-97.

Wang Li (1947) *Zhongguo yufa lilun* (Theories of Chinese Grammar). Shanghai: Commercial Press.

Wu, Guo (1997) '*The discourse function of the sentence-final particle le in Chinese*,' paper presented at the 6th International Conference on Chinese Linguistics, Leiden University, 20 June.

CHAPTER 14

COMPARATIVE STUDY OF THE INSTRUMENTS OF THE SARANGI FAMILY FROM AN ETHNOGRAPHIC PERSPECTIVE

SUVARNALATA RAO

Various social and cultural factors are known to affect aspects of music-making, including the stylistic evolution of musical instruments. This in turn brings about structural changes in the instrument. Whenever the existing form of an instrument fails to meet socio-cultural demands, it undergoes modifications. This facilitates the emergence of new performance techniques and styles. By and large, the basic structural form of the instrument is preserved and the modifications appear in the form of additions and alterations or one or the other, made in the original body of the instrument. Sometimes, the basic identity of the instrument is changed beyond recognition, giving birth to a new instrument. Hence, the changes that occur in the instrument with respect to its physical structure or the style need to be appreciated not only in the context of the musical tradition but in relation to the social and cultural contexts as well.

This study is based on observations made during the workshop on 'Ethnography of musical performance.'[1] It deals specifically with the instruments of the *sarangi* family,[2] viz. *Pyaledar sarangi*, *Sindhi sarangi*, *surinda/surindi* and *kamaicha* as practiced by professional *sarangi*-players of western Rajasthan. The similarity existing between these instruments, particularly the *Pyaledar* and *Sindhi sarangi* has motivated an in-depth inquiry into their musical traditions and their socio-cultural significance.

RAJASTHAN: GEOGRAPHICAL & CULTURAL FEATURES

After India gained independence in 1947, present-day Rajasthan emerged through a process of the integration of several princely states and the British-administered Ajmer-Merwar which comprised the erstwhile Rajputana. The Aravali ranges, running from northeast to southwest roughly divide the state into an arid zone to the west and a comparatively fertile region to the east, rising to a plateau towards the southeast. With an area about 3.4 million square km., area-wise it ranks second among all the states of India.

Rajasthan is a large state, abutting on several important cultural zones: Sindh and the Punjab (the former and part of the latter are now in Pakistan) to the west and northwest, Gujarat to the southwest, Malva to the southeast, the mid-western region of Uttar Pradesh to the east, and Haryana to northeast. Interaction between these cultures has enriched the folk-music tradition of Rajasthan with diversity and a great variety of genres and instruments.

The feudal division in medieval times established a plethora of centres of patronage for professional musicians. This gave rise to and also sustained a large number of communities of hereditary professional musicians. The financial security and localized patronage enjoyed by these musicians proved conducive to refining the folk traditions. Incidentally, the western, more arid parts of Rajasthan became the special preserve of a rich variety of music, perhaps, because of the harsh nature and scarce sources of other forms of entertainment.

LIFE OF MUSICIANS

In Rajasthan, every caste, whether high or low, is privileged to have its own family of musicians. Descendants of these musicians are also obliged to serve the descendants of their patrons. The Langa and Manganiar (also known as Manganihar) are two of several professional musician castes of western Rajasthan. Other musicians in this category are Damamis and Ranas. Collectively they represent a category, 'kalavant.' This is the highest rung, in a particular aspect of the folk tradition.[3] Like the other types of groups such as *bhat* (genealogists), *rao* (bards) and *nat* (acrobats-cum-genealogists) these musicians are also related to their patrons (*jajman*) by their provision of non-physical services which are of great importance to the maintenance of the social system. The musician castes and their patron families are linked by special traditional arrangements in which the rights of the musician caste (*jachak* or the server) are well protected. The significance of the musician castes and their music in the social system of Rajasthan is evident from the prevailing custom of unstringing one's instrument and burying the strings before the patron's house, in order to register a protest in case of a dispute between the patron and the client (musician). An unresolved dispute between the patron and a musician can even lead to the social isolation of the patron family.

These musicians have to attend ceremonies associated with the childbirth, marriage, and death in their patron families, as well as the major festivals and other private functions. In some cases, they even have to provide these services to the service castes (*kasbis*) attached to the patron. Singing and reciting laments during the death rituals are particularly important services rendered by the musicians. In fact, the attendance of a musician on such occasions is very important from the point of view of legitimizing the legal succession in the family. In return for their musical services, the musicians receive cattle, camels, goats, cash, and a share in the patron's agricultural income. In Rajasthan, professional musician castes such as the Langa, Manganiar, Dhadi, Dholi, and Nat. have continued to receive patronage from the common people and thus have been able to survive the political and economic upheavals in the society.

ETHNOGRAPHIC DETAILS OF THE LANGA AND MANGANIAR COMMUNITIES

This study is based on information provided by one representative each of the Langa and Manganiar communities, namely, Mehar Din Langa and Lakha Khan Manganiar. It should be noted that Lakha Khan belongs to that particular group of Manganiars who serve both Hindu and Muslim patrons and intermarry with the Langas as well as with Manganiars with Hindu patrons.

Sociologically, these communities are quite distinct from each other. Although both these groups are Muslims, their patrons are different i.e. Langas serve Sindhi *sipahi* who are Muslim, whereas Manganiars have Hindu patrons (mainly high-caste Rajputs). However, as mentioned earlier, Lakha Khan is supposed to serve both Hindu and Muslim patrons.[4]

The villages inhabited by these two castes are also different (with a few exceptions) and are found throughout the five districts of western Rajasthan, namely, Jodhpur, Jaisalmer, Bikaner, Badmer, and Jalor. In the social hierarchy, the Langas have a much higher status than the Manganiars. According to the census report of Marwar (1891), the Langas are descended from their patron community, viz. the Sindhi *sipahi*. It is also reported in this census that the Surnaya Langas (who play wind instruments such as *surnai*, *surinda*, and *murla*, and the like, but who do not sing) treat the *Sarangiya* Langas (those who play the *sarangi*) as occupying a lower place in the social hierarchy.

The dress worn by the men belonging to these groups is also quite distinctive and is generally designed to imitate the dress of their patrons.[5] Both, the Sindhi *sipahi* and the Langas appear to be converts from Hinduism, which is shown in the continued use of the *dhoti* (a white loincloth) by the men and *chuda* (large bangles covering the arm from the wrist to the elbow and from the elbow to the shoulder) by the Langa women. It is also evident from the occurrence of sub-caste names like Tunwar, Bhati, which are also used in Hindu communities. Like the Langas the customs, dress, and sub-caste names of the Manganiars are also indicative of their Hindu origin.

MUSICAL TRADITIONS

TEACHING AND LEARNING

Although the life of these musician castes is inseparably interwoven with the music-making activity, there is no system of formal training as such. Like many other things 'happening' in the lives of these unsophisticated people, music just 'happens.' Although we find a musical tradition that is a far cry from simple 'folk' music, it is a shock to discover that there is a total absence of formalized training methods. Passive exposure to the musical atmosphere all around motivates and also nurtures the musicianship. The art is kept in the family by the practice of marrying within the same caste or community. A child accompanying his father to a patron's house indirectly learns the dictates of music-making and the other etiquette pertaining to the patron-client relationship. It is rather interesting to note that every musician has to have a formal *guru* (preceptor, guide), even if it be a namesake, and to undergo an initiation ceremony to symbolize this relationship as also is the practice in the field of recognized classical music, which enjoys a high-brow image.

The communication of knowledge takes place in an 'in-the-field' situation. During the actual performance, the older musicians lead the way to be followed by the younger artistes. If required, the senior musicians also correct the youngsters using body language such as facial grimace or hand gestures, or even some sparing verbal remarks. Thus the youngsters learn, not only by intuition and association but also by interacting directly with fellow artists.

Until a number of years ago, women participated very actively in the music-making. Today, their musical activity is confined to composing and singing within the family. In fact, the songs composed by women are much sought after. Usually, these compositions have a wider tonal range and are appreciated for their tonal complexities.

The repertoire of an accomplished artist includes about 200-250 songs, *bhajan* and *duha* in 20-25 *raga*.[6] They have a whole range of terminology to describe different aspects of music-making such as the names of the notes, types of tuning, parts of the instruments, and the movements of a song.

It is interesting to note that these musicians are extremely receptive to other traditions of music as well. The music of Langas, especially, seems to be replete with some of the features of North Indian classical music. In fact, some of the stylistic elements in Lakha Khan's performances undeniably show this influence.

OCCASIONS FOR MUSIC-MAKING

During most ceremonial occasions, the musicians sing and play on their instruments without a formal audience being present. However, there is another performance situation in the context of weddings, known as '*kacheri*,' where serious music sessions are held in front of an audience of knowledgeable, appreciative listeners. It provides an opportunity for a musician to display his repertoire of compositions as well as his musicianship, including his ability to improvise. These occasions are fairly important to the musicians and they practice all their lives to make a success of these musical sessions.

Besides the presence of a formal audience, the songs played during a '*kacheri*' session are quite different from those performed on ceremonial occasions. They are associated with a specific *raga* and the musician even announces the name of the *raga* before commencing a song.[7] The session commences with one or more *duha*. These couplets are based on the melodic structure of a *raga* and their text may even include the name of that particular *raga*. A musician may elaborate on these couplets depending on his ability to improvise. After this, the song is rendered. It consists of several stanzas and is set to a fixed rhythmic cycle. After each stanza, the refrain line is repeated bringing in various rhythmic patterns, while still maintaining the metric structure of the set cycle. The subject matter of these songs is fairly diverse and varies from heroic tales to love songs.

A special musical game called *kankari* is played during a '*kacheri*.' The challenge of the game is to find the hidden object with the clues given by the music. The ten directions are symbolized by ten *raga*, and both the musicians and the listeners are expected to be adept in the directional connotation of these *raga*, which may differ greatly from each other melodically. The upshot is that the musical ability and the creativity of a musician are duly appreciated and they are rewarded financially on such occasions.

CHOICE OF THE RAGA

Raga like *Sameri*, *Soob*, *Sorath*, *Asa*, *Dhani*, *Goond Malhar*, *Khamaychi*, *Maru*, and *Salang* are performed by both these castes. However, *raga* like *Jungla*, *Sindhi Sorath*, *Mand*, *Shyam Kalyan*, and *Sindhi Bhairavi* are more specific to the Langa repertoire. According to the 1891 census report, these communities had some ideas about the specific times which are appropriate to certain melodies e.g. *Asa*, *Todi*, and *Bilawal* are to be sung in the morning, *Sarang* during the daytime, while *Shyam Kalyan* is performed in the evening. They also have an indigenous method for classifying their melodies.[8] Perhaps this classification has to do with the tuning of the sympathetic strings, e.g. when they tune the instrument to '*Sorath Ghar*' (tuning that includes natural and flat third as well as the seventh degree of the scale) they can play *raga* such as *Sorath*, *Salang*, *Desh*, and *Goond Malhar* without having to retune the instrument. Before the rationale for their method of classification can be established properly, further research work needs to be done.

CHOICE OF THE INSTRUMENTS

The instruments played by these groups are also quite specific. In fact, these professional groups are distinguished partly by the instruments they play. Langas play stringed instruments like the *Sindhi sarangi* and the Gujaratan *sarangi*.[9] In addition, a special group called Surnaya Langa play *surinda/surindi* as well as other wind instruments such as *sattara*, *algoja*, *pungi* and *murli*, whereas Manganiars prefer a chordophone such as a *kamaicha*, idiophone like a *kartal* (a wooden clapper), and percussion instruments such as *dholak*, *dhol*, *nagara*. Of these, the *dhol* and *surnai* are considered to be very auspicious instruments. A special group of Manganiars to which our informant belongs, prefers the *Pyaledar sarangi* and the *Sindhi sarangi*. Thus, we have an interesting picture regarding these groups, their patrons, and the instruments played.

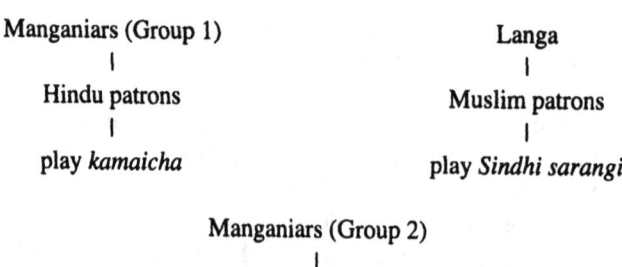

COMPARATIVE STUDY OF THE INSTRUMENTS OF SARANGI FAMILY

INSTRUMENTS

Despite some differences with respect to shape, size, tuning and other matters the instruments in this study have the following common features:

i   They are carved from a single block of wood with an integrated head (with a peg box) and body (finger board).
ii The belly is hollowed out and either partly or fully covered with a skin table on which the bridge rests.
iii The string holder is an extension of the base of the belly.
iv The neck is not fretted.
v   The peg box is more or less hollow and accommodates laterally placed pegs.
vi All these bowed lutes are held vertically in front of the chest.
vii The finger-board is situated along the upper end (away from the ground) of the instrument while the bowing is done along the lower end (closest to the ground) of the strings.
viii The bow is made by stringing together horse tail-hair to a shaft of wood.
ix Strings are made of gut, steel and brass.

PYALEDAR SARANGI

This is also known as *Jadi ki sarangi*. Considering its tonal resemblance to the *sarangi* used in classical music, it is rather surprising to find no mention of this type of *sarangi* in the literature available on the instruments of Rajasthan. According to Mr. Komal Kothari, today there are only a couple of players of this *sarangi* left.

This instrument measuring about 65 cm. in length is constructed out of a single block of *shisam* wood. A parchment made of goat-skin covers the front region of the belly, forming the main resonator called a *tabli*. The portion of parchment connecting the belly is marked by a fairly large sound hole. The rear portion of the belly is slightly rounded; giving it a shape of *pyala* (a glass-shaped vessel) and maybe therefore is known as *Pyaledar sarangi*. A bridge made of buffalo horn stands on the parchment, away from the finger-board, and carries all the strings.

According to our informant Lakha Khan, the instrument in his possession is seventy years old and was made by late Abat Darkhan Thalwadi in what is now Pakistan. The different parts of instruments are *choti* (head), *pirol* (peg box), *takhti* (finger-board), *peta* (region joining the resonator and finger board), *pyala* (resonator with goat-skin), *ghodi* (lower bridge), *bagad* (upper bridge), *hedi* (string holder), *gaj* (bow), *morna* (larger pegs), and *morni* (smaller pegs). In addition to pegs situated in the peg-box placed at the top end, there is a number of pegs including those corresponding to two of the main strings and *jeel* (sympathetic strings), accommodated along one side of the finger-board.

TUNING

There are three sets of strings situated at three different levels. Two strings each, of gut and steel, pass over the bridge. This can be considered as the main level because three out of these four strings are used for producing the main melody. They are tuned as follows:

The first gut string (fourteen twines) called *dadar* is tuned to the tonic.

The second gut string (twelve twines) is tuned to fifth and is called *agor*. Sometimes the same string is tuned to the fourth and is then called *dodha*, depending upon the song requirement and singer's pitch. The two steel strings are tuned an octave higher to the tonic and together they are known as *joda*. However, only the string on the far right is used for producing the melody and the adjacent string is used to provide a drone. A skilled player is able to bow both these simultaneously or sometimes concentrates only on the melody string, as desired. This manoeuvre is made possible owing to a specific curvature of the bridge.

At the second level there are five strings, collectively called *jhara*. They pass through the holes made at a lower level in the same bridge over which the main strings pass. The first three strings are of brass while the other two are made of steel. These strings are tuned to the third, fourth, fifth, sixth, and minor seventh, in relation to the tonic. This tuning may be changed according to the notes of the *raga* being played and they serve as sympathetic strings.

At the third level i.e. closest to the body of the instrument there are seventeen additional sympathetic strings, known collectively as *jeel*. These strings also pass through the same bridge along with the main strings and the strings of *jhara*, however, they run through the holes made at an even lower level. They decrease in length from right to left, and hence are tuned in progressively higher pitch. Our informant called his tuning *sabrang* (all purpose) and gave this tuning:

$$C\ ^bD\ D\ ^bE\ E\ F\ G\ ^bA\ A\ ^bB\ B\ C\ D\ E\ F\ G\ A$$

In this tuning the instrument can respond to all the notes over almost two octaves except $F^\#$. However, if the player shifts his tonic to the fourth, then with the existing tuning of the sympathetic strings he can also have access to $F^\#$. When necessary, these musicians use the shifting tonic. The complexity involved in tuning these strings certainly demands a high level of musicianship.

This instrument has a tonal range of three octaves. The lowest note corresponds to the white five. Generally, the right hand takes care of the bowing while the left-hand fingers (except the thumb), specifically the region of the nail near the cuticle is used to stop the string. It should be noted that this instrument is mostly used by a player to accompany his own singing. Our informant Lakha Khan is adept at singing and is a master of instrumental technique. While singing, he supports the vocal melody by playing either a part of the vocal phrases or by just standing on a note; and does not necessarily imitate the complete melody on the instrument. In between the vocal phrases he plays passages demonstrating his musical ability as well as his instrumental technique. In Laka's case, the fusion of voice and instrument is so harmonious that the two appear as if they are one! The man and his music-making instrument seem virtually inseparable!

While singing a song, the players are consciously aware of the metre (prosody) and use the bow accordingly. The concluding portion of the song or stanza often includes various rhythmic patterns created with jerky movements of the bow. A melodic piece called *lehra* allows a performer to display his instrumental technique.

SINDHI SARANGI

The name of the instrument suggests a possible connection with the region of 'Sindh,' now in Pakistan. It is also called '*Jode ki sarangi.*' Our informant Mehar Din Langa has a *sarangi* made at Nathu's shop in Pakistan. He says that the same instrument has been in his family for about three generations.[10] Though almost similar in construction, size, shape, left and right hand techniques and so forth to the *Pyaledar sarangi*, there are slight differences as listed below:

i The instrument we examined had a flat rear surface for the belly in contrast to the rounded *pyala* of *Pyaledar sarangi*. However, this feature might be totally dependent on skill and choice of the maker and may not be really characteristic of the instrument itself.

ii The number of twines used for weaving the main gut strings are twelve and nine respectively as against fourteen and twelve of the *Pyaledar sarangi*.

iii There are seven strings for *jhara* as against five in the corresponding set of *Pyaledar sarangi*. One of these strings is placed on the extreme left and is tuned to the lower octave fifth while the others are tuned as C E F G A ^{b}B or B.

iv   The lowest note is approximately equivalent to the white four and a half. However, because of the use of high-pitched notes it gives a general impression of being a high-pitched instrument.

vi   Compared to the timbre of *Pyaledar sarangi*, the tone of this instrument is quite sharp and piercing.

SURINDI

This is an instrument generally played by a special group of Langas called Surnaya Langa and is often used to accompany an aerophone called *murli*, also played by the same group. The instrument we studied was played by Mehar Din Langa. He said that this instrument (length of about forty cm.) was made by Redmal of Jodhpur in Rajasthan.

A slightly larger version of the instrument is known as a *surinda*. Instruments almost similar in structure and known as *sarinda*; are found in other states of India, such as the neighbouring state of Kachchh and also Assam, Manipur, and Tripura.[11]

The *surindi* is a heart-shaped, double-chested instrument made of *ruhida* wood. The lower chest is covered with goat-skin. There are three strings at the main level. The one in middle is a gut string (four twines) tuned to the fundamental note. This is used as a drone and is called *gram*.

While the strings on either side are made of steel and are tuned to the fifth and an octave above respectively. They are used for making the melody. The *jeel* consists of six sympathetic strings tuned to E F G A B C.

The instrument is much smaller than the other types of *sarangi* considered here. The fingering technique too, is different - the tips of the fingers of the left hand instead of the fingernails are used to stop the strings. A couple of brass bells are attached to the handle of the bow. Since the bowing movements are closely associated with the rhythmic patterns, the bells provide an additional melodic and rhythmic emphasis.

The lowest note on this instrument corresponds to black six and half and is therefore capable of producing very high-pitched tones; although limited in terms of tonal range as compared to *Pyaledar* and *Sindhi sarangi*.

KAMAICHA

It is a rather short necked and heavy instrument, about seventy-five cm. in length, which we found in the possession of Sakar Khan Manganiar of Jaisalmer. Its body is made of mango wood with *shisam* wood used for the finger board. The resonator is significantly different from that in the three other *sarangi* mentioned above, i.e. it is semicircular without any lateral indentation. Hence, the type of bowing that is possible in this instrument is very limited with respect to melody-making.

The instrument has three main strings of gut (twelve, eleven, and eleven twines respectively) which are kept in place by weaving them with horse-hair near the string holder. They are tuned to G C .C and only the string on the farthest right is used for producing the melody while the rest act as drone strings. Hence, the instrument has a tonal range of not more than one and half octaves. The specific terms used to denote these strings are *rodo*, *joda*, and *agor* respectively.

There are two sets of sympathetic strings consisting of six and eight metal strings respectively. They are tuned as:

set of six - five brass and one steel as - G A ^{b}B B C D

set of eight - all steel as - ^{b}E E F G A ^{b}B B C

Though sympathetic, they can be bowed to create particular rhythmic patterns. This is possible because all the strings pass over a notched bridge at the same level, unlike the strings of the other instruments described here. The bridge itself is characterized by the presence of a brass strip attached to the wooden structure; perhaps accounting for the rich timbre of the instrument.

Generally played by the Manganiar community, it can function both as a solo instrument or to accompany a vocal melody.

CONCLUSIONS

Our study based on the examination of one specimen each of the *Pyaledar sarangi* and *Sindhi sarangi* suggests that there is no significant difference between these instruments with respect to their physical structure, number of strings, their tuning and even the left and right hand techniques. Naturally, this raises the question about why these apparently similar instruments have survived side by side in the same culture?

The obvious and the only reason could be that these instruments are caste-specific i.e. the Langas play the *Sindhi sarangi*, while the *Pyaledar sarangi* is played by a special group of Manganiars who have both Hindu and Muslim patrons. Even though a musician from a particular caste may very well have the capability to play the instruments played by other musician castes, he prefers not to do so. Thus, despite the structural and stylistic similarities, these instruments have remained inseparably associated with the particular caste and have maintained their socio-cultural significance in Rajasthan. As far as the *kamaicha* and *surindi* are concerned, they have their own characteristic identity including a special timbre, and musical purpose to fulfill within the corresponding castes.

Another interesting issue which emerged during this investigation was the timbre of these two *sarangi*. The tone of the *Pyaledar sarangi* is found to be mellow, round, and sweet, as compared to that of *Sindhi sarangi*, which is quite sharp and piercing. The spectrographic analysis of the notes produced on the gut strings of these two *sarangi* revealed some interesting details to support our aural judgment. In the case of the *Sindhi sarangi*, the fundamental frequency is the most dominant one with a very weak harmonic content. The tones of the *Pyaledar sarangi* show consistent dominance of the second, forth and the seventh harmonic.

Considering the fact that both these *sarangi* employ very similar techniques of bowing, the effect of the method used for generating the sound in these cases ought to be quite similar. Then what could be the factors leading to such a difference in harmonic spectra?

The gut strings of this *Pyaledar sarangi* are much thicker (fourteen and twelve twines) as compared to those of *Sindhi sarangi* (twelve and nine twines). This could be one of the reasons affecting the spectral content and hence, also the quality of the tone produced by these *sarangi*s.

It should be understood that these observations are based solely on the examination of one specimen of each of either type of *sarangi*. In order to confirm the above hypothesis regarding their timbre, more such instruments need to be examined. However, considering the dwindling numbers of these instruments not to mention the demise of their makers and the players, this type of study needs to be undertaken with certain exigency before these instruments are relegated to oblivion, the remnants of a glorious tradition.

NOTES

1. This workshop was jointly organized by National Centre for the Performing Arts (Mumbai) and ARCE-AIIS (Delhi) during 1-15 Dec. 1996 at New Delhi, India. I am grateful to the organizers of this workshop and I feel deeply indebted to Mr Komal Kothari, Dr Ashok Ranade and the other faculty members for their valuable guidance during this workshop.
2. The *New Grove Dictionary of Music and Musicians* describes *sarangi* as, 'A bowed chordophone occurring in a number of forms in the Indian subcontinent. It has a waisted body, a wide neck without frets and is usually carved from a single block of wood; in addition to its three or four strings it has one or two sets of sympathetic strings. The *sarangi* originated as a folk instrument but has been used increasingly in

3   The other category comprises communities such as the Dholi, Dhadi, Mirasi, Jogi, and Kalbeliya.
4   According to Lakha Khan his ancestors were divorced from their Muslim patrons as a result of a serious dispute and hence, today, his family serves only the Hindu patrons.
5   E.g. Lakha wears a white *dhoti* (a loincloth), *khameez* (a shirt), and a colourful *pagadi* (a piece of headgear) like his Hindu patron (*Bishnoi*), while Mehar Din wears *kurta* (another type of shirt), *safa* (another type of headgear), and a special cloth called *ajrakh* round the neck. The dressing patterns and ornaments worn by their women are also quite distinct from each other.
6   *Raga* is a predominant concept in the Indian art music. As understood in the contemporary musical parlance it eludes a simple and concise definition. In a broader sense it could be defined as a melodic mode or a matrix possessing a rigid and specific individuality.
7   Usually it is customary, in the case of art music practitioners, to announce the raga to be performed. It is pertinent therefore to note the prevalence of such a practice among these musicians.
8   Specificity of time associated with the performance of *raga* and the concept of *raga*-classification, are also the important tenets of art music.
9   The other types of *sarangi* not considered here are Jogiya *sarangi* and Dhani *sarangi*.
10 We understand that this shop has been closed down but it is encouraging to know that a gentleman from Jodhpur, Redmal, and his nephew, Ibrahim, are engaged in making *Sindhi sarangi* and *surinda* to meet the local demand.
11 In Kachchh region this instrument is known as a *surnado* and is preferably made of *lahirro* wood.

Chapter 15

Karma Gling pa:
Treasure Finder or Creative Editor?

Henk Blezer

A Dream

'I have been 'seeing' peculiar dreams lately. It would not be appropriate to recount them here in full, but allow me to say this much, an ancient prophecy and auspicious signs coincided. In my dreams I clearly saw fragments of a text, the '*Bar do thos grol chung ba*'.[1] My '*Thos grol chung ba*' is a *yang gter*, a *re*-discovered treasure. With this treasure I revealed again an old kernel of the *Bar do thos grol chen mo*-cycle[2] that had been lost for many centuries. The *Bar do thos grol chen mo* is said to have been revealed for the first time by the illustrious visionary Karma gling pa (fourteenth century AD) at the sGam po gdar, a mountain near his birthplace in Dwags po,[3] in old Tibet close to six centuries ago, from a secret cache hidden by the great saint Padmasambhava.[4] Thanks to the support of a suitable consort I now have been able to render most of this re-discovered treasure into Tibetan. In this dark age, when the sun of the Good Doctrine is in eclipse, I humbly submit this treasure-text and fervently pray that it may be of benefit to all sentient beings!'

Now, if I were to introduce my present finds thus, would this encourage you, my academic colleagues, to take seriously what follows at all? Probably not! Let me try again.

Editing a Text

If I tell you that the text I present in Appendix III is a compilation of the passages that the *Man ngag snying gi dgongs pa rgyal ba'i bka' zhes bya ba'i rgyud* (*MNg*)[5] shares with (two texts from) the *Bar do thos grol chen mo* (*BTh*),[6] and point out that these passages, when compiled, yield a fairly readable (*Bar do thos grol*-like) text - as you can verify by reading Appendix III,[7] then I presume there is a real chance that a good percentage of you might feel inclined to give some credence to my words when I subsequently suggest that the compilation presented in the appendix below might well represent an old core or source of the *BTh* as we know it now.

Please rest assured, I am far from blaming anyone for adopting a sceptical attitude towards claims of unusual or miraculous revelations of *gter ma-s* (nor was I exposed to too much sunlight during fieldwork in India). There is a curious point, however, that, by means of the prelude I have used, I tried to bring to your attention. For a textual scholar a disclosure like the above dream-account would be tantamount to academic suicide, while conclusions based on text-historical and text-critical analysis would, if properly executed, be fully acceptable. For a treasure-finder (*gter ston*) like Karma gling pa, in his community, the acceptance of his work and, more in general, his respectability seem to have accounted to quite *opposite standards*. He was respected precisely for his visionary powers and the miraculous nature of his discoveries and not for his skill at reworking existing material. While, as I shall argue in this article, at least as far as some of the discussed *BTh*-texts attributed to him are concerned, he actually seems to have done something very much similar to what I did for the appended collation: cut, paste, and edit existing material![8]

MATERIAL USED

Especially in *rNying ma* or the 'old' traditions of Tibetan Buddhism (and, of course, in Tibetan '*Bon*' traditions as well) the phenomenon of purportedly hidden and later (re-)discovered treasures or *gter mas* is quite common. The *rNying ma gter ma*s usually are, one way or the other, traced back to the legendary figure of Padmasambhava (eight century AD), that is, they are said to have been concealed by him or by one of his associates for later discovery (usually by purported re-'incarnations' of his disciples). The technicalities of concealment and revelation need not be discussed here.[9]

For this paper I shall focus on texts from one specific treasure-cycle, which is available in many diverging compilations, the *Kar gling zhi khro*-cycle(s). Several core-texts of these cycles have been attributed to Karma gling pa - hence its name, 'The (Cycle on) Peaceful and Wrathful Deities (according to) Karma gling pa'. The *gter ston* and *gter ma*-cycle are traditionally dated to the fourteenth century AD, though I should like to emphasize here that both the historical accuracy of this attribution and the exact composition of the 'core-texts' still remain to be established.[10]

In the course of my work on *Kar gling zhi khro*-cycles, especially on one text, the *Chos nyid bar do'i gsal 'debs*[11] *thos grol chen mo* (ChB) (which can be grouped together with the *Srid pa bar do'i ngo sprod gsal 'debs thos grol chen mo* (SB)[12] - they are considered to constitute the core of what is often styled the *Bar do thos grol chen mo*, *BTh*) - it became quite apparent that this so-called revealed treasure might well have been a digest of earlier material on the subject, which, perhaps, was even expanded later at the hands of commentators and redactors. In this article I shall be concerned with localizing some of this source-material (mainly that which was incorporated into the *ChB*) in earlier sources that Karma gling pa - or whoever compiled the *ChB* - might have used. I shall limit myself to textual correspondences, the issue of a more general affiliation and convergence in (*rDzogs chen*[13])-theory will be the subject of another study.

This article will focus mainly on a comparison of the *ChB* and *SB* with the *MNg*.[14] Here I shall not again discuss the *Bar do 'phrang sgrol gyi smon lam*,[15] another *Kar gling zhi khro* (and *Bar do thos grol*) text, in this respect. But some correspondences with a text from the *rNying ma'i rgyud bcu bdun*,[16] the *Nyi ma dang zla ba kha sbyor ba chen po rgyud* (*Nyi zla kha sbyor*),[17] will also be mentioned briefly. Both texts have already been discussed elsewhere in a similar context.[18] However that may be, by far the most fascinating and tantalising text for this comparative exercise is no doubt the *MNg*.

The *MNg*, as far as I am presently aware, is extant in two major recensions, both contained in the *rNying ma'i rgyud 'bum*,[19] a shorter version of eight chapters (Taipei/ *mTshams brag*) and a longer one of thirteen (*gTing skyes*) or fourteen (Taipei/ *mTshams brag*) chapters. The longer versions merely contain extra chapters beyond the eighth. The most significant variant readings occur between the short *mTshams brag* edition and the longer versions. The *gTing skyes* and the long *mTshams brag* edition show only minor, usually negligible, variant readings. Unfortunately, at present I have no access to other *rNying ma'i rgyud 'bum* collections. The *MNg* is classified under the *Man ngag gi sde*. It comes with a *Sanskrit*-title (*Upacittajayatantrasamatināma* -- short version/ *Upacittajayasamatitantra-nāma* -- long versions), thus suggesting it is a translation.[20] All versions come without reference to date or author and so far I do not yet have any clue as to its possible inclusion in earlier *rNying ma'i rgyud 'bum* compilations. More than half (of the short version and approximately one third of the long ones) consists of phrases shared almost *verbatim* with the *ChB* and, to a lesser degree, also with the *SB*.

The absence of any explicit marker of a date is, of course, the main obstacle in this comparison. As far as my information now goes, I am afraid I can only submit the not so very enlightening statement that the *MNg* might be earlier than the *BTh* texts, but that it might also be later. As for now we obviously have to go by internal criteria. Judging by its contents, there are good cases to be made for *both* scenarios, there is no conclusive evidence pointing in either one direction or the other. Actually, the general picture that emerges is that the scattered nature of the shared passages *both* in the *MNg* and the *BTh* suggests instead that their authors have been 'drinking' at the same fountain. One of the main reasons it is difficult to ascertain a date on the basis of internal criteria is because the several versions of the *MNg* do not seem to be homogenous products in themselves. Instead they appear as somewhat rough-edged collations. Several points of extension and insertion present themselves when studying the contents of the various chapters. Since the seams of collation are easier to discern if we take a brief look at the correspondences of the *MNg* with the two *BTh* texts, I include a conspectus of the shared material in Appendix II.

AN (ATYPICAL) EXAMPLE

The number and also the nature of the matching passages will become sufficiently clear by studying Appendix II. The scope of this article does not permit me to present detailed analyses for all matching phrases, allow me therefore to elaborate just one of the less clear and more problematic sections of correspondence below.

In general, the *MNg* and the *ChB* feature their shared phrases in similar contexts and, apart from smaller or larger omissions and an occasional reversion,[21] the order and fabric of the presentation also remain alike. In the *srid pa'i bar do*[22] sections of the *MNg* and the *SB*, however, the passages that show correspondence seem to move around a little more, that is, relative to the order of appearance in the *SB* or *MNg* successively. The remarkably brief description in the *MNg* does not present much material that does not also appear in the *SB*. Needless to say, the *SB*, which is much more voluminous, obviously contains a quite a large amount of non-matching material. I think that considering the rather concise nature of the *MNg* here, this does not allow us to conclude that the 'extra' material of the *SB* should be interpolation. A more revealing feature of the correspondences is, indeed, that when tracing the material that the *MNg* shares with the *SB*, one has, at times, to jump back and forth in the *SB*. In the *SB* itself these passages appear in related contexts but nonetheless more or less discrete paragraphs. In order to clarify the exact nature of these 'movements', allow me to analyse in some detail a section of the *MNg*, starting after the description of the 'judgement scene', where the order in the *MNg* and *SB* is different. The general match, by the way, is much less close or literal here than in previous sections. This supports the perceived difference in history and provenance of the contents of the *ChB* and *SB*, which has already been discussed elsewhere (in brief, the *ChB* probably represents a more recent layer of speculation).[23]

After its description of Yama,[24] the *MNg* continues discussing the *srid pa'i bar do*.[25] Its 'introductory part' has no direct correspondence in the *SB* (though there is a general affinity to the subject discussed there):[26]

> Then, again, in the *bar do* of becoming, (his) senses are complete[27] and his (faculty of) discrimination is seven times sharper than at present.[28] He sees all those on the other side,[29] on this side[30] he does not see those that do not belong to his own class.[31] His awareness is without support, lifted up like a feather in the wind.

The part (immediately) following this, however, does match the *SB* fairly well. For reasons of clarity it is better to divide this *MNg* passage into three (contiguous) parts. First *MNg*1:[32]

> Awareness, straddling the horse of breath, becomes unstable[33] and languid.[34] While it is all over the place, scrambling for a body, and relatives and family are weeping, it realizes: 'I'm dead, what shall I do?' It is overcome by tremendous suffering, like a fish stretched out on hot sand. Awareness is without support. It moves unobstructed by rocks, houses, and the like. It says to all those weeping: 'Don't cry, for I'm here!' Since they do not hear it, it realizes: 'Seems I'm dead!', that really hurts. ...

Note that the description repeats itself, suggesting collation.
Secondly *MNg*2:[35]

> ... Thinking: 'If (only) I could obtain a body, wouldn't that be great!' it is all over the place scrambling for (a body).

Thirdly *MNg*3:[36]

> The terrible suffering in the *bar do* of becoming will continue for twenty-one days.

The *MNg*1 corresponds to parts of *two* passages in the *SB*. Tracing the matching phrases from *MNg*1 we have to jump to and fro from one *SB* passage to the other. Please note that after the corresponding Yama passages(!)[37] in the *ChB* and *SB*, the text that the *SB* shares with the *MNg* 'continues' four pages back[38] (that is, relative to the order of the brief compilation in the *MNg*). First *SB*1b:[39]

> Straddling the horse of breath, as it were, carried by the moving wind of *karma*, you proceed unstable and languid. You say to all those weeping: 'I'm here, don't cry!', but since they do not perceive that, you realize: 'I'm dead!' and experience a tremendous suffering - do not create suffering like that!

The second passage (*SB*1a) continues with thematically strongly related material that is also present in *MNg*1:[40]

> ..., though you speak to your close relatives, no answer comes your way, you see relatives and family weep and realize: 'I'm dead, what shall I do?', and experience a tremendous suffering, like a fish exposed[41] on hot sand, even though you now create suffering (thus), it is of no use.

Note well that this passage, *SB*1a, *precedes SB*1b in the *SB*.

*MNg*2 corresponds to a passage from the *SB* (*SB*2) for which we have to jump ahead four pages in the *SB*:[42]

> Once again seeing your home(land), family, relatives, your own corpse etc., you now realize: 'I'm dead,[43] what to do?' Your mental body again becomes depressed,[44] and, as you think: 'If I (only) could obtain a body now, wouldn't that be great!', you notice you are all over the place scrambling for a body.

*MNg*3 corresponds to a passage from the *SB* (*SB*3), which now again jumps to the 'later' section of *SB*1, *SB*1b (and not the 'earlier' one, *SB*1a):[45]

> In general, the suffering of the *bar do* of becoming is said to continue for twenty-one days, yet, because of the influence of *karma* (this) is not completely certain.

Most of the above passages from the *SB* - *SB*1a, *SB*1b, and *SB*2 - are appended to a commentary on a verse quoted from 'a *tantra*', introducing the qualities of the mental body of this intermediate state, that is, pertaining to the *srid pa'i bar do*. Though *SB*1(a&b) and *SB*2 are thematically connected to the subject matter introduced by the verse quoted and its commentary, they are not part of the commentary proper. The tantric verse (I have not tracked the source) apparently is already attested in the *Abhidharmakośa(bhāṣya)* (*AbhK(Bh)*) III, vss. 13-14:[46]

[*SB*, ka, p.72, ll.1-4] *de yang rgyud las%*
sngon 'byung srid pa'i sha gzugs can(1)%
dbang po kun tshang thogs med rgyu(2)%
las kyi rdzu 'phrul shugs dang ldan(3)%
rigs mthun lha mig dag pas mthong (4)% *zhes gsungs pas%* ...

Which, if we refer it back to the *Sanskrit* original - cf. *AbhK(Bh)* III, vs. 13-14, see Swāmī Śāstri (1981),[47] Vol.II, p.419, l.11 - p. 424, l.16, and Pradhan (1975),[48] p. 123, l.21 - p. 125, l.18:

ekākṣepād asāv aiṣyatpūrvakālabhavākṛtiḥ (1)/
sa punar maraṇāt pūrva upapattikṣaṇāt paraḥ //13//
sajātiśuddhadivyākṣidṛśyaḥ(2) *karmarddhivegavān*(3) /
sakalākṣo 'pratighavān(4) *anivartyaḥ sa gandhabhuk* //14//

cf. a Tibetan translation of *AbhK(Bh)* III, vs. 13-14 in the Peking Edition of the Tibetan Tripitaka,[49] p. 119, 2, ll.3-5:

de ni 'phen pa gcig pa'i phyir/ /sngon dus srid 'byung sha tshugs can(1)/ /
de ni 'chi ba'i sngon rol te/ /skye ba'i skad cig phan chad do/ /
rigs mthun lha mig dag pas mthong (2)/ /*las kyi rdzu 'phrul shugs dang ldan*(3)/ /
dbang po kun tsang thogs med ldan(4)/ /*mi zlogs*(!) *de ni dri za'o/ /*

- could be translated as follows (note that going by the Tibetan rendering only we would here, as so often, arrive at a different translation!):

With regard to this there is said in a *tantra*:
He[50] bears the form of the phase (after birth and) before death,
(His) organs of sense are complete, he knows no obstruction,
He is endowed with the swiftness of supernatural power by *karma*,
He is visible for (other) beings of his class and with the divine eye. ...

A BRIEF COMPARISON

The basic structure of the *MNg* and its correspondence with the two *BTh*-texts, as we can deduce this from the appended conspectus, can be condensed into the following points:

1. The first chapter of the *MNg* seems to present a more elaborate quotation of material that was also used for the *ChB*, it suggests a shared source rather than a scenario of borrowing one way or the other. But then, if there were to be a relation of borrowing, the *MNg* would seem to be the more likely

source here. This chapter could very well be read independently from the rest, not even necessarily as embedded in the context of an after-death phase.

2. The peaceful and wrathful deities (*zhi khro*) are 'listed' twice in Chapters Two to Five. The descriptions in the second listing, however brief, match those in the *ChB* better (almost literally). The descriptions of the peaceful (Chapter Five) and wrathful deities (Chapter Four) are reversed in the second listing. The two diverging descriptions suggest a different source. The *MNg* does not seem to provide enough 'space' to allow both descriptions of the *zhi khro-maṇḍala* to live comfortably or at all peacefully together, the repetition strongly suggests it is an unwanted by-product of compilation. I should like to point out that in many *Kar gling zhi khro* and *BTh* editions the peaceful and wrathful deities are contained in separate texts,[51] they need not necessarily be seen as an original unit. Please note that the *Rig 'dzin* or *Vidyādharas* do not appear in the *MNg*. Considering what I now know about the development of the *kar gling zhi khro-maṇḍala*,[52] I should like to interpret this as a sign for greater antiquity of the *MNg-maṇḍalas*.[53] Lastly, I should like to record here that the description of the wisdom lights in Chapter Two, which here precedes the (first) description of the peaceful deities,[54] in similar terms also appears in the *Nyi zla kha sbyor*.

3. In general, if there were to have been a scenario of borrowing between these texts (which I myself doubt), it seems as if much (but not all, see the next point) of the shared material in Chapter Six would have derived from *BTh* texts rather than the other way round. Especially the *srid pa'i bar do*-descriptions in the *MNg* look like a jumbled cut-and-paste digest of phrases from the *SB* or a similar text (which at this point seems more likely). It would be rather improbable that the more 'complete' (NB. not in the sense of elaborated or more ornate!) descriptions of the *SB* would derive or could be meaningfully (re)constructed from the few, somewhat loosely connected phrases in the *MNg*, that is to say, that anyone could construe the text as we now have it in the *SB* by lifting the minimal bunch of phrases contained in the *MNg*, scattering them and giving them the wider, often slightly diverging, context they have in the *SB*. The *MNg* on the other hand could easily be construed by presenting a digest of some *SB* phrases. The different order in the *MNg* (that is, relative to the order in the *SB*) seems especially to point to a mnemonic convergence of phrases in a brief description of a *srid pa'i bar do* by someone familiar with a *SB*-like text. But I hasten to add that such a mnemonic convergence might also have occurred in the composition of the *SB*. Again, the nature of the convergences suggests to me that both do not apply, but then, if a process of borrowing *were* to have occurred between these texts, the former option would seem to be somewhat more likely I think, that is, when I look at this particular section.

4. An absolutely fascinating point in the sixth chapter of the *MNg*, but one which serves to confuse the picture considerably, is that the discussion of the *chos nyid bar do*[55] jumps to that of the *srid pa'i bar do* in the middle of an, again, almost *verbatim* identical description of the appearance of *gShin rje chos kyi rgyal po, Yama Dharmarāja*[56], in such a way that the *MNg* presents one coherent description of Yama's appearance! That is to say, the *MNg* is free from the awkward split reference to Yama that the *BTh* has in its descriptions in the *ChB* (the wrathful deities as a whole appearing in his form) and *SB* (the well-known 'judgement-scene'). The *MNg* definitely presents a more convincing and maybe also more authentic narrative of Yama. This might, my preliminary perceptions presented above notwithstanding, argue for a greater antiquity or at least originality of the undivided story, or, in any case, for a single (and now I mean, without a disjointed narrative structure) source for the Yama passages in the *BTh* texts. Needless to say, this seamless connection of *chos nyid* and *srid pa'i bar do* descriptions in the *MNg* does give us some reason to assume that part of the *ChB* and, at least, the first part of the *SB* as we know it now, might originally have been one text. Whether this would be a text that Karma gling pa (or some later editor) used for a *BTh* or whether this maybe actually *was* Karma gling pa's treasure, which was subsequently enlarged by intervention of later editors, is impossible to establish at this point. However that may be, it would be fascinating, to say the least, to be able to lay hands on more textual evidence for such a coherent Yama-in-the-beyond narrative. Unfortunately, so far, I have not been able to locate it thus far in older Buddhist and Hindu literature.

The *MNg* might, in an earlier form, well have ended here, that is, at Chapter Six, with the *srid pa'i bar do* description. After the *srid pa'i bar do* description, the *MNg* continues with further material that is not, or only in starkly deviating form, included in the *BTh* (as we have it now). The seventh chapter discusses a *'khrul pa'i bar do*,[57] the eighth the three evil destinies. Chapter Eight seems to form a natural conclusion to the *MNg* recensions as we now have them, the further chapters in the longer versions, both from point of view of content and style, strongly suggest that they are additions.

In Chapters Nine to Twelve we find brief discussions of other *bar dos*:[58] a *rang bzhin gyi bar do*[59] in Chapter Nine; a *ting nge 'dzin gyi bar do*[60] in Chapter Ten; a *rmi lam gyi bar do*[61] in Chapter Eleven; and, once again(!), a more extensive description of the *chos nyid kyi bar do* in Chapter Twelve. The *chos nyid bar do*-description in Chapter Twelve provides detailed explanations of the significance of the deities presented in the previous chapters, which, as mentioned above, together with other 'earlier' sections, also deal with *chos nyid (bar do)* experiences. In these last, probably appended, chapters of the *MNg* we find a short list of four *bar do*s deviating from the six listed in the *ChB*.[62] In Chapter Nine, for instance, we find a separate listing of these four *bar do*s,[63] which are then discussed in the text.

I should like to note here that the *srid pa'i bar do* and the *'khrul pa'i bar do*, which are discussed at great length in Chapter Six and Seven, are not mentioned in the list in Chapter Nine. This discrepancy underlines even more clearly that the Chapters Nine and those which follow it were added later from a different source.

PRELIMINARY CONCLUSIONS

When compared to the *BTh*, earlier sections of the *MNg* suggest derivation from a common source. But some later parts especially might, in view of the nature of the matching phrases, well have been extracted or remembered from *BTh*-texts or similar material, rather than the other way round. If the *MNg* were later than the *BTh*, there is not much doubt that a *BTh* as we have it now or a precursor of it was indeed incorporated into the *MNg*. If, and as far as I can see now, this is highly speculative, (part of) the *MNg* predates the *BTh* texts, it would contain very important material, (similar to that) which the redactor(s) - let us *assume*(!) Karma gling pa - would have been most likely to have used for his (their) *BTh* texts; that is to say, considering the astounding number of shared phrases and ideas, the *MNg* would either have been used for the composition of the *ChB* and *SB* or reflect (part of) the contents of another source used for this purpose.

Whatever the relative dating of the *MNg* may be, based on the evidence available so far, I think I may tentatively conclude that a scenario where both the *MNg* and the two *BTh* texts drew upon a similar stock of material is the most likely one. I do not see any strong arguments in favour of the hypothesis that the *MNg* and the *BTh* as we have them now would have been 'communicated' directly, and in the unlikely case that this would have been so, I would certainly not prefer to support a derivation of the *BTh* from the *MNg* in the first place. As may have emerged from what I have already said, I seriously question the homogeneity of the *MNg* texts, and I also suspect that at least the later sections of the hypothetically older core of six (or eight) chapters of the *MNg* are a digest of (a text or texts) similar to the *BTh*, but then, I must concede that the *MNg* also contains more original elements (the Yama narrative).

In general, the *BTh* especially, which is much longer - and thus contains much more material than the *MNg*, when it features 'extra' text in the context of the more or less tightly woven passages that it shares with the *MNg*, more often than not this material consists of further explanations addressed to the deceased, making the option of interpolation quite likely. The *Mng*, especially the short version, seems much closer to a hypothetical common source than the *BTh*, its 'extra' material - except for the standard phrases pertaining to the narrative question-and-answer structure of the chapters, of course - usually do not suggest it to be interpolations, especially in the first chapter.

An evaluation of both the amount and the nature of the material that the *ChB* derives from other sources, especially as evident in the passages shared with the *MNg*, suggests that Karma gling pa, traditionally styled a discoverer of hidden treasures endowed with special visionary and magical powers, as a *gter ston*, might, at least as far as the *ChB* is concerned, be regarded as a creative editor rather than as a visionary revealer of Padmasambhava's hidden teachings. This only confirms my impression that an important aspect of *gter ma* traditions might well be that they grants the *gter ston*, or should I say author, more liberties in his work of editing and reworking earlier material without necessarily having to drop the reference to an authoritative figure or source. As long as the reshaping of older material is considered to be authentic in the sense of true to the perceived spirit of the authority to which it refers, it apparently still deserves to be styled a '(re)discovery' of an old teaching.

Judging by the information that I have been able to 'unearth' so far, a possible form of this hypothetical 'earlier material' used for the *ChB* (cum *SB*), as well as for the first chapters of the *MNg*, might well be what I presented as the '*Bar do thos grol chung ba*' below in Appendix III.

Please note that so far we have simply assumed, as a likely scenario, that Karma gling pa actually *was* the editor of the *BTh*. I should like to state explicitly that if the *BTh* as we have it now would be a product of later editing based on Karma gling pa's *gter ma* - which after all, also considering the editorial patchwork that, for instance, the *ChB* appears to be, is not *all that* unlikely - then, as far as my information now goes, the old core of such an extended '*BTh*' that was supposedly discovered by Karma gling pa (but nothing is certain at this point) might well have been a text similar to the '*Bar do thos grol chung ba*'. In that case it would, of course, be most likely that the *MNg* indeed is later than Karma gling pa. At the moment I am not aware of any conclusive evidence to support this no doubt interesting possibility.

I shall definitely come back to this issue as more information becomes available. I suspect this to take some time, as the process of discovery of crucial 'missing' links and clues usually only serves to confirm the tantalising level of serendipity involved in such wilful or 'co-ordinated' search efforts. As for now, the hypotheses I have attempted to support above, do not allow me to draw any more definite conclusions, lest this, my dream, turn into an ugly nightmare as I wake up to more information.

APPENDIX I, SOME BACKGROUND INFORMATION

For a general (and fairly late) picture of how Karma gling pa was perceived, I should like to refer briefly to information contained in the *gTer ston brgya rtsa'i rnam thar rin chen bai ḍūrya'i phreng mdzes*.[64] This is a collection of biographies of treasure-finders or *gter stons*, composed by the first 'Jam mgon kong sprul, that is 'Jam mgon kong sprul blo gros mtha' yas also called Padma gar dbang yon tan rgya mtsho (1813-99). It is contained in his *Rin chen gter mdzod chen mo*,[65] which is basically a large collection of *gter ma* texts, it is one of the five encyclopaedias (in Tibetan called *mdzod*) that the first 'Jam mgon kong sprul collected.

Somewhere in the fourteenth century, that is, in the sixth hexagenary cycle, anywhere between the years 27 and 87, Karma gling pa was born as the eldest son of Grub chen Nyi zla sangs rgyas, in Khyer grub, in the uplands of Dwags po.[66] He was a tantric adept, said to be endowed with special psychic powers, like the capacity to imbibe knowledge directly. According to tradition he was a reincarnation of the translator Klu'i rgyal mtshan of Cog ro, who is said to have been a contemporary of King Khri sroṅ lde btsan (676-704).[67]

At the age of fifteen, a purportedly ancient prophecy and auspicious signs coincided and at that time Karma gling pa extracted several concealed texts, so-called *gter mas* or treasures, from the sGam po gdar, a mountain near his birth-place in Dwags po, which is said to have the peculiar shape of a dancing deity (*lha bran*). Herewith he became a *gter ston*, a treasure-finder, hence his place in Kong sprul's 'Beauteous Rosary of Precious Beryl'. Amongst the texts he is said to have unearthed were teachings concerning the peaceful and wrathful deities of Padma,[68] as well as the now much celebrated *Zhi khro dgongs pa rang grol* cycle, a cycle of texts of the 'self-liberated' or *rang grol*-type,[69] in this case, texts pertaining to 'contemplating peaceful and wrathful deities' (*zhi khro dgongs pa*).

These hidden texts allegedly discovered by Karma gling pa are said to have been concealed six centuries earlier by the eighth-century legendary saint and *rDzogs chen* champion Padmasambhava (Padma 'byung gnas), who, in *rNying ma* circles, is considered to be a second Buddha, something like the founding father of Tibetan Buddhism.[70] The prophecies regarding *gter ston* Karma gling pa allegedly also originate with Padmasambhava.

Karma gling pa did not live very long. The reasons given for this are worth mentioning. He is said to have 'departed to another realm' at a tender age because 'the connection with the consort prophesied for him was not auspicious', that is to say, he could not get (or keep) the right spiritual female companion.[71] Despite this, he apparently did manage to produce some offspring. He entrusted the cycle concerning the *padma zhi khro* to his fourteen disciples, who thereby became masters of his doctrine (*chos bdag*). The *Zhi khro dgongs pa rang grol* cycle, however, he transmitted exclusively to his son, Nyi zla chos rje. Nyi zla chos rje was carefully instructed that for three consecutive generations the cycle should be transmitted to one person only. After three generations, it was Nam mkha' chos kyi rgya mtsho who spread the teachings of the *Zhi khro dgongs pa rang grol* cycle in the provinces of dBus, gTsang, Khams and especially in the southern and northern districts of mDo khams. The transmission of empowerment, oral tradition, and commentary (*dbang, lung*, and *khrid*) have remained intact over the centuries and the teachings have continued to spread until this very day. The *Bar do thos grol chen mo* section of this cycle became especially widely known and practised in Tibetan *Buddhism*, and can be found in many sects of Tibetan Buddhism nowadays.

A few of these *Bar do thos grol* texts were introduced to the English-speaking world in 1927 under the somewhat idiosyncratic and inaccurate title 'The Tibetan Book of the Dead' in a pioneering translation by Lama Kazi Dawa-Samdup, edited by W.Y. Evans-Wentz. It might be interesting to mention that an original annotated typescript by Evans-Wentz is at present kept in the library of the Kern Institute in Leiden, the Netherlands. Soon after their introduction in the English language these *Bar do thos grol* translations became what they still are today, the single most popular group of translated Tibetan Buddhist texts in 'The West'.

APPENDIX II, CONSPECTUS OF CORRESPONDENCES BETWEEN THE *MNG* AND THE *ChB* AND *SBi*

Man ngag snying gi dgongs pa rgyal ba'i bka' zhes bya ba'i rgyud		*Chos nyid bar do'i gsol 'debs thos grol chen mo* & *Srid pa bar do'i ngo sprod gsal 'debs thos grol chen mo*	*Nyi ma dang zla ba kha sbyor ba chen po gsang ba'i rgyud ces bya ba bzhugs*
Taipei-edition, Vol. LVI (Tib.Vol.*pa*), no. 4766 (= *gTing skyes* no.84?), pp. 311/580(6) – 315/607(5), eight chapters; see also no.4781 (= *gTing skyes* no. 84?), pp. 342/795(2) – 349/843(3), fourteen chapters plus concluding verses; except for minor variant readings this text is identical with the Dilgo Khyentse *gTing skyes*-edition, Vol.V, pp. 314-352, Thimphu 1973, which, however, stops at the thirteenth chapter.	*ka/*	*Bar do thos grol chen mo*, Kalsang Lhundup (1969) [*ChB*, text *kha*, and *SB ga*]	Text *Ma* from the *rNying ma'i rgyud bcu bdun*, Vol.III, reproduced from the A 'dzom-blocks by Sanje Dorjé, pp. 153-233, New Delhi 1973
	kha/	*bar do thos grol chen mo*, Library of the Kern Institute.ji [*ChB*, text *ka* & *kha*]	
	ga/	*Bar do thos grol chen mo*, Library of the Kern Institute, Nr. 28.452.4 [*ChB*, text *kha*]	
	nga / skor/	*gSang ba ye shes kyi chos*	
	ca/	*phrin las le lag dang 'pho ba man ngag*, Shuh et al. (1985), Nr. 235iii [*ChB*, text *jo*] *Bar do thos grol chen mo*, IASWR Microfiche R 285, Tachikawa (1983/88), Nr. 1233	
NB. the Taipei texts are print-identical with the *mTshams brag* editions.			

305

Taipei-edition, Vol. LVI (Tib.Vol.pa), no. 4766 (= gTing skyes no.84?), pp. 311/580(6) - 315/607(5)

[ChB, text ka & kha]
[ka 4] om% zab chos zhi khro dgongs pa rang grol las% chos nyid bar do'i gsol 'debs thos grol chen mo bzhugs so//

//@/ /rgya gar skad du / u pa tsitta dza ya tan tra / sa ma ti na ma / bod skad du / man ngag snying gi dgongs pa rgyal ba'i bka' zhes bya ba'i rgyud /sangs rgyas 'od mi 'gyur ba la phyag 'tshal lo/ /'di skad bdag gis bstan [581] pa'i dus gcig na / rgyal ba 'od kyi phung po chen po ye shes kyi gzhal med khang na / rigs lnga'i sangs rgyas dang / dbang phyug gi dkyil 'khor 'od gsal ba'i dgongs pa la bzhugs so/ /'di skad bdag gis thos pa dus gcig na / rgyal ba rdo rje sems dpa' ye shes kyi gzhi nas / thugs rje rang byung gi dkyil 'khor dang / sku dang ye shes 'du 'bral med pa'i dgongs pa la bzhugs so/ /

De'i tshe gsang ba'i bdag pos 'di skad ces zhus so/ /kye kye bcom ldan 'das sku

dang ye shes 'du 'bral med pa'i dgongs pa gsung du gsol/ zhes zhus so/ /bcom ldan 'das kyis bka' stsal pa / kye gsang ba'i bdag po / sangs rgyas chos kyi sku de sku dang ye shes kyi lus su bzhugs pas mtshan ma'i lus med do/ /kye gsang ba'i bdag po / sangs rgyas kyi sku la mtshan ma'i gzugs med pa de yin no/ /	... [p. 10, l.19 - p. 11, 1.13] kye [nga 254] rigs kyi bu khyed rang gi da lta'i shes rig gi ngo bo stong sang nge ba 'di% dngos po dang mtshan ma kha dog [ka 11] ci'i ngo bor yang ma grub par [kha-ka 8] stong sang nge ba 'dug pa 'di ka chos nyid kun tu bzang mo yin no%
Khyod ma yengs par nyon cig- /rang gi shes rig gi ngo bo stong sang nge ba 'di / dngos po dang mtshan ma ci'i ngo bor kyang ma grub par stong sang nge 'dug pa 'di ka chos nyid kun tu bzang mo yin no/ /	khyod kyi shes rig 'di stong pa de tsam na stong pa phyal chad du ma song bar rang gi shes rig ma 'gags [ga 7] par sal le sing nge % wal le ba% 'di ka rig pa sangs rgyas rgyas kun tu bzang po yin no%
Rang gi rig pa 'di stong sdo rtsa na stong pa phyang chad du ma song bar / rang gi rig pa sang nge sal le ba 'di rig pa kun tu bzang po yin no/ /	rang gi rig pa dngos po cir yang ma grub pa'i ngo bo stong pa dang % rang
Rang gi rig pa ngo bo stong [582] pa dang / rang gi shes pa wal le ba 'di	

dbyer mi phyed par 'dug pa de / sangs rgyas chos kyi sku yin no/ /

gi shes rig wa ler gsal bar 'dug pa 'di gnyis dbyer mi phyed par 'dug pa 'di ka sangs rgyas chos kyi sku yin no% ...

<<rang gi rig pa gsal stong dbyer med 'od kyi phung po chen por bzhugs pa 'di la skye 'chi med pas sangs rgyas 'od mi 'gyur ba 'di ka yin no% [nga 255] de ngo shes pas chog go% >>

Rang gi rig pa ma 'gags par gsal ba 'di / sangs rgyas su ngo shes nas / rang gis rang la longs spyod pa 'di / longs spyod rdzogs pa'i sku yin no/ /rang gi shes pa sdang nge gsal le ba 'di / sangs rgyas yin par rang gis ngo shes pas rang sangs rgyas yin no/ /gzhan la bstan pas gzhan sangs rgyas pa de / thugs rje sprul pa'i sku yin no/ /kye gsang ba'i bdag po / rang gi rig pa gsal le hrig ge gsal ba'i ngos nas/ chos kyi dbyings kyi ye shes yin no/ /rang gi rig pa gsal stong dbyer mi phyed pa'i ngos nas / mnyam pa nyid kyi ye shes yin no/ /rang gi rig pa de rang shes kyi shes rab ma dgags pa'i ngos nas / so sor rtogs pa'i ye shes yin no/ /rang gi rig pa thogs pa med pa'i ngos nas / bya ba grub pa'i ye shes yin no/ /rang gi rig pa wal le ba 'di sangs rgyas kyi sku yin no/ /rang gi

rang gi shes rig gi ngo bo sang nge ba
'di sangs rgyas su ngo shes nas rang gi
rig pa la rang lta ba de% sangs rgyas
kyi dgongs pa la 'jog pa yin no%

rig pa ma 'gags par gsal le gsal ba 'di
sangs rgyas chos kyi sku yin no/ sangs
rgyas kyi sku dang ye shes 'du 'bral med
par bzhugs pa yin no/ /kye gsang ba'i
bdag po /

Rang gi shes rig gi ngo bo stong sang
nge ba 'di / sangs rgyas su ngo shes na /
rang gi rig pa'i [583] mdangs la lta ba de
sangs rgyas kyi sku dgongs pa la 'jog pa
yin no/ zhes gsungs so/ /

Man ngag snying gi dgongs pa rgyal
ba'i bka' zhes bya ba'i rgyud las ! sku
dang ye shes 'du 'bral med pa gleng
gzhi'i le'u ste dang po'o// //

de nas yang gsang ba'i bdag pos 'di skad
ces zhus so/ /kye kye bcom ldan 'das
sangs rgyas kyi sku dang / ye shes ji ltar
bzhugs pa lags/ zhes zhus so/ /bcom ldan
'das kyis bka' stsal pa /

kye gsang ba'i bdag po khyod nyon cig/

sems can thams cad la rang gi snying gi dkyil na chos kyi dbyings kyi ye shes mthing kar bzhugs so//

[NB. moved from ka 34,1.20 - ka 36, 1.15] kye rigs [ka 35] kyi bu rigs lnga yab yum de dag gi thugs ka nas ye shes bzhi sbyor gyi 'od zer shin tu phra la dangs pa% nyi ma'i 'od zer ba thag sbrel ba lta bu re re khyod kyi snying khar 'char du 'ong ste

de yang dang po rnam par snang mdzad kyi thugs ka nas chos kyi dbyings [nga 294] kyi ye shes dkar la gsal ba% bkrag la nyam nga ba'i 'od zer

[p. 122,1.6 - p. 224,1.4] de'i tshe rang gi snying ga nas 'od shin tu phra ba zhig 'char te/ de sku thams cad [223] kyi thugs kar 'brel te 'char ro/ de la rang gis shes pa zin te/ mi rtog pa'i bsam gtan la rang bzhin gyis gnas so/ /de ni rig pa 'od la 'jug pa zhes bya ste/ snang ba de kun kyang rab tu 'phrigs par mngon par 'gyur te/ snying ga'i zer thag de la yang / thig le phra mo grangs med pa 'char ro/ /de nas yang rang gi snying ga nas 'od kyi zer thag tshon skud bsgril ba tsam zhig 'char te/ de nas sku de thams cad rang gi lus la thim pa snyam byed pa'i snang ba 'char te/ de ni 'od rig pa la tshul 'jug ba zhes bya'o/ /de'i tshe skyes bu rnams kyis yid ches pa ma pang bu 'jug pa lta bu'i thabs mchog tu dran par bya'o/ /

yang rang gi snying ga nas 'od kyi thag pa shin tu phra ba zhig 'char te/ de'i steng gi nam mkha' la gyen du zug par snang ngo //de la rang gi mig gis ma

me long lta bu'i ye shes sku mdog dkar por bzhugs so!!	gyi snam bu zhig khyod rang gi snying ga dang 'brel mar 'char du 'ong ngo % 'od zer gyi snam bu de'i nang du thig le dkar po zer dang ldan pa% me long kha sbub pa tsam shin tu gsal ba bkrag la 'tsher ba% de yang rang bzhin gyi thig le lnga lngas [ga 26] brgyan pa% de'i mtha' dang dbus med par thig le dang thig phran gyis brgyan pa 'char du 'ong ngo %	yengs par bltas pas/ /snang ba de dag ma 'dres par/ shin tu rgya che bar 'char te/ de yang dang po mthing ga'i snam bu'i steng du thig le zer dang ldan pa me long kha sbub pa tsam shin tu gsal la 'chor ba/ de la yang rang bzhin gyi thig le lnga lngas [224] brgyan pa'o//
mnyam pa nyid kyi ye shes sku mdog ser por bzhugs so//	rdo rje sems dpa' thugs ka nas me long lta bu'i ye shes mthing la gsal ba snam bu'i steng du thig le mthing ka g-yu'i phor pa kha sbub pa tsam thig le dang thig phran gyis brgyan pa 'char du 'ong ngo %	yang de'i steng du dkar po'i snam bu'i steng du thig le shin tu gsal ba gong dang 'dra ba 'char ro//
so sor rtogs pa'i ye shes sku mdog dmar por bzhugs so//	rin chen 'byung ldan gyi thugs ka [kha-ka 29] nas mnyam pa nyid kyi yes [ca-ka 23] ser la gsal ba snam bu'i steng du% thig [nga 295] le ser po gser gyi phor pa kha sbub pa lta bu'i thig le thig phran dang bcas pa 'char du 'ong ngo %	ser po'i snam bu'i steng du/ yang thig le gong dang 'dra bar 'char ro//
		de'i steng du yang dmar po'i snam bu'i steng du/ thig le gong ma ltar 'char ro//

	de'i steng du 'od zlum po shin tu gsal ba zhig gdugs ltar 'char ro/ /de dag kyang ye shes lnga'i snang ba ste/
	bya ba grub ba'i ye shes kyi rtsal ma rdzogs pas mi snang ngo / /de ni ye shes bzhi sbyor gyi snang ba zhes bya ste/ rdo rje sems dpa' khong seng gi lam zhes bya'o/

snang ba mtha' yas kyi thugs ga nas so sor rtogs pa'i ye shes dmar la gsal ba snam bu'i steng du% thig le dmar po 'od zer dang ldan pa dper na byi [ka 36] ru'i phor pa kha sbub lta bu% ye shes kyi gting mdangs dang ldan pa% shin tu gsal la 'tsher ba de yang rang bzhin gyi thig le lnga lngas brgyan pa% de'i mtha' dbus med par thig le dang thig phran gyis brgyan pa 'char du 'ong ngo % de rnams kyang khyod rang snying kha dang 'brel mar 'char du 'ong ngo % kye rigs kyi bu de rnams kyang khyed rang gi rig pa'i rang rtsal las shar ba yin te% gzhan [nga 296] zhig nas 'ong ba ma yin pas% de rnams la chags par ma byed la% skrag par yang ma byed par% rnam par mi rtogs pa'i ngang la lhod la shog cig% de'i ngang la sku dang 'od zer thams cad khyod rang la thim nas sangs rgyas par 'gyur ro%
bya ba grub pa'i ye shes sku mdog ljang khur bzhugs so/ /

kye rigs kyi bu bya ba grub pa'i ye shes

kyi 'od ljang gu ni khyod kyi rigs pa'i ye shes kyi rtsal ma rdzogs pas mi snang ngo % kye rigs kyi bu de mams ni yes bzhi sbyor gyi snang ba zhes bya ste% [ga 27] rdo rje sems dpa' khong seng gi lam zhes bya'o%

rang gi snying gi dkyil na sangs rgyas thams cad kyi mes po / sangs rgyas 'od mi 'gyur ba chen po chos kyi phung po chen por bzhugs so/ /

(Cf. [NB. moved from: ka 11, ll.8-11] rang gi rig pa gsal stong dbyer med 'od kyi phung po chen por bzhugs pa 'di la skye 'chi med pas sangs rgyas 'od mi 'gyur ba 'di ka yin no% [nga 255] de ngo shes pas chog go%)

[NB. moved from: ka 33, 1.20 - ka 34 l.20] kun tu [ka 34] bzang po dang % kun tu bzang mo dang % sangs rgyas thams cad kyi spyi mes kun bzang yab yum gnyis kyang 'char du 'ong ngo % longs sku'i lha tshogs bzhi bcu rtsa gnyis rang gi snying kha'i nang nas phyir thon nas% khyod rang [ga 25] [nga 292] la 'char du 'ong bas khyod rang gi dag pa'i snang ba la 'char ba yin pas ngo shes par gyis shig% kye rigs kyi bu zhing khams [ca-ka 22] de ye gsang ba'i bdag po rang gi mig rdo rje sems dpa'i me long la bcug nas ltas pas / sangs rgyas 'od mi 'gyur ba'i sku cha 'phra la dangs pa / gsal la 'tsher ba / rang bzhin [584] gyis bkra la nyams nga ba mdzes pa'i 'od zer 'phro ba / mngon sum du me re re 'char ro/ /kye rdo rje 'dzin pa chen po rang gi snying gi dkyil na / rig pa kun tu bzang po'i gdangs las / mtshan nyid 'dzin pa'i kun tu bzang po sku mdog dkar por bzhugs so/ /chos nyid kun tu bzang po'i gdangs las / mtshan nyid 'dzin pa'i kun tu bzang mo sku mdog mthing khar bzhugs so/ /kun bzang yab yum gnyis rang gi snying gi dkyil na 'od skur bzhugs so/ /

dag kyang gzhan zhig na yod pa ma yin te% snying gi nang nas da ltar phyir thon nas khyod la shar ba yin no% sku de rnams kyang gzhan zhig nas 'ong ba ma yin te% khyod rang gi rig pa'i rang rtsal la ye nas grub pa yin pas de ltar yin par ngo shes par gyis shig% [kha-ka 28]

kye rigs kyi bu sku de dag kyang mi che ba% mi chung ba% cha mnyam pa% rgyan cha lugs kha dog bzhugs tshul dang % gdan khri rang rang gi phyag rgya dang [nga 293] bcas te% sku de dag kyang lnga lnga'i zungs gis khyab pa% lnga tshan re re la 'od lnga'i mu khyud dang bcas pa% yab kyi cha 'dzin pa'i rigs kyi sems dpa' dang % yum gyi cha 'dzin pa'i rigs kyi sems ma dang % dkyil 'khor thams cad dus gcig la rdzogs par 'char du 'ong pas% de khyod kyi yi dam gyi lha yin pas ngo shes par gyis shig%

[p. 222, ll.4-6] sku de dag kyang mi che ba/ mi chung ba/ cha mnyam pa/ rgyan dang / kha dog dang / bzhugs tshul dang / gdan khri dang / phyag rgya dang bcas te/ sku de dag kyang lnga lnga'i gzugs kyis khyab pa/ lnga tshan re re la 'od kyi mu khyud dang bcas pa/ yab kyi 'dzin pa'i rigs dang / yum gyi cha 'dzin pa'i rigs dang / sems dpa' dang / sems ma dang / dkyil 'khor thams cad gcig la rdzogs par gnas so/ /

[p. 584, l.3 – p. 587, l.4] N.B. poorer match with *ChB*.	NB. Here the peaceful deities are mentioned after the wrathful ones! Summary of the *maṇḍala*	
[p. 587, l.5 – p. 593, l.3] N.B. poorer match with *ChB*.	[p. 597, l.7 – p. 599, l.5] N.B. best match with *ChB*.	[p. 17, l.12 – p. 39, l.15] N.B. matches second (summarizing) description *MNg* best.
	[p. 595, l.2 – p. 597, l.5] N.B. though summarising, best match with *ChB*.	[p. 47, l.19 – p. 61, l.2], N.B. matches second (summarising) description *MNg* best.
de nas yang gsang ba'i bdag pos 'di skad ces zhus so! /kye bcom ldan 'das bar do'i khro bo'i sku rnams kyi 'char tshul gsung du gsol/ zhes zhus so! !bcom ldan 'das kyis bka' stsal pa / kye gsang ba'i bdag po / mal gyi tha mar ni nyal / gos kyi tha ma ni gon / zas kyi tha ma ni za /		

skom gyi tha ma ni 'thung / gtam gyi tha ma ni smra ba'i dus su rang la 'chi ba'i sdug bsngal 'ong ngo / /rang gi dbugs ngar ngar phar 'gro tshur 'gro byed pa'i tshe / nye ba dang 'brel pa kun nged bcugs byed zer nas gdung ba'i smre sngags bton pa'i dus su ngas sdug rtsir byas pa la snyam nas nor rdzas 'dor ba'i sdug bsngal 'ong ngo / /da res mi thar 'dug pa ji ltar byed snyam pa'i sdug bsngal mi bzod [594] pa 'ong ngo / /snga ma'i lus dang mi 'dra bar song nas rang gi lag mgo mi theg- /lce yang mi 'gyur bar song ba ni / dus su lus kyi nyams so bri ba'i sdug bsngal 'ong / nga shi nas chir skye nas snyam nas / phung po nying mtshams sbyor ba'i sdug bsngal 'ong ngo / /kye gsang ba'i bdag po / sems can thams cad 'chi ba dang / nyin mtshan med par tshe la rku ba'i mi sdod par 'gro'ol /da res shi nas 'dir mi 'ong bas mi ldog par 'gro'ol /sang nang par mi 'chi ba'i dpang po med pas mgyogs por 'gro'ol /cha med pa'i yul du

'gro bas mgyogs por 'gro'o/ /da ji ltar byed snyam nas snying mi dga'o/ /gshin rje skungs par 'gro bas 'jigs pa che'o/ /skyel ma mi rnyed pas mgon skyabs med do/ /las dge sdig gnyis las mi shong ba 'phangs dog go-/	[NB. moved from ka 16, 1.8 - ka 17, 1.7] chos nyid dag pa'i snang ba phra la dangs pa% gsal la [nga 259] 'tshor ba% rang bzhin bkrag la nyam nga ba% sos ka'i thang la smig rgyu rgyu ba bzhin du me re re 'char du 'ong ngo % de la ma 'jigs shig% ma skrag cig% ma sdangs shig%
kye gsang ba'i bdag po / rang gi sems glo ba'i nang nas dbugs sna sgor chad pa'i tshe / chos nyid dag pa'i snang ba 'phra la dangs pa / gsal la 'tsher ba / rang bzhin gyis bkra la nyam nga ba / sos ka'i thang la smig rgyu rgyu ba ltar me re re 'ong ngo / de la ma 'jigs shig-/	de ni khyod rang gi chos nyid kyi rang mdangs yin pas ngo shes par gyis shig% 'od kyi nang nas chos nyid kyi rang sgra drag la ldir che ba% "brug stong dus gcig la ldir ba tsam du ldi ri ri 'ong ngo % de yang khyod rang gi chos nyid kyi rang sgra yin pas de la ma 'jigs shig% ma skrag cig% ma sdangs shig% khyod la bag chags yid
'od kyi nang thams cad nas chos nyid kyi rang sgra 'brug stong ldir ba tsam sgra drag la ldir che ba 'ong ngo / /de la ma dngangs shig- /'od las zer mtshon cha'i char bab pa 'dra ba sna tshogs [595] pa zing zing 'ong ngo / /de la ma skrag cig- /kye gsang ba'i bdag po / da lta ngo ma sprad na / bsgom bsgrub ci ltar byas kyang sangs mi rgya'o/ /gdam ngag dang ma sprad pas 'od kyis 'jigs / sgras sngangs / zer gyis skrag go-	

/gdams pa'i gnad ma shes na / sgra 'od zer gsum ngo ma shes par 'khor bar 'khyam mo/ /... .. *continued in second column* **khro bo'i lha** *above.*	kyi lus zhes bya ba zhig yod kyi% gdos bcas sha khrag gi lus ni med pas sgra 'od zer gsum gang byung yang % khyod [nga 260] la gnod pa mi yong ste% khyod [ka 17] la 'chi rgyu med do% khyod rang gi [kha-ka 13] rang snang du ngo shes pa rkyang bas chog go% bar do yin par shes par gyis shig% kye rigs kyi bu% de ltar rang snang du ngo ma shes na% mi yul du bsgoms bsgrubs ci ltar byas kyang da lta'i gdams pa 'di ngang ma 'phrad na% 'od kyis 'jigs so% sgras sngangs so% zer gyis skrag go% gdams pa'i gnad 'di ma shes na% sgra 'od zer gsum ngo mi shes pas 'khor bar 'khyam mo% >>
kye gsang ba'i bdag po / rang gi rang snang sku dang ye shes kyi zhing khams ngo shes par gyis shig- /	
kye kye rdo rje 'dzin pa chen po rang 'chi ba'i tshe 'khor ba'i ru log nas snang ba thams cad 'od dang skur 'char ro/ /...	[NB. moved from ka 17, ll.10-12] de'i tshe 'khor ba'i [nga 261] ru log nas snang ba thams [ca-ka 11] cad 'od dang skur 'char ro%

... *continued in second column*	*zhi ba'i lha above.*
zhi ba dang khro bo'i sku che ste / che ba nam mkha'i mtha' dang mnyam mo/ /'bring ri rab tsam gyis khengs nas 'char ro/ /zhag lngar snang srid thams cad 'od dang skur 'char ro/ /snang ba thams cad 'od dang skur 'char ba de rang rig pa'i mdangs su ngo shes pas/ /rang 'od dang sku la gnyis su med par thim nas sangs rgya'o//	[p. 61,1.2 - p. 62,1.7] kye rigs kyi bu% zhi ba dang khro bo'i sku de rnams kyang che ba ni nam mkha' mtha' dang mnyam pa% 'bring rnams ri rab tsam du% tha ma yang rang lus bco brgyad brtsegs pa tsam 'byung bas de la ma skrag cig% snang srid thams cad 'od dang sku ru 'char ro% snang ba thams cad 'od dang sku ru 'char ba de rang rig pa'i rang mdangs ngo shes pas% rang mdangs [nga 336] rang 'od dang sku gnyis su med par thim nas sangs rgyas so% bu khyod mthong snang 'jigs skrag gi snang ba gang byung yang rang snang du ngo shes par gyis shig% [ga 46] 'od gsal rang rig rang mdangs su ngo shes par gyis shig% de ltar ngo shes na da lta rang la sangs rgyas pa la the tshom med do% skad cig gcig gis rdzogs sangs rgyas% zhes bya ba de da res 'byung ba yin no% yid la dran par gyis

shig% kye rigs kyi bu%

rang gis da lta ngo ma shes nas skrag na% zhi ba'i sku thamd mngon po nag po'i skur shar ro% [kha-kha 17] khro bo'i sku thams cad [ca-kha 14] gshin rje chos kyi rgyal po'i sku ru shar nas rang snang bdud du song nas 'khor bar 'khyam mo% kye [nga 337] rigs kyi bu% rang snang ngo ma shes na% bka' mdo rgyud thams cad [ka 62] la mkhas shing bskal par chos byas kyang sangs mi rgya'o% rang snang ngo shes na gnad gcig dang tshig gcig gis sangs rgyas so% rang snang ngo ma shes na shi ma thag tu chos nyid bar dor gshin rje chos kyi rgyal po'i skur 'char ro% gshin rje chos kyi rgyal po sku che ba ni nam mkha' dang mnyam% 'bring po ni ri tsam gyis 'jig rten gyi khams khengs nas 'ong ngo % de yang yaso% sa mchu mnan pa% mig shel mig tu yod pa% skra spyi por bcings pa% gsus pa che ba% ske phra ba% lag na

rang gis da lta ngo ma phrod na / zhi ba'i sku mgon [600] po nag por shar / khro bo'i sku gshin rje chos kyi rgyal por shar nas / rang snang bdud du song nas 'khor bar 'khyam mo/ kye gsang ba'i bdag po / rang snang ngo ma shes na bskal par chos byas kyang sangs mi rgya'o/ /rang snang ngo ma shes na shi ma thag tu chos nyid bar dor gshin rje chos kyi rgyal po'i skur 'char ro/ /gshin rje chos kyi rgyal po sku che ba ni nam mkha' dang mnyam pa / "bring ba ri rab tsam mo/ /de yang ya sos ma mchu mnan pa / mig shel mig tu yod pa / skra spyi bor bcings pa / gsus pa che ba / ske phra ba ! lag na khram shing thogs pa / kha nas rgyob sod kyi sgra sgrogs pa / klad pa 'thung ba / mgo lus 'grel ba / don snying 'don pa / de lta bus 'jig rten gyi khams thams cad khengs nas 'ong ngo / /

NB. Here the text jumps to the *SB*, ka

80,1.15 - 81,1.10.	khram shing thogs pa [nga 338] kha nas rgyob sod kyi sgra sgrogs pa% klad pa 'thung ba% mgo lus phral ba% don snying 'don pa% de lta bus 'jig rten gyi khams khengs nas 'ong ngo % NB. the *MNg* continued with a passage corresponding to the *SB*, ka 80,1.15 - 81,1.10.iv
de'i tshe lhan cig skyes pa'i 'dres sdig pa byas tshad bsags nas rde'u nag po 'dren du 'ong ngo / /lhan cig skyes pa'i lhas dge ba byas tshad bsags nas rde'u dkar po 'dren du 'ong ngo / /de'i dus su rang shin tu bred pa / dngangs pa / skrag pa / 'dar ba byas nas / ngas sdig pa ma byas zer nas rdzun zer ro/ /der gshin rje na re / ngas las kyi me long la dri yi zer nas / las kyi me long bstan nas / dge sdig thams cad me long gi nang du khra lam gyis gsal bar [601] byung bas / rdzun byas pas ma phang par gshin rjes / ske la thag pa btags nas drud de ske 'breg- /snying 'don / rgyu ma bzeng / klad pa ldag- /khrag 'thung / sha za / rus pa mur	de ni lhan cig skyes pa'i lhas dge ba byas tshad thams cad bsags nas rde'u dkar po 'dren du 'ong ngo % mnyam por 'ong ba'i 'dres kyang sdig pa byas tshad thams cad bsags nas rde'u nag po 'dren du 'ong ngo % de'i dus su khyod shin tu bred pa dang % dngangs pa dang % skrag pa dang % 'dar bar byas nas ngas sdig pa ma [ka 81] byas zer nas rdzun smras kyang % der gshin rjes na re ngas las kyi me long blta'o zer nas% me long la bltas pas dge sdig thams cad me long nang du bkra lam me% gsal lam gyi byung bas% rdzun byas kyang ma phan nas% gshin rjes ske la thag pa btags te khrid nas% ske

321

/ yang zhag lnga 'chir mi sdod do/ /lus dum bur gtubs kyang sos so/ /yang gtubs pas sdug bsngal chen po zhag lngar 'ong ngo/ /

"bregs% snying 'don% rgyu ma phyung % klad pa bldag% khrag 'thung % sha za% rus pa mur yang % 'ching mi btub pas% lus dum bur gtubs kyang yang sos nas 'ong ngo % yang yang gtubs pas sdug bsngal chen po 'ong bas%

de tsam na rde'u dkar po bgrangs nas 'ong kyang % khyod rang ma zhed cig% ma skrag cig% rdzun ma zer% gshin rje la ma skrag cig% khyod rang yid lus yin pas bsad pa dang gtubs pa byung yang 'chi rgyu ni med do%

de nas yang srid pa'i bar ma do la / dbang po tshang ba shes rab da lta bas bdun 'gyur gyis che ba / pha rol thams cad mthong ba / tshur la rang gi rigs min pa mi mthong ba / rig pa rten med pa / bya sgro rlung gis bteg pa lta bur /

[NB. ka 76, ll.3-9] khyod g-yo ba las kyi rlung gis khyer ba lta bu'i

dbugs kyi rta la zhon nas rig pa phyo lang lang pa 'ong ngo / /thams cad du lus tshol du 'gro bas / nye drung bza' tshos

dbugs kyi rta la zhon nas% phyad phyod lang lang 'gro zhing % ngu ba kun la nga 'di na yod ma ngu byas ngus nas / nga shi nas 'dug pa ji ltar bya snyam pa / sdug bsngal drag po nya bye tshan la bres pa lta bu 'ong ngo / /rig pa rten dang bral bas / ri dang khang khyim la sogs pa la thogs pa med par 'gro- /ngu ba kun la nga 'di na yod pas ma ngu zer ro/ /de ma thos pas nga shi nas 'dug pa 'dra'o snyam nas / sdug bsngal shin tu che'o/ /

ngas lus cig thob na ci ma rung snyam nas thams cad du tshol du 'gro'o/ /sngar gyi lus de yod pa snyam du yang yod do/ /

kyang % de khong tshos ma tshor bas nga shi nas 'dug snyam nas sdug bsngal shin tu che ba zhig da lta khyod la yod de% khyod de lta bu'i sdug bsngal ma byed cig% nyin mtshan med par ston nam skya 'od lta bu'i skya tham me pa zhig rgyun du 'ong ngo %
[NB. cf. ka 75, ll.12-17] khyod kyis nye ba dang 'brel ba tsho la gtam smras kyang gtam lan mi 'ong ba dang % nye ba dang bza' tshang ngu ba mthong bas% nga shi 'dug pas ci ltar byed nyam nas sdug bsngal drag po nya bye tshan la bsgro ba lta bu'i sdug bsngal zhig khyod la da lta yod pas% da khyod rang sdug bsngal byas kyang phan pa med do%

[NB. ka 79, ll.10-15] rang gi yul 'khor nye du rang gi ro la sogs pa yang mthong nas% da ni nga shi par 'dug pas ci drag snyams te% yid lus de nan ltar skyob yang 'byung ste% da lus cig thob na ci ma rung snyam nas% thams cad du lus tshol du 'gro ba'i snang ba khyod la 'ong ngo %

brag dang sa rdo thams cad kyi gseb tu 'tshang ngo / /	
srid pa'i bar [602] dor shin tu sdug bsngal ba la zhag nyi shu rtsa gnyis 'ong ngo / /man ngag snying gi dgongs pa rgyal ba'i bka' zhes bya ba'i rgyud las / srid pa'i bar do bstan pa'i le'u ste drug pa'o// //	[NB. ka 76, ll.15-16] phal cher ni% srid pa bar dor sdug bsngal bzhag nyi shu rtsa gcig 'ong bar gsungs te% las kyi dbang gis gcig tu ma nges so%

APPENDIX III, *BAR DO THOS GROL CHUNG BA*

*** [p. 581, l.6 - p. 582, l.1:] *khyod ma yengs par nyon cig- /rang gi shes rig gi ngo bo stong sang nge ba 'di / dngos po dang mtshan ma ci'i ngo bor kyang(!) ma grub par stong sang nge 'dug pa 'di ka chos nyid kun tu bzang mo yin no/ /rang gi rig pa 'di stong sdo(!) rtsa(!) na stong pa phyang chad du ma song bar / rang gi rig pa sang nge sal le ba 'di rig pa kun tu bzang po yin no/ /rang gi rig pa ngo bo stong* [582] *pa dang / rang gi shes pa wal le ba 'di dbyer mi phyed par 'dug pa de / sangs rgyas chos kyi sku yin no/ /...* [p. 582, l.7 - p. 583, l.1:] *rang gi shes rig gi ngo bo stong sang nge ba 'di / sangs rgyas su ngo shes na / rang gi rig pa'i* [583] *mdangs la lta ba de sangs rgyas kyi sku dgongs pa la 'jog pa yin no/ zhes gsungs so/ /...* [p. 583, l.3 - p. 583, l.6:] <*kye gsang ba'i bdag po*> *khyod nyon cig- /sems can thams cad la rang gi snying gi dkyil na chos kyi dbyings kyi ye shes mthing kar bzhugs so/ /me long lta bu'i ye shes sku mdog dkar por bzhugs so! !mnyam pa nyid kyi ye shes sku mdog ser por bzhugs so/ /so sor rtogs pa'i ye shes sku mdog dmar por bzhugs so/ /bya ba grub pa'i ye shes sku mdog ljang khur bzhugs so/ /rang gi snying gi dkyil na sangs rgyas thams cad kyi mes po / sangs rgyas 'od mi 'gyur ba chen po chos kyi phung po chen por bzhugs so/ /...* [p. 594, l.2 - p. 595, l.3:] <*kye gsang ba'i bdag po /*> *rang gi sems glo ba'i nang nas dbugs sna sgor chad pa'i tshe / chos nyid dag pa'i snang ba 'phra la dangs pa / gsal la 'tsher ba / rang bzhin gyis bkra la nyam nga ba / sos ka'i thang la smig rgyu rgyu ba ltar me re re 'ong ngo / de la ma 'jigs shig- /'od kyi nang thams cad nas chos nyid kyi rang sgra 'brug stong ldir ba tsam sgra drag la ldir che ba 'ong ngo / /de la ma dngangs shig- /'od las zer mtshon cha'i char bab pa 'dra ba sna tshogs* [595] *pa zing zing 'ong ngo / /de la ma skrag cig- /*<*kye gsang ba'i bdag po /*> *da lta ngo ma sprad na / bsgom bsgrub ci ltar byas kyang sangs mi rgya'o/ /gdam ngag dang ma sprad pas 'od kyis 'jigs / sgras sngangs / zer gyis skrag go- /gdams pa'i gnad ma shes na / sgra 'od zer gsum ngo ma shes par 'khor bar 'khyam mo/ /**** [p. 595, l.3 - p. 597, l.4:] <*kye gsang ba'i bdag po /*> *dpal chen bud dha he ru ka zhes bya ba sku mdog smug nag- /dbu gsum pa / phyag drug pa / zhabs bzhi pa / zhal g-yas dkar ba / g-yon dmar ba / dbus smug nag la / 'od kyi phung po 'bar ba / spyan dgu sdang mig tu gzigs pa / smin ma glog bzhin 'khyug pa / mche ba zangs yag 'bar ba / a a dang ha ha la'i sgra skad can / bshug pa'i sgra chen po sgrogs pa / dbu skra dmar ser gyen la 'khyil zhing 'phro ba / nyi zla dang thod skam gyis brgyan pa / sbrul nag dang thod skam gyis dbu bcings pa / rkan sgra dang stug bcom dang / 'ur sgra dang stug bcom dang / 'brug stong ldir ba / rdo rje 'bar ba'i spu gseb nas ye shes kyi me 'bar ba ! khyung gis 'degs pa'i gdan la brkyang bskum du bzhugs pa / yum dang zhal sbyar nas rang gi klad pa'i nang nas thon nas*

rang la de skad ltar 'char ro/ /de la ma 'jigs [596] shig- /'khrag 'thung rdo
rje'i rigs sku mdog sngo nag yang(!) yum la zhal sbyar nas / snga ma bzhin
du klad pa'i shar nas rang la 'char ro/ /de la ma 'jigs par brod pa skyed cig-
/khrag 'thung las kyi rigs yab yum sku mdog ljang nag- /rang gi klad pa'i
byang nas thon nas rang la 'char ro/ /de la ma 'jigs shig- /shar nas ke'u ri
dkar mo thon no/ /lho nas rtse'u ser mo 'thon no/ /nub nas spra mo dmar mo
/ byang nas pe ta li nag mo / shar lho pu ka si dmar ser / lho nub nas karma
ri ljang nag- /nub byang nas tsan dha li ser skya / byang shar nas sman sha
li mthing nag- /gnas kyi ke ri brgyad rang gi klad pa'i nang nas 'thon nas
rang la de ka ltar 'char ro/ /de la ma 'jigs shig- /de'i phyi rol gyi shar na /
lho na bya tri mu ka dmar mo rta mgo can / nub na sri la mu ka nag mo wa
mgo can / byang nas shwa na mu ka mthing nag spyang mgo can / shar lho
nas dhi ta mu kha ser mo bya rgod can / lho nub nas skam ska mu kha dmar
nag kangka'i mgo can / nub byang nas kha kha mu kha nag mo bya rog mgo
can ! byang shar na hu lu mu ka(!) rkang khra 'ug pa'i mgo can / rang gi
klad pa'i dkyil na yul gyi phra men brgyad rang la 'char ro/ /de la ma 'jigs
shig- /rang gi klad pa'i [597] shar nas stag gdong lcags kyu ma / lho nas
phag gdong zhags pa ma / nub nas seng gdong lcags sgrog ma / byang nas
sbrul gdong dril bu ma / sgo ma bzhi rang gi klad pa'i dkyil nas thon nas
rang la 'char ro/ /de ngo shes pa gyis shig- /rang gi klad pa'i nang nas
khrag 'thung lnga bcu rtsa brgyad thon nas rang la 'char ba'i dus su ! rang
gi rig pa'i mdangs las / rang shar ba'i rig pas / rang khrag 'thung gi sku
dang gnyis su med par thim nas sangs rgyas so/ /da lta ngo ma sprad na
khrag 'thung gi lha thams cad gshin rje ru mthong nas / khrag 'thung gi lhas
'jigs so/ /dngangs so/ /skrag go- /brgyal lo/ /rang snang bdud du song na /
'khor bar 'khyam mo/ /... [p. 597, 1.5 - p. 599, 1.6:] <kye kye rdo rje 'dzin pa
chen po> rang 'chi ba'i tshe 'khor ba'i ru log nas snang ba thams cad [p.
597, l.7] 'od dang skur 'char ro/ /nam mkha' thams cad 'od kha dog mthing
gar 'char ro/ /mthing ka rnam par dag pas rig pa'i mdangs dkar po las /
rnam par snang mdzad kun [598] tu 'od sku mdog dkar po seng ge'i gdan la
bzhugs pa / phyag na 'khor lo rtsibs brgyad bsnams pa / yum nam mkha'
dbyings phyug ma dang zhal sbyar nas bzhugs so/ /'byung ba sa thams cad
'od mthing kha / rdo rje mi bskyod pa phyag na rdo rje rtse lnga pa bsnams
pa / glang po che'i gdan la yum sangs rgyas spyan dang zhal sbyar nas /
byang chub sems dpa' sa'i snying po dang byams pa mai tri gnyis / sems ma
la sem dang mā le gnyis kyis bskor nas sangs rgyas kyi sku drug 'char ro/
/'byung ba chu thams cad 'od ser po / rin chen 'byung ldan phyag na nor bu
rin po che bsnams pa / rta mchog gi gdan la bzhugs pa / yum mā ma ki dang
zhal sbyar nas / byang chub sems dpa' nam mkha'i snying po dang kun tu
bzang po gnyis / sems ma gīrti ma dang nir ti ma gnyis te / sangs rgyas kyi
sku drug tu 'char ro/ /'byung ba me thams cad 'od dmar po / snang ba mtha'

yas phyag na padma bsnams pa / rma bya'i gdan la yum gos dkar mo dang zhal sbyar nas / byang chub sems dpa' spyan ras gzigs dang 'jam dpal gnyis / sems ma pushpe ma ma dang dhū pe gnyis kyis bskor nas sangs rgyas kyi sku drug tu 'char ro/ /'byung ba rlung thams cad 'od ljang khu / don yod grub pa phyag na rdo rje rgya gram bsnams pa / nam [599] mkha' lding gi gdan la yum dam tshig grol ma dang zhal sbyar nas bzhugs so/ /byang chub sems dpa' phyag na rdo rje dang sgrib pa rnam par sel ba gnyis / sems ma ā lo ke dang gan dhe ma gnyis kyis bskor nas sangs rgyas kyi sku drug tu 'char ro/ /sgo ba khro bo rnam par rgyal ba dang / gshin rje gshed dang / rta mgrin dang / khro bo bdud rtsi 'khyil pa dang / sgo ma lcags kyu ma dang / zhags pa ma dang / lcags sgrog ma dang / dril bu ma'o/ / dbang po brgya byin dang / thag bzangs ris dang / shākya seng ge dang / seng ge rab brtan dang / kha 'bar ma dang / chos kyi rgyal po dang / kun tu bzang mo dang / longs sku rang gi lha bzhi bcu rtsa gnyis rang gi lus la 'char ro! /*** [p. 599, 1.6 - p. 601, 1.2:] zhi ba dang khro bo'i [p. 599, 1.6] sku che ste / che ba nam mkha'i mtha' dang mnyam mo/ /'bring ri rab tsam gyis khengs nas 'char ro/ /zhag lngar snang srid thams cad 'od dang skur 'char ro/ /snang ba thams cad [p. 599, 1.7] 'od dang skur 'char ba de rang rig pa'i mdangs su ngo shes pas/ /rang 'od dang sku la gnyis su med par thim nas sangs rgya'o/ /*** rang gis da lta ngo ma phrod na / zhi ba'i sku mgon [600] po nag por shar / khro bo'i sku gshin rje chos kyi rgyal por shar nas / rang snang bdud du song nas 'khor bar 'khyam mo/ /<kye gsang ba'i bdag po /> rang snang ngo ma shes na bskal par chos byas kyang sangs mi rgya'o/ /rang snang ngo ma shes na shi ma thag tu chos nyid bar dor gshin rje chos kyi rgyal po'i skur 'char ro/ /gshin rje chos kyi rgyal po sku che ba ni nam mkha' dang mnyam pa / 'bring ba ri rab tsam mo/ /de yang ya sos ma mchu mnan pa / mig shel mig tu yod pa / skra spyi bor bcings pa / gsus pa che ba / ske phra ba ! lag na khram shing thogs pa / kha nas rgyob sod kyi sgra sgrogs pa / klad pa 'thung ba / mgo lus 'grel ba / don snying 'don pa / de lta bus 'jig rten gyi khams [p. 600, 1.5] thams cad khengs nas 'ong ngo / /*** de'i tshe lhan cig skyes pa'i 'dres sdig pa byas tshad bsags nas rde'u nag po 'dren du 'ong ngo / /lhan cig skyes pa'i lhas dge ba byas tshad bsags nas rde'u dkar po 'dren du 'ong ngo / /de'i dus su rang shin tu bred pa / dngangs pa / skrag pa / 'dar ba byas nas / ngas sdig pa ma byas zer nas rdzun zer ro/ /der gshin rje na re / ngas las kyi me long la dri yi zer nas / las kyi me long bstan nas / dge sdig thams cad me long gi nang du khra lam gyis gsal bar [601] byung bas / rdzun byas pas ma phang par gshin rjes / ske la thag pa btags nas drud de ske 'breg- /snying 'don / rgyu ma bzeng / klad pa ldag- /khrag 'thung / sha za / rus pa mur / yang zhag lnga 'chir mi sdod do/ /lus dum bur gtubs kyang sos so/ /yang gtubs pas sdug bsngal chen po zhag lngar 'ong ngo //... [p. 601, 1.4 - p. 602, 1.1:] dbugs kyi rta la zhon *nas rig pa phyo lang lang pa 'ong ngo / /thams cad du lus tshol du 'gro bas / nye drung bza' tshos ngus nas / nga shi nas 'dug pa ji ltar bya snyam pa / sdug bsngal drag po nya bye tshan la bres pa lta bu 'ong ngo / /rig pa rten dang bral bas / ri dang khang khyim la sogs pa la thogs pa med par 'gro-/ngu ba kun la nga 'di na yod pas ma ngu zer ro/ /de ma thos pas nga shi nas 'dug pa 'dra'o snyam nas / sdug bsngal shin tu che'o/ /ngas lus cig thob na ci ma rung snyam nas thams cad du tshol du 'gro'o/ /*** srid pa'i bar* [602] *dor shin tu sdug bsngal ba la zhag nyi shu rtsa gnyis 'ong ngo / /****

NOTES

1 The Lesser (Cycle Styled) 'Released by Hearing when in the Intermediate State(s)', See Appendix III.
2 The form in which the *BTh*-cycle has reached us might well have changed over the centuries.
3 Dwags po is located in south-west Khams, roughly 200 kilometres east-south-east of Lha sa.
4 For the non-specialist reader who is not very familiar with Karma gling pa and the literature discussed, I shall briefly present some data and context and meanwhile also introduce some key terms and names that might facilitate reading this article in Appendix I.
5 'The Proclamation of the Victorious One (the *Buddha*), the Deepest Meaning of the Essence of the Secret Instruction.' The passages are extracted without emendations from one of the Taipei-editions, to wit, Vol. LVI (Tib.Vol.*pa*), no. 4766 (= *gTing skyes* no. 84?), pp. 311/580(6)-315/607(5), this edition features eight chapters and is print-identical to the *mTshams brag*-edition; other editions will be described below.
6 The Great (Cycle Styled) 'Released by Hearing when in the Intermediate State(s)'. Kalsang Lhundup (1969), Vol. *kha: Zab chos zhi khro dgongs pa rang grol las% chos nyid bar do'i gsol 'debs thos grol chen mo* and *ga: Zab chos zhi khro dgongs pa rang grol las% Srid pa bar do'i ngo sprod gsal 'debs thos grol chen mo*.
7 Or the (roughly) corresponding passages in translation, referred to in the notes.
8 Though, of course, technically speaking, I work in a reverse direction, i.e., I here attempt to extract the source-material that he, or (a) later editor(s), incorporated into the *BTh*.

9   I shall content myself here with referring to several of the well informed discussions that have been published so far, see Bibliography, Secondary Sources, Gyatso, Neumaier, Prats, Thondup and others.
10 These issues will not be addressed in this article, I should like to mention, however, that we can look forward to a detailed and in-depth study of the transmission history of the *Kar gling zhi khro* by Bryan Jare Cuevas that will most likely challenge the traditional claims regarding this treasure-cycle.
11 The Great 'Released by Hearing(-Text)': A Clarification of (or Reminder when in) the Intermediate State of (the Confrontation) with Reality as it is. Some editions feature *gsol 'debs* (prayer) instead of *gsal 'debs* (guidance, clarification, reminder?) in their title.
12 The Great 'Released by Hearing(-Text)': A Clarification or Reminder when Brought Face to Face with the Intermediate State of Becoming (Being Reborn). See Bibliography, Tibetan Sources; for further bibliographical references see Blezer (1997), p. 133, 139.
13 Great Perfection.
14 See Bibliography, Tibetan Sources, Buddhist. My thanks go to Bryan Jare Cuevas for pointing me in the direction of this interesting text.
15 The Prayer Liberating from the Perilous Passage through the Intermediate State.
16 The Seventeen *Tantras* of the *rNying ma pas*.
17 The Secret *Tantra* of the Great Union of Sun and Moon.
18 See Blezer (1997), pp. 85-8 and p. 90.
19 The Hundred Thousand *Tantras* of the *rNying ma pas*.
20 This claim is difficult to verify at this point (see following).
21 See the second description of the *maṇḍala*.
22 Intermediate state of becoming (or being reborn).
23 Blezer (1997), see especially pp. 4f. (for further references).
24 *MNg* no. 4766, p. 599 l.6 - p. 601, l.2.
25 *MNg* no. 4766, p. 601, l.2 - p. 602, l.1.
26 *MNg* no. 4766, p. 601, ll.3f.
27 I.e., unimpaired.
28 I.e., than ordinarily, when alive.
29 I.e., in the 'physical world', the 'world of the living'.
30 I.e., in 'the beyond'.
31 I.e., do not correspond to his destined realm of rebirth (see Blezer (1997), pp. 20f, esp. n. 97), we would have expected 'on this side he *is invisible to* those that do not belong to his own class'.
32 *MNg* no. 4766, p. 601, ll.4-6.
33 Read: *phyad phyod* (cf. *SB*).

34 Read: *lang long* or *lang nge long nge*.
35 *MNg* no. 4766, p. 601, ll.6f.
36 *MNg* no. 4766, p. 601, l.6 - p.602, l.1.
37 I.e., in the *ChB*, ka, p. 61, 1.16 - p. 62, 1.7 and *SB* p. 80, 1.15 - p. 81, 1.10.
38 I.e., from the *SB*, ka, p. 81, 1.10 to p. 76, 1.3.
39 *SB*, ka, p. 76, ll.3-9.
40 *SB*, ka, p. 75, ll.12-17.
41 Read: *bsgres pa*, naked.
42 *SB*, ka, p. 79, ll.10-15.
43 Read: *shi bar*.
44 The readings in edition ka and ga (f.8v, ll.3f.) are probably mistaken, a *tsheg* is missing: *yid lus de nan ltar skyob* (kyang, de?) *yang 'byung ste* (the mental body earnestly wards that (gloomy pondering) off, (yet) it arises again?). Probably this reading has to be emended to: *yid lus de nan ltar skyo ba yang 'byung ste*. This variant is supported by edition ca (f.8, ll.4f), kha (f.8v, 1.5, NB. only Inv.No. 2740/H12 has the *SB*, 2740/H19&187 are incomplete and do not have it), and the *Zab chos zhi khro dgongs pa rang grol las// bar do thos grol chen mo*, Delhi 1995, pp. 158, 1.5. Please note that the Dharamsala edition (*Zab chos zhi khro dgongs pa rang grol las bar do thos grol gyi skor*, Dharamsala n.d. (1994?), p. 208, 1.5) is basically just an emended version of edition kha. The Dharamsala edition was printed from the same, yet 'repaired', physical blocks that the three block-prints from the Johan van Manen collection (2740/H12, 19&187, kha-prints) were once produced from.
45 *SB*, ka, p. 76, ll.15-16.
46 Attributed to Vasubandhu, to be dated somewhere around the fourth or fifth century AD.
47 Abhidharmakośa & Bhāṣya (*AbhKBh*) of Ācārya Vasubandhu with Spūṭārthā Commentary of Ācārya Yaśomitra, two volumes, critically edited by Swāmī D. Śāstri, in Bauddha Bharati Series-5 & 6, Varanasi 1981.
48 Abhidharmakośabhāṣyam of Vasubandhu, edited by P. Pradhan, in Tibetan Sanskrit Works Series, Vol.VIII, Patna 1975.
49 Suzuki, D.T., ed. (1956), The Tibetan Tripitaka, Peking Edition, Tokyo/Kyoto 1956.
50 I.e., the intermediate state/being.
51 See for instance the subdivision into two volumes in the texts listed in Appendix III.
52 See Blezer (1997), esp. section 1.2, pp. 39-66.
53 Please note that in the long versions of the *MNg* the colour of *rNam par snang mdzad* is blue in both descriptions, thus making the colour of

both the *Tathāgata* and the light from which he appears the same, i.e., blue (*mthing kha*). The colour of the corresponding wisdom light of *chos kyi dbyings kyi ye shes*, is also blue here, in contrast to the *ChB*-ka-kha-ga-ca, but in accordance with the *ChB*-nga. Thus it is not, as in *ChB*-ka-kha-ga-ca, reversed relative to the description of the peaceful deities. See Blezer (1997), pp. 92f, esp. n. 289, discussing different conventions of associating *Tathāgata*, wisdom, direction, and hence colours).

54   Please note, in the *BTh* this section is appended after the description of the peaceful deities and is followed by a summarizing discussion of the six realms.
55   Intermediate state of (the confrontation with) reality as it is.
56   Yama Dharmarāja, the Lord of Death.
57   Intermediate state of 'straying'.
58   Intermediate states.
59   Intermediate state of the natural or, in this case, ordinary state (of waking consciousness/ existence).
60   Intermediate state of meditative absorption.
61   Intermediate state of the dream.
62   See Blezer (1997), p. 36.
63   Taipei edition, Vol. LVI (Tib.Vol. *pa*), no. 4781, p. 829, 1.6 - p. 830, 1.2: *kye gsang ba'i bdag po / phyi rabs kyi gang zag rnams la bar do bzhi'i gsang lam phye la ston cig- /'di bstan pa'i tshe zag pa med pa'i ye shes bzhugs pa / me long gsum gyis* [830] *gtan la 'babs te nang gsal du 'char rol /kye gsang ba'i bdag po / rang bzhin gyi bar do dang / ting nge 'dzin gyi bar do dang / rmi lam gyi bar do dang / chos nyid kyi bar do bzhi la ngo sprad do/ /*.
64   The Lives of the Hundred Treasure-Finders, a Beauteous Rosary of Precious Beryl.
65   Great Encyclopaedia of Precious Treasure-Texts, see Vol.I, pp. 291-759, for Karma gling pa's biography see especially, pp. 537f.
66   Literally, *dwags po'i yul gyi stod khyer grub*, p. 537, 1.3.
67   Cog ro Klu'i rgyal mtshan's name is as connected with the translation of (amongst others) the important *Āryāmitābhavyūhanāmamahāyāna-sūtra* into Tibetan, that is, with Amidist doctrines. This Cog ro Klu'i rgyal mtshan and a party which he led together with another translator, sKa ba dpal brtsegs of the 'Bro-family, is said to have been sent to India by King Khri srong lde btsan at behest of Nyang ting nge 'dzin bzang po, in order to procure *rDzogs chen*-teachings (about which some more will be said soon), by inviting the *rDzogs chen*-master Vimalamitra to Tibet (see Dargyay [1977a], pp. 57f. and [1977], pp. 44-7).

68 Padma Refers to the figure Padmasambhava who, as we shall soon see, is said to have concealed these texts, but also to the central figure in Amidism the Buddha of the Western paradise, Amitābha, who presides over the lotus or *padma*-family.

69 In the strictest sense, *rang grol* texts would be characterized by the implementation of a profound doctrine, stating that all appearances are liberated in themselves, that is to say, liberation is present in all perception and experience and is not to be sought for anywhere else. Such a reference in the title already marks the *rDzogs chen* influence or provenance for these texts. *rDzogs chen* might be introduced as a more direct approach in tantric Buddhism, in which the possibility of instantaneous enlightenment is emphatically promoted, there are some similarities with Chinese Chan. In a strict sense it is an approach to practice rather than a school, and as such *rDzogs chen* adepts appear throughout all schools of Tibetan Buddhism, though they definitely are most numerous among adherents of the old sect of Tibetan Buddhism, the *rNying ma s*chool, but they also appear among the *bKa' rgyud pa*s, the oral transmission-lineage, and they moreover are, and always have been, very numerous among '*Bon pos*', traditions that are not Buddhist, but in the form one can meet them now, nonetheless in doctrine and practice come very close to *rNying ma Buddhism*. Though originally referring to a most profound *rDzogs chen* tenet, the designation '*rang grol*' or 'self-liberated' soon seems to have turned into a fashionable ID, attached to many a ritual *rDzogs chen* text more profound in title than in content.

70 He is generally respectfully and affectionately referred to as Guru Rin po che (Precious Teacher).

71 Literally, *lung nas bstan pa'i gzungs ma dang rten 'brel ma grigs pas zhing khams gzhan du gshegs so* (p. 537, 1.6 - p. 538, 1.1), it seems that 'Jam mgon kong spru*l* is trying to be subtle here. We can expect a fuller more spicy account regarding this covert reference and the, perhaps, quite tragic events underlying it from my esteemed colleague, Cuevas, who is currently studying all the available biographical material of Karma gling pa, I shall not anticipate on his work here.

72 Please note that in the texts presented below I tried to maintain the orthographic peculiarities and mistakes of the originals, without attempting to emend them. Critical editions have been (and partially are in the process of being) prepared, but since this apparatus is not relevant to our present concern and the nature of the present publication does not allow me to clutter my text with a small forest of footnotes,

the quite lengthy annotation is not included here. Also note the following conventions used for the editions:

/	ordinary *shad*
%	*gter shad*
!	other *shad*
-	*shad* absent (mainly after *ka* and *rjes 'jug ga*)
...	part omitted from *MNg*
***	part omitted also from *BTh*
@	*dbu ̄*
[ ]	indication pages, lines, etc.
small print	passage taken out of its original context

Since the text presented in the '*Bar do thos grol chung ba*' corresponds fairly accurately to passages from the *ChB* and *SB*, which have been translated many, many times, allow me to refer to the corresponding English rendering from one of the more recent and widely spread translations in Fremantle, F. and Chögyam Trungpa (1975). Her (their) translation was apparently made under consideration of accessibility to a larger public of non-specialists, it seems especially geared to the style and ('psychological') terminology used by Chögyam Trungpa Rinpoche and the (then) Vajradhatu sangha. In short, their translation is rather free and does not claim to meet academic standards. I trust it may nonetheless serve to give those people that do not read Tibetan and have not been thoroughly introduced to the often technical terminology used when translating esoteric Tibetan material a general idea of what is discussed in the passages that I compiled in the '*Bar do thos grol chung ba*'.

Compare as follows:

MNg no. 4766 [p. 581, l.6 - p. 582, l.1], cf. Fremantle (1975), p. 37, ll.12-20;

MNg no. 4766 [p. 582, l.7 - p. 583, l.1], cf. Fremantle (1975), p. 37, ll.23-26;

MNg no. 4766 [p. 583, l.3 - p. 583, l.6], cf. much more elaborate passage from the *ChB* rendered in Fremantle (1975), p. 51, l.17 - p. 52, l.15, cf. also the corresponding passage in the *Nyi zla kha sbyor*, translated in Orofino (1985), p. 47, ll.14-33;

MNg no. 4766 [p. 594, l.2 - p. 595, l.3], cf. Fremantle (1975), p. 41, ll.1-22, cf. also Blezer (1997), pp. 121-4;

MNg no. 4766 [p. 595, l.3 - p. 597, l.4], cf. the much more elaborate description (with interpolations) of wrathful deities rendered in Fremantle (1975), p. 60, l.6 - p. 68, l.10;

MNg no. 4766 [p. 597, l.5 - p. 599, l.6], cf. the much more elaborate description of peaceful deities (here including descriptions of the six realms) rendered in Fremantle (1975), p. 41, l.26 - p. 50, l.36;

MNg no. 4766 [p. 599, l.6 - p. 601, l.2], cf. Fremantle (1975), p. 86, ll.11-18 and p. 86, l.24 - p. 87, l.6;

MNg no. 4766 [p. 601, l.4 - p. 602, l.1], cf. Fremantle (1975), p. 77, ll.2-15 and p. 74, l.33 - p. 75, l.1, cf. also p. 74, ll.24-7 and p. 75, l.3-5.

73 Johan van Manen Collection, Inv.No. 2740/H187,12,19.
74 Microfilms of the cycle *mKha' 'gro gsang ba ye shes kyi rgyud* are preserved in the 'Staatsbibliothek Preußischer Kulturbesitz Berlin'. This *gter ma*-cycle is also extant in the library of the Kern Institute in Leiden (no systematic catalogue-number) as a xylographic reprint of block-prints from the library of Dudjom Rinpoche.
75 Note that the order of the two deities in the *MNg* and the *SB* is reversed.

REFERENCES

TIBETAN SOURCES

rNying ma'i rgyud bcu bdun, Collected Nyingmapa Tantras of the Man ngag sde Class of A ti yo ga (rDzogs chen) (reproduced from a set of prints from A 'dzom blocks preserved in the library of bDud 'joms Rin po che by Sanje Dorje), three volumes, edited by Sanje Dorje, New Delhi 1973-77:
- *Nyi ma dang zla ba kha sbyor ba chen po gsang ba'i rgyud*, Vol.III, pp.153-233.

rNying ma'i rgyud 'bum-section of the Taipei edition of the Tibetan Tripitaka (Taipei 1991):
- Taipei-edition, Vol. LVI (Tib.Vol.*pa*), no. 4766 (= *gTing skyes* no. 84?), p. 311/580(6) - 315/607(5), eight chapters; see also no. 4781 (= *gTing skyes* no. 84?), pp. 342/795(2) - 349/843(3), fourteen chapters plus concluding verses; except for minor variant readings this text is identical to the Dilgo Khyentse *gTing skyes*-edition, Vol.V, pp. 314-52, Thimphu 1973, which, however, stops at the thirteenth chapter; NB. the Taipei-texts are print-identical to the *mTshams brag*-editions.

Karma gling pa (fourteenth century AD), *Kar gling zhi khro*, see Kalsang Lhundup (1969), for further bibliographical references see Blezer (1997), p. 133:
- *Chos nyid bar do'i gsal 'debs thos grol chen mo* (*ChB*), pp. 4-69.
- *Bar do 'phrang sgrol gyi smon lam*, p. 115-16.

- *Srid pa bar do'i ngo sprod gsal 'debs thos grol chen mo* (*SB*), pp. 70-109.

Rin chen gter mdzod chen mo compiled by *'Jam mgon kong sprul blo gros mtha' yas* (1813-99), *mKhyen brtse*-edition based on the *sTod luṅ mtshur phu*-redaction supplemented with texts from the *dPal spuṅs*-redaction and other manuscripts (IASWR-microfiche-edition)
- *gTer ston brgya rtsa'i rnam thar rin chen bai ḍūrya'i phreng mdzes*, Vol.I, pp. 291-759.

SECONDARY SOURCES

Aris, M. (1988) *Hidden Treasures and Secret Lives, A Study of Pemalingpa (1450-1521) and the Sixth Dalai Lama (1683-1706)*. Delhi.

Back, D.M. (1979) *Eine Buddhistische Jenseitsreise, Das sogenannte 'Totenbuch der Tibeter' aus philologischer Sicht*. Wiesbaden.

Blezer, H.W.A. (1997) *Kar gliṅ Źi khro, A Tantric Buddhist Concept*. Leiden.

Chökyi Nyima Rinpoche (1991) *The Bardo Guidebook*. Translated by E. Pema Kunsang. Hong Kong/Kathmandu.

Cuevas, B.J. (1997) *Catalogue to an exhibition on The Tibetan Book of the Dead*. Charlottesville.

--(forthc.) 'Rgya-ra-ba and the Institutionalization of Tibetan Funeral Liturgy in the Late Fifteenth Century', forthcoming in *Fifteenth-Century Studies*.

Dargyay (Neumaier), E.K. (1969) 'Einige Aspekte der gTer-ma-Literatur der rÑiṅ-ma-pa-Schule', *Zeitschrift der Deutschen Morgenländischen Gesellschaft, Supplementa I*, pp. 849-62. Wiesbaden.

--(1977) (trsl.) *Das tibetische Buch der Toten*. Bern/ München/ Wien (1978).

--(1977a) *The Rise of Esoteric Buddhism in Tibet*. Delhi (1979).

--(1978) 'Probleme einer Neubearbeitung des Bar-do-thos-grol', in: M. Brauen and P. Kværne (eds) *Tibetan Studies, Presented at the Seminar of Young Tibetologists, Zürich, June 26-July 1, 1977*: pp. 91-112. Zürich.

Dudjom Rinpoche (1991) *The Nyingma School of Tibetan Buddhism, Its Fundamentals and History*. Two volumes, Volume One: The Translations, Volume Two: Reference Material, translated and edited by Gyurme Dorje with the collaboration of Matthew Kapstein. Boston, Massachusetts.

Ehrhard, F.K. (1997) 'Recently Discovered Manuscripts of the rNying ma rgyud 'bum from Nepal', in: E. Steinkellner (ed.) *Tibetan Studies,*

Proceedings of the 7th Seminar of the International Association for Tibetan Studies, Graz 1995. Two volumes, Vol.I, pp. 253-67. Wien.

Evans-Wentz, W.Y. (editor of translation) (1927) *The Tibetan Book of the Dead, The After-Death Experiences on the Bardo Plane, according to Lāma Kazi Dawa-Samdup's English Rendering*. London/Oxford/ New York 1960.

Fremantle, F. and Chögyam Trungpa (1975) (trsl.) *The Tibetan Book of the Dead, The Great Liberation Through Hearing in the Bardo*. Berkeley/London.

Germano, D. (1994) 'Architecture and Absence in the Secret Tantric History of the Great Perfection (rdzogs chen)', *Journal of the International Association of Buddhist Studies* 17:2, pp. 203-335.

--(1997) 'Dying, Death, and Other Opportunities', in: D.S. Lopez Jr. (ed.) *Religions of Tibet in Practice*, pp. 458-93. New Jersey.

Gyatso, J.B. (1986) 'Signs, Memory and History: A Tantric Buddhist Theory of Scriptural Transmission', *Journal of the International Association of Buddhist Studies* 9:2, pp. 7-35.

--(1992) 'Autobiography in Tibetan Religious Literature: Reflections on Its Modes of Self-Presentation', in: Shôren Ihara and Zuihô Yamaguchi (eds) *Tibetan Studies: Proceedings of the International Association for Tibetan Studies, Narita 1989*. Two volumes, Vol.II, pp. 465-78. Narita: Naritasan Shinshoji.

--(1992a) 'Genre, Authorship, and Transmission in Visionary Buddhism: The Literary Traditions of Thang-stong rGyal-po', in: S.D. Goodman and R.M. Davidson (eds) *Tibetan Buddhism: Reason and Revelation*: pp. 95-106. Albany.

--(1993) 'The Logic of Legitimation in the Tibetan Treasure Tradition', *History of Religion* 33:2, pp. 97-134.

--(1994) 'Guru Chos-dbang's gTer 'byung chen mo: an Early Survey of the Treasure Tradition and its Strategies in Discussing Bon Treasure', in: P. Kværne (ed.) *Tibetan Studies, Proceedings of the 6th Seminar of the International Association for Tibetan Studies, Fagernes 1992*. Two volumes, Vol.I, pp. 275-87. Oslo.

--(1997) 'From the Autobiography of a Visionary', in D.S. Lopez Jr. (ed) *Religions of Tibet in Practice*, pp. 369-375. New Jersey.

--(1998) *Apparitions of the Self, The Secret Autobiographies of a Tibetan Visionary*. Princeton.

Kalsang Lhundup (ed) (1969) *The Tibetan Book of the Dead by the Great Acharya Shri Sing-ha*. Varanasi.

Kunsang, Pema (1989) v. Rangdröl, Tsele Natshok 1989.

--(1991) v. Chökyi Nyima Rinpoche 1991.

Lati Rinbochay and J. Hopkins (1979) (trsl.) *Death, Intermediate State and Rebirth in Tibetan Buddhism*. Ithaca 1985 (London 1979).

Lauf, D.I. (1970) 'Initiationsrituale des tibetischen Totenbuch', *Asiatische Studien* XXIV, pp. 10-24.

--(1975) *Geheimlehren tibetischer Totenbücher, Jenseitswelten und Wandlung nach dem Tode, Ein west-östlicher Vergleich mit psychologischen Kommentar*. Freiburg im Breisgau 1979 (1975).

(Lama) Lodö (1982) *Bardo Teachings, The Way of Death and Rebirth*. Ithaca 1987 (San Fransisco 1982).

Martin, D.P. (1997) *Tibetans Histories, A Bibliography of Tibetan-Language Historical Works*. London.

Mayer, R. (1996) *A Scripture of the Ancient Tantra Collection, The Phur-pa bcu-gnyis*. Oxford.

Mullin, G.H. (1986) (trsl.) *Death and Dying, The Tibetan Tradition*. London/New York (1987).

Orofino, G. (1985) (ed. & trsl.) *Sacred Tibetan Teachings on Death and Liberation*. Translated from the Italian (Roma 1985), Bridport 1990.

Prats, R.N. (1980) 'Some Preliminary Considerations Arising from a Biographical Study of the Early gTer-ston', in: M. Aris and Aung San Suu Kyi *Tibetan Studies in Honour of Hugh Richardson, Proceedings of the International Seminar on Tibetan Studies Oxford 1979*, pp. 256-60, Warminster.

--(1996) (trsl.) *El Libro de los Muertos Tibetano, La liberación por audición durante el estado intermedio*. Madrid.

--(1997) 'Towards a Comprehensive Classification of rNying-ma Literature', in: E. Steinkellner (ed.) *Tibetan Studies, Proceedings of the 7th Seminar of the International Association for Tibetan Studies, Graz 1995*, Two volumes, Vol.II: pp. 789-801. Wien.

Rangdröl, Tsele Natsok (1989) *The Mirror of Mindfulness, The Cycle of the Four Bardos*. Translated by Pema Kunsang. Boston/Shaftesbury.

Reynolds, J.M. (1989) (trsl.) *Self-Liberation through Seeing with Naked Awareness*. Barrytown, New York.

Sagaster, K. (1978) 'Grundgedanken des tibetischen Totenbuches', in: H.J. Klimtheit (ed.) *Tod und Jenseitsglauben der Völker*. Bonn.

Sogyal Rinpoche (1992) *The Tibetan Book of Living and Dying*. San Francisco.

Schuh, D. and P. Schwieger (1985) *Tibetische Handschriften und Blockdrücke*. Teil 9, Die Werksammlungen Kun-tu bzaṅ-po'i dgoṅs-pa zaṅ-thal, Ka-dag raṅ-byuṅ raṅ-śar und mKha'-'gro gsaṅ-ba ye-śes-kyi rgyud, in: Verzeichnis der orientalischen Handschriften in Deutschland Band XI, Teil 9, Stuttgart.

Tachikawa, M. et al. (1983f.) *A Catalogue of the United States Library of Congress Collection of Tibetan Literature in Microfiche*. Part I, by The International Institute for Buddhist Studies, in: Bibliographia Philologica Buddhica, Series Major III. Tokyo 1983. Part II, Series Major IIIb. Tokyo 1988.

Thurman, R.A.F. (1994) (trsl.) *The Tibetan Book of the Dead, Liberation through Understanding in the Between*. New York.

Trungpa, Chögyam (1975) v. Fremantle (1975).

(Tulku) Thondup Rinpoche (1986) (trsl.) *Hidden Teachings of Tibet, An Explanation of the Terma Tradition of the Nyingma School of Tibetan Buddhism*. Edited by H. Talbott, Buddhayana Series I. London.

Varela, F.J. (1997) (ed.) *Sleeping, Dreaming, and Dying, An Exploration of Consciousness with the Dalai Lama*. Boston.

Wallace, B.A. (1998) (trsl.) *Natural Liberation, Padmasambhava's Teachings on the Six Bardos, commentary by Gyatrul Rinpoche*. Boston.

Winkler, J. (1997) '"The Net of Compassion for the Benefit of Others": A Death Ritual of the rDzogs chen klong chen snying thig Tradition', in: E. Steinkellner (ed.) *Tibetan Studies, Proceedings of the 7th Seminar of the International Association for Tibetan Studies, Graz 1995*. Two volumes, Vol.II: pp. 1069-80. Wien.

For Product Safety Concerns and Information please contact our EU
representative GPSR@taylorandfrancis.com
Taylor & Francis Verlag GmbH, Kaufingerstraße 24, 80331 München, Germany